Global Activism

CW00521032

In this age of globalization, activists are going global. Ruth Reitan traces the transnationalization of activist networks, analyzes their changing compositions and characters, and examines the roles played by the World Social Forum in this process.

This book compares four of the largest networks targeting the "neoliberal triumvirate" of the World Bank, the IMF and the World Trade Organization: those of the Jubilee anti-debt campaigners, Via Campesina peasant farmers, Our World Is Not For Sale, and the anarchistic Peoples' Global Action. This work finds, first, that despite their diversity, these collective actors follow a similar globalizing path. Second, networks in which solidarity is based on a shared identity perceived as threatened by neoliberal change are gaining strength. These networks reject the centralized, NGO advocacy model based on altruistic solidarity and instead adopt more horizontal, direct action, and transformative approaches, while building reciprocal solidarity ties with others mobilizing against the harms of globalization. Finally, this work depicts the social forums as a fertile ground to strengthen networks and a common ground for cooperative action among them, but also a battleground over the future of the forum process, the global anti-neoliberal struggle, and "other possible worlds" in the making.

Written by a scholar-activist, this text will strongly appeal to those interested in globalization, International Relations, IPE and social movements.

Ruth Reitan is Visiting Assistant Professor at University of Miami's Department of International Studies, USA.

Rethinking Globalizations

Edited by Barry K. Gills
University of Newcastle upon Tyne, UK

This series is designed to break new ground in the literature on globalization and its academic and popular understanding. Rather than perpetuating or simply reacting to the economic understanding of globalization, this series seeks to capture the term and broaden its meaning to encompass a wide range of issues and disciplines and convey a sense of alternative possibilities for the future.

1 **Whither Globalization?**
   The vortex of knowledge and globalization
   James H. Mittelman

2 **Globalization and Global History**
   Edited by Barry K. Gills and William R. Thompson

3 **Rethinking Civilization**
   Communication and terror in the global village
   Majid Tehranian

4 **Globalisation and Contestation**
   The new great counter-movement
   Ronaldo Munck

5 **Global Activism**
   Ruth Reitan

Global Activism

Ruth Reitan

Routledge
Taylor & Francis Group

LONDON AND NEW YORK

First published 2007
by Routledge
2 Park Square, Milton Park, Abingdon, Oxon, OX14 4RN

Simultaneously published in the USA and Canada
by Routledge
270 Madison Ave, New York NY 10016

Routledge is an imprint of the Taylor & Francis Group, an informa business

Transferred to Digital Printing 2007

© 2007 Ruth Reitan

Typeset in Baskerville by
Taylor & Francis Books

British Library Cataloguing in Publication Data
A catalogue record for this book is available from the British Library

Library of Congress Cataloging in Publication Data
Reitan, Ruth.
    Global activism / Ruth Reitan.
        p. cm. – (Rethinking globalizations)
    Includes bibliographical references and index.
    1. Social movements – International cooperation. 2. Social movements –
    International cooperation – Case studies. 3. Social action –
    International cooperation – Case studies. 4. Globalization – Social
    aspects. 5. Anti-globalization movement. 6. Neoliberalism. I. Title.
    HM881.R45 2007
303.48'4 – dc22   2006021382

ISBN10: 0–415–77036–X (hbk)
ISBN10: 0–415–45551–0 (pbk)
ISBN10: 0–203–96605–8 (ebk)

ISBN13: 978–0–415–77036–1 (hbk)
ISBN13: 978–0–415–45551–0 (pbk)
ISBN13: 978–0–203–96605–1 (ebk)

For Andreas

Contents

List of illustrations   viii
Acknowledgments   ix
List of abbreviations   x

1   The globalization of neoliberalism and of activism:
    an introduction   1

2   Global activism: methodology and scholarly review   25

3   Toward Jubilee 2000 and beyond   66

4   Our World Is Not For Sale   108

5   Via Campesina   148

6   Zapatista-inspired Peoples' Global Action   188

7   Concluding reflections on present and future scholarship
    and activism   230

Appendixes   259
Notes   269
Bibliography   309
Index   330

Illustrations

Figures

1   Scale shift process and constituent mechanisms   42
2   The scale shift process model amended   50

Tables

1   Composition and character of transnational activist networks:
     six conceptual continua   52
2   First- and second-generation transnational networks: NGO
     advocacy and direct activism social justice   58
3   Operational paradigms for transnational activist networks   60
4   Social justice claims-making: redistribution vs. recognition   62

Acknowledgments

For their careful reading, thoughtful comments, and guidance, I would like to thank Paul Wapner, Diane Singerman, Julie Mertus, Barry Gills, Sidney Tarrow, Louis Goodman, and Robin Broad. I would also like to thank those scholars and activists who have shared their thoughts on my work and publications of their own, including Teivo Teivainen, Peter Waterman, Jackie Smith, Jan Aart Scholte, John Cavanagh, Bob Edwards, Andreas Bieler, Thomas Olesen, Jim Mittelman, and Patrick Jackson. To my friends Amal Khoury, Anne-Claire Hervy, Elisabeth Michelon, and Felipe Agüero for helping with translations. To American University's School of International Service in Washington, DC, the University of Miami in Coral Gables, Florida, and the University of Trento, Italy, for their institutional support of my project.

To all of the activists who gave me their time and attention to participate in interviews, surveys, and conversations at the social forums, street protests, and WSF international council meetings, all of which was truly invaluable. My sincere apologies for any omissions or misunderstandings. To the alternative media activists, including those working with indymedia, truthout.org, wikipedia and all those doing the thankless job of posting to activist websites: consider yourselves greatly thanked. This sort of research could not be done without all of you.

On a personal note, many thanks to friends, landlords, students, farmers, and vintners in South Tyrol, Italy, for sharing their time, stories, produce, mountains and water with me. A year abroad from American University to our Graduate Research Center in Trento quite naturally turned into three. This optimistic of a work could not have been written in DC beginning in 2002, at least not by such a sensitive soul as myself. Finally, an existential thanks goes to my husband, Andreas Neufeld, and my parents, Carol and Hank Reitan, whose love and support have made my world possible.

Abbreviations

ABONG	Brazilian Association of Non-Governmental Organizations
AFL–CIO	American Federation of Labor–Congress of Industrial Organizations
AFRODAD	African Network and Forum on Debt and Development
AGOA	Africa Growth and Opportunity Act
AIPAC	American Israel Public Affairs Committee
ANAP	Asociación Nacional de Agricultores Pequeñas of Cuba
APEC	Asia-Pacific Economic Cooperation
ASOCODE	Asociación de Organizaciones Campesinas Centroamericanas para la Cooperación y el Desarrollo
ATTAC	Association for the Taxation of Financial Transactions for the Aid of Citizens
CAP	European Union Common Agricultural Policy
CAFOD	Catholic Agency for Overseas Development
CBJP	Brazilian Justice and Peace Commission
CCRI	Clandestine Indigenous Revolutionary Committee
CAFTA	Central American Free Trade Agreement
CEO	chief executive officer
CGIL	Confederazione Generale Italiana del Lavoro
CIRCA	Clandestine Insurgent Rebel Clown Army
CIVES	Brazilian Business Association for Citizenship
CJG	Center for Global Justice
CLOC	Coordinadora Latinoamericana de Organizaciones del Campo
CNSTP	Confédération Nationale des Syndicats de Travailleurs Paysans
COBAS	Comitati di Base
COC	Council of Canadians
CONFEUNASSC	Ecuadorian Confederación Nacional del Seguro Campesino
CP	Confédération Paysanne
CPE	Coordination Paysanne Européene
CPT	Pastoral Land Commission of Brazil
CUT	Central Trade Union Federation of Brazil
DOC	Dynamics of Contention
DSM!	Serbian Drugaciji Svet je Moguc!
ESF	European Social Forum

EU	European Union
EURODAD	European Network on Debt and Development
EZLN	Ejército Zapatista de Liberación Nacional
FAO	Food and Agricultural Organization
FARC	Revolutionary Armed Forces of Colombia
FIAN	Food and Information Action Network
FIPs	Five Interested Parties in WTO negotiations
FDC	Freedom from Debt Coalition (Philippines)
FDP	Foundation for Deep Ecology
FMRA	World Forum on Agrarian Reform
FNSP	Fédération Nationale des Syndicats Paysans
FOEI	Friends of the Earth International
FONDAD	Forum on Debt and Development
FTAA	Free Trade Area of the Americas
FZLN	Frente Zapatista de Liberación Nacional
G7	Group of Seven industrialized countries
G8	Group of Eight industrialized countries (G7 plus Russia)
G20	Group of Twenty developing countries
G33	Group of Thirty-three
G90	Group of Ninety
GATS	General Agreement on Trade in Services
GATT	General Agreement on Tariffs and Trade
GAAWM	General Assembly of the Anti-War Movement
GCAP	Global Call to Action Against Poverty
GDP	gross domestic product
GM	genetically modified
GMO	genetically modified organism
HIPC	highly indebted poor countries
HIV/AIDS	Human Immunodeficiency Virus/Acquired Immune Deficiency Syndrome
HKPA	Hong Kong-based People's Alliance Against the WTO
IBASE	Brazilian Institute for Social and Economic Studies
IC	International Council of the World Social Forum
ICCO	Interchurch Organization for Development Cooperation
IFG	International Forum on Globalization
IMC	independent media (indymedia) center
IMF	International Monetary Fund
INB	Infernal Noise Brigade
IPE	international political economy
IPS	Institute for Policy Studies
J2000	Jubilee 2000
JAFIP	Joint Action Forum of Indian People against the WTO
KOPA	Korean People's Action against the Korea–Japan Free Trade Agreement and the World Trade Organization
KRRS	Karnataka State Farmers' Association (Karnataka Rajya Raitha Sangha)
MAI	Multilateral Agreement on Investment
MGJ	Mobilization for Global Justice
ML	Communist Party India

MST	Landless Rural Workers' Movement (Movimento dos Trabalhadores Rurais Sem Terra, or Movimento dos Sem Terra)
NAFTA	North American Free Trade Agreement
NATO	North Atlantic Treaty Organization
NFU	Canadian National Farmers' Union
NFFC	National Family Farm Coalition
NGO	nongovernmental organization
Novib	Oxfam Netherlands
OECD	Organization for Economic Cooperation and Development
OPEC	Organization of Petroleum Exporting Countries
OWINFS	Our World Is Not For Sale
PAR	Participatory Action Research
PFS	Paolo Freire Stichting (Holland)
PGA	Peoples' Global Action
PPP	Plan Puebla Panama
PRS	poverty reduction strategy
PT	Brazilian Workers' Party (Partido dos Trabalhadores)
RICA	Intercontinental Network of Alternative Communication (Spain)
ROR	Rhythms of Resistance
SAP	structural adjustment program
SAPRI	Structural Adjustment Policy Review Initiative
SAPRIN	Structural Adjustment Participatory Review International Network
SLPI	Solidarité et Luttes Paysannes Internationales
SMA	Social Movements Assembly
SMIN	Social Movements International Network
SMWN	Social Movements World Network
STARC Alliance	Students Transforming and Resisting Corporations
SWP	Socialist Workers' Party
TNC	transnational corporation
TNI	Transnational Institute
TRIMS	Trade Related Investment Measures
TRIPs	Trade Related Aspects of Intellectual Property Rights
TWN	Third World Network
UN	United Nations
UNAG	Nicaraguan Unión Nacional de Agricultores y Ganaderos
UNEP	United Nations Environment Program
UNESCO	United Nations Educational, Scientific and Cultural Organization
UNORCA	Mexican Unión Nacional de Organizaciones Regionales Campesinas Autónomas
VC	Via Campesina
WEF	World Economic Forum
WMW	World March of Women
WOMBLES	White Overalls Movement Building Libertarian Effective Struggles
WSF	World Social Forum
WTO	World Trade Organization

A key question, and yet one that is not often asked in studies of the so-called "global justice" movement, is: "how are coalitions formed at a scale that is much greater than the local interpersonal networks that compose these coalitions?" ... For many observers, it is as if "globalization" automatically produces "resistance".

Sidney Tarrow, "Confessions of a Recovering Structuralist"

Over the last two decades country after country adopted the structural adjustment programs prescribed by the IMF. But in every country, people are now reeling under the disastrous impact of the World Bank, WTO and IMF triumvirate. So the resistance is also building up.

W. R. Varada Rajan, World Social Forum (WSF) delegate

What exists for the majority of people that are here is that capitalism, *this* capitalism no longer works for the great majority of countries. It does not offer dignified conditions for most of us; only for some, and all the time fewer. ... Therefore, people are seeking an alternative that, paradoxically, globalizes in the reverse.

Comité Mercosur de Organizaciones de Trabajo Social, WSF delegate

We believe that the forum attracts so many people because ... of neoliberal politics globalized in the entire world that creates exclusion, illiteracy, brain drain, infant mortality. All the human rights that the last generation fought for are being violated by ... the neoliberal economic model. Now, this model that is globalizing itself ... is fracturing at all sides because of the great amount of social exclusion, because the communities that protest are hungry and are everyday growing. This is demonstrated by the number of people here. They are representatives of all the countries where neoliberalism has played havoc. ... They are demonstrating that there are new social protagonists, and the people go out to the streets in order to be heard. Sometimes, the governments will listen to them. If they don't listen, we will continue fighting.

Madre de la Plaza de Mayo, WSF delegate

We all want, what it says there in the slogan, that another world is possible.

Aldo Caliari, WSF delegate

1 The globalization of neoliberalism and of activism

An introduction

Over the last quarter-century, we have witnessed a sea-change in the nature of leftist activism. Formerly grassroots or nationally focused social movements, nongovernmental organizations (NGOs), and other collectivities are increasingly sharing information, networking, coordinating action, launching campaigns, petitioning, lobbying, protesting, and framing their claims, targets, and visions at the transnational level of contention. These emerging, cross-border networks have even forged a unique and autonomous space, the World Social Forum (WSF) along with a web of regional and local offshoots. Here and through their proliferating joint campaigns, they deepen and broaden their ties and struggle toward "another possible world" beyond the current (dis)order, which activists decry as a globalizing neoliberal rule plagued by worsening poverty and inequalities within and among societies, the corporate takeover of land, the theft of the commons, ecological devastation, the feminization of poverty, the exacerbation of conflicts, and the erosion of democracy. This work seeks to address, first, why and how this shift to the global is taking place among activists (and, in doing so, what is the relationship between transnational activism and economic globalization); second, what is the composition and character of these emerging networks; and, third, what is the role of the WSF in this transnationalizing process.

The networks to be investigated in this work are among the largest that have come together in recent decades to directly target the "neoliberal triumvirate" of the World Bank, the International Monetary Fund (IMF) and the World Trade Organization (WTO). These include the Jubilee networks against debt and structural adjustment programs (SAPs), Via Campesina peasant farmers and Our World Is Not For Sale, which both target the WTO and other trade agreements, and the anti-capitalist, Zapatista-inspired Peoples' Global Action (PGA). Though beyond the scope and space confines of this study, it is important to bear in mind that these four networks are increasingly forging ties, coordinating action such as joint pressure campaigns and mass protests, and building the social forum process with other networks whose main targets and concerns have not traditionally been neoliberal globalization. As a consequence, environmental, workers', women's, immigrant, minority, indigenous, and peace networks are all becoming entwined with those struggling against neoliberal globalization. Together they are constituting what is today being called by a range of names, from the misnomer "anti-globalization movement" to the nondescript, but apt, "network of networks." Stated more generally, this is the global – and globalizing – left at the cusp of the twenty-first century.

Neoliberal globalization: an overview

In order to understand the globalizing left today, we must first get a sense of the complex phenomena *within* which and *against* which so many struggle: that is, neoliberal globalization. The footings of a neoliberal world order were laid with the establishment of international economic institutions following the Second World War, chief among them the World Bank, the IMF, and the General Agreement on Tariffs and Trade (GATT), which eventually would be expanded into the WTO.[1] But neoliberalism did not begin its climb to global orthodoxy until the 1970s economic recession and debt crisis, which led to the erosion and discrediting of the Keynesian social economic state in Europe and the developmentalist models of the Third World. In their place arose Reaganite and Thatcherite policies favoring capital investments, open markets, and limited state intervention as a recipe for spurring economic growth and reducing debt.

The spread of these policies both helped to precipitate and was in turn greatly legitimized by the implosion of the USSR and the dissolution of the Soviet bloc. The collapse was widely hailed as the triumph of the capitalist free market over the socialist planned economy, and of democracy over authoritarianism. Margaret Thatcher's declaration that "there is no alternative" seemed borne out by events of the late 1980s and early 1990s. With the demise of the bipolar order, the emergent "Washington Consensus" could be spread to every corner of the globe, unrivaled and unimpeded as never before. This presumed consensus called for states to adopt a number of economic policy changes which have also had wide-ranging social and political ramifications, many of them painful to broad sectors of society and thus extremely unpopular. These policies include state fiscal discipline to ward off deficits, cuts in public expenditures including the removal of subsidies, lowering tax rates, liberalizing finance toward interest rates determined by markets, floating exchange rates, trade liberalization through the reduction of tariffs, removing barriers to foreign direct investment, privatization of state-owned industries and services, deregulation to stimulate competition, and the safeguarding of private and foreign-held property rights. This bundle of policies comprising the Washington Consensus forms the substantive core of neoliberal globalization.[2]

The avenues through which these policies have been diffused over the last few decades are numerous, and go far beyond national governments deciding freely to adopt them. Here is where the post-Second World War footings of the neoliberal artifice gain importance. The Bretton Woods "twins" of the World Bank and IMF along with a strengthening GATT/WTO were the main instruments in neoliberal expansion throughout the last three decades of the twentieth century.

While a number of governments have on their own accord adopted these policies, many others have had little choice in the matter due to their indebtedness to foreign lenders and their relatively weak position in international trade *vis-à-vis* the wealthier North. Indeed, the debt trap in which many developing countries are mired compels their leaders to adopt the World Bank and IMF's neoliberal SAPs as a condition for further loans or debt write-offs. Meanwhile, a global, neoliberal free trade regime has been advancing under the WTO and regional and bilateral agreements, such as the North American Free Trade Agreement (NAFTA) and the Free Trade Area of the Americas (FTAA).[3] Smaller economies have little choice but to join these bodies and little effective voice for advancing their own interests once they do. Taken together, these international institutions and agreements constitute the main arteries for the dissemination of neoliberalism to more and more countries.

The debate over neoliberal globalization

Coinciding with the rise of neoliberal globalization is the contentious debate surrounding it, centering on its contemporary scope compared with previous historical periods, its virtues and vices, and the degree to which its transformative processes and effects are inevitable or could be rolled back, softened, steered, or strengthened and spread.[4] And given all that is at stake, these arguments over neoliberal globalization are likely among the most portentous of our time. The scholarly literature reflecting and contributing to this debate has mushroomed to the point where globalization is considered by some to be an ascendant paradigm in its own right, while globalization studies is emerging as a trans-disciplinary field bridging international relations theory, international political economy, sociology, development studies, geography, history, anthropology, post-colonial studies and cultural studies.[5]

Participating in these growing debates are scholars, policymakers, and concerned citizens and activists weighing in across the spectrum. Along the supportive side are its outright champions and defenders,[6] while moving toward the center are what might be called "recovering neoliberals" along with its long-time skeptics.[7] The latter are critical of some of its policy outcomes and call for reform in order to address the growing chasm between rich and poor as well as the political, social, and economic tensions it foments. But while critical of neoliberalism's excesses, the underlying assumption is that global capitalism can and should be righted. Moving into the oppositional side of the spectrum, we have a range of scholars and activists who by and large are united in their opposition to neoliberal globalization, but differ in their stance toward capitalism itself. Here again we find a continuum, this time from reform to total rejection and, often, revolution. Toward the reformist middle are calls for a return to Keynesian social democracies and/or to Polanyian re-embedded economies at the local, national, or macro-regional level,[8] while toward the anti-capitalist edge we find various strains of Marxism and anarchism.[9] Furthermore, we must step outside a strictly economistic barometer if we are to locate, for example, feminist calls for the need to address and root out patriarchy as part and parcel of any struggle against neoliberalism or capitalism, in addition to non-Western, pre-/ post-/anti-modern, indigenous, ecological, and spiritual approaches that propose more holistic ideas for transforming human relations and our relations with other species and the planet.[10]

Given this vast array of analysis and opinion surrounding neoliberal globalization and capitalism today, this debate will certainly not be settled herein. What *is* the central concern of this study, again, is the process by which and the reasons for which activists expand their critique and struggle from the local and national to the transnational level of contention in order to counter various aspects of neoliberal globalization. In this limited sense, then, this work contributes to our understanding of economic globalization's darker side of who loses, who suffers, and who pays for what is widely heralded as the only path to prosperity today, and who is attempting to construct another kind of globalization. But at the same time, in illuminating the collective actors and their proposals countering neoliberal globalization, we also get a glimpse of potential, alternative, and hopefully brighter futures beyond the contemporary global (dis)order in which we find ourselves. My perspective therefore is congruous with critical globalization studies, which is an emerging subsection of the literature comprised of scholars and activists most concerned with neoliberal globalization's negative outcomes and with studying and proposing alternatives to the current economic order.[11]

It must be stressed that this work does not pretend to be the complete story on neoliberal globalization. But by viewing neoliberal globalization through multiple lenses and from distinct vantage points – in this case from the perspective of those feeling so threatened, harmed, or dismayed that they are actively mobilizing against it – the research contributes to a fuller understanding of the complex, highly contested, and dynamic phenomenon, or, better, *syndrome*,[12] that is globalization. Simultaneously, we will gain a greater understanding of the transnationalizing activist networks themselves which are arrayed against neoliberal aspects of globalization. These groups comprise a significant part of the network of networks and the social forum process, and thus the global left today. It is to this diverse array of collective actors that we can now turn.

Distinguishing global activists from transnational civil society

This study focuses on *global activists* rather than *transnational civil society*, for the former term most clearly identifies which slice of civil society we are in fact referring to when we speak of transnational collective action against neoliberal globalization. As with globalization, the concept of transnational or global civil society is itself rife with debate over its definition, importance, and virtues.[13] While some, such as Ann Florini and P. J. Simmons, banish "profit-seeking private entities"[14] from their definition of transnational civil society – a move that accurately reflects the common usage of the term among many activists themselves – other scholars include financial actors as an important part of civil society, regarding them as instrumental in forging contemporary transnational ties. In his recent historical investigation of the concept, John Keane asserts that global civil society is comprised of "charities, think-tanks, prominent intellectuals, … campaigning and lobby groups, citizens' protests … small and large corporate firms, independent media, internet groups and websites, employers' federations, trades unions, international commissions, parallel summits and sporting organisations."[15]

The difficulty with broad definitions such as Keane's is that they tend to gloss over the very real tensions and conflicting interests occurring among non-state actors: that is, *within* civil society itself most broadly defined. To Keane, "General Motors plus Amnesty International plus the Ruckus Society" all have a place in a global civil society "marked by a proclivity toward non-violence and respect for the principles of compromise, mutual respect, even power-sharing among different ways of life."[16] Based on my research, I would venture to say that the bulk of activists resisting what they perceive to be the nefarious effects of neoliberalism would take exception to such a lumping of multinational corporations in with human rights NGOs and direct action groups; I would also suspect that many Fortune 500 chief executive officers (CEOs) would balk at being considered of the same *genre* as those raising a ruckus in the streets of Seattle. It is perhaps more reasonable to take our cue from the framers of the WSF in thinking of civil societies – both domestic and global, if the latter indeed exists – as a *space* or *terrain* rather than a collective entity or set of actors. Similarly, following Margaret Keck and Kathryn Sikkink, civil society is most accurately viewed as "an arena of struggle, a fragmented and contested area where 'the politics of transnational civil society is centrally about the way in which certain groups emerge and are legitimated (by governments, institutions, and other groups).'"[17] I would only add to this definition that, in the current struggle to shape globalization, seeking legitimacy is a crucial, yet tactical, battle; the substantive war is cast in terms of who will govern domestically and have the power to establish transnational rules, the people or global capitalists.

We therefore need to identify more precisely which actors within domestic and transnational civil society constitute this study's protagonists. They are *activists*, which I define as:

> A role assumed by individuals or collective actors either to resist what they consider to be a political wrong or to act to bring about political change, through either contained or transgressive tactics, excluding political violence.[18]

An activist therefore may be a member of a social movement, popular struggle, trade union, collective, network, NGO, or civic or religious organization, a scholar or student, or an individual unaffiliated with any group. I use the term *role* in order to emphasize that actors can and often do play more than one such role engaging with the same political issue.[19] For example, I distinguish the role of activist from that of *state actor*, who nevertheless may act as a *state ally* to activists in his governmental capacity and may assume the role of activist in his free time – or while checking e-mails from a political listserve while at his government office. I also distinguish the activist role from that of *armed militant*, who, like the state actor, may work toward similar goals as activists and might be considered, by some, as an ally.[20] An indigenous Zapatista woman who donned a mask and took up a gun to help occupy her town hall in southeastern Mexico on 1 January 1994 may have joined other peasant farmers years later under the banner of Via Campesina in street demonstrations against the WTO Cancun Round. Apropos of the Zapatistas in particular, just as individuals can play different roles around the same issue, so can organizations: In their relationship with the Mexican authorities they are armed militants and, indeed, when they are occupying a town hall by force they are actively playing this role (even though in that action sympathetic activists may consider them allies). But in their popular *consultas* with the Mexican people and their *encuentros* with international activists, they are activists.

Furthermore, the range of contemporary activism against neoliberalism runs from routinized and contained activities of lobbying and information-sharing to transgressive acts of street demonstrations and civil disobedience. In the latter, I include political acts against private property, such as squatting land or buildings, dismantling multinational fast-food restaurants, destroying genetically modified crops, and defacing advertising billboards. I also include obstructionist tactics like physically blocking entrances to prevent delegates from attending trade meetings, as well as symbolic, physical contact meant to publicly shame but not cause bodily harm, such as *entarteurs* flinging pies in the faces of James Wolfensohn and Bill Gates (he got twenty-five) and other unlucky figureheads of neoliberal rule.[21]

This shift in language toward *activism* and away from *civil society*, in addition to giving us greater definitional precision, also reflects the more assertive tone of political contention in recent years. This is witnessed, for example, in the rise of massive street protests, the startling array of opinion and approaches housed within the same transnational networks, and the growing willingness on the part of some NGOs and other Northern solidarity groups to listen to, learn from, and cooperate with those most adversely impacted by neoliberal globalization, who are often demanding more thoroughgoing structural transformations than the policy or lifestyle changes that have often been advocated by reformist NGOs. Indicative of this shift toward activism is the recent experience of Amnesty International, relayed by its European and Asian campaign coordinator:

> There are all kinds of individual actions that contribute to the change and I think that it is extremely important to recognize this. And we as an organization are recognizing that ourselves. We are talking about *activism, activists*. We don't talk about "Amnesty members" anymore. We're moving away from this old thing about *belonging to*. It's about *doing what* as opposed to belonging to. ... It's about activism, it's about change. ... If we help, if we change, [then] in which organization and in which form we are, that doesn't matter.[22]

This trend has been identified by W. Lance Bennett as the emergence of a second generation of transnational activism. It is characterized by inclusive organizational models that favor diversity, linking issues through horizontal networks, and adopting social technologies that facilitate greater autonomy and leaderless networks and that provide political capacities for communication. This new generation of activism, according to Bennett, differs from the more centralized NGO model and social movement coalitions that predominated in the first generation of transnational activism, chronicled, for example, in earlier works by Keck and Sikkink and by Jackie Smith, Charles Chatfield, and Ron Pagnucco.[23] These above distinctions, as we will see later on in this chapter, will be a useful point of departure for analyzing the diverse networks comprising today's so-called network of networks. Before doing this, however, we must first overview the genesis and magnitude of contemporary transnational activism.

The rise and scope of transnational left activism

Transnational collective action has recently been described by social movement scholars Donatella della Porta and Sidney Tarrow as "the most dramatic change we see in the world of contentious politics."[24] This is a change not only in frequency of interactions across borders but also in the complexity of campaigns, the density and design of networks, the adaptability to rapidly changing events, the fluidity of alliances that bring together a wide range of issues, actors, and perspectives, and the boldness, assertiveness, and creativity with which demands for profound, systemic change are put forth.[25] This trend toward increased transnational activism has coincided and accelerated alongside the global spread of neoliberalism. Between 1973 and 1993, the number of transnational social movement organizations concerned with human rights, the environment, women's rights, peace, and development more than tripled, rising to over 600 organizations, with groups having members from over twenty countries on average.[26] Furthermore, since 1983 these organizations have markedly increased their networking activities with other NGOs.[27]

This trend has been magnified in the last ten years as transnational organizations and ties matured and solidified. Parallel summits are often organized in tandem with meetings of states and intergovernmental bodies such as the World Bank, IMF, WTO and regional trade organizations, United Nations (UN) conferences, the World Economic Forum (WEF), the Group of Seven/Group of Eight industrialized countries (G7/G8),[28] the European Union (EU), the Organization for Economic Cooperation and Development (OECD), and the North Atlantic Treaty Organization (NATO). These parallel summits are further being supplemented with a growing number of independently organized events that allow non-state actors to set their own agenda and timetable. The most notable example is the annual WSF. Initiated in Porto Alegre, Brazil, in 2001, it has quickly inspired a number of macro-regional, national, local, and thematic forums modeled after it. Autonomous events such as these, rare in the early 1990s, have grown to comprise about 40 percent of international activist summits since 2001 and attract anywhere from 1,000 to over 100,000 participants.[29]

While tensions between "reformist" NGOs and more "radical" or direct action social movements and networks exist today as they have in the past, the nature and frequency of contemporary activist forums have helped to bring this diverse spectrum into contact with one another, and can therefore be credited with some softening of the reformist-radical polemic among contemporary activists. This is witnessed by the fact that four out of five parallel summits organized by NGOs and social movements in recent years have included both conferences and street demonstrations – that is, both contained and transgressive activities – up from only one out of two in the recent past. As another indication that this reformist-radical gulf is being somewhat narrowed by a greater willingness or perceived necessity to work together to achieve common goals, "networking" has emerged as the stated primary aim of these parallel summits, followed by public education and proposing alternatives.[30]

A final important indicator that activism is truly going global, and not just North Atlantic, is the diversification in the locales of parallel summits. Whereas in the late 1980s nearly nine out of ten events were held in North America or Europe, in 2001 the majority were being hosted in the Global South. Roughly one-third were set in Latin America, corresponding to the number held in Europe. Africans organized the same amount of summits as did North Americans – about 20 percent each – and nearly one in ten was held in Asia and Oceania.[31] Southern activists' increasing capacity and willingness to host autonomous social forums in addition to parallel summits that accompany nearly every meeting of global and regional financial institutions, trade bodies, and security organizations demonstrate that the trend toward building truly global ties, campaigns, and networks is likely to continue.

The anti-neoliberal struggle and the network of networks

What is animating this rise in transnational activism? A crystallization around exactly who to fight and why has slowly emerged in recent years. In my interviews and conversations with activists at global forums, the enemy goes by many names, but almost always entails the global spread, and perceived mounting failures, of specific neoliberal policies, or institutions, and/or global capitalism overall: "structural adjustment," "the IMF," "World Bank," "Multilateral Agreement on Investment (MAI)," "WTO," "NAFTA," "FTAA," "multinationals" or "transnational corporations (TNCs)," "neoliberalism," "*this* kind of capitalism," or "capitalism" in general are the common culprits. One activist shared the sentiment of countless others in stating:

> Capitalism has become global, much more global, and much more *explicitly* global in its reach. In its ascendance, it's eliminating governments and their agencies. The IMF, WTO, the World Bank, all these other regional banks are basically taking over functions of government. They're trying to impose their decisions on the rest of the world, and it happens in Brazil, it happens in the USA, in Canada, in Asia, in Africa, everywhere. So people coming

from there, they experience this. Not to be simple, but to simplify: We are really facing a global enemy. ... In a sense, we all throughout the whole world experience it in different forms and different shapes, but it's the same enemy.[32]

Because of its complexity, global, neoliberal capitalism is seen as requiring a multi-pronged and multi-level resistance. There are first and foremost the points at which economic globalization "touches down," to use Mittelman's phrase: the sweatshop floor union-busters; the countryside loggers, poachers, miners, and dam builders; the military, police, or hired guns sent to disperse an angry crowd or move off a squatter encampment; the mayoral office or national parliament. But activists are also increasingly feeling compelled to pull at the strings of globalization and follow them up and away from their localized manifestations, leading to a more complex web of struggle, coordinated via internet, fax, phone, and face-to-face meetings, and aimed at linking with others across borders to publicly denounce and explicitly target what once were shrouded entities. These new targets are embodied especially in neoliberalism's three pillars, the World Bank, IMF, and the WTO, as well as regional and bilateral trade agreements patterned off of the latter, the TNCs who most profit from these new policies, wealthy governments – especially the G7 advancing the neoliberal agenda – the less formalized spaces where world elites meet, such as the Davos, Switzerland-based WEF, as well as national leaders and parties who acquiesce to or promote these often unpopular policies.

Resistance locally to neoliberalism's "touchdown" has been building within national borders since the early 1980s and has taken myriad shapes. In what was then known as the Third World, "IMF riots" against IMF and World Bank-imposed SAPs have intermittently erupted for some three decades. Social unrest and industrial conflicts in both poor and rich countries have taken the forms of strikes, work stoppages, and blockades. Democratic movements have driven from office governments and politicians responsible for squandering or stealing public funds, and others who promoted or caved in to neoliberal policies by dismantling the welfare and developmentalist state. Greater organizing to counter neoliberal reforms has also been seen among the most vulnerable constituencies of societies, such as poor women, immigrants and asylum seekers, indigenous peoples, ethnic and sexual minorities, and people with HIV/AIDS. Land seizures by peasants have been on the rise in many parts of the Global South. Small farmers, indigenous communities, and urban activists have waged ongoing resistance against the encroachment of corporate agriculture, pharmaceutical companies, and energy and road-building projects, in an attempt to defend their communities and life-ways, protect the environment, and preserve the commons. Armed uprising, most notably in Chiapas as NAFTA came into effect, has also been launched in opposition to free trade agreements. More recently, anti-war efforts have arisen to counter the US-led invasion and occupation of Iraq and the ongoing "war against terror," which many activists equate with neoliberal imperialism.

This brief overview of the diverse forms that local and national resistance has taken suggests that there are many differences of opinion, emphasis, tactics, organizational composition, and stated purposes among the various groups and individuals mobilizing today. Yet, as we shall see throughout this work, there is also growing articulation, overlap, cooperation, and even convergence among them around shared spaces, issues, campaigns, and alternative visions. This confluence is so remarkable that many participants and observers have begun referring to these vast mobilizations as one single movement or network, calling it differently depending on their vantage point: anti-corporate globalization, anti-capitalist, anti-imperialist, globalization from below, global justice and solidarity, global social justice, or simply a movement of movements or a network of networks. Revealing how this collectivity is still very much a work in progress, one leading activist-scholar noted:

> We are increasingly calling it the Global Justice Movement. This, of course, is an illusion, because there are thousands of different movements, they aren't just one movement. But starting with MAI and then the WTO Battle in Seattle, many people are beginning to see that these movements add up to more than the sum of their parts. The World Social Forum is a place where people get to know one another and, in effect, make a reality of the Global Justice Movement.[33]

The World Social Forum in brief

Indeed, the WSF is remarkable in a number of ways. It has been an unrivaled success in drawing diverse social movements and NGOs together into one global space/institution/organization. This embrace of diversity is encapsulated in the WSF Charter of Principles:

> The World Social Forum is a plural, diversified, non-confessional, non-governmental and non-party context that, in a decentralized fashion, interrelates organizations and movements engaged in concrete action at levels from the local to the international to build another world. The World Social Forum will always be a forum open to pluralism and to the diversity of activities and ways of engaging of the organizations and movements that decide to participate in it, as well as the diversity of genders, ethnicities, cultures, generations and physical capacities, providing they abide by this Charter of Principles.[34]

This unprecedented ability to attract actors and organizations diverse in issues, goals, type, and demography can be demonstrated both quantifiably and qualitatively. The first gathering held in Porto Alegre, Brazil, in January 2001 attracted 15,000 people, while its numbers have grown dramatically since then, as some 100,000 have participated in each of the annual events since 2003. While the first forum was coordinated by a coalition of twelve NGOs and social movements from Latin America and Europe, the process is now overseen by the WSF International Council (IC), drawn from over 100 NGOs, networks, social movements and campaigns from around the world.[35] Macro-regional, national, and local forums are proliferating in Europe, the Americas, the Mediterranean, Asia, Africa, and the Middle East, coordinated by over sixty mobilization committees. The forums' wide-ranging themes include democratic sustainable development, principles and values, human rights, diversity and equality, media, culture and counter-hegemony, political power, civil society and democracy, democratic world order, the fight against militarization, and promoting peace. Reflecting the diversity of left activism today, the solutions advocated by WSF participants are equally broad, ranging from rolling back globalization processes and strengthening the local and/or the state, to reforming neoliberalism and global institutions, to tearing down existing structures and building a post-capitalist, post-state world order.

The forum's genesis can be traced to a convergence of political activism taking place on both sides of the Atlantic. By the late 1990s, social movements and citizens' networks had matured to the point where there was a widely felt need to construct an autonomous space in which they could continue to expand and strengthen their global links, and to discuss, strategize, and develop alternatives to neoliberalism, militarism, and all forms of discrimination and marginalization. As one of its key supporters, John Cavanagh of the Washington, DC-based Institute for Policy Studies, reflected:

> Beginning in 1997–8, citizens' movements that make up the global justice movement began to get strong enough to check the dominant institutions – we defeated fast-track, the MAI, the WTO in Seattle. We were at the point of a critical mass. We could block their moves. So the onus shifted to us. If we wanted to move to the next stage, we needed to develop alternatives. The World Social Forum is one space committed exclusively for the task of developing alternatives.[36]

The WSF indeed was the embodiment of an idea whose time had come. The confluence of a number of processes served to create an environment ripe for the WSF: the mounting failures of neoliberal policies and the attribution of these policies and their promoters as a common source of suffering and, thus, target; the increased awareness of, communication among, and identification with more and more streams of resistance from around the globe, greatly facilitated by the internet; the coordinated action across borders brokered by ever more experienced activists; the de-legitimization of UN conferences which were coming to be seen as a waste of activists' time and resources; and the recent, successful mass actions and events such as the defeat of the MAI and the Battle in Seattle. Cavanagh elaborated on this auspicious timing:

> This is the moment. The dominant institutions of economic globalization are in crises of legitimacy. The public debate has opened up for the first

time since the 1970s to different approaches, different alternatives. The WSF offers the space for these alternatives to be born and to spread.[37]

But if these larger processes provide the backdrop for the birth of the WSF, the trigger event was the refusal by organizers of the Davos-based WEF to open those meetings to activists.[38] In response, the Brazilians Oded Grajew and Francisco (Chico) Whitaker, in discussions with the French director of *Le Monde diplomatique* Bernard Cassen, conceived the idea of an organization, or rather a space, to oppose Davos, choosing its name carefully. The WSF was to be, first, a *social* economic counterpoint – thus the name social forum – to the neoliberal economic WEF. They soon brought together eight Brazilian organizations to begin planning for the first forum.[39] Around the same time, the new network that Cassen helped to initiate, that of the Association for the Taxation of Financial Transactions for the Aid of Citizens (ATTAC), joined with three other European groups mobilizing against unfettered financial flows and SAPs to convene an alternative conference in late January 1999 in Switzerland. This they termed "The Other Davos," to coincide with and counter the annual WEF meeting.[40] The Europeans invited scholars and activists from around the globe, including the Brazilian coalition, to participate.[41] At this and subsequent meetings, the plan for the WSF was brought to fruition.

In addition to promoting social economic alternatives to the prevailing neoliberal doctrine, another component of the WSF's name – that is, *world* – encourages activists to shift their scale to the global level of contention. This scale shift is enshrined in the WSF Charter:

> The World Social Forum is a world process. All the meetings that are held as part of this process have an international dimension. ... The World Social Forum is a process that encourages its participant organizations and movements to situate their actions, from the local level to the national level and seeking active participation in international contexts, as issues of planetary citizenship, and to introduce onto the global agenda the change-inducing practices that they are experimenting in building a new world in solidarity.[42]

The third and final part of its name – *forum* – is also salient in that its founders adapted an innovative design for a transnational political entity: horizontal, non-deliberative, and non-representational, and thereby avoiding becoming a locus of power over which to be fought. Its Brazilian founders have worked hard to establish and maintain the WSF as neither an organization, nor a movement, nor an event, nor a political party, but instead as a place for encounter, dialogue, and free exchange of ideas. This battle – at once ideological and methodological – rages on, as we will see throughout this work. The proper metaphor, as Whitaker and other framers continually remind us, is rather an open space or a town square. The WSF Charter outlines and seeks to safeguard this unusual transnational structure:

The meetings ... do not deliberate on behalf of the World Social Forum as a body. No-one, therefore, will be authorized, on behalf of any of the editions of the Forum, to express positions claiming to be those of all its participants. The participants in the Forum shall not be called on to take decisions as a body, whether by vote or acclamation, on declarations or proposals for action that would commit all, or the majority, of them and that propose to be taken as establishing positions of the Forum as a body. It thus does not constitute a locus of power to be disputed by the participants in its meetings, nor does it intend to constitute the only option for interrelations and action by the organizations and movements that participate in it. ... Nonetheless, organizations or groups of organizations that participate ... must be assured the right, during such meetings, to deliberate on declarations or actions they may decide on.[43]

Although it is too early to conclude with certainty, many share Cavanagh's ambitious and hopeful view stated at the beginning of this section that the WSF is a key stepping stone toward building one global movement or, to my mind more accurately, one network of networks. This sentiment is reflected in initial characterizations of the forum on the part of scholars. Heikki Patomäki and Teivo Teivainen, for example, see the WSF as "the first serious attempt to organize the political forces of global civil society into a unified space of positive agenda-formation and planning of collective transformative actions."[44] Thomas Ponniah and William Fisher hailed it as "the most recent, vibrant, and potentially productive articulation of an emergent global civil society."[45] Bennett concurs, stating: "these gatherings of the social justice tribes also represent the first steps toward a global civil society populated not just by NGOs, but by citizens who seem to be making direct democratic claims beyond borders."[46]

The importance and impact of the network of networks

While the progress is slow and the defeats are many, the groups comprising the emerging network of networks and organizing in and around the social forums can claim at least partial credit for a number of significant victories through their transnational collective action against neoliberal globalization. One of the first came when a fledgling network, which would eventually grow into Our World Is Not for Sale (to be analyzed in Chapter 4), organizing largely over the internet successfully defeated the OECD's MAI in 1998. Members of this network, including Public Citizen's Global Trade Watch, the Third World Network, and Focus on the Global South, were also instrumental in organizing the Battle in Seattle at the WTO's third ministerial meeting in late 1999. These activists co-ordinated much of the week's activities – including marches and mass actions, public lectures and debates, and an NGO tribunal – which helped to disrupt the official meetings, led to the talks breaking down, and earned this nascent movement a second win, and its first major press coverage (albeit much of it negative).

Another victory came in late 2003 at the fifth WTO ministerial in Cancun. Tens of thousands of peasant farmers organized within the Via Campesina (Chapter 5) joined with other activist organizations such as the World March of Women in a parallel summit and street demonstrations, which emboldened delegates inside the meetings to stand their ground, leading to the talks' stalemate with no agreement. Furthermore, a vast network of debt-eradication campaigns, social movements, church and civic associations, NGOs, and political entities, organized into the Jubilee 2000 initiative (Chapter 3), were successful in appealing to religious values and beliefs and attracting media attention and celebrities to their cause. Their efforts culminated in a global petition signed by 24 million people in support of a "Jubilee year" of debt forgiveness. This campaign is widely credited for getting G7 governments and banks to agree to write off $110 billion of poor-country debts, and their follow-up campaigns have kept the pressure on rich nations to make good on the promises made and to go further still.

Meanwhile, a citizens' movement begun in France but which has since spread rapidly across the globe, ATTAC, has been working to avert future catastrophes like the Asian financial crisis by shoring up national democratic control over financial flows. Their core demand is to push governments to pass legislation that would levy a small tax on financial transactions. Through a combination of public education, lobbying, working through existing political parties, and mass actions, ATTAC now enjoys a considerable degree of legitimacy among politicians and the media, especially in Europe, and is credited with getting a number of European national parliaments to begin proposing EU-wide legislation toward this tax. ATTAC France is also widely hailed as one of the lead organizations of the successful "*non*" campaign rejecting the EU constitution in the summer 2005 referendum and thereby bringing the elite-driven integration process to a screeching halt. In voting down the proposed document, they demanded instead a constitution that enshrines Europe's social democratic legacy, not the contemporary neoliberal doctrine.[47]

There have also been victories away from the media spotlight trained on major international meetings, and rather on the "frontlines" where communities are everyday battling corporate encroachment and government rollbacks. For example, the massive protests over the privatization of water witnessed from Canada to South Africa won an important battle in Cochabamba, Bolivia, where hundreds of thousands of workers and peasants mobilized to beat back Bechtel corporation's efforts to privatize the community's water supply. Meanwhile, Indian villagers, farmers, and consumer NGOs – waging simultaneous campaigns against Monsanto, Coca-Cola, Kentucky Fried Chicken, Cargill, and Enron, among others – recently pulled off a successful village blockade that thwarted DuPont's plans to relocate a nylon manufacturing plant to Tamil Nadu. The Karnataka State Farmers' Association, which is the largest single organization participating in both the Via Campesina and the Peoples' Global Action network (Chapter 6), has been crucial in these struggles.

Through activists' adaptability and willingness to synergize diverse struggles, the nascent network of networks survived – and arguably reemerged stronger from – the post-September 11th restrictions on civil liberties and democratic oversight in the name of heightened security and fighting terror.[48] By shifting emphasis and expanding agendas to bring the issues of peace, war, and military violence to center-stage, as well as through dialoging on how these issues inter-relate with those of economic justice, the environment, and struggles for equal rights, the network of networks was able to launch a formidable, collective come-back on 15 February 2003, a date that was decided upon at the Social Movements Assembly following the first European Social Forum in Florence the previous fall. In a massive mobilization without historical precedent, an estimated 30 to 60 million people – up to 1 percent of the earth's inhabitants – mobilized for peace in more than 100 countries before the war against Iraq had even begun. Many who came together for that day of struggle have continued to coordinate their efforts, coalescing into the General Assembly of the Anti-War Movement (GAAWM)[49] that now convenes at and between the annual WSF and regional social forums.

While this impressive mobilization against war in early 2003 failed to prevent the United States from launching an attack, it nevertheless sent a strong message to political leaders that has had far-ranging impacts from Europe to Latin America to Asia, and can be partially credited for the erosion in US allies' willingness to main-tain troops in Iraq.[50] The event also won for the emerging global justice and peace movement – as some have since been calling it – a greater legitimacy in the main-stream press. A *New York Times* commentary the following day exclaimed:

> The fracturing of the Western alliance over Iraq and the huge antiwar demonstrations around the world this weekend are reminders that there may still be two superpowers on the planet: the United States and world public opinion. … President Bush appears to be eyeball to eyeball with a tenacious new adversary: millions of people who flooded the streets of New York and dozens of other world cities to say they are against war.[51]

When compared with the same newspaper's editorial page upon the network of network's debut in Seattle just a couple of years earlier, the difference is striking: At that time, Thomas Friedman flippantly dismissed the emerging collectivity as "a Noah's ark of flat-earth advocates, protectionist trade unions and yuppies looking for their 1960's fix."[52] Three years on, the old feminist adage "you've come a long way, baby," seemed particularly fitting.

Summary of findings

How and why activist groups comprising the network of networks have come that long way from localized contention to transnational collective action capable of these considerable successes, in addition to what are their compositions and characters, and finally what is the role of the WSF in this transnationalizing process, is the focus of this work. I will briefly overview the main findings from exploring these three questions. In Chapter 2, I will detail the research approach and methodology used that resulted in these conclusions, and will situate them within the appropriate scholarship from which they draw and to which they contribute.

Findings I: why and how activists shift scale

While there is growing evidence that activism is in fact "going global," there have been remarkably few studies to date that empirically investigate how and why this process is occurring. Thomas Olesen and James Rosenau observed:

> A spate of recent publications suggests that social movements are going global. ... The scholarly work of the last ten years has made important strides in theorizing this development. This is why we find it surprising that the majority of these accounts pay no, or only little, attention to questions of distance. Negotiating distance and traversing scales, from the local over the national to the global and back again, is perhaps the most important, and also complex, task for many of today's movements.[53]

Their sentiments echo Tarrow's admonition at this chapter's opening: "A key question ... not often asked in studies of the so-called 'global justice' movement, is: 'how are coalitions formed at a scale that is much greater than the local interpersonal networks that compose these coalitions? For many observers," he continues, "it is as if 'globalization' automatically produces 'resistance.'" Taking Olesen, Rosenau, and Tarrow's critique seriously, I have placed at the center of my empirical research and theorizing the relationship between the globalization of neoliberalism and resistance to it, by asking both *why* and *how* activists are shifting from the local and national to include the transnational level of contention.

The most general – and thus generalizable – finding is that, despite their tremendous diversity, each network nonetheless has followed a similar trajectory in "going global." Specifically with regard to *why* this process is taking place, as was alluded to earlier in the context of rising anti-neoliberal sentiment and reaction, this work concludes that what triggers localized resistance across the globe today and what spurs activists to seek their targets, solutions, and allies transnationally is the widely perceived *structural violences* of neoliberal globalization, experienced as palpable threats and suffering in people's day-to-day lives. In denouncing neoliberalism as the source of widespread danger and harm, activists are not denying that benefits have accrued to some under these policies. What they are asking, however, is: "*Who* has benefited, and how many in relation to the whole of humanity, and at what cost to the rest of us, to other species, and to the planet?" And given the adverse global changes coinciding with neoliberalism's broad processes, or what I term structural violences – namely, the unprecedented concentrations of wealth and power and the rapid destruction of life-ways and livelihoods, eco-systems and species – activists are questioning whether the price of neoliberal globalization is not in fact too high, and the risks too great, for too many.

My usage of the term structural violence deserves elaboration. This term is rooted in both peace studies and neo-Marxist dependency theory, and is experiencing a renewed interest among some critical globalization scholars.[54] The classic conception of structural violence within peace studies comes from Johan Galtung's identification of three forms of violence. The most obvious is *direct* violence, whereby an actor intending to cause physical or mental harm can be identified. A second form is indirect, or *structural*, violence. The social structure itself is the medium through which the violence is conducted in this case. Exploitation, the penetration and segmentation of identities, and marginalization and fragmentation are all forms of structural violence, and can occur between individuals, societies, and regions, as well as globally. The structural violence of colonialism is one of the most pervasive transnational examples, wherein "there was an input of mega-violence which was used to build the structure … , still to a large extent operational after formal decolonization."[55] A third kind of violence, which to Galtung is the most insidious, is *cultural* violence: "all of it symbolic, in religion and ideology, in language and art, in science and law, in media and education."[56] Cultural violence serves to legitimize direct and structural forms of violence: "The culture preaches, teaches, admonishes, eggs on, and dulls us into seeing exploitation and/or repression as normal and natural, or into not seeing them (particularly not exploitation) at all."[57] When referring to cultural violence, he argues that one should really speak of cultural *power*, or the ability to shape actions by framing what is right and wrong. Here Galtung is very close to the Gramscian notion of hegemony, or the legitimization of particular relations of power as "common sense."

To illustrate the nature and interrelationship of these various forms of violence, let's take the example of Brazilian poverty and landlessness and the growing Movimento dos Sem Terra (MST) to reclaim land on which to feed themselves and rebuild self-sufficiency, community, and dignity, and which is also a driving force behind the transnational network the Via Campesina. Despite being a leading food exporter, some estimates claim that as much as two-thirds of Brazil's population is malnourished, perhaps double the figure of thirty years ago. This means that an estimated 56 million Brazilians go hungry every day. This, in Galtung's conceptualization, would be structural violence. Legitimating and perpetuating this structurally violent situation is a more general cultural violence, reflected by one rural activist as "hav[ing] been trained always to obey, to obey the landowner, the priest, the political boss. They learnt this from their families and from the short period they were in school."[58] But due to a growing willingness to question cultural violence and challenge structural violence by occupying land, Brazil's poor are experiencing increased direct violence. An estimated 1,600 peasants have been murdered in agrarian conflicts since the 1980s, in addition to the beatings and threats that are apparently commonplace on behalf of powerful landowners to intimidate the movement and maintain the status quo. In sum, *direct violence* is rising now that *cultural violence* has failed to shore up the *structural violence* of the unequal distribution of land, wealth, rights, and dignity in that country.

This example is illustrative of the spirals of violence being set off across the globe, as more and more people come to challenge as nonsensical the hegemonic "common sense" of neoliberal globalization and, in the words of the International Forum on Globalization (IFG), "reject as absurd the argument that the poor must be exploited and the environment destroyed to make the money necessary to end poverty and save the planet."[59] Challenging this logic is what global leftist activism today is about. In the case studies that follow, we will begin each chapter with a closer look at the nature of the perceived violence against which that particular network is mobilizing, shifting transnationally, and participating in the social forums to do so. While those who protest against neoliberal policies are at times met with direct violence as a consequence – as the Brazilian example showed – what will be focused on in this work is what I call the structural violence of neoliberal globalization, which I view as a more general concept into which we can adequately group activists' diverse claims.

My use of the concept of "structure" also needs further explanation. Following the constructivist scholar Nicolas Onuf, I understand structures to be "social arrangements," which are any stable patterns of rules, institutions, and unintended consequences which manifest themselves in the social world for observers to experience. Rules, along with their conglomerations into institutions and regimes, lead to *rule*, defined as a condition in which some agents use rules to exercise control and obtain advantages over other agents.[60] From this perspective we can interpret neoliberalism as a condition of rule where some privileged actors use rules to control and obtain advantages over others. Furthermore, the main collective actors propagating neoliberal policies – the WTO, the World Bank, the IMF, numerous state governments and the multinational corporations who greatly influence them, along with the structural adjustment programs, "free" trade agreements, and loans to heavily indebted countries – constitute neoliberal rule's powerful agents, institutions, and regimes. Finally, structures should be thought of as not only political and socioeconomic institutions but also cultural formations, and therefore the violence they entail is also varied.

Turning from what structures are ontologically to *how* we might be able to identify their existence, the hermeneutic philosopher Peter Winch posited that a system – or in our case a structure – can be said to exist if there is enough of a set of explicit, tacit, or latent rules that actors share and follow.[61] This understanding of structure is consistent with much of the work within cultural studies, where structures are said to exist as long as people act or behave in accordance with such structures or make use of them in activities.[62] Reflecting on activism against neoliberal globalization, I would add that structures can also be said to exist if people are explicitly *re*acting to them, blaming them for causing harmful changes and heightened insecurities in their lives, and joining together to denounce, discredit, and resist their rule.

Once we have located the source of localized resistance to be broad change processes and triggers of neoliberal policies that I subsume under the rubric of structural violence, we can next turn to the question of *how* activism is going global. By tracing the "how" question in addition to that of the "why," we are refusing to rush to a second conclusion on globalization and resistance which is often assumed. This one presumes that the spread of neoliberal policies, touching down to trigger *localized* resistances in various sites around the globe, automatically produces *transnational* collective action. In order to avoid this assumption and rather to turn it into an empirical question, we must next identify a series of relational and cognitive shifts, or *mechanisms*, that contribute to the scale shift process, in order to understand the "how" question of transnational activism.

This work shows that, once localized action has been triggered against a specific aspect of neoliberal policies, what often occurs is the following sequence of actions, or mechanisms:

- a *realization of the need to "go global"* fueled by frustration in not getting desired results at the local or national level;
- *relational and non-relational diffusion* of information through existing ties and networks, in addition to *relational and non-relational brokerage* wherein movement entrepreneurs reach out to forge ties with new actors or to reinvigorate ties with former allies;
- both diffusion and brokerage require some efforts at *frame alignment*, often entailing frame extension of one issue into another in a search for common ground for joint action and, eventually, constructing a global transformative frame that could serve as an alternative to neoliberal globalization overall;
- via diffusion, brokerage, and frame alignment, a *shift in objects and claims* occurs among existing or newly brokered umbrella groups, often identifying a common transnational object of contention – such as the IMF, World Bank, or WTO – in addition to a similar shifting in claims made against those and other proponents of neoliberal globalization;
- through this process, three types of *attribution* may take place among activists involved:
  - *attribution of worthiness*, for example in distant-issue, Northern NGOs finding recipients or so-called partners in the South deemed worthy of their altruistic advocacy efforts; and/or
  - *attribution of interconnectedness*, characterized by groups with diverse goals and constituencies identifying each other's struggles as related to their own, and seeking to link up as autonomous but articulated movements; and/or
  - *attribution of similarity*, witnessed, for example, in activists increasingly identifying others across borders as sharing the same identity – peasant, debtor, indigenous, precarious worker, youth, etc. – threatened by neoliberal change.
- each of these forms of attribution produces *solidarity*, that is, support for a group cause as well as its tactics,[63] but as we will see in the next section, the solidarity evoked is of differing qualities and has distinct impacts on the cohesiveness of networks themselves;
- finally, all three forms of attribution and solidarity lead to *transnational collective action*, completing the scale shift process.[64]

Structured around the above framework, this work is able to explain both why and how scale shift has occurred, tracing this process from localized beginnings to transnational collective action across four major activist networks countering neoliberal globalization. And in doing so, we are also able to better grasp the complex relationship between globalization and resistance.

Findings II: transnational activist network composition and character

Another set of findings regards the changing composition and character of today's activist networks.[65] These directly follow from the previous conclusion that the type of attribution – of worthiness, interconnectedness, or similarity – impacts the nature of solidarity and the cohesiveness of the transnational network overall. First and perhaps foremost, in contemporary networks globalizing to counter neoliberalism we can detect a decided trend away from *altruistic solidarity*, based upon attribution of worthiness and *sympathy* for the suffering of *distant* others. What this means is that so-called "first-generation" advocacy networks, typified by the Northern-based NGO standing up and in for an oppressed (usually) Third World constituency, are increasingly being superseded. Foreseeing this likely development while simultaneously pioneering the study of such networks in the 1980s and 1990s, Keck and Sikkink observed that the advocacy model would tend to break down as the once-perceived passive beneficiaries became activists themselves.[66]

Sikkink has recently identified one of the primary reasons for this rising tension leading to eventual network breakdown. NGO legitimacy in the eyes of those they petition – usually state actors but increasingly powerful corporations – depends upon their "moral authority," stemming from their appearance of impartiality and independence. NGOs, especially those acting across borders, have traditionally assumed a position of distance from those directly suffering, and thus an independent vantage point from which to judge who is worthy of their sympathy and altruistic advocacy. This, according to Sikkink, is the font of their legitimacy. They cannot therefore be seen as promoting their own political or economic interests if they are to retain their credibility.[67] Here lies the inherent tension and marked difference between traditional, first-generation NGOs and those social movements and networks increasingly struggling in their own name for their own interests and rights, and in some cases for their very survival.

What is coming to replace altruism are two kinds of solidarity, one being *reciprocal* and the other *identity*. A number of scholars have identified the former as prevalent today. Thomas Olesen, Peter Waterman, Ivana Eterovic, and Jackie Smith call it by various names, including mutual, reciprocal, or political solidarity, or the new transnationalism.[68] Reciprocal solidarity comes about when individual activists, collectivities, NGOs, and social movements draw a *connection* between the suffering of others and their own plight and claims. This perceived connection invokes *empathy with*, rather than sympathy for, others' struggles, leading to a solidarity among them based on reciprocity and a sense of ultimately interconnected fates. This kind of solidarity helps to hold together the diverse activists and issues that comprise contemporary transnational networks.

In addition to reciprocity, a second – and I would argue more potent but often dismissed or derided – form of solidarity also binds networks today, one based in a shared *identity*. Identity solidarity prevails among activists mutually regarded as sharing a similar fate, threat, or harm, suffered as a consequence of a common identity. Furthermore, as those who *immediately* and *personally suffer* the structural violence of neoliberal changes increasingly become agents themselves at the transnational level of contention, this new, or more accurately old,[69] form of solidarity serves as a powerful adhesive for contemporary networks. Often these identity-based networks spring from prior, disenchanting experiences in networks at the receiving end of altruistic solidarity, or in others where reciprocity among partners is the stated norm, but where those possessing greater funds, experience, access to politicians or other resources still control the agenda. The lessons drawn from these frustrated alliances can and do lead some to establish new networks among those like themselves: that is, with others suffering in a comparable way due to a shared identity and possessing a similar urgency and commitment to rooting out the causes.

Former "beneficiaries" demanding a greater voice in issues that impact their lives and in the networks that purport to advance their interests are also causing a shift in how networks are structured. We see a general trend away from the first-generation, centralized, *NGO advocacy model* of limited, policy-oriented campaigning aimed at governments toward a hybrid model, falling somewhere between that of NGO advocacy and what Bennett refers to as a second-generation, *direct activism social justice network*.[70] The latter is characterized by a polycentric structure of mass activism and multi-issue, diversely targeted campaigns proliferating via the internet and therefore difficult to turn off. Bennett claims that much activism today has taken on this character. This investigation, by contrast, provides a more nuanced picture of organizational models in that the networks studied were found to be *hybrids*, yet with a tendency toward the second-generation model. Furthermore, as the following chapters will show, each network model carries with it strengths and weaknesses, potential successes as well as uncertainties and failures, and points of convergence with other networks as well as those of contention and, at times, outright confrontation.

One of the more significant outcomes of this evolution in network structure pertains to the relative importance of NGOs in contemporary activism. While they continue to play key roles in a number of networks resisting neoliberalism, they are no longer their sole initiators or directors. This work, rather, corroborates Bennett's assertion that NGOs are increasingly finding themselves *embedded within* larger webs of activism sprouting around them,[71] a process which they have partially helped to initiate but which is now beyond their control. Further, I will argue that NGOs are not only being hemmed in by networks growing up around them. They are also increasingly being shut out of some networks altogether, either explicitly through "identity-group only" rules barring their participation, as with the Via Campesina, or implicitly by the more radical and confrontational stance adopted by networks such as Jubilee South and the PGA, which make them unpalatable partners for most traditional NGOs.

Yet attempts at exclusion also run in the opposite direction, as many NGOs and other contained or reformist tendencies struggle to hold onto their privileged position atop the "civil society" heap. Toward this end they seek to distance themselves or to banish from "our movement" advocates of more transgressive tactics and claims, who are usually organized within the direct action and/or identity-solidarity networks. But this is only one of two reactions that NGOs are having to the shifting terrain upon which they find themselves, as we shall see. Others are adapting to their new role of embedded NGO and thus have emerged as key facilitators and supporters of the nascent identity-based networks, in coalitions based upon hard-won trust, mutual respect, and reciprocal solidarity.

Finally, network claims and operational paradigms are also changing. As those who are most directly impacted by neoliberal violence assume greater roles in transnational activism, the nature and scope of claims, and thus the paradigm within which they operate, have shifted. Even among those most closely modeled upon NGO advocacy, but *especially* among hybrid and second-generation direct action networks, we see an expansion in the framing of both problems and solutions to encompass a wider spectrum of political claims, objects and allies. Today's activists work hard to achieve common ground and a contingent unity within and across networks, while recognizing and even "celebrating" (at the risk of sounding clichéd) the diversity that exists among them. Given the broad scope of suffering and threats, or structural violences, seen as caused by neoliberalist globalization, the nature of claims is equally wide-ranging and *bivalent*. These perceived violences range from economic ills of poverty and exploitation to cultural harms of devaluing or threatening different ways of life and peoples. Their claims are also therefore bivalent, taking the forms of both *economic redistribution* and *cultural recognition* and protection. The results of this study serve to further erode what is coming to be considered a false choice between the social politics of equality and the cultural politics of difference, just as it enriches our understanding of contemporary struggles for both simultaneously.

Yet despite these modern networks actively bridging and extending the framing of their objects and claims in order to build broad alliances, considerable paradigmatic divergences persist along the strategic range from policy reform to institutional/structural transformation, as well as in how, tactically, to reach desired goals. While networks modeled more closely as first generational still tend to operate within a *domain-specific, policy reform paradigm*, we see a general shift among all networks studied herein toward a *transitional paradigm*, and even on to a *multi-sector paradigm* of *structural transformation* seeking to replace neoliberal globalization with comprehensive alternatives. Given this range of operational paradigms today, considerable disunity within the network of networks is apparent, and is likely to continue. This latter point is bound up with the previously mentioned practices of exclusion between NGOs on the one hand and identity-based and direct action networks on the other. Together, they reveal the limits to the inclusive diversity mantra that prevails among many contemporary activists.

Findings III: The role of the WSF in transnationalizing activism

A final cluster of findings pertains to the various roles that the WSF plays in the transnationalization of activist networks. The forums can be seen, first, as *fertile ground* for individual networks to grow upon and, second, as *common ground* for activists to come together to network with others, but, third, as a *battleground* for the future of the forum process and the global network of networks itself. Regarding the former, we find that involvement in the forums both reinforces the networks' scale shift process to the transnational level and, at the same time, often strengthens networks locally, nationally, and macro-regionally. This is achieved primarily through holding internal meetings and workshops – and, for some, staging direct action – during the social forums.

Further, we will learn that the social forums are a space for encounter, fostering rejuvenation, learning, cooperative action through joint campaigns, and the construction of a network of networks. This is witnessed in three clusters of activities. First, there is concerted networking and strategizing among networks aimed at strengthening global and regional partnerships, working toward a common analysis of complex problems and solutions, and coordinating action. Second, activists have enthusiastically helped to found the WSF, participated in its coordination on the IC, and spread the process to the regional, national, and local levels. Third, certain networks organize their own autonomous spaces which are connected to, but distinct from, the social forums, toward facilitating encounter and mutual learning, and building cooperative, autonomous practices and action.

But finally, just as the social forum "space" is a joint creation of these networks, it continues to be contested and challenged by each of them to become more like the networks themselves in composition and character, be they "vertical" or "horizontal": that is to say, more centralized and resembling an NGO, a social movement organization, or a political party, or more radically open, decentralized, networked, spontaneous, and autonomous spaces of self-organized action. Regarding the social forums as contested terrain is crucial, in that many WSF observers believe that it is precisely the ways in which activists and their various organizations engage each other in spaces such as the WSF that will indelibly impact any "possible world" beyond neoliberalism/capitalism. Here scholars have pointed to the paramount importance of *how* the social forum is being conceived and constituted, through practice, and specifically between a conception of the forum as *open space* and *process* versus that of an *event*, which is akin to the hierarchical planning tendencies of the old left.

Massimo de Angelis has pitched the terms and stakes of this contest, and the role of the WSF in this process, as follows:

> *How* struggles circulate, organise and are able to coordinate alternatives is the *key* question around which *an alternative* to capitalism as a mode of organising

social production can emerge. In other words, the alternative to capitalism is an alternative mode of relating, and hence also requires and must manifest alternative *processes* of social production. The SF [social forum] might represent an important element in the constitution of this alternative.[72]

Thus, the process and outcome of this contestation among networks, when combined with their cooperative efforts within and around the WSF, will greatly impact not only the shape of the forum, but that of a network of networks that is in the process of becoming, and, indeed, other possible worlds in the making.

Overview of the book

The rest of this work will proceed as follows. Chapter 2 will introduce and overview the research approach and methodology that includes *comprehending*, participatory action research, and critical globalization studies. In addition it will explicate the frameworks for analysis utilized for the case study chapters, namely the *Dynamics of Contention* scale shift process, the six-by-three conceptual continua table for analyzing network composition and character, and the three facets by which the relationship between the WSF and networks is to be examined. Chapters 3–6 entail case studies of the Jubilee anti-debt networks, Our World is Not for Sale, the Via Campesina, and Peoples' Global Action. Each will follow the trajectory of addressing this study's three research questions. Hence, after a brief introduction to the network, I will identify the particular structural violence that was the change process and/or trigger for localized contention, and then trace the mechanisms that constitute that network's shift in scale to the transnational level of coordinated action; next, I will analyze the composition and character of the network, including activists' proximity to the problem, affective response, forms of solidarity, network model, paradigm, and nature of claims within which it is operating; finally, each chapter will conclude with an examination of the network's involvement with the WSF as it impacts the network individually, its cooperation with other networks, and its distinct competitive actions to shape the social forum process and the emerging network of networks. We will conclude with Chapter 7's summary of findings and their implications for present scholarship and future research, as well as for popular action against neoliberalism and for, as the saying goes, another possible world.

2   Global activism

Methodology and scholarly review

This chapter will explicate the research methodology, broadly defined, by which I have undertaken this project, engaging with relevant scholarship throughout. It will begin by retracing my reflexive process of becoming a scholar-activist, wherein I try to show the co-constitutiveness of normative commitments, methodology, and political activism. Although not commonly done in a scholarly work, this critical reflection on my role as a scholar and activist is what International Studies Association (ISA) president J. Ann Tickner has called for in her address "Politics, Policy and Responsible Scholarship" given at the 2006 annual convention, and is also in the spirit of past ISA president Steve Smith's address following the September 11 attacks on the US and the start of the war on terror.[1] In doing so, I also argue that this sort of research requires us *both* to explain and understand, and to consider individual, relational, and structural factors involved. Toward the first goal, I attempt to reconcile explaining and understanding through *comprehending*, or taking up and grasping together. Next I situate the aspiration to comprehend within participatory action research. I then turn our attention to the emerging field of critical globalization studies, showing that empirically based, participatory research aimed at comprehension is what is most called for in order to advance critical globalization scholarship today.

From this broader discussion I then move to a more circumscribed one of deciding upon both my research questions and the main analytical framework for studying them. This is oriented around the process of scale shift and the constituent mechanisms that comprise it. I next overview how I went about investigating activist networks' shift from the local and national to the global level. Based on my empirical findings, I then propose an amended scale shift model. I next introduce a second analytical framework developed in order to answer another set of questions not captured within the scale shift process, but which called for more systematic treatment: namely, the different forms of solidarity among activists today, their network structures, and the scope and nature of their claims. Here I engage extensively with various streams of social movement literature in order to develop six conceptual continua with which I analyzed transnational networks' composition and character. I finish by reflecting on the emerging literature on the WSF itself in light of my own research, and offer what I think to be a fruitful way of conceptualizing and comprehending the co-construction of the social forums and transnationalizing networks.

The personal is methodological as well as political: the co-constitution of normative commitments, methodology, and political activism

If the personal is political, I would say it is also methodological. The methodology we utilize as scholar-activists – which I now consider myself to be – stems from our own normative commitments, the privileges and limitations of our social locations and identities, and the people, events, and ideas with which we engage prior to and throughout the research process itself. I therefore wish to reflect on these aspects in negotiating my role and approach as a scholar-activist while researching and participating in transnational activist networks and the WSF process over the last few years for this book. To foreshadow my methodological approach a bit, I have come to see both activism and research as reflexive and dialectical processes. To study activism is to change it, and also to be changed by the experience of engagement. I have found this to be true in reflecting on my own normative commitments, which could be summarized as striving to ameliorate human suffering and to deepen and broaden democratic practices. My commitment to these two social projects or values has in fact grown considerably stronger and more enthusiastic through my study of and participation in activism against neoliberal or corporate-led globalization and the nascent process of the social forums. I am now able to articulate these commitments with a greater clarity and certainty than I would have at the start of the research process. So in my presentation here, I am beginning at the end, so to speak. It is therefore more accurate to think about this process not as a linear one, but rather as reflexive, co-constituted, dialectical.

Normative commitments of a scholar-activist

I would venture to say that a core question for many scholar-activists approximates the Buddha's age-old query of "Why does suffering exist in the world?" Two intervening assumptions enter here – one normative and the other about human agency – which are that it is both *good* and *possible* to help reduce suffering. A more direct question then follows: What can we do to lessen our own suffering, that of other sentient beings, and the harm done to the planet? I submit that the motivation and product of activist-scholarship largely centers on these questions and assumptions, which one might ambitiously term a normative research program or project. If one accepts this cluster of questions and assumptions as the bane and charge of human existence, as I do, and therefore as deeply coloring social relations and humanity's relationship with the natural world, then when we turn to the realm of politics – that is, to the struggle over power – scholar-activism assesses actors, actions, ideas, social practices, structures, and distributions and forms of power based upon their likelihood to foment or mitigate suffering at the interpersonal, community, national, transnational, and global levels.

I have only just recently identified the above as the normative research program/project/agenda underlying my – and perhaps other scholar-activists' – work. Identifying this project has allowed me to relax into the realization that innumerable interesting and important questions can contribute positively to this program. Three of them are my project's actual research questions, which again are: why and how are once locally and nationally focused activists expanding their networking, campaigns, targets, demands, frames, and visions to forge transnational networks; what are these networks' changing compositions and characters; and what is the role of the WSF in this scale shift process? Again, to answer these questions, the activist networks I am investigating are the Jubilee 2000 anti-debt campaign and the networks that have spun off from it, the Via Campesina peasant farmers, the Our World Is Not For Sale anti-WTO campaigners, and the Zapatista-inspired Peoples' Global Action.

One commonality I have found among all of these networks – and which links the more circumscribed research questions to my normative program described above – is that each is mobilizing around and resisting a distinct form of suffering: that caused by poverty and debt, landlessness, the loss of the commons and ecological devastation, IMF and World Bank SAPs and "free" trade agreements, which together I call structural violences. But, importantly, they are also increasingly naming the cause of these violences as neoliberal globalization and are coming together in greater coalitions and in the spaces of the WSF and regional and local forums to forge alliances, campaigns, and alternative, transformative projects and visions of other possible worlds where these kinds of suffering are drastically mitigated. Whether this other world, or worlds, is indeed possible – as the WSF slogan boldly declares – is another matter. But given my core normative commitment stated above as a research agenda, I was drawn to the prospect of such a transformation, and therefore to study and participate in the project itself.

In the process of engaging with these activist networks, I have also come to recognize another commonality among them: their commitment to strengthening and reinvigorating democracy from the grassroots to the national to the transnational level. A shared, fundamental grievance across the board is that local communities' and nations' decision-making processes and powers are being challenged and siphoned off by the institutions, policies, actors, and effects of neoliberal globalization. This concern is interrelated with the suffering noted above, in that many activists are finding that established channels and practices by which they could formerly express and attempt to redress grievances are being closed off, just as new grievances and threats are arising. Also, as activists are more and more realizing that decisions are being taken at the transnational level which seriously impact their everyday lives, they are turning their attention to democratizing decision-making at that level as well. They are, furthermore, making efforts to internalize their goal of deepening and broadening democracy, by, first, undertaking self-critique and then implementing changes within their own networks, organizations, and movements towards becoming more inclusive, participatory, and horizontal in decision-making practices. Second, they are experimenting with, learning from, and attempting to improve upon new autonomous spaces for encountering each other, mutual learning, building networks, and planning action. The most notable example is that of the WSF, which has spurred hundreds of thousands to participate in this annual transnational event and which, perhaps more importantly, has inspired countless others to initiate their own local, national, and macro-regional forums.

By studying and participating in this process of building the social forums, my own dedication to devolving decision-making power to the people – that is, to the *demos* – has crystallized. I can now say that I believe in democracy as a basic principle not only out of habit or because it seems like the right or obvious thing to do because I happen to be socialized in a society that purports to value such a form of government as a universal human right. Additionally, in experiencing its mundane and exasperating practices and glimpsing its transformative and emancipatory potential firsthand, I have emerged not only a sharper critic of existing democratic processes and institutions; I have also developed greater sensitivity to and awareness of relations of power, of manipulation, of subtle and structural silencing, and of overt oppression. I have refined my own skills on how to practice democracy at home, in the community, and at the state and transnational levels. Furthermore, based on what I have learned about and experienced, my conviction has deepened that the greatest challenges facing humanity on the planet today can best be met through a radical devolution and dispersion of decision-making power, coupled with transparent, democratic, and transnational decision-making bodies. And despite much evidence and rhetoric to the contrary, this "other possible world" of genuine democracy in which ameliorating human suffering and learning to live in disciplined harmony with the planet are central concerns seems tantalizingly possible. The spirit of resistance which began with the Zapatista uprising in Chiapas against the Mexican government and the NAFTA on New Year's Day 1994 and which has permeated the mass mobilizations and the social forums is rightly being called the "globalization of hope." And it is contagious, if one risks being "contaminated" by it. In this way, through studying and engaging with transnational activism and the social forums, I am making some small contribution toward changing them, just as my own normative commitments have also been clarified and deepened by the experience.

As was just demonstrated, being able to articulate the bedrock values and motivations for one's work is important, for it has direct implications, first of all, on what we "see" ontologically in international relations/global politics in general, and in the phenomenon we choose to study in particular.[2] This is not to say that we merely project our biases or values onto the phenomenon; but rather, as I described above, in engaging with the networks and the social forums, I not only came to "see" suffering and the strong desire to ameliorate it via democratization as fundamentally shared across a wide swath of activists; but also, I recognized that these concerns are fundamentally shared by *me*. I began to see these values or goals as important out there, so to speak, as well as to recognize that these are important – and increasingly so – *in here*, for my own scholarship and political engagement. Second, as I will argue in the following sections, articulating these values is also important because they have a bearing on *how* we ought to ethically relate to, study, and engage with actors or phenomena if we are to remain consistent with our values. That is to say, our values should not contradict the methodology we adopt as scholar-activists and should rather inform our approach.

Evolving the research question: explaining vs. understanding?

I have arrived rather late at the realization that there is one methodology that a scholar uses to evolve the research question and framework themselves, and then another related, yet distinct, methodology once the commitment has been made to that question and framework. The first will be taken up here, and the second in the subsequent sections on the frameworks used to analyze activist networks' shift in scale and their composition and character. Regarding the former, while I had gravitated early, as explained above, toward these emerging transnational networks and the social forum process and while I felt intuitively confident that these were the people, practices, and events that I wanted to study and become involved in myself, the actual research questions did not come easily. It was in fact not until near the *end* of the entire project that I locked in the final three queries. For quite some time, then, I seemed to be unable to internalize the "proper" sequence, beginning with formulating the research question and proceeding forward through data collection to analysis and then the final written output. Entering upon a research project *sans question* made me appear and indeed feel somehow suspect, undisciplined, or dangerously adrift.

The research process, the story seems to go, *begins* with a burning question, problem, puzzle, or glaring inconsistency that wakes one from blissful slumber in the night. Since this is the sequence presented in most scholarly books, it gives readers unfamiliar with the research process the false impression that this is also the way the project unfolds. I've therefore long been an admirer of scholars who seem to be visited by angels (or demons, or maybe the ghost of Popper) whispering precision-point questions in their ears; or, to switch metaphors, those who appear to have Magic 8 Balls for brains, needing only to swivel their heads back and forth for a few seconds, causing one clear and concise Question to gurgle to the surface. My attempts at such illuminating divination heretofore have only produced the messages: "UNCERTAIN," "ASK AGAIN LATER," and the infuriatingly coy "BETTER NOT TELL YOU NOW."

The problem, at bottom, was my inability – or unwillingness – to decide to explain or to understand. Am I observing behaviors (and perhaps structures) from the "outside" with an eye toward explaining correlations and/or causation, or am I understanding meanings and motivations from the "inside" and therefore interpreting regularities as (usually) rule-following? It continued to escape me how one aspiration could *really* be disentangled entirely from the other. The pragmatist Quine, after all, convinced most of us (with the possible exception of those with Magic 8 Balls for brains) that the senses give us no "unvarnished news" and no "brute facts" independent of the concepts and theories we use to classify and interpret them.[3] And yet, scholars such as Steve Smith warn of the pitfalls that await attempts to synthesize or reconcile the two positions, and rather urge us, for the sake of clarity and consistency, to just choose one.[4]

Individualism vs. holism

Along with the distinction between explaining (objective) and understanding (subjective), we must add another apparent dichotomy to the mix when contemplating how to craft a question and which methods to use to investigate it: that of the individual versus the social. The scholar-activist therefore seems to have four choices on how to proceed. If we wish to *explain* activism, we can focus *either* on individual actions or on the broader material and social conditions and interrelations which constitute action from an external "observer" standpoint. The methods would usually be observation and data collection, coded into variables upon which to perform correlational analysis or quasi-experimental methods. If one is to remain consistent with the objective/outsider/explanatory logic, the appropriate relationship of this scholar-activist to those she is studying and participating with would be largely an instrumental one, viewing them as objects whose behavior is to be explained and, perhaps, modified to achieve better results.[5]

On the other hand, if we wish to *understand* action, we can attempt to reconstruct the intentions, meanings, and values as they seem to constitute practices according to the individual activists involved, or more broadly seek to understand the language, traditions, and discourses which may constitute collective action, as viewed from their subjective social perspectives. Scholar-activists of this sort would generally use phenomenological, idiographic, autobiographical, clinical or critical ethnography, and other qualitative research methods. If we are to remain consistent with this understanding/subjective/insider logic, this scholar-activist would assume a "practical" relationship to those being studied, respecting them as responsible, cognizant, and autonomous subjects or representatives of such traditions.[6]

So far so good … and yet, I was still not convinced that getting at what is most interesting, relevant, or important for the scholar-activist and her audience can be constrained within one of these boxes, not least because the process of negotiating and deciding upon what *is* most interesting, relevant, and important to study *entails* both. I therefore have determined that, in order to arrive at one's research questions, these two aspirations of explaining and understanding are to be treated sequentially, or, better yet, in a deepening spiral which circles between the two. This is because even the most pristine ivory tower-dwellers must consider their audience and learn what is meaningful to or valued by those select few with whom they wish to be conversant. This requires them, first, to *understand* what is deemed worthy of further understanding or explanation. For scholar-activists, who are by definition conscious of a much wider audience, learning what is worthwhile understanding or explaining is even more arduous.

The scholar-activist's audience: two tough crowds

I have now come to the conclusion that scholar-activists in particular are well advised to hold off on committing to their research question; In fact, given our dual audiences, we really have little choice. For evolving our question or questions is doubly difficult in that we must be conversant with and relevant to not one but two rather distinct communities, each bearing its own criteria for what passes muster. Our discipline – or *disciplines*, since most of us are propelled by our research interests to traverse the boundaries of international relations and its subfields of international peace and conflict resolution, (transnational) civil society and globalization studies, in addition to sociology, anthropology, cultural studies, linguistics, and comparative politics – demand that we are well read, contribute to knowledge and theory-building in virtually any field we draw upon, have rigorous research designs, frameworks, and methodology, and the like.

But for scholar-activists, the considerations do not end there, for we have our other audience to bear in mind, that of activists themselves, who will judge our work's worth by another set of criteria. Here understanding what is a potential contribution is decidedly more difficult than in academia. Scholarship is by definition public, and thus tracing the trajectory of a debate as well as finding its cutting edge is a rather straightforward process. These debates are essentially on paper or, if discussions or oral presentations are to be remembered and to compete to become valuable to their field, they must be recorded in written form and made available to the community of scholars. In addition, there are also clear indicators of the status of knowledge in academic fields, based on the reputation of journals and publishers and a work's date of publication, where today newer often seems to be better.

With the activist audience, consistent publicity is not at all the norm. Much of what is deemed important by activists themselves – that is, the key debates or questions, and even who the "important" or popularly legitimate actors are – comes about through contested communication, action, and the interpretation of those activities and debates among the activists involved, those they are contesting, the media, and a broader public. Therefore, scholars who wish to understand what is important or meaningful to activists must access these debates using a variety of methods, such as: observing and/or participating in planning meetings, discussion forums, and protest events; locating and interviewing a wide range of participants; monitoring debates on activist listserves; reading internal accounts and critiques posted on their websites, in alternative media sources, and in activist publications; and reviewing the few scholarly analyses that are produced on these topics, which are usually detailed, single case studies. All of these methods were undertaken in this study.[7] And each, I would add, has the finesse – and indeed resembles the actual process – of stumbling around in the dark, groping for the outer walls of a room while simultaneously trying to make out its main pieces of furniture. But I find that it is precisely these methods, with all of the logistical challenges and methodological concerns they give rise to, that are crucial to discovering what are the salient issues and parameters of debates for this second audience, as well as which are the relevant actors with whom to engage.

Explaining vs. understanding revisited (and transcended?): toward comprehending

Beyond this discovery process described above, which I feel must begin with understanding before we can know what is worth explaining or understanding, further, I wish to explore the possibility of treating explaining and understanding dialectically throughout the entire research process. We should remember that Max Weber, in making his seminal distinction between *erklären* and *verstehen*, bid us to do both: that is to say, to achieve adequacy at the level of meaning (understanding) and at the causal level (explanation).[8] While I part company with the solution Weber proposed in his theory of social action, which is to apply a microeconomic model of rational action and a classification scheme for understanding individual decision-making, I nonetheless share his conviction that as social scientists, and as scholar-activists, we should strive for adequacy both in understanding and in explaining. Or as Hollis and Smith put it, "with the former for making possible sense and the latter for identifying actual causes."[9]

Still, how is it possible? In my own work, I have come to think of reconciling, or overcoming, the *erklären–verstehen* divide with the practice of *begreifen* or *umfassen*, which, translated from German, mean to *comprehend*. I am not enough of a Weberian buff to know if he'd considered either of these terms before opting for the former two; but, in any case, I find "comprehending" to be a particularly instructive term methodologically for scholar-activists, especially those dedicated to democratizing practices and actively working to lessen suffering. It comes from the Latin *comprehendo*, meaning to take up or grasp together, to unite, to gather, and to include. *Comprehending* a phenomenon, then, connotes engagement, participation, co-constitution, shared experience, collective and inclusive efforts, and merging or uniting with the "object" of inquiry. It strives to see phenomena intersubjectively, from both the "inside" and the "outside."[10]

In my search for a methodology that approximates *comprehending*, or melting or transcending the boundaries between explaining and understanding, I have found participatory action research to be especially apropos for scholar-activism. It is to this methodological approach that we can now turn.

Comprehending through participatory action research

Participatory action research (PAR) includes a number of different approaches, yet the one I find to be most relevant to scholar-activists who are engaged with social movements, NGOs, and networks is that of "participatory research." This approach emerged from engagement on the part of activists and scholars in various struggles in the Third World, and has roots in liberation theology, Paulo Freire's educational philosophy, neo-Marxist theories of development and dependency, Frankfurt School critical scholarship, feminism, and liberal human rights activism. Scholar-activists working in this tradition are committed to participatory methods and are responsive to the ideas and needs of local people, often working in poor, urban *favelas* or *barrios* doing research in concrete settings geared toward social, economic, and political development, or in "consciousness-raising" activities which lead to "unmasking" power and dominating structures, and thereby fomenting political awareness and collective action.[11] "The aim of action research," write two of its proponents, Stephen Kemmis and Robin McTaggart, "is to make a difference in these day-to-day lived realities – the ordinary settings in which people live and work, in which some thrive and some suffer."[12] This approach, then, closely matches my normative commitment to ameliorating suffering and addressing the conditions that create and sustain various forms of violence, and is sympathetically tied to local struggles themselves.

The participatory action approaches also clearly reflect and reinforce my second commitment, that of democratizing social practice and institutions. Democratic values inform each step of the PAR process, from deciding on the question, to the purposes for and methods used to study the phenomenon, to the relationship to those being investigated, to the status of and criteria for evaluating results. While there is debate between top-down versus bottom-up theorizing, many scholars of this orientation believe that the research agenda and questions should emerge from the movements themselves. This is in keeping with my own "understanding" process described in the previous section. This perspective is also shared by Anthony Giddens, and by extension international relations constructivism, who holds that activists are not, in fact, "cultural dopes." They often can voice cogent reasons and well-articulated motivations for their actions, as well as rather sophisticated understandings of their own situations and analysis of problems, actors, and forces against which they are struggling. They are, furthermore, able to shift between multiple perspectives and can draw connections between their local situations and global phenomena. They are also aware of, or believe in, the potential efficacy of their own agency and collective action in the sense that they are *choosing* to act to make change. They are often engaged as well not only in a struggle against something, but simultaneously in a critical reflection process to improve their own efficacy, democracy of social practices, and the like.[13]

Flowing from this genuine respect for the ideas and aspirations of participants themselves, the role of the scholar is more one of being in service to the movement as a sympathetic insider. The entire process is therefore one of joint creation and of shared ownership, which some have called *accompaniment*. This means collaboration based on trust, common understanding and analysis of the problem, and a commitment to solidarity and equality.[14] The role of the researcher from this perspective is to articulate a "common sense" that will be widely seen as authentic and relevant by the participants, and to produce results that will be judged on their authenticity in light of the participants' lived experience.

According to the ethos of PAR, the scholar-activist should not strive to uncover insights that supposedly have remained hidden from the participants themselves, a stance that is consistent with much ethno-methodological research, which refuses the temptation that the researcher could compete with participants themselves in interpreting meanings or offering the "ultimate" interpretation.[15] The proper role should rather be to illuminate and clarify the interconnections and overt or latent tensions that those involved find salient.[16] The results therefore are also jointly anticipated and owned, in that they must give something back to the movements and activists from whom they "took," based on reciprocity and on being held accountable for the results by those involved.[17]

Reflexive dialectical perspective of PAR

Let us now take a closer look at how PAR seeks to transcend the boxes that divorce explaining from understanding, and individualism from holism, and move toward something similar to what I had earlier called comprehending, or taking up together. Recall the four possibilities that seemed to be available to the scholar-activist who accepted these divisions previously delineated. While those undertaking PAR would likely admit that a broad and unifying synthesis still eludes us, they rather view these divisions of individual/social and objective/subjective as false dichotomies. They further assert that it is more useful to consider them to be dialectically related; that is, in opposition or contradiction to the other, but also mutually necessary in the sense that each aspect – human, social, historical – constitutes the other. Practice, then, is seen as historically embedded and reflexively altered over time.[18] This reflexive dialectical perspective takes the view that we must understand activism

> as enacted by individuals who act in the context of history and in ways constituted by a vast historical web of social interactions among people. Similarly, it is also necessary to understand [activism] as having both objective (externally given) and subjective (internally understood and interpreted) aspects, both of which are necessary to understand how any practice is really practiced, how it is constituted historically and socially, and how it can be transformed. ... [It] does its best to recognize not only that people's actions are caused by their intentions and circumstances, but also that people cause intentions and circumstances – that is, that people are made by action in the world, and that they also make action and history.[19]

In attempting to get at this co-constitution of agents with society and structure, some researchers try to take into account each of the aforementioned orientations and methods of objectivism, subjectivism, individualism, and holism, by striving to find a place for all in a broader framework. A notable example is the attempt to operationalize Habermas's theory of communicative action.[20] Scholars who promote this search for a broader framework, however, also readily admit the difficulties of implementing such an approach, and rather find it more fitting as "symposium research," or interconnected studies which specialize in various traditions but which coordinate around a particular phenomenon. Partly in response to the complexity of organizing such a symposium project and partly due to taking the view that PAR is better as a solitary process of systematic self-reflection, others working alone often find it necessary or prudent to adopt methods mainly from one or the other of these traditions.[21] In either case, researchers adopt a strategic use of methods that help both to explain and/or understand at the individual, societal, and/or structural levels. In this regard, they share much with cultural studies' eclectic, pragmatic, and strategic mixing of methodologies, referred to as *bricolage*, in their investigations of the multiple manifestations and meanings of culture.[22] They further are fellow-travelers with constructivists of all stripes, who focus on relationships, connections, language, dynamics, and change. In PAR, the study of complex social practices such as activism

> is a study of connections – of many different kinds of communicative, productive, and organizational relationships among people in socially, historically, and discursively constituted media of language (discourse), work, and power – all of which must be understood dynamically and relationally. ... At its best, such a research tradition aims to help people understand themselves both as "objective" forces impinging on others and as subjects who have intentions and commitments they share with others, and both as people who act in ways framed by discourses formed beyond any one of us individually and as people who make meaning for ourselves in communication with the others alongside whom we stand, and whose fates – one way or another – we share.[23]

This notion of shared fate is important because it assumes a first-person relationship between the researcher and the researched. Furthermore, the idea of standing beside others is also in keeping with my normative commitments to help relieve suffering and promote democratic practice, by taking an unapologetic "emancipatory" view of the reason for and goal of research. It therefore allows us to regard our work as explicitly engaged with other activists in actions that are making history. In this sense, we are given permission to consider research *as* social practice and, stated a bit differently, to view research *as* activism. The research project then becomes one of self-discovery and learning together from interaction and from history. This is a project and a process undertaken *within* activism and history, in the role of companion – or *compañer@* – not of recorder, commentator, or outside critic, or of controller or conductor from above.[24]

This insider perspective, however, is strengthened by the capability of shifting between the inside and outside and the individual and collective. This multi-perspectivism is described as:

> Seeing themselves, their understandings, their practices, and their settings from the perspective of *individuals* in and around the setting, and then from the

perspective of *the social* (in terms of both system integration and social integration, under the aspect of both system and life world); from the "*subjective*" / *insider* perspective, and from the "*objective*"/*outsider* perspective; and from the *synchronic* perspective of "how things are" and from the *diachronic* perspective of "how they came to be" or "can come to be."[25]

In addition to striving to analyze from multiple perspectives, a final commonality shared among those using PAR is the focus on concrete experience and practice as central to their study. While abstraction does of course take place, researchers begin from the material and actual practices of people in particular settings. Any abstraction or generalizations that are undertaken are approached with care, for PAR is rooted in time and in place, and in the meanings and understandings that practices have to those involved.[26] In this regard, we see that theory in PAR is often – although not always – *emic*: that is, it emerges from engaging with others in shared practice and reflection on meanings and through the processes of learning by doing and communicating. Theory is therefore bound up with practice. Kemmis and McTaggart regard this to be what makes PAR *research*: "not the machinery of research techniques but an abiding concern with the relationships between … theory and practice."[27]

The critique of PAR

As was intimated above, PAR is not slavish to academic methodological criteria, nor does it claim outsider objectivity or value neutrality. In fact, some have suggested that while its unapologetic commitment to active accompaniment will always win it adherents, it is equally probable that governments and some scholarly traditions will make greater efforts to coopt or domesticate these approaches. "To the extent that these efforts are *not* successful," averred Kemmis and McTaggart, "it is likely that participatory action research will be eschewed and rejected as 'unscientific' – even renegade."[28] If this is the case, then a range of criticisms will likely continue to be leveled against the approach. These critiques take the form of, first, accusations that those who undertake it confuse or conflate activism and community development with "proper research," charging that the approach lacks sufficient scientific rigor. Second, with regard to the manner and quality of data and its collection, it is decidedly low tech and usually qualitative in the sense that each piece of evidence is regarded as unique and of its own kind. It is thus charged with sampling error and biases, and, further, its results lack generalizability. Third, given the marginality and vulnerability of many participants themselves, some worry that PAR places their studies' "objects" at risk through their collaboration. And finally, authoritarian governments at times label these activist-researchers as politically dangerous and subversive.

As a partial response, PAR is guilty of not (uncritically) subscribing to the methodological criteria of its critics, or to the normative commitments that often tacitly underlie these methods. That said, many strive for methodological rigor appropriate to qualitative researchers and, further, utilize quantitative methods when deemed valuable and appropriate. Whatever methods are chosen, they entail a special concern for protecting those who participate and a greater awareness of the work's potential repercussions in specific contexts. Regarding the allegations that PAR is politically conscious and potentially subversive, many would plead "guilty as charged," but only if investigating inhumane, undemocratic, and unjust conditions and practices is a crime.

With regard to the view that PAR is insufficiently analytical, in my own experience I have found the reverse to be true. This approach demands extreme flexibility of analysis, in that the researcher must remain open to the prospect that a new encounter will not only add *content* or *evidence* within a pre-existing framework or set of questions, but can also potentially force a revision or even a significant transformation of the extant framework and questions themselves. I would submit that PAR is analytical not only on the level of data or evidence, but at a most fundamental level of constantly scrutinizing the very categories, framework, and appropriate questions in need of investigating. My own experience in adopting PAR will be detailed throughout the rest of this chapter to better illustrate what this analytical process entails.

Since PAR is a dynamic, reflexive, and contested methodology, it is therefore also fruitful to examine the *internal* critiques among its practitioners. A first concern was already noted above in the context of symposium research, namely that co-constitution has proven difficult for individual scholars to operationalize on their own, meaning that the applied methods almost always falls short of the ideal. Yet this is true not only for PAR, but for the broad swath of constructivism/constructionism across academic disciplines, and indeed for other methodologies as well.[29] A second internal concern stems from a danger that the researcher can become overly identified with the study's participants. This could lead to becoming blinded to activists' faults and perhaps overstating their importance or virtues and understating their weaknesses and vices, and therefore losing one's ability to judge or critique. There are various strategies for keeping this in check, which are similar to those utilized by qualitative researchers across disciplines. But in the end much of this depends on the researcher choosing and then maintaining his or her focus of inquiry as well as his or her maturity, commitment to constructive criticism, and ability to consider multiple and, at times, contradictory perspectives and claims. And again, this is not a danger that befalls PAR alone.

If anything, this type of research methodology requires considerable reflection on and discipline of one's *own* biases. In accompaniment, or what I call comprehending, one must attempt to place oneself in the mindset and indeed the physical spaces of those whose motivations and actions one wishes to understand and/or explain. This calls for skills of listening and of non-judgmental questioning, of quickly orienting oneself in unfamiliar terrain so as to focus outwardly, and of being able to eventually weigh criticisms and contradictory perspectives: one's own, those of other activists, and those of outside critics or interested parties.[30]

Additionally, those who write from an interested insider's vantage point, such as scholar-activist and farmer Annette Desmarais in her decade-long involvement with the Via Campesina, argue that the benefits of becoming a committed insider outweigh those of striving to be an objective outsider. Specifically, she notes the access to resources and informants, the trust and rapport gained, and the ability to support and accompany an organization or movement in its efforts for social change.[31] While my own broader study of multiple transnational activist networks and the social forums has not allowed for day-to-day participation on par with Desmarais's involvement with the Via Campesina, it nonetheless corroborates her experience with regard to the advantages of being what I would call an empathetic participant. Furthermore, researchers such as Desmarais have also democratized the research process, helping to "emancipate" it, so to speak, from the exclusive purview of the academy, institutes, or government agencies. Finally, the trade-off for methodological sophistication seems to be greater participation by and relevance for the audience who are most interested and invested in our process and its results: that is, the activists themselves. For scholar-activists, this is a compromise worth making.

Introducing PAR into critical globalization scholarship

I will next conjoin the methodological approach of PAR, or comprehending, with my ontological focus. As stated in Chapter 1, given my central task of studying transnationalizing activist networks challenging neoliberal globalization, my work closely fits within critical globalization studies, or those scholars and activists most concerned with the negative aspects of neoliberal globalization as well as the potential for reforming or transforming them.[32] Although diverse, critical globalization scholars share common features, which are also consistent with the ethos of PAR. These, according to one of its lead proponents, James Mittelman, include: *reflexivity*, or an understanding that all knowledge is embedded in material and political conditions and specific interests; *historicism*, or incorporating notions of time and history into one's analysis; *decentering*, or bringing in multiple, grounded, and critical perspectives from the margins in order to generate new discourses and questions; *crossovers* among academic disciplines providing key research on globalization's many facets; and *strategic transformations* that work toward upending hegemonic concentrations of power and giving voice to emancipatory visions that reflect one's values and ethics.[33]

Studying globalization critically, then, means challenging the notion that *this* globalization is a timeless or inevitable development. It entails examining whether and how globalization processes reinforce certain interests of historically situated actors. It gives voice to local, peripheral subjects and those negatively impacted by globalization with the aim of revealing critical discourses and new insights and questions. It looks beyond a single academic discipline's boundaries for assistance in understanding and explaining these complex phenomena. It calls into question neoliberalism's core ethics – competition, efficiency, extreme individualism, and consumption – which serve to reduce human beings to *homo economicus*.

It instead strives to revalorize cooperation, citizenship, and autonomy from the local to the global levels and to promote the concept of work as a human *right* and a *social* contribution.

I have come to think of critical globalization studies as a nascent, self-organizing project of symposium research akin to that proposed by PAR researchers. Each scholar has a unique orientation and method with regard to objectivism, subjectivism, individualism, and holism, and some ambitiously try to incorporate a number of these approaches into broader frameworks. Together, these critical analyses can be seen as distinct but interconnected studies of the myriad facets of neoliberal globalization and their alternatives. Yet within this emerging symposium, critical scholars Catherine Eschle and Bice Maiguashca have identified two main theoretical weaknesses. First, they claim that theory has been insufficiently grounded in empirical investigations into the actual practices of activists involved. A second and related criticism entails the conceptual language used to analyze and theorize these movements, which they claim has been largely inconsistent, unreflexive, or ignorant of the considerable literature on social movements in fields such as sociology and political science.[34] Eschle further suggests that critical globalization scholars could learn from their feminist counterparts, many of them pioneers in PAR. Specifically, they could better engage in organic theorizing, which considers activists themselves as primary producers of theoretical categories and generators of knowledge.[35] Following Eschle and Maiguashca's advice and critiques, my own empirical and activist-oriented research can be seen as a corrective to critical globalization's extant weaknesses.

To recapitulate, so far I have traced my reflexive process of becoming a scholar-activist, whereby I attempted to show the co-constituted nature of normative commitments, methodology, and political activism. I posited that this type of research requires both explanation and understanding at the individual, relational, and structural levels, and proposed to reconcile these through comprehending, or taking up and grasping together. I then situated comprehension within PAR and, finally, introduced this approach to the sub-discipline of critical globalization studies as a way to address what some critical researchers see as weaknesses in current theorizing. Throughout, I demonstrated my conviction that *what* we study – that is, ontology – cannot be de-linked from *how* we go about studying it – that is, methodology. Below I will develop this theme further as I delineate another co-constitutive process, that of my research questions with the analytical frameworks chosen or developed to study them and the methods used to obtain evidence. Here I will describe the co-evolution of my three questions alongside the frameworks for analysis and methods.

Review of primary and secondary print and electronic sources

After deciding early on that my focus of inquiry was to be activist networks coming together in and around the social forums to counter neoliberal globalization, I then began a multi-pronged literature review, the salient results of which are presented both in Chapter 1 and in this chapter. This literature consisted of, first, documentation on social movements and NGOs mobilizing in recent years and, second, on the WSF process. Sources included scholarly books and articles, popular journals and newspapers, and activist books, websites, and alternative media. Through these primary and secondary print and electronic sources, I familiarized myself with the major transnational protest events and campaigns, the groups organizing and/or participating in them, their membership or adherents, organizational structures, campaigning allies, targets, tactics, claims, and operational paradigms. A third area of academic literature reviewed was on globalization; a fourth dealt with transnational civil society; a fifth focused on regionalism, and a sixth concerned theories of social movements, networks, and contentious politics. In perusing the latter, I decided upon Doug McAdam, Sidney Tarrow and Charles Tilly's "dynamics of contention" approach from their work of the same name.[36] In order to be able to illustrate the reasons for doing so, I will first overview the approach.

The dynamics of contention (DOC) approach

In recent years there has been a growing desire among social movement scholars to break out of the strict confines demarcating the three main approaches – structuralism, rationalism, and culturalism – from one another. They are instead seeking more eclectic ways to comprehend the complexity and richness of human practice.[37] One of the most systematic and ambitious efforts in this area is McAdam, Tarrow, and Tilly's DOC. Their work is informed by and attempts to integrate the main strands of social movement theorizing into a cross-disciplinary, comprehensive approach to studying a broad range of contention.[38] While acknowledging the important contributions made by the prevailing approaches,[39] the DOC takes the "constructionist turn" pioneered by sociologist Alberto Melucci and other scholars of new social movements, in admitting that we still know very little about the *dynamics* that account for the observed regularities that the structural program has identified.[40] They therefore join others in their call for moving away from static, variable-driven models in order to identify the dynamic *mechanisms* that cluster or form sequences within *processes* that shape contentious politics. In this way they take up McAdam, John McCarthy, and Mayer Zald's critique of two decades ago, that scholars "have focused the lion's share of our research ... on the before and after of collective action. ... But we haven't devoted a lot of attention to the *ongoing accomplishment of collective action*."[41] The DOC therefore turns our attention away from the "before" and "after" toward the "how," or to the process questions of ongoing political accomplishment. To be clear, they are not proposing general covering laws, but rather seek to interrogate "many different episodes of contentious politics to find out whether intuitively important processes have consistent foundations in their constituent mechanisms and are similarly constituted across a range of types of contention."[42]

The DOC centers around three main analytical concepts: *episodes*, *processes*, and *mechanisms*. An episode is the broadest category, processes are in the middle, and mechanisms the most precise. Mechanisms form causal sequences or concatenate into processes, and a cluster or sequence of processes comprises an episode. Where one draws the line between a mechanism and a process is left open to the researcher's best judgment and may vary from case to case depending on the amount of detail one wants to draw out of a particular phenomenon. Mechanisms can be *environmental/external* (such as the availability of communications technology), *relational* (connections among people, groups, and interpersonal networks), or *cognitive* (individual and collective perception). Some of the same mechanisms and processes occur in other episodes of contentious politics, albeit in different combinations, yielding distinct outcomes in other historical settings. Finally, the processes for which McAdam, Tarrow, and Tilly hypothesize constituent mechanisms included mobilization, actor constitution, polarization, and scale shift.

Based on the prior discussion of my desire to overcome the bifurcations between explaining and understanding and between individualism and holism and to undertake PAR toward *comprehending*, the DOC has much to offer. This integrative approach calls on us to both explain and understand: that is, to step back and identify causes or mechanisms as well as to make sense of these mechanisms from the perspectives of those involved. It therefore allows us to consider activism as being comprised of both objective, or externally given, and subjective, or internally perceived, aspects. It further enables us to overcome the individualism versus holism bifurcation by identifying three sorts of mechanisms: cognitive (individual), relational, and environmental (structural). The way to go about identifying these potential mechanisms also fits with my research approach, in that we should study actual practice and find out the interpretations of that practice among those involved. Hence it is open to whatever methods allow us to uncover these mechanisms. It follows that since this research focuses on actual practice it is both historically and empirically grounded. Finally, the DOC provided me with a flexible yet orienting set of concepts and organizational frameworks with which to begin my research.

Scale shift process introduced

The DOC process chosen to be the centerpiece of this investigation is *scale shift*. This process is defined by the authors as "a change in the number and level of coordinated contentious actions leading to broader contention involving a wider range of actors and bridging their claims and identities."[43] In analyzing scale shift across a wide variety of historical cases, these scholars have identified a set of social phenomena, or a cluster of *mechanisms*, which often recur and which they therefore call "robust" mechanisms constitutive of the scale shift process. Specifically, for scale shift to occur, we often see a pattern in which *localized collective action* spawns broader contention when information concerning the initial action reaches – via *brokerage* and/or *diffusion* efforts – a geographically or institutionally distant group. On the basis of this information, this group defines itself as sufficiently similar (i.e. *attribution of similarity*) to the initial activists as to motivate *emulation*, leading ultimately to *coordinated action* between the two sites.[44] The mechanisms hypothesized to comprise scale shift are illustrated in Figure 1.

Let's take each of these mechanisms in turn. *Localized collective action* is just that: activism focused predominantly in the sub-state level – and in our study the national level as well – but which does not undertake significant, coordinated action with others beyond its regional or national confines. This localized action nonetheless can spawn wider contention when at least one of two mechanisms is present: either *diffusion*, defined as the transfer of information along already established lines of interaction, or *brokerage*, which is information transfers that depend on the linking of two or more previously unconnected social sites.

At this point we must go deeper, because key to successful brokerage is *frame alignment*, or the linking of individual and social movement organization "interpretive orientations." The way brokers portray the activities, goals, and ideology of their organization must be perceived by non-affiliated individuals or groups to be congruent with their own interests, values, and beliefs for alignment to occur.[45] Over the years social movement scholars have developed precise categorizations for different types of framing, ranging from those that require little effort or change to those that are transformative in their effects on activists' claims, paradigms, and even identities. The framing strategy needing the least effort is *frame bridging*,

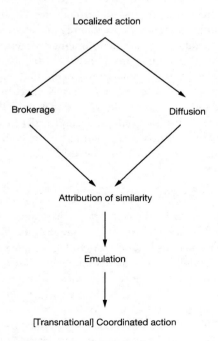

Figure 1 Scale shift process and constituent mechanisms.

Source: Doug McAdam, Sidney Tarrow, and Charles Tilly, "Figure 10.3. Scale Shift," *Dynamics of Contention* (Cambridge: Cambridge University Press, 2001), 333.

which successfully links ideologically congruent but unconnected frames *vis-à-vis* a particular issue or problem. Frame bridging assumes that there are individuals or groups out there that share one's views but only need to be contacted by means of organizational outreach and information diffusion through interpersonal or intergroup networks, media, telephone, direct mail, e-mail, or websites.

A second framing strategy is *frame amplification*, or the attempt to clarify and emphasize an interpretive frame that bears on a particular issue. Amplification can be of two kinds: *value amplification*, which seeks to identify, idealize, and elevate one or more values presumed to be basic among the target of brokerage but which have not inspired collective action due to the value having fallen into disuse, been suppressed, taken for granted, not been sufficiently challenged, or because of the lack of an organizational outlet; or *belief amplification*, or homing in on beliefs about the seriousness of the problem or grievance, the locus of causality or blame, stereotypes of the antagonists or targets of influence, the potential for change or the efficacy of action, and the necessity or responsibility to "stand up." A third, more profound, framing strategy is that of *frame extension*. This type of framing is said to be in play when a social movement organization feels either compelled or drawn to extend the boundaries of its primary framework in order to encompass interests or points of view that were previously incidental to its primary objectives, but which are of considerable salience to those with whom the organization wishes to broker ties.[46]

A final brokering strategy is that of *frame transformation*, which occurs when "new values may have to be planted and nurtured, old meanings or understandings jettisoned, and erroneous beliefs or 'misframings' reframed in order to garner support and secure participants."[47] Transformative frames can be both *domain-specific*, which are self-contained but substantial changes in the way a particular domain of life is framed, and *global interpretive*, wherein the scope of change is broadened considerably to the point where a new, primary framework largely replaces others and comes to function as a kind of "master frame" that interprets events and experiences in a new way. A global interpretive frame transformation has been described as the "displacement of one universe of discourse by another and its attendant rules and grammar for putting things together."[48]

After information reaches new actors via brokerage – which utilizes the above framing strategies – or diffusion, the next mechanism in the scale shift process according to McAdam, Tarrow, and Tilly is *attribution of similarity*. This occurs when actors in different sites identify themselves as sufficiently similar to justify common action. This mechanism mediates between receiving information and taking adoptive action. Such identification may be inherent (that is, an identification that comes about through frame bridging among already likeminded sites) or constructed (i.e. arrived at through frame amplification, extension, or transformation efforts on the part of brokers), and in most cases is likely to be a combination of both. *Emulation* often follows attribution of similarity. This mechanism is defined as collective action modeled on the actions of others. Finally, *coordinated action* on a new level often occurs after emulation among groups, making the scale shift process complete.

Comprehending through semi-structured interviewing, theory-driven participant observation, internet research, and activist surveys

Now that I have laid out the main framework around which this study has been oriented, I wish to explicate the overall research methodology. Again, it is *comprehending*, or taking up and grasping together with those whose practices I wish to understand and explain. This has entailed combining a number of methods. I adapted an extended case method by including, first, semi-structured interviews and, second, theory-driven participant observation; the latter necessitated extensive reviews of multiple streams of scholarly literature. Third, taking up together means interacting with activists not only in physical field sites, but also in their virtual fields. Toward this end, I perused network members' websites and subscribed to and monitored the European Social Forum listserve. Fourth, I attempted to triangulate – or more accurately *quadrangulate* – my qualitative methods by surveying all organizations and social movements actively participating in the WSF International Council and in the Social Movements Assembly that has sprung up around the forums. This approach closely resembled ethnographer Michael Burawoy's extended case method, as well as Paul Lichterman's synthesis of Burawoy's with other techniques from Barney Glaser and Anselm Strauss's grounded theory, in order to devise his own theory-driven participant observation.[49] In addition, semi-structured interviews also proved central to this study. These were conducted in field sites while engaging in participatory action, and were largely congruent with the technique defined by Kathleen Blee and Verta Taylor.[50]

Briefly, the task of the extended case method is to *extend* cases by synthesizing evidence gleaned through participant observation – and in this study, semi-structured interviews and other documentary sources – with broader theories. The goal is to reconstruct or improve existing theory, so that it can accommodate new cases. In posing and then answering my three research questions, I sought to better theorize these complex social phenomena. Specifically, I consider the activist networks to be, first, *cases* of the scale shift process; second, *types* of transnational network models; and, third, *illustrations* of efforts to shape the social forum process in their own image through distinct forms of participation. Studying these networks as cases of something more abstract allows us to improve upon – that is, substantiate, refine, alter, or reconstruct – pre-existing theories and hypotheses.

Furthermore, semi-structured interviewing has a number of advantages for studying phenomena such as activist networks, and for doing so in a way consistent with my desire to comprehend. Blee and Taylor have found it particularly useful in helping us to, first, understand social movements from activists' perspectives themselves; second, gain knowledge about organizations that are loosely networked and where little documentation already exists; third, broaden the diversity of participants more widely than is usually represented in other methods of inquiry, which tend toward larger or more mainstream NGOs and transnational social movement organizations; fourth, counter-balance the bias in availability of information on existing groups, whose spokespersons, platforms, websites, and other publications usually reflect the voices of a few leaders, more often than not older, Northern, male, well educated, and wealthier than other participants; fifth, gain summaries of longitudinal and other evidence through conversations with expert informants which could be gotten in no other way except by extensive field research or other prolonged involvement with organizations; sixth, probe cause and effect which is often missed in other sorts of data collection methods; and, finally, discover, explore, and interpret complex social processes, especially when triangulated with participant observation and other document research.[51]

Methods applied

Between 2002 and 2005, I attended one WSF annual gathering in Porto Alegre, three European Social Forums (ESF), a week of meetings of the WSF International Council and Commissions, and numerous protest and planning events in Washington, DC, at which I conducted participant observation and semi-structured interviews. In total, I recorded 125 interviews and participated in over fifty social forum workshops, seminars and assemblies, protest planning meetings, strategy sessions and committee meetings, activist teach-ins, trainings, and cultural events, small protest actions, and massive street marches.[52]

When beginning participant observation and interviewing, my main objective was to gain a sense of the breadth of the activist organizations involved in anti-neoliberal struggles as well as their motivations for, and expectations of, participating in the social forum process at various levels. Given my dual audiences, as I explained above, I felt it necessary to ask broad-ranging questions at that point and not decide upon my main theoretical lens, concepts, and categories prematurely. Although I had already identified a potential framework for inquiry in McAdam, Tarrow, and Tilly's DOC approach that I knew would contribute to scholarship on transnational contention, I needed to better ascertain whether studying activism and the social forums from this particular lens would also be of interest to my other audience, that of activists themselves.

At that exploratory stage, I interviewed two Washington, DC-based activists participating at both ends of the social forum spectrum, one actively involved in the WSF and the other in attempting to form a local social forum. I also immersed myself in DC-based, anti-neoliberal and anti-war activism within the umbrella group Mobilization for Global Justice, which coordinated the protests during the World Bank and IMF Spring 2002 meetings and whose members continue to play a role in mass mobilization around these issues. I further joined some of them in planning meetings toward establishing a local, DC social forum. In total I attended twenty-six planning and educational meetings and protest events where I took notes, collected literature, and participated in discussions and action.[53] At these events I fully disclosed my dual roles as activist and researcher. Through these experiences I began to get a better sense of the vast scope of issues and actors involved, as well as what ties, if any, they had to national and transnational organizations and networks.

In autumn of 2002 I relocated from Washington to northern Italy and attended the first ESF in Florence in early November, where I continued to conduct exploratory interview-conversations with participants. I questioned attendees as to the groups and issues with which they were affiliated, their expectations and level of involvement in the social forums, and their ideas about European integration, regionalism, and collective identity construction.[54] I also attended workshops and seminars on alternative European integration, neoliberalism and war in Asia, student mobilizing, and the role of religion in contemporary Europe, and joined a massive anti-war march as well as the SMA at the close of the forum. These interviews and participatory actions were helpful in uncovering tensions, internal debates, and marginal voices difficult to access in other ways. Furthermore, from these and subsequent ESFs in Paris and London, I was able to compare and contrast the European and US activist milieus. Here I noted the ongoing relevance of and tensions surrounding Marxist debates and political parties in Europe, the strong social democratic aims of many of the largest European NGOs and movements, the significant presence of labor unions in Europe's anti-neoliberal struggle, and the resurgence of anti-consumerist and anti-capitalist activism among youth, especially in Italy, Spain, the UK, and Greece.

My participation and interviewing at subsequent social forums grew more focused with each experience. In January 2003, while attending the third WSF in Porto Alegre, interview conversations were directed toward eliciting the cognitive, relational, and structural mechanisms activists, as expert informants, saw as relevant in their shift to the transnational level, both in general and specifically *vis-à-vis* participating in the WSF. Their responses allowed me to begin testing McAdam, Tarrow, and Tilly's hypothesized mechanisms against new empirical evidence.[55] From these interviews I learned about the wide variety of neoliberal change processes and triggers touching down and sparking localized protest. Further, participant after participant relayed a cognitive shift that they perceived to be widespread among those present, stemming from a recognition borne out of frustration and experience of the need to seek targets, allies, and solutions beyond their borders. Said another way, I gained significant evidence of two additional mechanisms, one structural, the other cognitive, comprising scale shift. These I termed the *structural violence of neoliberal globalization*[56] and the *realization of the need to go global*.

I also elicited opinions and expectations of the WSF process itself, in order to gather empirical evidence to weigh against the nascent theories about the social forum and its participants. Specifically, I wanted to better assess to what extent we can say one collective actor or movement is emerging, and if so, how best it can be characterized. I was at the same time considering applying a second DOC process, that of actor constitution, while also contemplating the appropriateness of Hardt and Negri's concepts of *multitude* and *posse* as counter-hegemonic forces against *empire*. I came away from Porto Alegre, however, with the sense that this phenomenon was too overwhelming in size and diversity and lacking in coherence – save for participants' opposition to neoliberalism and war and their desire for global alternatives, in the plural – to be able to theorize it as a collective actor at this stage in its development.

While impressing upon me the massive range of my subject matter, this field experience also gave me a better idea of the varied networks involved in anti-neoliberal struggles and the search for alternatives. This was aided by my participant observation at a trade union forum, marches and rallies, small workshops and gigantic seminars, a planning meeting among Asians in preparation for the WSF to be held in India the following year, and informal observations and discussions on buses, in communal kitchens and bars, and at the youth camp. Furthermore, this field site, attended mainly by Southern Cone activists, gave me another point of comparison to my prior experiences in Europe and the US. I also got a better feel for the coordinating and tacit leadership roles of the Brazilian committee and the WSF IC, whose meetings I had requested to observe but was denied access to due to their being too full. I further learned of the SMA coming together within the WSF, which issued a "Call of the Social Movements" at its close in an attempt to coordinate transnational action over the next year and build toward one global movement.

Upon transcribing and coding these interviews, I gained confidence that the DOC's scale shift process – and potentially others – was a sound framework with which to go forward with additional field visits. In interviews and participant observation conducted at the second ESF in Paris in November 2003, I focused on three processes – scale shift, actor constitution, and polarization – in addition to activist involvement in and expectations for the social forums. There, I found questions that attempted to elicit evidence of actor constitution and polarization to be awkward or confusing to respondents, while the scale shift process, which had guided my questioning at previous forums, seemed again most fruitful, as was eliciting general thoughts on the ESF and WSF.

In Paris I also attended assemblies, plenaries, and workshops dealing with women's rights, the global anti-war movement, human rights, anti-capitalist youth, and political art. In these spaces I experimented with a method of treating these political workshops as focus groups, whereby I selected which workshop to attend based on the likelihood that the discussion would shed light on a particular process or network on which I wanted more evidence. By audio-taping these discussions (with disclosure and consent of those present), I was able to capture insights on youth mobilization today, anti-war coalition-building, tactics for bringing about "other possible worlds," tensions as well as *rapprochement* between younger Marxists and anarchists, and methods and motivations for creating political art. All provided rich, varied, and firsthand evidence which would have been difficult to gather in other ways.

In coding and reflecting on this evidence and continuing my documentary research, I narrowed my project in two important ways. First, I whittled the investigation down to the single process of scale shift and to the role of the social forums in this process. Second, I was now able to identify specific networks focusing on eight distinct issue areas that I surmised to be strong cases of transnationalizing networks actively participating in the social forums. These included the Jubilee 2000 and Jubilee South anti-debt networks; the Via Campesina peasant farmers, the Our World Is Not For Sale (OWINFS) anti-WTO campaigners, the autonomist/anti-capitalist/youth Peoples' Global Action, the ATTAC network lobbying for a tax on financial transactions, the World March of Women against poverty and patriarchy, the environmental justice federation Friends of the Earth International, and the Global Anti-War Assembly. These were chosen because they appear to be the largest transnational networks in their particular area of concern. I could therefore plausibly make the claim that this study captured a large swath of the global left today, and more specifically, of what is being depicted as the network of networks, movement of movements, *alterglobalisation*, globalization from below, the anti-corporate globalization movement, or global peace and justice movement.

I then began drafting case studies of each of these networks' scale shift processes, reflecting on the hypothesized mechanisms from McAdam, Tarrow, and Tilly in light of the evidence coded from my interviews and documentary sources. In this task, organizational websites, personal activist accounts, and scholarly case studies were particularly useful in identifying mechanisms that constituted scale shift in these cases. I found similarities across all of them, as well as ambiguities or holes where more evidence was needed. For my next two field site visits to the third ESF in London in fall 2004 and the WSF IC and Commission meetings in Amsterdam and Utrecht in spring 2005, I determined in advance which organizations were key to the eight transnational networks so that I could interview them. I then conducted directed interviews with activists knowledgeable about the networks under investigation in order to elicit the evidence needed.

Following these last two field visits, I coded the evidence once more into mechanisms constituting scale shift. This led me to make further revisions to the model. As stated earlier, I had already identified two additional mechanisms, one being the environmental change processes and triggers that I called structural violences, and the other being the cognitive shift toward a realization of the need to go global. At that point, I also found significant support for DOC hypothesized mechanisms of *brokering* new relations and *diffusing* information through existing ties, and further specified these with relational and non-relational pathways,[57] as well as various frame alignment strategies used by networks.[58]

These three latter mechanisms – realization of the need to go global, brokerage, and diffusion – appear to produce two additional mechanisms, which in my amended model are depicted together, since they are largely entwined: Following from the prior three mechanisms, we see a similar *shift in the objects and claims* toward the transnational level as well. Furthermore, while my evidence corroborated the DOC hypothesis that *attribution of similarity* often plays a salient role in networks' transnationalizing, I came to conclude that this mechanism was insufficient in explaining how and why such a diverse array of activists are motivated to band together into collective action. What was missing, first, was that which attribution evoked: that is, *solidarity*, or agreement with another's cause and tactics.

Second, in further reflection on the process of attribution leading to solidarity, I questioned whether identification of another group as *similar* captured all significant ties in these networks. Specifically, I queried: What of the motivations behind professional NGOs, charity organizations, and sympathetic individuals who actively take up the cause of others suffering on the other side of the world, such as many Northerners comprising the Jubilee campaigns of debt forgiveness? Further, what of those social movements, think-tanks, or individual activists that identified in another group not a similarity or a shared identity but rather a *reciprocity* or an *interconnectedness* among their distinct concerns and struggles, as I saw comprising giant umbrella networks such as OWINFS? In reflecting on my disparate cases, therefore, I found there to be not one but at least three attributional roads to solidarity, with an important, although not exclusive, route being attribution of similarity.

Two final amendments needed to be made to the scale shift process. First, my evidence suggested that the DOC mechanism *emulation*, although sometimes occurring through the sharing of information about tactics among activist organizations, was not so "robust" or important as to be maintained as a constituent mechanism of scale shift. Groups or individuals join together into transnational networks and campaigns without *necessarily* adopting one or the other's tactics. And joining on to an existing transnational network or campaign is not at all the same as emulating another group's tactics. Second, participating in transnational collective action loops back to impact *local* activism as well, whereby activists participating in transnational campaigns take initiative and ownership in bringing transnational networks down to earth, so to speak, as a form of "glocalization."[59] This needed to be reflected in the scale shift model as well.

Hence, while I have found McAdam, Tarrow, and Tilly's initial hypotheses to be invaluable for orienting the research, as detailed above, the new evidence from my case studies called for significant amendments.[60] Figure 2 better explains both how and why networks shift to include the transnational level of contention in contemporary struggles against neoliberal globalization.

A final, necessary narrowing of my work became obvious as I began to revise the eight case studies toward explicating how these mechanisms manifested in each one. I realized this would be a daunting, and most likely impossible, task to undertake in a single book. So while I had in fact found a recurrent pattern of mechanisms constituting scale shift across eight transnational networks in preliminary research, a significant reduction in the number of cases presented in my final work was necessary, in order not to erase their unique qualities in the process of demonstrating their commonalities.

I decided to focus exclusively on those networks whose primary target is one of the "neoliberal triumvirate" – the IMF, World Bank, and WTO – and save for future revisions and publication the other case studies. The four networks retained constitute the anti-neoliberal core of the network of networks, and can thus be regarded as the anchor, base, or engine of global left activism today. As we move forward to the in-depth case analyses, it is nevertheless important to retain what was learned from the entire research process: These four networks which are central to the anti-neoliberal struggle share common spaces, actions, and aspirations

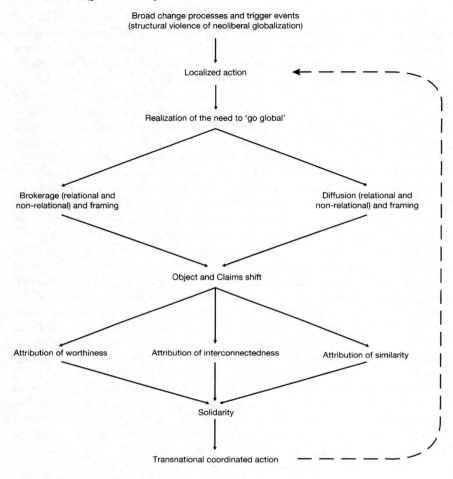

Broad change processes and trigger events
(structural violence of neoliberal globalization)

Localized action

Realization of the need to 'go global'

Brokerage (relational and
non-relational) and framing

Diffusion (relational and
non-relational) and framing

Object and Claims shift

Attribution of worthiness

Attribution of interconnectedness

Attribution of similarity

Solidarity

Transnational coordinated action

Figure 2 The scale shift process model amended.

with a much broader range of activists, chief among them those promoting tax justice to aid developing countries, international peace, women's rights, and environmental sustainability.

Transnational network composition and character

With the amended scale shift framework, we are able to answer questions of both why and how activism is shifting scale to include the global. Yet in researching this process, another cluster of issues and questions came to the fore. Tensions and conflicts among activists, as well as debates over how best to move forward together toward what world and through what organizational forums, all seemed increasingly important. However, they could not be addressed within the scale shift framework alone, save for my addition of three routes to solidarity. In speaking and participating with activists, reading their documentary web and print sources, and reflecting on various streams of literature dealing with transnational activism, social movements, NGOs, and globalization, certain distinctions as well as commonalities among these networks grew apparent. I began to ask myself, and others: What holds a transnational network together across time and space? What creates fissures or causes complete ruptures in them? How are they structured? How do they conceive the problem, that is, the nature of their claims, as well as the solution, or their operational paradigm?

This evolving interest in the differences in composition and character among transnational networks necessitated a comparative, organizational tool for more systematic analysis. But unlike the DOC's scale shift, there was no comprehensive model readily available for application, testing, and amendment. In reflecting on what I was hearing, seeing, and experiencing in the field, I returned to the social movement literature for insight into these questions. I found particularly salient the work related to solidarity, distance, network structure, and the type and scope of claims-making. From this I developed Table 1, comprised of six continua concepts which illustrate these important differences.

Proximity to problem, affective response, and nature of solidarity

Let's take a closer look at the first three concepts, which are interrelated, individual/cognitive level features, namely *proximity to the problem*, *affective response*, and type of *solidarity* evoked. The relative proximity to a perceived threat or harm tends to trigger different affective responses and produce distinct forms of solidarity, all of which correlate horizontally. First, among activists at a considerable *distance* from a threat, *sympathy* with the suffering of others who are deemed worthy of one's support seems to be the prevailing affective response among those who choose to act, leading to solidarity based upon *altruism*. Second, a *perceived connection* between one's own problems or struggle and that of others tends to lead to *empathy* with another's suffering and a sense that its source is at least *remotely threatening* to oneself, which evokes a solidarity based on *reciprocity*. Third, *immediate* proximity to a threat or harm produces *personal suffering*, which can lead activists to seek solidarity relationships with others sharing the same threatened *identity*, be it peasant or recently landless, tribal member, woman, immigrant, or citizen suffering under debt and SAPs or environmental contamination.

Activist networks, especially complex transnational ones, are comprised of a mixture of the above tendencies. That is to say, those who are experiencing an immediate threat posed by some facet of neoliberal globalization are involved in more traditional solidarity relationships with altruistic distant others; yet they are increasingly linking up with activists like themselves who are threatened based on a shared identity, as well as with those with whom they perceive a reciprocal connection among struggles. These are the complex, cognitive and affective bonds that hold transnational networks together. But as well, differences in proximity to

Table 1 Composition and character of transnational activist networks: six conceptual
continua (PASMOC table)

Individual level / cognitive features P-A-S			Group level / relational features M-O-C		
Proximity to problem	Affective response	Solidarity	Model (see Table z2)	Operational paradigm (see Table 3)	Claims (see Table 4)
distant	sympathy for others' suffering	altruistic	NGO advocacy	domain-specific policy reform	economic redistribution
perceived connection	empathy with others' suffering; remote threat	reciprocal	hybrid (embedded NGOs)	transitional	bivalent
immediate	personally felt suffering/ threat	identity (shared fate)	direct activism social justice	multi-sector structural transformation	cultural recognition

the problem, threat perceptions, experienced suffering, and kinds of solidarity
can also account for differing perspectives on the problem itself and its potential
solutions. These can also help explain variance in levels of involvement and
commitment to a cause. The dizzying diversity encompassed in a contemporary
transnationalizing network can also lead to tensions, frustrations, and accusations
of paternalism, on one side, and of radicalism, intransigence, or exclusionism on
the other. All can strain, and eventually rupture, a network.

As intimated above, altruistic solidarity has waned as the driving force within
transnational networks. Instead, contemporary networks are increasingly comprised
of and even driven by the would-be beneficiaries of Northerners' sympathy and
advocacy. Those who are immediately suffering firsthand the structural violences of
neoliberalism are more and more becoming transnational agents themselves, and
are building alliances among those identified as sharing a similar identity and a
common fate with themselves. They are, however, forging these networks with
borrowed – or, to adopt an anarchist term, "liberated" – resources and existing
relationships that were facilitated by NGOs offering altruistic solidarity. These
identity-based solidarity networks are furthermore often enhanced by *reciprocal
solidarity*: that is, by relations with activists with whom they empathize, perceive a
connection, and grant reciprocal solidarity. Many of these are small collectives of
seasoned and deeply committed activists playing key brokerage and diffusion roles.

Transnational solidarity under conditions of globalization

A broad range of scholars are considering anew the possibilities and limitations
of solidarity in the contemporary era of globalization; so much so that Fuyuki

Kurasawa has recently asserted, "Solidarity is becoming the central problem animating social sciences at the dawn of the 21st century," while Pierre Bourdieu, Jacques Derrida, Jürgen Habermas, and Ulrich Beck have each called for a new internationalism in the face of globalization.[61]

Although my nuanced findings speak directly to this increasingly important subject, they cut against the grain of much contemporary thinking on the nature of transnational solidarity. First, altruistic solidarity still takes pride of place in Northern social movement scholarship and mainstream press alike. This is exemplified in research on solidarity movements concerned with distant issues and problems far from home, such as recent works by Dieter Rucht and by Thomas Olesen and James Rosenau.[62] It is also witnessed in media-grabbing, star-studded campaigns such as the summer 2005 Global Call to Action Against Poverty (GCAP), which culminated in the globally broadcast Live 8 concerts held in tandem with the G8 meetings in Scotland.

Altruism can indeed spur many to take part in one-time, low-risk campaigns such as signing a petition or e-mailing a politician. It can also spark changes in lifestyle or personal preferences requiring little if any sacrifice, such as attending a concert that purports to have a political purpose, switching to fair trade coffee, or wearing "no-name" clothing as a political (anti-)fashion statement. But altruism cannot, it would seem, sustain mass-based, transnational activism.

Decades ago, economist Mancur Olson identified this problem in his now infamous exposition of the "free rider." This propelled social movement scholars to begin to take a hard look at the difficulties of motivating individuals – assumed to be rational and self-interested – to act to achieve common goods, let alone to win benefits for others.[63] This in turn opened the way for resource mobilization scholars to conclude that "conscience constituents," or those who expect to receive no benefits from their activism, can often be fair-weather friends to the beneficiaries of their altruistic efforts. For while providing much-needed resources, they can also pose risks to an organization in that they tend to withdraw support in rough times or when a new interest catches their fancy.[64] In addition, neo-Marxist scholars of poor people's movements Francis Fox Piven and Richard Cloward found that leaders and elites often derail mass-based struggles and prevent them from attaining what little is possible through their efforts to channel popular rebellion into social movement organizations or bureaucratized politics.[65]

More recent critiques of altruistic allies and the solidarity they offer reinforce this previous scholarship. They furthermore reflect criticisms voiced by a growing chorus of Southern activists denouncing Northern NGOs as self-appointed representatives of their plight. These alliances have been derided as often a one-way relationship characterized by paternalism and inequality between Northern providers and Southern beneficiaries. Ivana Eterovic and Jackie Smith, for example, point out that action motivated by altruism is often cast as apolitical charity or service work, and rarely challenges underlying, structural causes of grievances.

Peter Waterman has termed this *substitution solidarity*, connoting standing "up" or "in" for those who cannot, it is assumed, speak for themselves. He claims that substitutionism has been the main form of international solidarity over the last three decades on the part of development activists and "First-World Third-Worldists." This has bred a "single community of guilt and moral superiority within 'donor countries,' whilst creating or reproducing further feelings of dependency and/or resentment in countries where social crises have evidently been worsening."[66] By itself, altruistic solidarity serves to reproduce and perpetuate existing inequalities.

In response to their legitimacy being increasingly questioned, NGO-led networks of this nature have accepted or even invited greater participation on the part of their "partners" in the South, with mixed results. For in this very process of former beneficiaries winning a greater voice in networks that claim to advance their interests, altruistic solidarity networks are often challenged to the point of breakdown, as Keck and Sikkink foresaw.

My work's findings also depart from another trend in scholarship with respect to the relative importance and desirability of the kinds of solidarity that have overtaken altruism in transnational networking, those of reciprocal and identity solidarity. Again, my case studies evidence a turn toward popular, transnational networks based upon mass participation by those in immediate proximity to perceived threat or harm and thus personally experiencing an injury. Stated more specifically, identity-based solidarity is increasingly foundational to transnational activism. But in addition, this type of solidarity is facilitated, sometimes greatly, by relationships of reciprocity with those with whom activists empathize and perceive some connection among struggles.

This primacy of identity solidarity, with reciprocity playing an often crucial but largely facilitative role within networks, seems missed – or rather dismissed – by a number of scholars today who have crowned reciprocal solidarity king of transnational networks, termed, alternatively, "reciprocal," "mutual," "political," or "the new transnationalism."[67]

Waterman, for example, writes, "*Reciprocity* suggests mutual interchange, care, protection and support. It could be taken as *the* definition of the new global solidarity."[68] Olesen, following Eterovic and Smith, claims that "mutual solidarity" is a two-way, reciprocal relationship that "blurs the distinction between providers and beneficiaries" and entails "a 'higher' level of global consciousness than the [other] solidarity forms ... [for] it constructs the grievances and aspirations of physically, socially and culturally distant people as deeply interlinked."[69]

On a related note, Donatella della Porta speaks about contemporary activists within the ESF as bearing dynamic, tolerant, flexible, and relaxed identities, while she and Tarrow observe the growing importance of "rooted cosmopolitans" in recent activism. These are said to embody multiple belongings or overlapping memberships in networks, giving them flexible, inclusive identities that promote diversity and cross-fertilization of issues, campaigns, and identities.[70]

Yet in heralding reciprocal solidarity, they simultaneously fail to acknowledge the role that identity plays in these very same networks. Or, if acknowledged, it is done so warily. Waterman, for example, warns:

Identity or identity creation is what commonly underlies socialist calls for international solidarity, usually in reference to oppressed and divided classes or categories in opposition to powerful and united oppressors (capitalists, imperialists). By itself, however, an *Identity Solidarity* can be reductionist and self-isolating, excluding unalikes. In so far as the identity is oppositional, it is a negative quality, often determined by the nature and project of the enemy or opponent (as with much traditional socialist internationalism).[71]

Olesen largely concurs, expressing concern that politicization may lead us back to identity-based forms of solidarity, which he calls ideological. In his eyes this would be an unfortunate reversal which could and should be avoided through mutuality or reciprocity based, in his words, on a "'higher' level of global consciousness" than identity or altruism.[72]

This disparaging of identity solidarity seems to stem at least in part from an aversion to revisit or resurrect the Marxist category of *proletariat* that so captivated and constrained political thinking and practice around identity solidarity throughout much of the twentieth century. Marxist sociologists' analysis of collective action has realistically centered on the interest-based claims of solidarity groups.[73] But while successful in reorienting the discourse away from earlier social breakdown theories and toward rational claims made by collective actors, Marxist theories have been roundly challenged and considerably discredited on other grounds.

Earlier criticisms centered on the empirical observation that those who were actually mobilizing rarely corresponded to the Marxist categories defined by groups' relations to production, and that class conflict in industrial societies often waned, not intensified, in direct contradiction to the theory's predictions.[74] In recent decades, the conception of the working class has been further challenged on two points: first, for the ongoing, and many would say futile, search for the *real* working class, thereby clinging to the assumption that this is the only legitimate identity upon which international solidarity should or could be built; and, second, for assuming that "worker" and "working class" are objective categories, given by the structural relations of production, and not dynamic, contingent, contested, and socially constructed.[75] Waterman summarizes the arc of this critique when he writes:

> The social movement that Marx considered the bearer of human emancipation was, however, the proletariat of the industrialised capitalist world. This working class later spread internationally but became less internationalist with the development of the industrial(ising) nation state, a liberal-democratic/state-collectivist/populist polity, social services, and nationalism/chauvinism/imperialism. It has also become increasingly socially differentiated and dispersed, both nationally and internationally. Whilst labour internationalism is slowly beginning to revive, the major international(ist) social movements of our day are rather those concerning human rights, peace, women, ecology, indigenous peoples.[76]

While Waterman correctly acknowledges that "the *new internationalisms* must therefore be thought of in the plural, with no ontological or teleological privilege granted to one of them," he nonetheless fails to make explicit precisely on what basis this "global solidarity movement ... addressed to the increasing number of global problems produced by a globalised networked capitalism" coalesces and moves forward. It is rather comprised, as he rightly admitted, of indigenous peoples, of women, of peasant farmers – that is of *identities* – as well as of people fighting to uphold *their* rights and preserve *their* immediate environment, not solely, or even in the main, *the* environment or human rights *in general*.

The popular base of support for these networks is not, therefore, built upon altruism or some "higher" reciprocal consciousness. Yet I would argue that this is a healthy strength not a debilitating weakness. For the agency, and thus power, of transnational activist networks increasingly is embodied by those who have the dedication, and indeed the necessity, to make most sure that their grievances are redressed, for they are the very ones whose lives are impacted by the problem, and thus by the fruits of their efforts.

This research suggests that for a transnational network to be genuinely mass-based and to be dedicated to the struggle for the long haul, its rank and file – to perhaps misappropriate a term – must be activists who bear and share a certain identity which is seriously threatened by neoliberal globalization. While others can and do play important facilitative and supportive roles, the onus is shifting to those whose identity as a member of a specific community in a physical place engaged in particular ways of living and working is felt to be under attack. Herein lies these networks' trenchant strength.

I therefore find little reason to privilege the still somewhat ambiguous notion of reciprocal solidarity, in an effort to avoid going down the garden path toward the reified "worker" or to isolationist, in-group/out-group identities. My research shows, first, that this is not an either/or choice. Complex transnational movements today are comprised of identity, reciprocal, and altruistic solidarities alike, in different mixes towards different outcomes. But, perhaps more importantly, the identity solidarity that forms the foundation of contemporary, mass transnational networks is decidedly not reducible to "worker," neither the Procrustean, Marxist proletariat nor the latter-day catholic revival of Hardt and Negri's *multitude*. It is based upon concrete identities – debtor, peasant, indigenous, youth, woman, and, indeed, worker[77] – that have been activated as political due to their being threatened in some concrete way by neoliberal globalization touching down in a specific place.

Highlighting the role of threatened or harmed identities in constructing solidarity networks, when combined with mechanisms shown earlier to constitute scale shift – that is, structural violences of neoliberalism triggering localized contention, brokerage, diffusion, framing, and object and claims shift – speaks to the decades-long debate among social movement scholars over the relative importance of structure, agency, and process.[78] First, it lends credibility to the rather unfashionable "disorganization" and "deprivation" scholarship, which holds that suddenly imposed grievances and disruptions in social roles and institutions cause protest. But, that said, this work also demonstrates that a series of further steps, or mechanisms, are needed for localized contention to grow into transnational collective action. Therefore, in answer to the question of which factors are most useful in explaining contention – social-psychological, structural-organizational, or constructionist-processual – this work finds all of the above.

Network model

Let us now move into the second half of Table 1. These last three columns consist of group or relational features, namely *network model, operational paradigm*, and *claims*. Unlike with the first three concepts, the latter do not necessarily correlate horizontally. That is to say, these three should not be read across but rather treated as distinct categories with which to analyze networks. Nonetheless, there is a degree of consistency along the rows. Networks in which altruism plays a key role tend to bear the features of the *NGO advocacy model* and work within a paradigm of *domain-specific policy reform*; but while these networks often advocate *economic redistribution* in the forms of charitable giving or economic relief, this is not always the case, and they may also call for *cultural recognition* or a *bivalent* mix of both. Moving down to the bottom two rows, networks where both identity and reciprocal solidarity predominate tend either to be modeled as *hybrids* or lean toward the *direct activism social justice model*. Additionally, their operational paradigms tend to be *transitional* and moving toward *multi-sector structural transformation*. Finally, their claims are usually bivalent in nature, encompassing both cultural recognition and economic redistribution.

The above categories can be explained in light of the following literature. First, with regard to network models, Bennett's work has been particularly insightful. He distinguishes between what he calls *first-generation, NGO advocacy networks*, which he sees as still prevalent but increasingly in conflict with emerging *second-generation, direct activism social justice networks*.[79] According to Bennett, the NGO advocacy model is characterized by limited, policy-oriented campaigning aimed at governments, while a direct activism social justice network is typified by a polycentric structure of mass activism and multi-issue, diversely targeted campaigns proliferating via the internet, which are therefore difficult to turn off. For purposes of illustration and also as a tool with which to analyze my four cases, I have condensed Bennett's two tables into one, as shown in Table 2.

My findings both corroborate and challenge Bennett's assertions. These case studies reinforce his observation that NGO-led networks are becoming embedded in more loosely connected networks, which can lead to tensions.[80] Yet the current study departs from his in two primary ways. First, although we must be cautious in generalizing to all transnational networks based on analytic comparisons of four cases, these findings lead us to question his assertion that more centralized NGO and social movement coalitions of the first-generation model still in fact "hold sway."[81]

Second, the current study further shows that a pure second-generation direct activism network is extremely difficult to sustain, as the analysis of the PGA will demonstrate, and thus is itself far from becoming the prevalent model. Rather, Bennett's two categories are best viewed as ideal types, against which contemporary

Table 2 First- and second-generation transnational networks: NGO advocacy and direct activism social justice

	First generation: NGO advocacy network	Second generation: direct activism social justice network
organization	NGO-centered issue networks	mass activism, multi-issue
structure	centralized with lead organizations	polycentric, distributed
formation	brokered strategic coalitions	affinity ties and permanent campaigns
bridging	high brokerage costs	low brokerage costs
scale	limited by brokered coalitions	expanded by technology networks
diffusion	within homogeneous networks	across diverse networks
membership	sign up/pay up; limited agenda control	opt in/opt out; collective agenda setting
stability	issue/goal framing and organizational identity create fracture lines	organizational code of inclusive diversity creates dense network of weak ties
capacity	reform advocacy and crisis intervention	mass protest and value change
mobilization tactics	strategic campaigns turned on and off by leading organizations, member alerts	technological infrastructure generates continuous protest calendar and permanent campaigns difficult to turn on and off
targets/objects	government (all levels), some corporations	corporations, industrial sectors, economic blocs (G7, WEF, IMF, WTO)
goals	government (national and international) regulation, establish information regimes, maintain organizational identity; limited and directed political goals	personal involvement in direct action, establish communication networks, hyper-organizations to empower individuals; diverse and evolving political goals
scope of claims	policy issue advocacy	diverse social justice agenda

Source: Adapted from W. Lance Bennett's Tables 9.1 and 9.2 in "Social Movements beyond Borders: Organization, Communication, and Political Capacity in Two Eras of Transnational Activism," *Transnational Protest and Global Activism*, eds. Donatella della Porta and Sidney Tarrow (Lanham: Rowman & Littlefield, 2005), 214–15.

networks can be analyzed. So while networks approximating the ideals do exist, contemporary activism tends to be organized into a hybrid of the two. My findings therefore provide a more nuanced picture of today's network structures. Furthermore, as the following chapters illustrate, each model carries with it strengths and weaknesses. Negotiating a workable balance between centralized coordination and autonomous action is an ongoing challenge faced by all contemporary transnational networks, the WSF, and the emergent network of networks.

Operational paradigm

Activists have long faced two apparently conflicting paradigms, those of reform versus revolution. The former works within the current institutional framework to promote fairer rules of the game in specific domains, such as labor and environmental standards in trade agreements or provisions for poverty reduction for SAPs, whereas the latter seeks to challenge the current "game" itself of neoliberal globalization or capitalism and replace it with some form of deep democracy based on local autonomy and/or socialism. The Third World Network's Martin Khor speaks of this dilemma confronting activists both at the personal level and in larger groups and networks. Since "the real world is moving ahead in the first paradigm ... I personally often work in the context of the first ... whereas emotionally I really belong to the second one."[82] He goes on to argue that both paradigms should be kept in mind and eventually bridged if mass-based movements are to advance toward transforming global structures.

Khor therefore urges activists to be more explicit as to which assumptions and paradigm they are situated in when making certain claims. In addition, even if one feels compelled to work for now within the first paradigm, he argues that activists should strive to "infuse the second paradigm into the first paradigm as a kind of transition." This could be done, for example, by seeking ways of changing institutions and policies to become more environmentally sound while at the same time reducing the suffering of the poor and transferring costs of pro-environment adjustments to the wealthier countries and entities which can more easily bear them. These incremental reforms, further, should be conceived as steps along the way to transforming the global system. Finally, with regard to working toward the second, transformative paradigm, Khor calls for *evolution* rather than revolution. Table 3 illustrates these three possible paradigms.

It must be said that many would disagree with Khor's strategy on a number of grounds. First, some activists neither desire nor propose thoroughgoing, structural transformations, and rather seek specific policy reforms that address concrete problems, and therefore would have little need for transitional planning toward some world radically different from the current one. Others on the other end of the spectrum would decry Khor's "transformation-in-parts" approach as an impossible strategy toward achieving their desired revolutionary outcomes, and would therefore dismiss his "evolutionary" tactics as futile reformism and, thus, as destined to fail. Both reformists and revolutionaries alike may fault him for leaving out the seizure of state power as a desired goal.

These critiques notwithstanding, I find Khor's distinctions among three paradigms of reformist, transitional, and transformational to be useful categories for analyzing transnational networks, for they adequately reflect the breadth of operational paradigms held by those seeking change, if not their entire content. My research has found that considerable paradigmatic divergences do indeed persist along the strategic range from policy reform to structural transformation. Those networks modeled most closely as NGO advocacy tend to operate within a domain-specific, policy reform paradigm. Meanwhile, there seems to be considerable effort among other networks where identity and reciprocal solidarity

Table 3 Operational paradigms for transnational activist networks

Domain-specific policy reform	Transitional paradigm	Multi-sector structural transformation
work within the current system of neoliberal globalization	promote reforms as objectives to be reached within a strategy of transformation	challenge the current system of neoliberal globalization/capitalism
Fight to make "rules of the game" more fair for weaker parties	Fight to radically reform rules of the game; long-term objective of transforming "the game"	Fight to change "the game" itself
promote labor and environmental standards in trade agreements; industrial jobs and technology transfers to the South	reform trade agreements and development objectives to protect the poor and the environment; costs borne by wealthier parties	promote community-based self-reliance as a model for sustainable living on the planet
short-term pragmatism seen as necessary for immediate survival of some	short-term pragmatic objectives set as part of long-term transformative strategy	long-term vision seen as ultimately necessary for survival on the planet

Source: Adapted from Martin Khor, "Commentary," in *South–North: Citizen Strategies to Transform a Divided World*, ed. John Cavanagh (San Francisco: International Forum on Globalization, November 1995); reprinted in Cavanagh *et al.*, *Alternatives to Economic Globalization*, 13–14.

are salient to develop a multi-sectoral paradigm of structural transformation, which strives to replace neoliberal globalization with comprehensive alternatives. And consistent with Khor's recommendations on how to get from this world to that one, we find that these networks have developed transitional tactics, such as networking broadly to launch or join pragmatic campaigns with concrete objectives, as steps along the way to another possible world.

We should keep in mind that operational paradigms are dynamic and fluid concepts. Individuals, organizations, networks, and indeed "the network of networks" are constantly engaged in action, reflection, study, dialogue, and debate among themselves and others. This dialogic process shapes and reshapes activists' views and their collective actions as to what they are fighting against and for and how to succeed in that struggle.

Nature of claims

Lastly, with regard to the nature of claims being made by transnational activist networks, I have found feminist political philosopher Nancy Fraser's work to be particularly clarifying.[83] She helps us think through the broad scope of harms and injustices faced by many today so as to neither silence nor privilege one set of claims over another. Fraser's work is synthetic along the lines of Khor's thinking above, in that she explores the tension between two seemingly contra-dictory tendencies in activism – the so-called *social politics of equality* and the *cultural politics of difference* – with the aim of combining or reconciling them.

Her larger goal is to reconstruct the left in the most broad, inclusive, and sensitive manner. Toward that end, she highlights the difficult challenge confronting both theorists and movement activists of how to do justice, so to speak, to the claims of multiculturalism without abandoning the left's historic and still worthy commitment to economic equality. Said another way, how do we broaden our conceptualization of injustices to include both cultural insult and economic injury?

Fraser notes that increasingly claims regarding social justice are dividing into two types: redistributive claims, which have for over a century and a half been paradigmatic for theorizing social justice, and the newly ascendant "politics of recognition." These two kinds of justice claims are today often dissociated from one another, both in practice and in scholarship, especially in Northern-based activism. Within certain movements a polarization between the two has even emerged, wherein one side sees the other as bearing a "false consciousness," while the other accuses the former of being an outmoded materialism incapable of redressing certain injustices.

Further, the politics of recognition is said to have gained favor over that of redistribution in contemporary justice claims-making, a development which is attributed to the demise of communism, the rise of neoliberal ideology, and the increase in identity politics – both progressive and regressive. This presents scholars and activists with an apparently either/or choice between redistribution, class politics, and social equality, on the one hand, versus recognition, identity politics, and multiculturalism, on the other, which is depicted graphically in Table 4.[84]

Yet Fraser encourages us to reject these as false antitheses, and rather posits, "justice today requires *both* redistribution *and* recognition, as neither alone is sufficient." The question of how to combine the two is her major task, and she argues that "emancipatory aspects of the two problematics should be integrated in a single, comprehensive framework."[85]

In my own research, I have found considerable empirical evidence that transnational movements are doing precisely this. The reason is because neoliberal globalization is, at least in the short term, making *economic distribution* even more skewed while at the same time it seems to create or exacerbate *misrecognitions in status*. Said another way, the structural violences of neoliberal globalization create or magnify both *economic harms*, such as poverty, exploitation, and inequality, and *cultural harms* of cultural imperialism, misrecognition, and disrespect.

Let us take the most striking example of the rising threat to peasants in regions of the world which had until recently been out of the reach of global capital. The externally imposed changes brought about by the spread of neolib-eralism are not only economic threats or injuries; they are also perceived as an existential assault on identity, for they threaten the very possibility and capacity of individuals and communities to survive and to evolve *as* a community, tied to

Table 4 Social justice claims-making: redistribution vs. recognition

	Social politics of equality / redistribution	Cultural politics of difference / recognition
location of injustice (realm of struggle)	political economy; economic structure of society	cultural; social patterns of representation, interpretation, and communication
collectivities who suffer	economically defined class or class-like groupings in relation to production: exploited working class, economically marginalized racialized underclass, gender-based unwaged laborers, intersecting class/race/ gendered economic inequalities	Weberian culturally defined status groups in relations of recognition; lesser esteem, honor, prestige relative to other groups: low-status ethnic groups, gays and lesbians, racialized groups, and women; race/gender/ sexuality as intersecting cultural codes of misrecognition
harm or injustice suffered	poverty, exploitation, inequality, deprivation, economic marginalization	cultural imperialism or domination, mis- or non-recognition, disrespect
remedies / claims	economic restructuring/ transformation: income redistribution, reorganizing the division of labor, democratizing procedures of investment decisions, etc.	cultural/symbolic change: revaluing disrespected identities and cultural products of maligned groups, recognizing as a positive value cultural diversity, radically transforming society's practices, leading to identity shifts
understanding of differences among groups	differences as socially constructed, unjust differentials resulting from unjust political economy	differences as either pre-existing and benign cultural variations, or co-constituted with value hierarchies
goals	economic redistribution; social equality; abolish difference	cultural recognition; multiculturalism; recognize and celebrate, or deconstruct, difference
types of politics encompassed	"class politics": class-based, New Deal liberalism, social democracy, socialism, socioeconomic feminism and anti-racism	"identity politics": cultural feminism, black cultural nationalism, gay identity politics, deconstructive queer politics, critical "race," and deconstructive feminism

Source: Adapted from Nancy Fraser, "Social Justice in the Age of Identity Politics: Redistribution, Recognition and Participation," The Tanner Lectures on Human Values, Stanford University, 30 April–2 May 1996; and Nancy Fraser, *Adding Insult to Injury: Social Justice and the Politics of Recognition*, ed. Kevin Olson (London: Verso, 1999).

a place and to forms of work and to ways of life that they have collectively developed and that are meaningful to them. Thus, the violences, grievances, and claims made are by necessity *bivalent*.

The best way to regard these violences and claims, following Fraser, is as primary and co-original, and to comprehend this relationship between political economy and culture "integratively." This is done through what Fraser calls a standpoint of "perspectival dualism," rendering visible and open to criticism both the cultural subtexts of apparently economic processes as well as the economic subtexts of ostensibly cultural practices.[86] By extension, this entails evolving alternatives that take both redistribution and recognition seriously.

Fraser's thinking is important in helping (activist-)scholars achieve a perspectival dualism through which to accurately read the bivalent claims articulated among transnational activist networks today. In adapting her categories into an analytic tool, illustrated in Table 4, we are better able to observe that as those who are most directly impacted by neoliberal violence assume greater roles in transnational activism, the nature and scope of claims have shifted. Even among those most closely modeled upon NGO advocacy, but particularly among hybrid and second-generation direct action networks, there has been an expansion in the framing of both grievances and remedies.

Given the broad scope of suffering and threats, or structural violences, seen as caused by contemporary globalization, claims-making is increasingly *bivalent*. Under conditions of neoliberal globalization, redistributive gains are not perceived as achievable without also winning a genuine recognition of diverse individuals' and communities' rights to exist and to determine – or at the very least to have a voice regarding – the pace and nature of change. Activists therefore seek redress across a broad spectrum, ranging from economic ills of poverty and exploitation to cultural harms of devaluing or threatening distinct ways of life and peoples. By studying the multiple claims-making against neoliberalism and the solutions proposed, we see quite clearly that networks today are involved in *both* the social politics of equality and the cultural politics of difference. These results help to throw further into doubt what Fraser and others deem a dubious split within left politics.[87]

Transnationalizing networks and the World Social Forum

My third and final research question deals with the mutual construction of the WSF and contemporary transnationalizing networks. Through interviewing and participant observation at a number of forums in addition to documentary research on the topic, I have concluded that the significance of the social forums for activists, their organizations, and the networks they comprise can be conceptualized as the widening rings surrounding a stone dropped in water. The activist is the stone plunging into the relational, political water of the WSF, while the rings are various dimensions or levels of engagement with others.

This begins with the forums' importance for the individuals and for the organizations to which they belong, moves out to the wider network they are becoming part of, continues on to their encounter with others beyond their specific concerns, and finally toward shaping the nature of an emerging network of networks itself. In engaging in the space of the forums, individuals, organizations, networks, and a global network are shaped and strengthened; at the same time, these people and practices constitute and actively reshape what *is* the social forum itself.

Since the unit of analysis throughout this work is the transnationalizing network, as well as key organizations and activists that are constructing it, my examination of the WSF remains consistent with this network-level focus. It also goes one step further, however, to begin to explore the role of the social forums in forging one global network of networks.

First, I find that the social forums serve as fertile ground for the distinct networks themselves, reinforcing their shift to the transnational level and often strengthening the networks locally, nationally, and macro-regionally at the same time. Second, the forum is a common space of encounter which fosters rejuvenation, learning and reflection, networking, cooperative action, solidarity, and even construction of a new identity. It is a place where activists and their networks meet others and share ideas, build alliances, launch joint campaigns, develop solidarity based on shared identity or interconnectedness of struggles and thus reciprocity, and work toward forging one global network of networks.

But finally, it is a terrain for not only cooperation but also competition and, at times, open conflict, wherein the very nature of the forum is contested, challenged, and prodded to become more like the networks themselves in composition and character: that is, more radically open, decentralized, horizontally connected, spontaneous, autonomous spaces of self-organized action, or more centralized and resembling an NGO, a social movement organization, or a political party; furthermore, will actions coming out of the forum process be guided by visions for a new world that is radically different than the current neoliberal order, or will they seek reforms that leave much of the global economic and political architecture in place. The outcome of both this cooperation *and* this competition will determine not only the future shape of the social forums, but also that of any unified global movement that is to emerge.

With regard to the latter point, the forum can therefore be viewed as something of a multi-faceted, shape-shifting mirror of the transnationalizing networks themselves. Many activists welcome the forum's aspiration to being a non-deliberative and non-hierarchical space, and work to make it more genuinely so. Some do this through sympathetic critique or suggestions to WSF organizers and the IC, others through provocative direct action, as will be seen, for example, in Chapter 6.

These so-called "horizontal" critiques include charges that the WSF embodies informal hierarchies and opaque decision-making structures masked by claims of being an open, non-hierarchical space. This lack of transparency allegedly serves to promote more traditional Marxist or reformist groups and ideas, and perpetuates gender and racial hierarchies while marginalizing more radical, alternative, or oppressed groups.

In response to these criticisms, the WSF's planning and administration have become more open and less centralized in the hands of its Brazilian founders through an expansion of the IC, by the forum's move to Asia and establishment of the Indian committee, and through the creation of an open source website allowing participants to propose and coordinate their own themes and events.

In addition to the "horizontal" critiques, we must add what could be called the "vertical" ones. These come from those who are either bewildered by the non-deliberative, non-hierarchical model, have grown frustrated with it, or have never really bought into it in the first place. All seek to turn the forums into the more familiar – they would argue effective – types of leftist political entities, namely the social movement, NGO, political party, or even communist international.

This tendency has led to the creation of the Call of the Social Movements/ Social Movements Assembly process by a number of the largest networks and movements participating in the WSF, many of which also sit on the WSF IC. Although the assembly is not a recognized part of the forum itself and usually takes place on the day following a forum's close, it has to a considerable degree become entwined with the forum process, as preparatory meetings and coordination run between and throughout the forums themselves. So while the assembly, which reaches consensus on a final call to action, allows participants to come away with some semblance of a collective plan, it also pushes the forum in the direction of a movement and away from a non-deliberative space.[88]

These horizontalist and verticalist tendencies collide in and seek to pull the forums in different directions. And in the process, they have rendered these forum spaces the most dynamic and fertile sites for contention – as well as for mutual learning and cooperation – among activists forging the network of networks today.

Looking ahead to the case analyses

Now that we have overviewed the research questions and the appropriate analytical frameworks through which they will be investigated – those of the scale shift process, network composition and character, and three salient facets of analysis *vis-à-vis* the WSF – we can turn to the case studies themselves, those of the Jubilee anti-debt networks, Our World Is Not for Sale, the Via Campesina, and Peoples' Global Action.

Each chapter begins with a brief introduction of the network, followed by the change processes and/or triggers viewed as structural violence sparking localized contention. This begins the tracing of the mechanisms that constitute that network's shift in scale to the transnational level of coordinated action. Next we examine the composition and character of the network, including proximity to the problem, affective response, forms of solidarity, network model, operational paradigm, and nature of claims. Each chapter concludes with a brief examination of the network's involvement with the WSF, looking first at the impact on the network itself, next its cooperation with others within the forum, and finally the ways in which, through its competitive participation, it is shaping the nature of the social forum, and potentially that of an emerging global network.

3   Toward Jubilee 2000 and beyond

"Jubilee" is the name shared among a web of debt-eradication, anti-SAP and trade justice campaigns taken up by social movements, church and civic associations, NGOs, celebrities, and political entities over the last decade. It is comprised of over two dozen loosely affiliated "Drop the Debt" national coalitions as well as an umbrella network, Jubilee South, made up of anti-debt groups from Africa, Latin America, the Caribbean, and Asia-Pacific. These activists' most visible and successful campaign has been the church-based, grassroots Jubilee 2000 initiative, which sought to press G7 governments and banks into canceling unpayable debt owed by the poorest countries by the end of the year 2000.[1] Participants framed their campaign in moral terms, challenging people of faith to celebrate the 2,000th anniversary of Christianity by proclaiming it a "jubilee year" wherein creditors ought to forgive the debts of the poor. In this five-year campaign, Jubilee 2000 organizations spread to some fifty countries and circulated petitions in twice as many, which were signed by 24 million people. This campaign was successful in getting debt on to the global agenda and was partially rewarded with world leaders agreeing to write off $110 billion of the poorest countries' debts as 2000 approached.

Yet this victory proved pyrrhic for the network itself. The promised debt forgiveness was made contingent upon these countries' adopting austere, SAP-like conditionalities, which split the campaign roughly along North–South lines. On the Northern side were many who cautiously welcomed the G7 offer as a partial victory, while from the South came denunciations of the offer being too little, too late, and with too many strings attached. Southerners and their allies broke away to form Jubilee South, while others linked to the UK-based Jubilee Research developed the Jubilee Framework for debt arbitration. In addition to rupturing the coalition, the much-touted 2000 initiative also led to a premature demobilization on the part of Northern activists on the debt issue, only to be revived with the GCAP launched in the lead-up to the July 2005 G8 ministerial in Scotland. Below we will trace the scale shift process of these campaigners fighting debt and SAPs, beginning with the broad change processes and triggers that I term neoliberal globalizations' structural violences. Once the mechanisms that comprise this network's shift in scale to the transnational have been fully explored, we will turn to an analysis of its changing composition and character.

Finally, we will examine the interrelationship between the WSF process and various strands of Jubilee.

Broad change processes: the global debt crisis and SAPs

Meeting in Bretton Woods, New Hampshire, in 1944, the world's major powers designed a post-war economic system anchored in the TNC and to be managed by the World Bank (then the International Bank for Reconstruction and Development) and the IMF. But it took some time, and persuasion, for these organizations to attain the power they hold today. A seminal initiative was launched at the end of decolonization, when the Bank set up a program to educate Southern bureaucrats and economists about the export economic growth model. This model was to be financed through foreign debt and investment under the guidance of the Bank and IMF. But when initial loans for infrastructure and imports failed to stimulate the desired results, larger loans were needed just to service the growing debt. These failed policies marked the beginning of the global debt crisis, as well as the growing influence and intervention of Bretton Woods' organizations into newly independent states.

These mammoth loans also helped to create the "developmentalist state" of the post-war and post-colonial period. This model was forged in the context of the US–USSR rivalry to secure allegiances of Third World governments, and was therefore characterized by development assistance and active trade relations from abroad. Domestically, this model entailed the growth of state-owned enterprises, targeted state investment, import-substitution industrialization, and capital and exchange rate controls. A minimal social pact developed as well between government and citizens, which strove to guarantee a social wage, social security, health care, education, minimum wage, and trade union rights.[2] This minimal welfare state was maintained as long as development assistance, economic growth, and generous loans continued.

But the flush lending of the 1970s spurred by Northern banks swamped with money from the Organization of Petroleum Exporting Countries (OPEC) bred a Third World debt load that soon threatened the global financial system. Mexico defaulted in 1982, and was the first, of many, to be structurally adjusted. The benefit of accepting an SAP, however, amounted to little more than the opportunity to become further indebted. Consequently, with the onset of the Third World debt crisis, the growing pervasiveness of SAPs, and the withering of First World patronage as the Cold War ended, the developmentalist state could no longer be sustained. As we shall see in the later exploration of the roots of the Jubilee network, this retreat of the state set off a wave of contention that has yet to abate across the formerly Third and Second Worlds.

It is important to ask how successful the SAPs have been in what they were intended to do, that is, rein in debt. Though other factors certainly come into play, the overall results have been disappointing to their designers and disastrous to the societies which have been put through them. At the start of the crisis in the early 1980s, poor countries owed $609 billion. Today, that debt has tripled to

$2.4 trillion. One of the main culprits in the widening North–South income gap is debt service alone, never mind repayment: Over the past two decades, indebted countries have paid hundreds of billions more to service the debt to Northern creditors than they have received in government aid or private loans. In human terms, this has meant that Africa now spends four times more on repaying its debts than on health care for its people.[3]

Let's now more closely examine the SAPs. Largely as a precondition for new loans or aid, these programs have been quite literally thrust upon nearly a hundred developing countries over the past two decades. Furthermore, since the IMF has come to act as both an advisor and a loan accreditation body, countries have little choice but to accept the program as a condition of eligibility in order to qualify for *any* international financing. Under the SAPs, national governments must slash social spending on education, health care, and subsidies for food staples; devalue their currency; increase exports, which often leads to destruction of natural resources and falling wages; open financial markets, which invites instability through short-term speculative investments; increase interest rates to attract foreign capital, which threatens domestic businesses and employment; and remove tariffs and other import controls, allowing for consumer goods and agricultural products to flood the country, and which tends to worsen the external debt and destroy local businesses, agricultural markets, and jobs.

The explicit goal of these programs is to make governments prioritize debt repayment and macroeconomic stability in order to spur economic growth and development. But as we saw in the previous section, the cumulative results have been an increase, not a decrease, in overall debt burden. Hence, after two decades of further indebtedness, impoverishment, societal upheaval, and economic stagnation, pressure for change has built to the point where both the World Bank and the IMF have at least formally abandoned the SAPs, in favor of "poverty reduction" schemes that include some lending for social services. Yet many NGO experts who closely monitor these agencies caution that this reversal has been largely in words and not, as of yet, deeds.

They further conclude that, despite the failure to meet the stated goal of debt reduction, the *tacit* objective of the SAPs has been achieved, which was the elimination of the last vestiges of the developmentalist state. They explain that, beyond precipitating the end of the minimal welfare state through forcing cuts in basic services, it is the economic policies of import substitution, or national self-reliance, that have been the real target of adjustment, because this formerly widespread economic model is anathema to maximizing foreign corporations' profits. In contrast, SAPs work to dismantle most government policies that stand in the way of foreign investment. As evidence of this assertion, activists point out that the IMF programs not only stipulate what must be privatized – which is considerable – but often also specify which multinational corporations are to receive contracts on the formerly publicly owned enterprises. This means that some of the greatest indirect recipients of development loan funds are in fact Northern corporations. Therefore, given this decades-long track record of both growing debt and mounting foreign ownership under the SAPs, many activists have concluded that the World Bank and the IMF in their current form, as embodiments of neoliberal globalization theory and major instruments of its practice, are simply incapable of and uninterested in reversing the debt crisis and all that accompanies it, suffered by much of the world's people.[4]

Neoliberal globalization touches down via debt and SAPs, sparking localized contention

Now that we have overviewed the interrelated, broad change processes of growing poor-country debt and control over these economies via World Bank and IMF-imposed SAPs, we can now readily grasp the trigger events that sparked localized contention and initiated a process that would wend its way through additional mechanisms toward transnational coordinated action. The roots of the high-minded Jubilee year campaign to put faith into action can be traced to a riot; or, more accurately, a rash of riots, street demonstrations, and general strikes popularly referred to as "IMF riots." The effects of the SAPs on national economies and day-to-day lives have been stark, beginning with the forced deval-uation of currencies, which in turn sent prices for basic goods soaring and real wages plummeting.[5] Making matters worse, SAP privatizations often came quickly and without proper regulations or transparency. Many nations consequently experienced massive lay-offs and unpaid wages, political corruption, financial fraud, money laundering, the rise of organized crime, social and income polar-ization, and shrinking tax bases as foreign ownership skyrocketed and profits were sent out of the country.[6]

In reaction to these suddenly imposed and widely felt hardships and insecuri-ties, local protests erupted in more than three dozen countries beginning in 1976, peaking in the mid-1980s and continuing to the present. These actions have been diverse, taking the form of food riots in Morocco, Brazil, and Haiti, general strikes in Peru, Ecuador, and Bolivia, and violent protests in Sudan, Turkey, and Chile. Often one form of protest has morphed into another, as demonstrations turn into riots and violent mass actions grow into political organizations. Most participants have been urban and poor: shantytown dwellers, unemployed youth, precarious laborers, and working-class trade unionists who share a common fate of being negatively impacted by the SAPs.[7] Furthermore, a few keen observers in the 1980s understood the tremendous potential for this widespread suffering under austerity measures to provide a firm foundation upon which common frames, claims, and enemies could be articulated, broad identity-based solidarity constructed, and collective action among a wide array of groups waged: "The implementation of austerity policies," wrote Walton and Ragin, "is far-reaching and likely to affect virtually all currently mobilized collectivities, providing them with an opportunity to act in concert. Austerity may forge broad political alliances that would be impossible to sustain otherwise."[8] Walton and Ragin's predictions were largely borne out. Poorer groups often identified with and combined their protests with students, teachers, public employees, shopkeepers, professionals, middle-class consumers, and business organizations. And crucially, as will be seen below, for the scale shift process to move forward, they also came together with church groups who had at their disposal considerable transnational diffusion channels, organizational structures, and access to and credibility with a vast public, the media, and governments.

Erosion and de-legitimization of the state spur realization of the need to go global

The SAP reforms that countries were forced to undertake not only sparked localized contention. They also invoked citizen anger and disillusionment with their own governments. On the one hand, former officials were blamed as corrupt, unaccountable, and responsible for the excessive international borrowing that precipitated these crises. On the other, politicians, regardless of their intentions or actions, were seen as increasingly impotent in this more austere, global environment. The Third World developmentalist state had traditionally been characterized by patron–client relationships, and therefore politicians' legitimacy rose and fell on their ability to respond to their constituencies' material demands. But as leaders' room for maneuver was constricted under the SAPs, people in all sectors reacted. Citizens who were able channeled their discontent into already existing organizational networks, launching national protest campaigns and strikes. Claims on behalf of an emergent "civil society" also surfaced in many countries, where elements such as the Catholic Church and other Christian mission agencies, student groups, and professional organizations were called upon to fill the gaps in the shredding webs of patronage of the retreating state.[9]

What was underway was in fact a double shift away from the state and toward the transnational sphere. First, the fulcrum of decision-making was seen as becoming more remote and removed to powerful global nodes of the IMF, World Bank, and other international creditors. Second, and as a consequence, those non-state organizations that were increasingly asked to provide what were formerly public services were *also* international in nature. These were largely faith-based and humanitarian organizations. A Northern leader of the Jubilee 2000 campaign noted that this phenomenon has become commonplace under neoliberal globalization, and has occurred through relational diffusion of information and requests on the part of Southern congregations to their richer Northern counterparts:

> Churches are always asked to pick up the tab for education and health care when they are cut under structural adjustment. Churches from the South have turned to their counterparts in the North. So US churches have joined the [Jubilee] campaign not only because of the moral issues but because their Southern counterparts are pressuring them.[10]

Laying the groundwork for Jubilee: early brokerage, diffusion and framing of the debt crisis through Christian institutional channels and actors

As SAPs, and resistance to them, spread throughout the Global South, missionaries and Christian aid workers – some of whom were influenced by liberation theology, which stressed actively working to eradicate poverty – sent impassioned eye-witness accounts back to their home countries, urging NGOs and communities of faith to take up the issues there. These appeals to Northern churches and hierarchies for a response bolstered the pleas for help of the Southern church leaders. In addition to this relational diffusion along existing church channels, some of the earliest brokerage activity was undertaken by the Maryknoll priest Reverend Thomas Burns. In the early 1970s Burns brought together Catholic and Protestant missionaries from the US to form the lobbying organization Peru Solidarity. Early efforts included staging small protests at IMF and World Bank annual meetings, lobbying Congress, and conducting popular education through public talks and newsletters. In the main, however, brokerage leading to sustained coordination among diverse groups was limited until the late 1980s.

As pressure, testimonials, and locally gathered statistics continued to flow from South to North via existing church and humanitarian channels, awareness, interest, and coordinated action at the national level began to grow. National efforts were further aided by incipient, international information-sharing via diffusion efforts among already connected Northern groups. Christian organizations and economic justice NGOs brokered ties with domestic activists and supporters in order to exchange information and coordinate conferences and mailings. Notably, Washington, DC, and New York-based NGOs, including the Institute for Policy Studies (IPS), the Jesuit's Center of Concern, Bread for the World, the Development GAP (Development Group for Alternative Policies), and Methodist Church Women United, established the Debt Crisis Network to achieve these goals. Utilizing their already considerable diffusion channels, these international church organizations and NGOs drew on contacts in Europe, Canada, Latin America, and the Philippines to pool information so as to develop educational and lobbying materials in the Global North. Through developing and distributing pamphlets and illustrated books via church networks – especially Methodist and Catholic – activists were able to make, in the words of one pioneering anti-debt activist, "complex, technical issues that are both far a field from the everyday experience of Northern constituencies and insufficiently covered in the mainstream media ... more understandable to a wider audience."[11] This popular education was arguably crucial in developing a sizable base that could lobby for change, and laid the groundwork for broader action in subsequent campaigns. The Debt Crisis Network, in addition, lent its endorsement to Southern-led initiatives. Most notable was the 1987 Campinas Declaration calling on Latin American countries to collectively repudiate the debt and work together to form a new international economic order.

What was dawning on activists in the North was what had already emerged, under different conditions, in the South: a realization that in order to address injustices in the global financial system activists needed a coordinated response on that level. This is illustrated by one Catholic Agency for Overseas Development (CAFOD) campaigner, who reflected on the motivations for organizations to link up transnationally to campaign against debt and for development. Citing the realization of the need to go global as an important motivator, she saw a growing

> appreciation that global problems need global solutions, that to make a difference we have to work together. ... That we need to be putting pressure on our government in the UK while people in Brazil are putting pressure on their government simultaneously. ... The fact that multinationals/transnationals *are* transnational, ... if they're globalized we need to be globalized.[12]

CAFOD was not the only Northern-based agency to arrive at this conclusion of the need to coordinate globally. The campaigns director of Oxfam Netherlands (Novib), which is one of twelve national affiliates comprising Oxfam international, spoke of a similar realization among the vast anti-hunger organization:

> The corporate sector became internationalised at a much earlier stage. The same also applies to governments: within the European Union, at institutions such as the World Trade Organisation (WTO), the International Monetary Fund, the World Bank, etc. The global rules of play have always been determined primarily by leading players like the transnational corporate sector, large countries and a few powerful international institutions. ... We soon discovered that this is the only way to get things done. We are better off trying to join in with the forces that want to change the rules so that citizens throughout the world can live decently rather than having to help people because they are no longer able to survive.[13]

Another activist, based in Washington, DC, with the Center of Concern, further elucidates the complex dialectic among globalization forces and popular resistance in recent decades. In his view, the global diffusion of technology made transnational organizing possible, just as the mounting suffering, insecurities and exclusions caused by the spread of neoliberal policies make cross-border mobilizing necessary:

> On the one hand we regard as a positive aspect of globalization this increased, facilitated communication. In movements and in campaigns before the 90s what would take three or four weeks ... now takes seconds because of the internet [which] helps organizing something global. ... At the same time, the bad side, the economic side of globalization is [that] the increased flow of capital and goods across borders has brought a lot of problems. It has brought a lot of prosperity for very select groups, for privileged

people, and that has created a wider array of places where people live in very degrading levels of poverty, and it has exaggerated the already existing likelihood of environmental disasters. All this has created big movements of people [who are] being left out of the benefits of the system, and basically are being marginalized. ... The social movements in increasing number, the increasing mobilization power, the increasing connection that they draw between policies at the global level and their conditions at the local level, the fact that their voices are usually not heard, all that creates an environment that didn't exist twenty years ago.[14]

Forerunning efforts against debt and SAPs spread through Europe, Africa, Asia, and the Americas

In Europe, concern over the debt crisis was simultaneously growing among faith-based, humanitarian, and environmental NGOs and political parties. In 1986 Oxfam UK launched a "Hungry for Change" campaign to emphasize the local roots of global poverty and advocate for a policy shift within Britain. In this campaign they held weeklong fasts to draw attention to British culpability in perpetuating world poverty through that country's policies on debt, aid, trade, agriculture, and arms. The campaigners were partially successful in gaining an audience by casting these new issues within an extended frame of African famine – a topic that had been popularized by the LiveAid concerts spearheaded by the musician Bob Geldof.

Around the same time, activists from Oxfam and War on Want established the UK Debt Crisis Network, which went on to broker relations with a wider range of Christian aid and secular development groups throughout the UK in order to share information. In 1987–8, Dutch foundations and NGOs including Novib and the Interchurch Coordinating Committee on Development Projects brought together an international coordinating committee, called the Forum on Debt and Development (FONDAD). This forum set up a European secretariat in the Hague along with a network of regional offices around Latin America.

A second, more successful attempt to establish a European-based, international network on debt came in 1990 in the form of the European Network on Debt and Development (EURODAD), based in Brussels and partially funded by the European Community. After conversations with African NGOs, these same groups in 1994 helped to found and fund the African Network and Forum on Debt and Development (AFRODAD), based in Harare and seeking to establish coordination among national coalitions of church groups, NGOs, unions, and professional organizations throughout the continent.

The European-based groups led by EURODAD and Novib linked up with more moderate US NGOs in 1993 to launch a still-ongoing Debt Treaty movement. This network's efforts have included public lectures, press conferences and other media outreach, research, drafting of joint platforms, and lobbying of donor governments and Bretton Woods institutions. The goal throughout has been multilateral debt reduction for the most highly indebted poor countries

(HIPC). The Debt Treaty movement, having some 200 international NGOs as signatories, has been widely cited for, first, getting G7 and World Bank officials to put debt reduction on the table and, second, sustaining the attention needed to win their eventual promise of writing off over $100 billion in debts.[15]

Meanwhile, in Asia campaigning around debt reduction has been led since the late 1980s by the Philippines Freedom from Debt Coalition (FDC), representing over ninety organizations. In 1993, the FDC brokered ties to establish the Manila-based Asian Campaign on Debt and Structural Adjustment, which coordinated research efforts, grassroots organizing, and macro-regional campaigns. Similar to the establishment of the Latin American FONDAD, this Asia-wide campaign coincided with activist groups extending their focus out from mainly debt forgiveness to include a broader critique of the IMF and World Bank's interference in national policy-making and of the SAPs in general.

Coordinated campaigns based in the US against debt and SAPs grew as well in the early 1990s. These nascent attempts were highly unstable, dissolving and regrouping with many of the same members no less than six times in just a few years. The Debt Crisis Network gave way to the Debt Action Coalition, the Rethinking Bretton Woods project, the Debt Study Group, the Religious Working Group on the World Bank and the IMF, the Multilateral Debt Coalition, and finally the Fifty Years Is Enough campaign.[16] Despite their differences, each of these groups followed in the Debt Crisis Network's footsteps of prioritizing grassroots education in order to cultivate a critical mass of citizens in creditor countries willing, and crucially *able*, to authoritatively argue for debt forgiveness. Organizing just prior to the widespread availability of the internet, these networks distributed thousands of informational booklets and research reports, gave talks to church and civic groups, and developed religious reflections and sample letters to send to legislators.[17]

Of these networks, one in particular stands out as being most critical and action-oriented, Fifty Years Is Enough. This network was founded in 1993 by environmental and development groups including Friends of the Earth, Development GAP, the Environmental Defense Fund, and the Maryknoll Justice and Peace Office. Reflecting the expanded frame from debt to include SAPs, these activists demanded a "profound transformation" of the World Bank's and IMF's processes, policies, and projects in the lead-up to these institutions' fiftieth anniversary. While sharing some overlap of leadership, demands, and actions with the other US-based networks mentioned above, Fifty Years Is Enough has from its inception emphasized coordinated action among grassroots organizations both at home and abroad.

This network's more assertive stance in comparison with others in North America is partly due to the fact that the majority of its members are from the Global South. They have thus experienced firsthand the effects of debt and SAPs, and are therefore less likely to express satisfaction with or gratitude for public promises or what they consider half-measures on debt relief. Today, over 185 organizations in 65 countries exchange information and coordinate literacy training, mass mobilizations, and policy advocacy with some 200 grassroots organizations in the United States. Network board member organizations include the Bangkok-based Focus on the Global South, the Senegalese Forum for African Alternatives, the Brazilian Social Network for Justice and Human Rights, the South African Anti-Privatization Forum, and the US-based Sisters of the Holy Cross and the Religious Working Group on the World Bank and IMF.[18]

This network's more critical perspective may also be attributed to an ill-fated joint project between members of Fifty Years Is Enough and the World Bank. In the mid-1990s, network members approached Bank president James Wolfensohn proposing a joint civil society–World Bank assessment of the effects of SAPs. Two years later, Wolfensohn agreed to a multi-country, field-based study, to be named the Structural Adjustment Policy Review Initiative (SAPRI). As the project neared completion, the cumulative results were overwhelmingly negative. Researchers linked adjustment policies to worsening poverty, falling employment, and restricted access to essential services. When the civil society team publicly released its final report, "The Policy Roots of Economic Crisis and Poverty," the World Bank at first distanced itself from the project and then published its own alternative take on the study, called "Adjustment from Within: Lessons from the Structural Adjustment Participatory Review Initiative." While not disputing the devastating social impacts relayed in the NGO report, the Bank nonetheless defended SAP performance on the basis of optimism for future growth: "The overall result in the 1990s," the Bank report assured, "is that the people of these countries have been lifted from living in economically stagnant countries to *potential* emerging economies."[19] The joint venture collapsed shortly afterward in frustration and condemnation.[20]

From foundations to fruition: the brokered beginnings of Jubilee 2000

Above we have traced anti-debt and anti-SAP activism from its roots in broad change processes and trigger events sparking localized reaction and a realization of the need to go global across the South. We next followed various nascent attempts at cross-border brokerage and diffusion toward joint initiatives, identifying in the process a similar cognitive shift among Northern-based activists of the need to go global as well. We will now build on the above in order to more precisely identify the mechanisms comprising the scale shift process of the Jubilee 2000 campaign, followed by the various networks it has spawned as that important year came and went but debt and SAPs stayed.

The direct lineage of the Jubilee name and campaign itself can be traced to one of the original members of the UK Debt Crisis Network, whose genesis and early activities were described above. Martin Dent, a network activist and politics professor, organized a group of students into a "Jubilee campaign" in 1990 calling for debt relief. He soon joined up with former UK ambassador Bill Peters and others to start the Cambridge-based Jubilee Foundation. The latter brought together individual activists such as Isabel Carter and Ann Pettifor as well as relief organizations, namely CAFOD, Oxfam, Anglican Christian Aid, the World Development Movement, and Tearfund. Together they launched the first "Jubilee 2000" campaign in 1996. One year later, they combined their energies with the UK Debt Crisis Network in order to form the Jubilee 2000 Coalition, and chose Ed Mayo of the former organization to chair their coalition board for the duration of the campaign.[21]

Jubilee 2000's objects and claims

The Jubilee 2000 campaigners' key arguments had been worked out over the many years of anti-debt networking that had come before, and were therefore conceptualized in transnational terms from the outset. Poor countries, they held, devote too much money to paying interest on debt and thus leaving little for health, education, shelter, and job creation. They furthermore criticized SAPs for exacerbating this situation. Their demands were for significant reductions, and preferably outright cancellations, of unpayable debt and for modifying or completely eliminating the SAP "conditionalities" imposed on poor countries. The campaign's targets went immediately beyond their national government to take aim at commercial banks, all creditor governments of the Paris Club, and international financial institutions, especially the IMF, World Bank, and regional development banks.

As was shown in previous sections, considerable efforts that had already gone into transnational networking for debt forgiveness and against SAPs failed to catch on outside of small circles of the already committed. What, therefore, made the Jubilee 2000 campaign so successful in motivating millions of ordinary people to act, in garnering considerable sympathetic press coverage, and in eventually winning a commitment from creditors for significant debt reduction? This success seems largely due to the types of brokerage, diffusion, and framing strategies employed, namely: network brokers' frame amplification strategies emanating from and speaking to people of faith worldwide; second, capturing media attention, which helped diffuse their message and portrayed the campaign in a positive light through innovative tactics, including attracting celebrities and "branding"; and, third, the increased use of the internet, which greatly facilitated "framed" information flows via the pathways of relational and non-relational diffusion and brokerage. Let's take each of these in turn.

Religious frame taps into church networks and leadership, inspires mass solidarity and activism

The centrality of the religious frame to this network meant that faith-based organizations were at the forefront of Jubilee 2000. The frame resonated with and drew religious people the world over to the campaign. As one observer put it, "The secret of Jubilee 2000's success is simple but unfashionable: it is the Christian churches."[22] In Britain, for example, church involvement was seen as key for two reasons:

Their backing brought with it millions of churchgoers in the UK and the ready-built structure and parishes, along with their publications. News could – and did – spread fast, and Jubilee 2000 found the idea taking off as an integral part of the churches' celebration of the millennium. Alongside plans for parish parties and fireworks was debt cancellation. Jubilee 2000 found itself addressing church meetings up and down the country.

Secondly, the churches brought an international structure. As the idea gained ground in the UK, it began to spread through diocesan links, between bishops' conferences and via parish twinning to the southern countries. Missionary societies and orders spread the word.[23]

Oxfam, Christian Aid, CAFOD, the Catholic National Episcopal Conferences, the World Council of Churches, the bishops of the Anglican Communion, as well as Pope John Paul II all played central roles in the campaign. Worldwide, Jubilee 2000 also attracted support from Jewish and Muslim communities. In the US, the Religious Working Group on the World Bank and the IMF took the lead in organizing interested activists and local groups into a national coalition, restoring former ties and brokering new ones among the Multilateral Debt Coalition, the US Conference of Catholic Bishops, Bread for the World, and the Center of Concern. In 1997 these groups came to a consensus on a national Jubilee 2000 campaign, officially launching it at the G8 Summit in Denver that year.[24] The call for the campaign was disseminated quickly through pre-existing church structures. Northern countries, using the channels already established with Southern debt activists in the 1980s and 1990s, sponsored and financed dozens of Jubilee 2000 national campaigns across the South beginning in 1998.

The reason Jubilee campaigners were able to invigorate these pre-existing transnational and local ties and broker new relationships seems plausibly due to their successful frame amplification of both beliefs and values. The frame was rooted in the Judeo-Christian Book of Leviticus's prescription that anniversaries should be celebrated with the freeing of slaves, the return or redistribution of land and wealth, and the cancellation of debts. It was further tied to Christianity through the Gospel of Mark's reporting of Jesus's own declaration of such an anniversary.[25]

Setting their collective sights on 2000 as God's "acceptable year of favor" created an inspirational momentum for debt forgiveness as the important date approached. The Jubilee 2000's "Statement of Purpose" framed it as follows: "The Biblical tradition calls for a Jubilee year, when slaves are set free and debts cancelled. As the new millennium approaches, we are faced with a particularly significant time for such a Jubilee."[26] The Anglican Archbishop of Cape Town, Njongonkulu Ndungane, eloquently preached:

We are at the doorstep of the next one thousand years in the history of humankind. The first Christians stood on the threshold of the first millennium in a state of hopelessness after the Crucifixion of Christ. But God raised him from the dead: hence our age is one of hope, an age of new beginnings, an age of the Resurrection faith. The opportunity to start anew must be seized. Through an act of immeasurable power and grace, let us reshape the world's economy. In this way the third millennium can be a Jubilee celebration.[27]

Countless religious leaders echoed Ndungane's millennial call to action. Probably the most visible was Pope John Paul II's endorsement of debt cancellation in his 1994 *Tertio Millennio Adveniente*. In it he prodded:

> Christians will have to raise their voice on behalf of all the poor of the world, proposing the Jubilee as an appropriate time to give thought … to reducing substantially, if not canceling outright, the international debt which seriously threatens the future of many nations.[28]

Millions of people of faith and conscience around the globe were moved by these public appeals to the values of compassion and justice for the poor and to the amplified belief that something *can* and *must* be done. One UK activist shared this experience of participation in a Jubilee 2000 transnational action in profoundly personal and religious terms:

> The G8 leaders were in Okinawa. A small group of us were in a West London church. As we followed the Summit Watch vigil guide I realised that this was not just a routine ceremony. It was another step of faith; on a path that for many had included Birmingham and Cologne, the petition clipboard on the village green and outside the polling booth, the postcards and letters to Tony and Gordon and the Japanese Embassy. As the vigil ended, we were invited to light a candle, and place it at the front of the church. At first no-one moved. Then, in deep silence, one and another solemnly took their candles forward. The silent movement spoke eloquently: of commitment, of determination, of faith, of hope. The candle flames flickered, as the highest aspirations of the human spirit were fuelled again by God's compassion and justice. The spirituality at the heart of Jubilee 2000 had never felt so powerful. Never had ultimate victory seemed so certain.[29]

Yet departing from the traditional notion of Christian charity, and thus a solidarity based on sympathy for the poor, the Jubilee 2000 frame called on Northerners to reflect on their own culpability in the debt crisis and to struggle *at home* in solidarity with debtor nations. The frame therefore de-emphasized poverty reduction and rather focused on economic justice and rebalancing an exploitative, and thus immoral, historical relationship between debtor and creditor countries. In this way, campaign organizers reached out to the type of person who was unaccustomed to taking political action, but who nonetheless was an engaged church member, generally supportive of the Jubilee principle and concerned about poverty in foreign countries:

Not that he must do something about a starving child in Africa, but that he must do something about what is going on here, on our doorsteps. And that you can do it by going to your own Member of Parliament, and by addressing your own economy and your own lifestyle and actions. That is empowering in a way that talking about victims in far away places is not. Feeling guilty only makes one feel paralysed and immobilised.[30]

This type of frame amplification seemed particularly successful, at least for a time, in evoking a solidarity tied to a religious identity and based on a recognized interconnectedness between the actions, lifestyles, and governmental policies of Northerners and their effects in other parts of the world. And this Christian frame motivated more than apolitical churchgoers. It also seemed to have a considerable effect on key politicians. British Chancellor of the Exchequer Gordon Brown, for example, who is reportedly a Christian socialist, took up the issue personally and thus was crucial in convincing other finance ministers to consider debt forgiveness.[31] In another example, US Representative Spencer Bachus credited his support for a bill favoring debt forgiveness on Bread for the World's lobbying efforts, in which they framed their appeal in terms of an action demanded of him as a Christian.[32]

Innovative tactics capture media attention and diffuse message

A second important factor in Jubilee 2000's (J2000's) success was its ability to attract media through celebrity and branding. This opened another non-relational diffusion channel through which was disseminated a message that nevertheless remained consistent with Jubilee's religious frame amplification strategy. This success with the press was unusual when compared with most earlier debt campaigns, which prioritized grassroots education and lobbying and largely neglected attempts to court mainstream media.[33] In stark contrast, for "J2000" US boxer Muhammad Ali, Senegalese singer Youssou N'Dour, and UK musician Bob Geldof all lent their talents. Anthony Minghella made a film on the campaign that was shown all over the world. Irish rock star Bono organized benefit concerts and accompanied Archbishop Oscar Rodriguez Maradiaga of Honduras to meet German Chancellor Gerhard Schroeder at the G8 meetings in Cologne. This wide array of celebrity participation won coverage in popular magazines and television, which in turn helped raise awareness of the issue globally. Some of the notables involved also had access to top public officials. For example, a rather different type of celebrity, Pope John Paul II, garnered sustained media attention as a spokesperson for the campaign. Throughout the last years of his life he continued to raise this issue in public proclamations, official visits to heads of states and international forums such as the UN.[34]

By this celebrity support and popular media coverage, Jubilee gained considerable "brand recognition," which also helped the network control the framing of its image in the non-relational diffusion pathway of the international media. Maintaining this control was not accidental. Campaign strategists Ann Pettifor and others studied franchising models such as McDonald's and became interested in the concepts of quality control and consistency across disparate actors in order to construct a similar identity among them. These notions of standards of quality and consistency were brought to bear among the considerably autonomous and diverse local and national campaigns North and South. Pettifor reflected on the strategy and its effectiveness:

> We had a brand, a style of organising on the basis of a coalition and we had a franchise which we offered to whoever wanted it. To our astonishment, people did like it and it did get picked up. The IMF travelled to over one hundred and sixty countries around the world and kept coming up against Jubilee 2000 chains. It must have terrorised them and made them think that we were powerful and huge. We were not. We were a coalition of some very wobbly campaigns and some much more effective campaigns (largely because of the churches) in some sixty countries, who shared a single mission statement which was the petition that we wanted the debts cancelled by the year 2000 under a fair process, and who shared a logo. … I am very proud to say that in four years we turned this simple brand into a global brand.[35]

Diffusion and brokerage via the internet

A final aspect of Jubilee 2000's successful take-off as a transnational activist network has to do with their putting to good use recent technological advancements in communication. The spread of personal computers and internet access in the last years of the millennium facilitated all channels of information flow: It helped in its diffusion, largely on listserves, through pre-existing international channels (i.e. relational diffusion); in spreading information about the campaign to groups with which Jubilee activists hadn't prior contact (non-relational diffusion); and in serving as a virtual space to broker relations among previously unconnected actors by providing contact information for local or national Jubilee chapters (non-relational brokerage).

Let's take a look at each more closely. First, with regard to relational diffusion, Jubilee listserves were coordinated by some of the largest NGOs and participating groups and managed to keep around 180 key activists connected, allowing them to swap strategies and news. These web interactions were so efficient that at times campaign members received information regarding debt negotiations before their own state treasury departments, giving them a degree of leverage and respect in negotiations in their home countries that they would not have had without access to this up-to-the-minute knowledge.

In addition, with the increased availability of internet technology, it has become difficult to distinguish when a network – via its website – is playing which of the two diffusion roles and when it is brokering new relations. A further consideration with the use of websites is that, since the receiver of framing is often unknown, multiple framing strategies are underway simultaneously on websites, and must be seen as interactive, rather than one-way, in nature. For example, depending on the content of the posting and the perspective of the site visitor, the same web page could be simply frame *bridging* to a member of a Christian group already working independently to alleviate Third World poverty; or the same information could also be introducing a *transformative* frame to a person who had little knowledge of the Jubilee idea or the debt crisis prior to visiting the site.[36] In its complex role as broker/diffuser, the Jubilee website hosted over 2,000 visitors a day in the many months of the campaign.[37] Therefore, these varied information pathways made possible by the increased usage of new technologies were crucial in forging a diverse coalition without precedent, made up of churches and grassroots organizations, trade unions, environmentalists, development NGOs and human rights activists.

As we have seen, by a combination of a powerful religious frame amplification that resonated through pre-existing international church ties and structures, a publicity strategy combining secular and religious celebrity with name-branding that garnered widespread media attention, and the utilization of the internet, formerly local and national debt groups were able to coalesce into an increasingly transnational networked campaign, capable of launching considerable coordinated action. We can now turn to the innovative tactics and mass actions employed by Jubilee 2000 to attempt to reach their goals.

Transnational collective action

J2000's repertoire of contention contained both non-confrontational tactics such as popular education, petitioning, and lobbying, as well as more assertive ones like civil disobedience, mass marches, and the media-grabbing "human chain." Each will be described briefly below. An important activity that network members carried over from their earlier campaigns was popular education. This took the form of educational pamphlets, illustrated books, fake newspaper issues – such as the *Financial Crimes* – and workshop material made available to churches seeking economic and theological perspectives on debt relief. Prominent academics, such as Harvard development expert Jeffrey Sachs, played increasingly important roles as the campaign progressed. These experts provided credibility, innovative alternative proposals, and, importantly, access to mainstream media outlets such as the *New York Times*. Jubilee's massive popular education efforts gave many the confidence and determination needed to press their political representatives to action. The groundswell of US church groups writing letters to their congresspersons, for example, was credited for bringing about the proposed legislation on debt relief linked to poverty reduction that we have seen in recent years. This popular education-*cum*-mass lobbying was complemented by Washington, DC-based NGOs meeting regularly with Bretton Woods institutional representatives and US government officials, encouraging them to hold public hearings and pass regulatory reform *vis-à-vis* Third World debt.[38]

Another central activity of this campaign was the global petition drive calling for a one-time cancellation of HIPC debt by the end of 2000. Over the course of five years, activists went door to door and church to church in over a hundred countries, gathering the signatures of 24 million people. The delegation that delivered this voluminous petition to Chancellor Schroeder at the G8 in Cologne displayed the diversity – and star power – of the Jubilee network. It was comprised of representatives from the Philippines, Cameroon, Peru, Spain, and the US, and included a Honduran archbishop and a ubiquitous Irish rocker.[39]

Yet Jubilee activists' tactics did not stop with popular education, petitioning, and lobbying. Assertive actions such as massive demonstrations, marches, and civil disobedience became a hallmark of the campaign as the millennium year approached. This more confrontational stance was nevertheless consistent with Jubilee's core message: These acts were all framed in terms of religious values and beliefs and presented in a media-friendly way. For example, on Good Friday over 100 members of the Religious Working Group on the World Bank and the IMF held an "Economic Ways of the Cross" pilgrimage around Washington, DC. On the steps and in the doorways of sites of wealth and power, activists prayed for victims of economic injustice, and were often arrested for obstruction.[40]

Jubilee 2000 also played a key role in organizing protest marches at international financial meetings. The network's first major international outing was at the G8 Summit in Birmingham, England, in May 1998, where an estimated 60,000 marched under the banner of "drop the debt!"[41] Around 35,000 turned out for a procession two years later in Cologne, at which the J2000 global petition was presented. Network members also helped organize demos in Washington, Paris, Seattle, Tokyo, Okinawa, Prague, and New York. In these spaces, Jubilee activists have innovated a mass action tactic that is consistent with their religious frame and media savviness, that of the "human chain" formed around their target's meeting site. Their first encirclement was a 10-kilometer ring around the Birmingham G8. Since then, Jubilee activists have enclosed the IMF and World Bank in Washington, DC, in addition to forming "solidarity" chains in Madras, Osaka, Durban, Denver, Buenos Aires, and Lima.[42] Participating in this transnational collective action of the human chain can evoke feelings of common suffering and common purpose, and therefore attribution of similarity or interconnectedness upon which solidarity is formed among those present. One participant described this powerful symbol and affect as:

> represent[ing] the enslaving nature of the debt burden which undermines development, dignity and even people's sovereignty. It is a sobering fact that in the last four years the debt crisis has led to the deaths of more people than the brutal Atlantic slave trade carried out over decades. Yet the stark imagery of the chain has always had a double meaning. When people form a human chain, alongside anger there is an immense sense of the power of people linked for a common cause. … The chains of debt are not yet broken, but they have been loosened; and as people continue to join hands against debt bondage, we will prise the chains of debt apart.[43]

Jubilee and the Battle in Seattle: or how transnational networks touch down

The largest human chain in the US was staged during the Millennium Summit of the 134-member WTO in Seattle, which saw some 60,000 protesters over the week of 26 November to 3 December 1999. Again, Jubilee's strengths for broadly resonant moral framing and media attractiveness were used to good effect during what many have hailed as the global coming-out party of the network of networks. Recalls one local participant reflecting on their efforts in Seattle: "The Jubilee events … set the spiritual stage for WTO week. It was an all-souls gathering that cast the widest possible net and drew in everyone, from the outright devout to the downright unbelieving."[44] If a global movement was indeed birthed in Seattle, then the J2000 network could rightfully be named its *comadre* – godmother and midwife.

The organizing behind Seattle's human chain is a microcosm of the scale shift process at work more broadly in J2000 and other networks, from localized action to the realization of the need to go global, diffusion, brokerage, object and claims shift, attribution of interconnectedness and similarity leading to solidarity, and transnational coordinated action. It also demonstrates that, just as globalization "touches down" differently in distinct locales, so too do transnational activist networks: In this case, activists with whom the network's message resonates seize an opportunity to draw the global network down to earth in their local context. This, it seems, is the only way transnational networks actually take root, that is, *locally*.

Planning was initiated six months prior to "WTO week" by Ethiopian-born and Seattle-based activist Hannah Petros, director of a local NGO called Ustawi, concerned with African women. Petros had learned about Jubilee 2000 and then contacted Episcopalian Reverend Peter Strimer of Seattle's St. Mark's Cathedral. Together they convened members of Catholic Workers, the Women's International League for Peace and Freedom, the Church Council of Greater Seattle, and the Washington Association of Churches to study the issue of poor-country debt with an eye toward establishing a local J2000 campaign. Petros traveled to the Cologne G8 protest and participated in the human chain there. After experiencing this moving collective action firsthand, she returned to her Seattle group converted, reporting the chain to be a "beautiful event." Through discussion, they began to amplify their target from the G8 – which was Jubilee's focus in Cologne – to include the WTO, which would soon be convening in their hometown. Recalls Reverend Strimer, they came to the realization together that "those are the very same trade ministers [of the G7] who run the IMF and the World Bank, so we decided to do a human chain in Seattle."[45]

This core group of activists then began to reach out to others in the community, including Jobs with Justice sponsored by the AFL–CIO, the Christian *Sojourners* magazine and Jim Wallis's Call of Renewal, and the Baptist Reverend James Orange, a long-time civil rights activist with the Southern Christian Leadership Conference and a crucial broker to the African American Christian community.

Their group, Jubilee 2000 Northwest, sponsored a number of events during WTO week. These included an ecumenical service calling for cancellation of the debt, an interfaith gathering of 3,000, and the march on and human chain encirclement of the Kingdome where the WTO ministers were to assemble for an opening night party. This action, in which some 20,000 local, national, and international activists participated, was led by Petros, Ann Pettifor of Jubilee 2000 UK, Njoki Njehu of Fifty Years Is Enough and Jubilee 2000 USA, John Sweeney of the AFL–CIO, and California Representative Maxine Waters, who symbolically closed the chain in a Seattle downpour to the chants of "We're here! We're Wet! Cancel the Debt!"[46]

The above synopsis of the crucial role played by local activists in coordinating an international Jubilee action illustrates a number of important points about the structure of Jubilee 2000, as well as its relationship to local activism. Local campaigning groups usually came together at the initiative of one or more activists introducing the idea into their already close circle of activists, who then went on to revitalize dormant ties or broker relations with new groups. These local organizations therefore functioned as autonomous units, which allowed them to take initiative and assume considerable leadership and responsibility for a period of time within the global network. They were also free to emulate other actions already in Jubilee's repertoire or to innovate new ones, tailored to their unique constituency and to the opportunity or challenge that presented itself in that local context. As was the case with J2000 Northwest, local and national coalitions were usually initiated and led by a small group of church activists brokering relations with other faith-based, peace, and economic justice groups.

Yet since most local groups didn't have the opportunity to host tens of thousands of activists for such a battle as was had in Seattle, the main activity of the local network affiliates was to gather signatures for the Jubilee petition.[47] That being said, other nationally tailored actions included massive lobbying campaigns and public consultations and demonstrations: For example, the Bolivian Jubilee organized large citizen consultations calling for debt relief to be funneled into social development spending. The Ugandan Jubilee network organized a campaign targeting parliamentarians to reject new loans that had been made to their highly indebted country. Guyana Jubilee forged alliances with government and opposition parties to collectively denounce their debt. And Jubilee India organized a march against debt in which tens of thousands, mostly women, participated.[48]

Transnational collective actions result in pyrrhic victory

The accumulation of all the local J2000 groups' creative endeavors, as well as their acting in concert through the global petition drive and at mass demonstrations, made Jubilee 2000 one of the most successful transnational activist networks in recent history, if judged in terms of both popular participation in the network and, crucially, the degree to which it won concessions to its demands from powerful international actors. Regarding the latter, after making verbal commitments to reduce multilateral debt at their 1996 Lyon Summit coinciding with the Bretton Woods institutions' launching of the HIPC initiative, the G7 governments took significant further steps toward answering Jubilee's call in Cologne in 1999. There they revised and deepened the HIPC initiative to promise debt forgiveness of $100 billion for forty-one of the world's most indebted countries. These leaders also promised further bilateral debt relief linked to poverty reduction, toward the ultimate goal of 100 percent debt cancellation for the poorest nations.[49] In 2001, the IMF Deputy Director Anne Krueger echoed UN Secretary-General Kofi Annan's and US Treasury Secretary Paul O'Neill's calls to set up debt arbitration or international bankruptcy procedures to deal more comprehensively with all poor-country debt. Toward those ends, the IMF added a Sovereign Debt Restructuring Mechanism, which they hailed as a "fair and transparent process" for insolvent debts of so-called emerging market countries that didn't qualify under the HIPC framework.[50]

But getting governments and the Bretton Woods institutions to make good on these commitments, while winning greater concessions for all poor countries, continues to animate, and frustrate, many debt activists. Hence, although the targeted jubilee year has passed, activists still press government and bank creditors on two main points: namely that the amount of promised relief is insufficient and has been made available to too few countries; and that due to the conditionalities imposed as a term of debt forgiveness, which include first implementing SAPs before even being considered for the HIPC process, the World Bank and IMF have actually managed to *increase* their control over the poorest countries through the newest "debt forgiveness" regime.

In important ways, then, Jubilee's has proven to be a pyrrhic victory. This is evident first and foremost in the glaring fact, mentioned above, that the promised relief has been slow in coming. Almost a decade into the Bretton Woods–G7 initiative, only fifteen of the forty-one designated HIPC countries had received any debt relief at all, and that which has been written off amounts to only about one-third of the average debt stock. But more generally, critics have judged the scheme a failure by the World Bank's own criteria. Approximately one-third of the countries that have gone through the HIPC process still have what the Bank deems "unsustainable" levels of debt, while half of those in the HIPC process have seen their external debt significantly worsen.[51]

Furthermore, as stated above, all of the proposed debt relief thus far from the G7 and Bretton Woods institutions comes with the usual SAP strings attached. Patomäki and Teivainen of the Network Institute for Global Democratization hit upon the crux of the problem when they observed:

> In democratic terms, however, both the HIPCs initiatives are questionable because in exchange for minor compromises they impose even stricter neoliberal economic policy conditionality, thereby reducing the eligible countries' opportunities for autonomous policy-making. Moreover, the creditor institutions lead the whole scheme of negotiations within the HIPCs framework. In other words, while the HIPC scheme may have been

intended to meet a tiny part of the debt advocacy groups' demands for debt relief, it makes no concessions to their demands for fair and transparent procedures, neither does it release control over the economic policies of these countries.[52]

The fact that the Bretton Woods institutions have recently shifted the language used to define conditionalities away from structural adjustment and toward "poverty reduction strategies" does not seem to reflect a significant change in substance. Pettifor recently admonished the UK government not to delay bilateral debt cancellation in order to make it contingent on economic prescriptions of the IMF and World Bank: "The terminology," she warns, "may have changed from 'structural adjustment' to 'poverty reduction,' but these remain essentially the same policies that have failed the developing world for the last quarter century."[53] Many activist organizations that have long been involved in the anti-debt struggle concur with Pettifor's analysis. A statement recently signed by over sixty of these groups from across the globe advised others to stay away from a World Bank-sponsored Global Policy Forum in April 2005, warning that, in addition to it being little more than a bad faith publicity stunt, "participation in the forum also risks lending legitimacy to the PRS [poverty reduction strategy] process, when its flaws are so serious that it may not be reformable."[54]

A second way in which the Jubilee "win" has come at a high price is in terms of mass mobilization. Declaring victory, however partial, with the G7 declaration in Cologne served to prematurely demobilize Northern supporters. The issue appeared to have been addressed in the eyes of many distant do-gooders and a fickle media, leading to dwindling attention on the part of the international press to what was largely an unchanged situation. An immediate follow-on campaign to Jubilee 2000, that of Drop the Debt, which was kicked off in the run-up to the Genoa G8 Summit in the summer of 2001, managed to keep the issue of debt in the minds of state leaders, yet one of the main organizers of the campaign acknowledged that "after the [Genoa] Summit, campaigners began to disperse, and momentum began to be lost."[55]

The fracturing of Jubilee 2000 and the emergence of Jubilee South

A final way in which J2000's victory turned pyrrhic was that it proved to be the last straw of mounting tensions that would break the network, largely – though not exclusively – along North–South lines. Since the inception of transnational ties around debt, SAPs, poverty, and development, Southern groups have struggled to overcome their resource and access deficiencies and to make their opinions and experiences determine the global campaign's agenda. This aspiration grew more pressing throughout the Jubilee 2000 campaign. Some Northern-based groups seemed more ready to view as a victory the promise of partial debt reduction and reforms of the SAPs pronounced by world leaders. By contrast, the Southern position – which was also held by a number of Northern activists such as those within the Fifty Years Is Enough coalition – grew into a near-consensus demand for the complete write-off of debt without conditionalities, and many further called for reparations for damages incurred under colonialism and under what they call the neo-colonialism of debt and SAPs. They also diverged as to whether seeking legislative reform was a worthwhile endeavor or rather only undercut their efforts by coopting network members and thus weakening their collective position.[56]

Consequently, while some within the Jubilee coalition celebrated the G7 promises in Cologne, others – usually from debtor countries – denounced the concessions as falling far short of what was needed to effect real changes in their own lives and for others like them. Many Southerners dismissed outright the HIPC initiative as a "cruel hoax." Maintaining the J2000 values frame, they decried the Cologne initiative for its "refus[al] to acknowledge the moral dimensions of the debt crisis and the historical responsibility of the rich countries for the current state of affairs."[57] These tensions surfaced publicly in the Tegucigalpa Declaration of January 1999, wherein Latin American J2000 affiliates publicly appealed to Northern coalition members not to accept any compromises that were not pre-approved by their Southern partners. A follow-up, South–South Summit held in Johannesburg in November of that year solidified the North–South fissure. In a move akin to a declaration of independence from the Jubilee 2000 network and its Northern directors, about 120 representatives from three dozen debt-ridden countries founded a successor network, Jubilee South, with the explicit goal of building an international, Southern-led movement to articulate a united perspective, position, and agenda on debt.

The new network is organized by an international coordinating committee and a global secretariat. Membership currently numbers around eighty-five groups from over forty countries, including the Freedom from Debt Coalition of the Philippines, Diálogo 2000 of Argentina, Mozambican Debt Group/Christian Council of Mozambique, Ecumenical Service for Peace from Cameroon, Fiji Council of Churches, and a number of national J2000 groups.[58] These organizations have developed a "Declaration of Unities" defining Jubilee South's membership. This document maintains that the external debt of developing countries is immoral, illegitimate, and used as a tool to exploit and control people and resources with the effect of causing great harm to whole nations and their natural environment. Jubilee South calls into question the legal status of this debt and, given the considerable funds already paid out in interest, coupled with the theft of resources and labor on the part of colonial powers that has never been compensated, they turn the tables by asking, "Who owes what to whom?" This network's strategy, which clearly reflects a long-held Southern position within J2000, is to therefore pressure poor governments to collectively repudiate these debts as a first step toward complete debt annulment, so that public funds can instead be re-channeled away from debt servicing into much-needed social services.

Reflecting on their years of struggle in the debt movement, Jubilee South members have come to perceive their indebtedness as inextricably caught up in a complex web of global rule. They therefore have expanded their target objects and have deepened and broadened their claims to include abolishing all SAPs and decommissioning the Bretton Woods institutions. In addition, they demand that restitution and reparations be made to Southern countries by the Bank and IMF for damage done. They further advocate for global and national income redistribution policies, reform measures to prevent future debt crises, and the eventual transformation of the global capitalist system into one that prioritizes people, equity – including gender equity – democracy, and environmental sustainability.

To achieve these goals, they focus on strengthening grassroots campaigns on debt in the Global South by facilitating information and materials exchange, through education and research, and by promoting solidarity and political support. This they see as a necessary step toward forging South–South solidarity and consensus around debt and bringing to the forefront Southern voices and participation in global debt campaigns. This is to be done through dialogue, joint action, and devising global initiatives that put forward and complement local and national campaigns and perspectives and that critically challenge the global economic and financial architectures. Not completely renouncing ties with Northern groups, they instead seek Northerners' cooperation and support, but this time on their terms. As those who suffer the brunt of the debt burden and SAPs, Jubilee South activists have sought to first strengthen this South–South identity-based solidarity. Only after undertaking this internal process could they then establish relations of reciprocal solidarity as full partners with Northern groups, ensuring that Southern perspectives would be given the full weight they feel they deserve.

Relations among Jubilee South and their former J2000 allies are therefore in flux: Some are weak to non-existent, others have been strengthened, while still others are being reconsidered and renegotiated. One telling indicator of these ambivalent relations can be found on their websites. To Northern Jubilee groups which have maintained themselves post-J2000, as, for example, Jubilee USA, Jubilee South is considered an "international partner," and links to the latter can be found on the American website. Yet one finds no such partner reference or link to Northern Jubilee national campaigns on the Jubilee South website.

Beyond exemplifying the ambivalent North–South relations today among former alliance partners, Jubilee USA illustrates a more general point regarding the continuation of local and national coalitions after the year 2000. There remains a loose coordination among highly autonomous national and local campaigns, which are often tied to one or more of the follow-on transnational campaigns, and which tend to maintain the Jubilee moniker. Currently there are twenty-six such national campaigns on every continent with their own websites, which continue to carry out grassroots educational initiatives, church outreach, lobbying, and mass demonstrations, in addition to some transnational coordination in order to maintain pressure on creditor governments and institutions to drop the debt. Following a similar trajectory to Jubilee South, most of these national groups are coming to frame the debt issue as part of an interrelated complex of transnational problems with local effects, which include unfair trade rules, environmental degradation, abuse of workers' rights, and unsustainable agricultural policies.[59] This leads one to speculate that, through the Southern affiliates' crying, "Ya Basta!" and quitting the J2000 network, their former Northern partners were spurred into seeing a bigger, more complicated picture.

Two other transnational networks emerging from J2000: Jubilee Framework and GCAP

Jubilee South is only the most rebellious among three sibling initiatives spawned to sustain transnational action to drop the debt post-2000. The other two campaigns have emerged from the core of the J2000 NGOs, yet stem from a divergence over the central aim: one-time debt forgiveness or the establishment of debt arbitration processes. Like that which led to the founding of Jubilee South, this fissure also grew throughout the J2000 campaign, maturing into distinct initiatives, one calling for the implementation of a Jubilee Framework and another broader campaign, the GCAP. Both networks are coordinated by groups that were central to J2000 and thus tend toward the NGO advocacy model preferred by their lead organizers. Yet each has come to view the resolution of the debt issue in decidedly different ways.

The first UK-based network to have emerged is that promoting the Jubilee Framework. This network's main organizational hub is the New Economics Foundation, which sponsored the transitional Jubilee Plus program and which houses J2000 campaigner Ann Pettifor's project Jubilee Research. Pettifor joined with likeminded J2000 groups such as the German Erlassjahr campaign for a Fair and Transparent Arbitration Process, AFRODAD, and the Ecuadorian and Indonesian national Jubilee coalitions in a move away from campaigning for greater debt forgiveness. They instead chose to concentrate on developing and promoting a fair, transparent, and independent framework for arbitrating current and future national debts. This comprehensive Jubilee Framework is modeled on the US Chapter 9 code of bankrupt municipalities. It would allow all indebted countries to file for a standstill on the repayment of their debts and to have their cases adjudicated in front of an independent, jointly appointed, ad hoc arbitration body under the supervision of the UN secretary-general. As a crucial component of this arbitration process, the citizens of the indebted country would also have the right to participate in proceedings and to comment or object to the ruling.

Far beyond appealing for a one-time charitable or "safety valve" gesture from creditors to alleviate the mounting debt crisis, those advocating the Jubilee Framework target the very rules and structures of the global financial architecture which have created and perpetuate the debt cycle. "We became convinced," writes Pettifor, "that only by altering structural injustice, i.e. the balance of power between international creditors and sovereign debtors, could we achieve our goal."[60] This network therefore has shifted away from a single issue, reformist paradigm to one of global structural transformation, albeit centered on the particular domain of debt. In this way Pettifor and her colleagues envision their proposal as "the first vital step towards democratising international capital markets." Theirs is a conscious attempt to dismantle the particular artifice of the global financial regime and reconstruct it upon democratic principles and procedures, and thereby tame a considerable facet of neoliberal globalization. But this cannot be done, they acknowledge, without mass mobilization and participation in this process on the part of those who are personally suffering under national debt. The Jubilee Framework concludes:

> Much greater democratic involvement by ordinary people in crises that impact directly on the quality of their lives will, we believe, transform the project that has come to be known as "globalisation," and embed it more firmly in political, social and environmental relations.[61]

A third and most recent network to have emerged out of J2000 is the GCAP, which has grown rapidly into a worldwide alliance of hundreds of organizations. These include grassroots movements, trade unions, women's groups, NGOs, human rights advocates, international debt networks, and faith groups. The campaign was centered around three key "white band days" in 2005: the G8 Summit in Scotland in July, the UN General Assembly in September, and the WTO ministerial meeting in Hong Kong in December.[62] This choice of targeted days of action demonstrates what *has* changed between J2000 and GCAP 2005: The claims, or demands, have broadened, as have the objects or targets. For, unlike the domain-specific message of debt forgiveness of the 2000 campaign, GCAP places debt cancellation on an equal footing with trade justice and enhanced aid to the world's poorest countries. This campaign therefore reminds world leaders of their prior commitments made, first, to cancel poor-country debt pledged in Cologne; second, to halve extreme poverty and hunger by 2015 through signing the Millennium Development Goals; and, third, to establish fair trade rules by launching the WTO "development round." With regard to aid and debt, they call on the G7 and the Bretton Woods institutions to support new initiatives such as the International Finance Facility and plans for international taxation that would make more money available for development. With regard to trade, they particularly target the European Union and the US to halt agricultural dumping and reduce existing barriers to trade and development, and to generally work toward a more democratic trade regime. GCAP further opposes "free" trade agreements such as the Central American Free Trade Agreement (CAFTA) and the WTO Trade-Related Aspects of Intellectual Property Rights (TRIPs) agreement. They also criticize Bretton Woods loan conditionalities, and demand that governments and corporations respect labor rights. Finally, linking the issue of peace to development, they urge all governments to engage in the Arms Trade Treaty and work within the United Nations.[63]

Aside from this expansion in objects and claims, the GCAP nonetheless shares five commonalities with its predecessor J2000, leading to perhaps similar results. First, it was launched in the UK in September 2004 as a national campaign, called "Make Poverty History" (each country chooses a unique name for their particular GCAP) by many of the same charities, churches, unions, and celebrities who had planned and promoted the original. The impetus behind reviving J2000's core themes and demands in the year 2005 was to seize an opportunity to push G7 leaders to finally make good on their promise for debt cancellation when they met in Scotland that July. UK groups furthermore sought to press Tony Blair to use their country's EU presidency rotation to influence macro-regional policies toward trade justice.

Second, as with J2000, British campaigners activated existing ties and brokered new ones in order to build this campaign into a global one. Toward that end, they organized a meeting in Johannesburg where some eighty-five agencies from sixty countries were present.[64] Third, like J2000, the GCAP is a hybrid network model which nonetheless tends toward NGO advocacy in the sense that a small group of activists have largely determined the goals, targets, main tactics, and time frame of this campaign in advance; further, through their ability to attract celebrities to publicize their cause, they have established a global brand that people around the world can recognize and groups are able to "franchise" at the national level. Such franchising has occurred in the US, Canada, France, Germany, Spain, and Japan, among others.

Fourth, the campaign strategy has been largely reminiscent of J2000: a media blitz to spur public interest and solidarity – although the desired affective response is "justice, not charity" according to their website – toward massive involvement in petitioning politicians, this time through coordinated e-mailing since access to the internet is now more common than it was in the late 1990s. The fast-growing campaign made its official global debut with much fanfare at the fifth WSF in Porto Alegre in late January 2005. In a crammed stadium with considerable media, coalition members presented Brazilian President Lula da Silva with a white band, which is the symbol of support for the nascent campaign. Lula was only one of a number of notable political figures to throw his support behind the GCAP, including Nelson Mandela, UK chancellor Gordon Brown, French finance minister Hervé Gaymard, former general director of the United Nations Educational, Scientific and Cultural Organization (UNESCO) Federico Mayor Zaragoza, former prime minister of Denmark Poul Nyrup Rasmussen, and World Bank presidential nominee Bono.[65] Passed over for the position by a much less popular American, Paul Wolfowitz, the Irish rocker kept his day job (and his unfortunate blue "fly" shades as sported throughout Africa and the Vatican, which one assumes did not help his chances in landing the Bank gig) and teamed up with Band Aid mate Geldof to help recruit a new crop of celebrities to promote GCAP, which included Brad Pitt, George Clooney, and Claudia Schiffer.

Apropos to Geldof and Bono, a fifth way that GCAP has been reminiscent of J2000 is in the tensions and fissures that have surfaced in the wake of the G8 Scotland Summit. Indeed, the two major sources of derision are precisely what led to the rupturing of its predecessor. These entail, first, charges of Northern actors controlling the agenda and, second, the latter's comparative readiness to praise wealthy countries' pledges for "major debt forgiveness," which most Southern campaigners and other critical groups denounce as falling far short of what is needed.

The first allegation stems from organizing around the GCAP-related Live8 concerts, headed up by Geldof, Bono, and the British anti-hunger charities Comic Relief and Oxfam, and held in conjunction with the G8 meetings at various locations around Europe, North America, Japan, and South Africa. The lead organizers invited people to join "the long walk to justice" across Europe and to come to the Scottish capital to show the world's elite leaders "that they must act to stop the scandal of extreme poverty now." These big stars and big NGOs were thinking "big" for the event. They hoped for "the largest ever TV audience; The busiest website in the world; The largest ever online petition – The LIVE 8 list; The largest ever text petition; The largest ever response to a TV show."[66] Their logo was equally grandiose: an evocative image of Africa serving as the body of an electric guitar with its neck twisted into an "eight". An estimated 3 billion people tuned in to see pop stars sing their hits while Bono and Geldof reminded viewers of the message behind the spectacle: "It's not about charity [or Madonna or Robbie Williams, etc.], it's about justice." After the show, its organizers christened July 2 "the day that rocked the world!" and their event "the greatest, greatest show on earth."[67]

Yet in their drive for global greatness, Africa's plans, like the Live8 logo, got a little distorted by the designers themselves. Among the growing critics of the UK organizers as being self-anointed experts on and judges of the Third World debt crisis was the South African/UK network Fahamu.[68] They alleged that Geldof, Comic Relief, and Oxfam essentially pulled the rug out from under the GCAP African coalitions' preparations. This multi-country coalition had planned to launch their continental campaign on the UN's Africa Day of the Child and build toward the WTO meeting in Hong Kong, with concerts scheduled in the townships of Johannesburg, in Accra and Nairobi. These locations were chosen by the coalition in order "to encourage maximum participation of the people who suffer the greatest effects of globalisation and neoliberal policies" and were to feature local and national activists engaged in a wide range of struggles linked to poverty and debt, including landlessness, homelessness, and privatization of services. Yet in an apparent response to criticisms that Live8's line-up contained no performers of African descent, Geldof hastily added a South African venue for the global event without fully consulting the African coalition, and thus seriously jeopardizing their own campaign. When emergency meetings were held in an attempt to solve this crisis, Oxfam is said to have stacked the meetings with their staff in order to assure that Geldof's would prevail as the official Live8 event in South Africa. Recalls a Fahamu member:

> The loose coalition, now estimated to involve more than 100 organisations in Africa, affirmed that it was taking ownership of the mobilisations over GCAP in Africa, and would use it to build the confidence of the movement to make its own voice heard. There was a profound resentment about the

attempts by Geldof and Comic Relief to seize the agenda, promote their own paternalistic pity-based slogans on the campaign, and resentment about the frank appropriation of their own initiatives.[69]

Adding insult to injury, in addition to having the venue and date changed, this now more expensive event apparently consumed the local budget and threw into doubt whether the other events organized by the Africans would be able to go ahead. Worse still, the organic political content of the African program was replaced by dictates from above. The original plans to feature concrete struggles being waged by Africans today were apparently no longer welcome in the streamlined show, "presumably because they are viewed as not being 'on message,'" one African activist decried. "Instead of reflecting the genuine voice of those fighting the causes of impoverishment, we are to be treated to the razzmatazz of celebrities and eulogising of St Bob, the white supposed saviour of Africa."[70]

The second, related problem stems from the divergence in responses to the G7 pronouncements at the meeting's close. The heads of state agreed to a total package of roughly $55 billion in debt forgiveness from the Bretton Woods institutions and other multilateral banks, pending their approval, to be granted to eighteen of the world's poorest countries and with the possible addition of nine others, as long as they meet the G7 conditionalities.[71] The reactions that this announcement provoked varied along an inverse continuum: The less one personally experiences debt and SAPs, the more one was apt to applaud the announcement. The "two man Irish rock-poverty NGO," as they were now being called, were characteristically congratulatory about the whole deal. Geldof hailed it as a "qualified triumph. ... Never before have so many people forced a change in policy onto the global agenda, and that policy has been addressed. ... A great justice has been done." Bono declared: "The world spoke, and the politicians listened." And further, "If an Irish rock star can quote Churchill," he mused, "this is not the end of extreme poverty, but it is the beginning of the end."[72]

Oxfam UK's reaction largely echoed that of their celebrity friends. They posted a web response entitled "Steps in the Right Direction," complete with helpful pictures of a green first aid kit, a torn US dollar bill, and bronze scales with an eagle atop, illustrating, on aid: "Good news here but not enough"; on debt: "good news but we're pressing for many more to get the same support"; and on trade justice, they admitted: "little progress to make trade fair."[73] Their sister campaigners in the US's One Campaign seemed generally pleased with the offer, hailing it "a positive step forward in a comprehensive debt-aid-trade deal." Their statement claimed that the folks at One were "encouraged by the commitment" shown by the G8 and "welcome the pledges." They furthermore encouraged the 1.4 million Americans who participated in the campaign "to take satisfaction" in their president's commitments made at the meeting.[74]

It is striking that while many Northerners perceived the G7 offer as a "triumph," a "great justice," and a "positive step forward" for which we should "take satisfaction," Southerners, along with their more empathetic allies, received the news as a disappointing sleight of hand designed to mask and perpetuate the miserable status quo. The Southern partners in the GCAP issued a joint statement that departed markedly from that of their distant comrades in the UK and US:

> Simply put, we are disappointed in the outcomes of Gleneagles. The resolutions fall far short of our expectations for a comprehensive and radical strategy to make poverty history in Africa. The Summit has simply reaffirmed existing decisions on debt cancellation and doubling of aid. The debt package ... provides only 10% of the relief required and affects only one third of the countries that need it. A large component of the US $50 billion pledged is drawn from existing obligations. Further, both packages are still attached to harmful policy conditionality.[75]

The Southern GCAP campaigners pledged their determination to continue mass mobilization to achieve complete and unconditional debt write-off, better terms of trade, and greater development funds. In a tone betraying both frustration and defiance reminiscent of the J2000 Southerners just before leaving that coalition, the Southern GCAP members warned that if debt, trade, and aid are not forthcoming, they will push their governments to refuse payment altogether and rather use these funds at home.[76]

Indeed, with the notable exception of those UK celebrities and large charities to which the media mostly listen, the overwhelming response to the G7's announcement from within the GCAP was consistent with the critical statement issued by the Southern alliance members above, as seen, for example, in reactions by CAFOD, Jubilee Debt Campaign, and Action Aid. Harsher words still came from Christian Aid, Fifty Years Is Enough, and Jubilee South. The latter denounced the proposal as "still clearly tied to compliance with conditionalities which exacerbate poverty, open our countries further for exploitation and plunder, and perpetuate the domination of the South."[77] Given this breadth of reactions to the G7 pledge, it is amazing that such diverse actors holding such divergent standards on what constitutes "triumph" can inhabit the same transnational network. More incredible still is how out of step the GCAP's leadership is with the sentiments of those who must actually live with that supposed triumph.

Changing network composition and character: analysis based on conceptual continua

In order to better explain the tensions that led to the break-up of the Jubilee 2000 network, the founding of Jubilee South, and the more recent problems within the GCAP, we should begin our analysis of network composition and character with the earliest debt protests and incipient transnational organizing. To review, the six concepts to be analyzed are proximity to the problem, affective response, solidarity, network model, operational paradigm, and claims, each of which will be explicated below in various contexts as the network has matured.

In the localized actions on the ground, protests spontaneously erupted among diverse sectors which had for some time endured the deleterious effects of mounting debt but were triggered into action by suddenly imposed grievances due to the imposition of SAPs. But simultaneously, the widespread personal suffering and insecurity caused by the austerity measures allowed diverse actors to identify with others as sharing a common fate and identity as fellow citizens harmed by neoliberal policies. Based on this identification, they joined together in direct, mass actions, which initially targeted local and national governments with angry denunciations or with appeals to redress their grievances. Yet simultaneously, local actors were realizing that decision-making power was shifting away from regional and national governments and toward remote, transnational bodies.

Those who were suffering firsthand therefore turned to non-state entities to provide help and to appeal for support and allies from abroad. Christian churches and their relief and development agencies were prime targets in this regard, and quickly became active participants and facilitators of these nascent cross-border efforts. Densely rooted in these locales while simultaneously having vast global networks, institutional actors' proximity to the problem ranged from immediate on the part of local pastors and parishioners, missionaries, and aid workers, to distant, entailing members of various church hierarchies throughout the world. Likewise, affective responses ran the gamut from those who experienced the hardships firsthand in the debtor countries to those who received the reports back and responded with empathy or sympathy for those suffering at great distances. Hence, solidarity also ranged from those who identified with and shared the fate of local citizens, through those who attributed interconnectedness and thus a reciprocal relationship between their governments' actions and suffering in remote places, to still others who assigned worthiness to their plight and developed altruistic solidarity, inspiring the desire to alleviate suffering and perceived injustices.

The models of these earliest, cross-border anti-debt and SAP networks were a hybrid of hierarchical Christian institutions and the advocacy networks they supported. Regarding the paradigms within which these nascent efforts were operating: If on a philosophical level the guiding paradigmatic vision was one of global structural transformation through Christian mission and working toward a world of peace and justice, at a more practical level these were domain-specific relief efforts. Initially, this work was not so much policy reform advocacy as apolitical service provision unthreatening to, and even serving to perpetuate, the status quo. But as the debt crisis mounted and pleas for help diffused to the North, the faith-based actors' efforts became more overtly political. They began brokering relationships among likeminded groups and individuals to then lobby their national governments, and advocating policy reform for debt forgiveness, thus moving toward a first-generation network. Their claims therefore were largely cast in terms of economic redistribution. They further launched the first coordinated efforts for popular education in order to sensitize their Northern constituencies to these complex issues of debt and neoliberal adjustment policies, in the hopes of inspiring sympathy that could translate into altruistic solidarity actions at home.

As news of suffering and rebellion under crippling debt and SAPs continued to diffuse from the localized settings through church networks, brokerage efforts were extended to secular humanitarian, development, and environmental sectors in Europe, Africa, Asia, and the Americas. Members of faith-based hierarchies brokered these new relationships, and in the process completed the transition to an NGO advocacy model network. Northern groups forged alliances in the South and then launched the first transnational campaigns targeting their governments for limited policy change toward debt forgiveness and development aid, still centering their claims largely on economic redistribution. They also appealed to public sympathies, guilt, and a sense of moral responsibility over Northern culpability in perpetuating world poverty.

At the same time, we saw the emergence of more sophisticated transnational networking in debtor countries themselves. Led by a Philippines-based coalition in Asia, these efforts were unique in that they were spearheaded by groups with immediate proximity to the problems wrought by debt and SAPs, and were brokered largely by and among Southern organizations based on a shared iden-tity as citizens of debtor countries. Their critique (and thus paradigm) moved beyond limited policy reform or the single domain of debt, toward a broader focus on structural constraints and inequalities imposed by the debt/SAP regime promulgated by international financial institutions. Between the two models of altruistic, Northern, NGO policy reform advocacy and the identity-based, Southern structural critique and activism emerged transnational hybrid groups such as Fifty Years Is Enough. These were rooted in identity solidarity among Southerners, while at the same time they encouraged connections that created empathy and reciprocal solidarity with Northern network members. Combining grassroots education, lobbying, and mass mobilization, the largely Southern-comprised but Washington, DC-based Fifty Years Is Enough has attempted to articulate a critical, transitional paradigm of "profound transformation" of transna-tional financial institutions and debt/SAP regimes which perpetuate Southern poverty. In so doing, it also advances bivalent claims for both economic redistri-bution and cultural rights and survival.[78]

Turning now to examine the composition and character of Jubilee 2000, the full range of distance to the problem, affective response, and solidarity endemic in forerunning debt groups was brought into this vast North–South network. On the one hand, it was based upon – and very successful at – evoking sympathy among Northern Christians at great distances, unleashing a considerable outpouring of altruistic solidarity. On the other, the growing Southern participa-tion within J2000 sought to forge identity-based solidarity with people like themselves in other countries burdened by debt and increasingly constricted by SAPs. Flowing from this hybrid mixture of solidarity was a hybrid network model: part first-generation NGO advocacy, part second-generation direct activism social justice. Below I will trace both tendencies within the network, showing how the first-generation features helped the network win its partial victories, yet also precipitated its splintering. Next I elucidate its second-generation qualities, arguing that these actors and their practices would eventually assert independence from the larger coalition by forming Jubilee South.

Consistent with an NGO advocacy network model, J2000's organization was first comprised of faith-based, humanitarian, and development NGOs in the UK. These groups took the lead in coordinating the campaign and in brokering strategic relations. From the beginning, diffusion of information flowed largely through pre-established, rather homogeneous church networks. Mobilization tactics consisted of encouraging mass participation in a strategic campaign launched to gather signatures on the Jubilee petition. Their goal was a clear one: to press wealthy governments for a one-time debt write-off. Given this well-defined aim, mobilization was unwittingly "turned off" when their collective efforts were seemingly rewarded by the G7 governments' pledge in Cologne.

The network's capacity was this very ability to extract a one-time concession from wealthy governments. Yet it was also this circumscribed capability that was one of the contributing factors in the rising tensions within the network. A second factor regards the network's stability and membership: Lead NGOs' tight framing of debt "forgiveness" as a religious and moral obligation coupled with creating a brand identity that other groups could buy into succeeded in capturing celebrity, media, and popular attention; but these framing strategies appealed largely to Northerners' sympathies and lent a degree of trendiness and even glamour to the issue of debt, allowing individuals to sign on to a low-risk, feel-good, and pre-set agenda. This caused tensions among some Southern participants who were living the raw and decidedly unglamorous lifestyle of debt and structural adjustment day in and out. The latter sought not pity but rather justice and, increasingly, retribution. After colonialism and all that has been paid out in debt servicing, they asked who exactly owes what to whom, and knew full well the answer. It is perhaps ironic that it was this other internal success of J2000 – that of attracting significant numbers from across the Global South who were experiencing firsthand the ill effects of debt and SAPs – that eventually destabilized J2000 as a network. It is worth recalling Keck and Sikkink's observation that a first-generation, NGO advocacy model "breaks down at the point where the intended beneficiaries of advocacy campaigns play a significant role in carrying them out."[79]

That said, J2000 also bore characteristics of what Bennett labels a second-generation network, that of direct activism social justice. From early on, South–South solidarity was growing, based on the attribution of a shared identity of citizens harmed by debt and SAPs. In addition, North–South reciprocal solidarity was emerging in groups within the network – like Fifty Years Is Enough and the Transnational Institute – around the strongly felt conviction that those who were closest to the effects of debt and SAPs should be the ones to guide the campaign and decide the scope of claims, while the Northern NGOs should play a supporting role. So while centralized around the hub of UK NGOs, as the campaign spread its structure increasingly became polycentric, dispersing to far-flung areas and groups, intermingling with pre-existing local, national, and regional networks, and providing a vehicle through which to forge new ones. The fact that 24 million people signed the petition worldwide is evidence of the considerable reach and distribution of J2000. The scale of the network was also greatly expanded by the growing access to and use of internet technology as the decade, and campaign, progressed, which also lowered the costs of bridging, or brokering new ties. Although government officials remained the objects of their appeals, they were not targeted in isolation from one another but were rather treated as a bloc of G7/G8 countries; they furthermore targeted the Bretton Woods institutions, over which these wealthy countries exert de facto control.

J2000 was further a hybrid in that its capacity and mobilization tactics were, in part, second generation. For in addition to advocating reform as mentioned above, it also mobilized mass, innovative protests, including civil disobedience that emphasized individual involvement in direct action and the human chain that was adapted and organized by local activists and not directed from above. Finally, although the campaign was in some sense "turned off" as the target Jubilee year came and went, the technological infrastructure supporting affinity ties remained, out of which came three follow-on networks. These networks embody distinct tendencies that gestated within J2000; upon its dissolution, various actors carried forward their own agendas and practices into the subsequent networks. While Jubilee South forged itself more in the mold of direct activism social justice, the Jubilee Framework and GCAP/Make Poverty History came directly from the UK-based NGOs which first launched J2000, and thus bear the strongest resemblance to first-generation, NGO advocacy. Each of their compositions and characters will be briefly overviewed below.

Jubilee South grew out of the more critical, Southern-based trend that was a part of J2000. Its network's membership, therefore, is largely comprised of those with immediate proximity to the problems caused by debt and SAPs. They are either personally touched by this suffering or have close contact with those who are, and therefore strongly identify with one another as the basis for their solidarity. A network bias favoring the immediate, local level is evident: Their bottom-up approach seeks to strengthen grassroots debt campaigns by, first, coordinating and sharing information and resources among them and, second, articulating global initiatives that advance and complement already existing local and national campaigns. Through these processes they seek to create a consensus voice among Southerners to then bring to global debt campaigning.

Here is where the cautious opening to transnational allies becomes necessary, and where we detect an expansion from solely a network based upon identity solidarity to one that seeks reciprocity as well. Stemming from their prior experiences with charity-based, altruistic NGOs, Jubilee South has sought first to build within their own identity-solidarity group, and then open the network to others who perceive an interconnection with their own fate and struggle and empathize with them. They have therefore attempted to forge transnational relationships based on reciprocity and mutual respect, including with Northern-based think-tanks and NGOs, on the condition that they recognize that those who have the most intimate experience with these complex problems should be the determining voice in setting the network's agenda and judging what is to be considered a "triumph."

Reflecting the shift in solidarity from one of moral duty and charity toward others to one of restitution and justice demanded by those who suffer, Jubilee South has distanced itself from the strictly Christian frame of its predecessor, and, with it, the more circumscribed targets, claims, and reformist paradigm. It instead envisions nothing short of multi-sector, global structural transformation, based on the historic argument that the North owes a great economic and moral debt to the South after centuries of slavery and imperialism. This has only been exacerbated in recent decades by TNCs and banks reaping considerable profits through deals with corrupt governments, and via SAPs and "free" trade agreements biased in favor of foreign capital. Their claims therefore reflect this diverse, transformational social justice agenda from the local to the national to the global levels, including income redistribution both within countries and from North to South in restitution and reparations, massive refusal to pay debt in an effort to gain complete debt write-off, the decommissioning of the Bretton Woods institutions, and instead working toward replacing capitalism with a system that prioritizes the needs of people and the planet.

Unlike Jubilee South, the other two follow-on networks, originating in the UK, are more traditionally first generation. While the Jubilee Framework is also rooted within a justice frame and seeks to democratize the rules of the global financial architecture in order to root out the structural injustice of chronic debt, its main features are reminiscent of J2000's hierarchical tendencies: While its leaders recognize the necessity of participation by those immediately suffering, Jubilee Framework is organized and administered by a core group of NGO advocates presenting a clearly defined agenda, framing of the issue, and desired outcome which others are invited to join. Yet given that many Southern groups have grown increasingly disillusioned with the G7 promises and are now calling for complete debt write-off as well as restitution, it is doubtful that this initiative will gain the mass support that its organizers know it needs in order to push the framework onto the international agenda.

Conversely, the second follow-on campaign, that of GCAP, has managed to garner considerable popular support where its sister network has not. It has gathered a worldwide coalition of hundreds of organizations, helped to mobilize a quarter-million people to protest at the Scotland G8 meetings, and staged a televised event that organizers say reached half of the world's people. Furthermore, its claims and thus target objects have expanded from an exclusive focus on debt to include trade and aid as well. Yet allegations that UK coordinators overrode and even jeopardized the African coalition's plans are only the most dramatic evidence of the GCAP's top-down, first-generation approach. It is centralized around an elite group of celebrities and NGOs friendly with (and even funded by) their wealthy governments, who brokered a strategic coalition of member organizations and then invited "the masses" to franchise or join onto a predefined campaign, with apparently varying levels of interference by the key organizers. Externally imposed media extravaganzas aside, all who "franchised" the GCAP campaign slogan were to adhere to a strategic campaign of three "white band days" advocating that governments and multilateral lending bodies reform their policies on three issues. Given the divergent reactions to the G7's tepid announcement in Scotland – which ranged from qualified praise from GCAP's core to disappointment and denunciations the further one moves out to its periphery – the lessons that could have been learned from the demise of J2000 appear lost on those at a privileged distance, who see the debt crisis only via televised pop concerts or through rose – or blue – colored lenses.

Anti-debt networks' involvement with the WSF

Finally, let us turn to the analysis of the anti-debt networks' engagement with the social forums. To review, this analysis centers around three arguments: first, that the social forums are a fertile ground for networks in that the space provides the opportunity to both reinforce their shift to the transnational level and strengthen the networks locally, nationally, and macro-regionally; second, that the forum is a common space of encounter and dialogue which fosters rejuvenation, learning and reflection, networking, cooperative action, solidarity – both identity based and reciprocal – and even construction of a new identity in the form of building one global network of networks; but, third, it is not only a space for cooperation, but also a terrain of competition, where the nature of the forum itself is contested, challenged, pushed, and pulled into being more like the networks themselves in composition and character.

Upon this competitive terrain, some actors seek to make the forum more radically open, decentralized, horizontally connected, spontaneous, and an autonomous space of self-organized action. Others, via their actions, move the forum in a more centralized direction, hence making it more like a traditional NGO, a social movement organization, or a political party. Some in these social forum spaces attempt to gain support for significant reforms that nonetheless leave much of the global economic and political architecture in place, while others see the forum as a space for jointly articulating visions for a new world radically different from and antagonistic to the current neoliberal order. The outcome of this struggle is important, for it will greatly affect the future shape not only of the social forums, but also of any unified global movement – or network of networks – that may grow out of it. To illustrate these three main themes, below I will compare and contrast the two largest networks following from the Jubilee 2000 campaign, those of Jubilee South and the GCAP, and in the latter case will focus especially on its lead NGO Oxfam.

WSF strengthens networks and reinforces shift to the transnational level

Let us first take up the issue of the WSF as a space to strengthen the network and to assist in its shift to the transnational level. Jubilee South has taken advantage of the annual gatherings to organize its own internal meetings. For example, in the days prior to the third WSF in early 2003, the network held a conference entitled New Perspectives and Insights on Globalization and Debt: A Critical Review of Current Trends and Initiatives. Likewise, a year later in Mumbai, the Southern-led network held two major internal meetings where they discussed plans for upcoming international conferences and revisited their campaigning strategy. Furthermore, the constituent national- and regional-level campaigns that comprise Jubilee South also use the forums to strengthen ties within their own smaller networks. For example, the American and Brazilian Jubilee activists have organized their own network members' seminars on regional trade agreements, militarization, and debt. Finally, they have devised ways to ensure that their activists who are unable to attend the WSF are informed of their activities there. After the forums they hold report-back meetings in local communities and post information and commentary on their websites.[80]

Similarly, constituent member organizations of the GCAP use the social forum to strengthen the network internally and reinforce their shift to the global. Oxfam Netherlands participants have commented that they attend the forum in order to feel a part of a "global civil society" that is emerging in order to meet the challenges posed by globalizing neoliberal policies via powerful transnational bodies.[81] "Porto Alegre is a clear expression of a rapidly growing international social movement," explains Jan Bouke Wijbrandi, Novib campaigns director. He continues by stating:

> This movement is also very important to Novib since the Forum partly determines the future development of Oxfam and Novib. The reason is that what we are seeing here is the globalisation of the civil society. … Here in Porto Alegre there are signs that the civic society – and that includes us – is also becoming international.[82]

As part of that movement, Oxfam holds its own meetings to strengthen its network in addition to helping launch and build the GCAP in the space of the forum. And, similarly to Jubilee South, they are also concerned with transmitting the results from the forum to their network members who were not able to attend. Oxfam does so by providing regular updates from the WSF in the form of daily diaries, press releases, and speeches by its staff, in order to both keep its own network informed and publicize the WSF to a broader audience beyond its organization and participating networks.[83]

The forum as a space for encounter and building toward one global network

Let's now take up the second theme, that of the social forum as a space of encounter which helps foster rejuvenation, learning, cooperative action through joint campaigns, and construction of a "network of networks." Oxfam members hail the WSF as a unique place to learn from each other and to network and strategize toward coordinated action, all of which help activists maintain or regain hope. One member reflected:

> Wherever the WSF may take place in the coming years, Novib will be present. Because the WSF offers a unique opportunity for networking, exchanging experiences, debating, developing ideas, and for joining hands in action with other organisations and many counterparts. If there is somewhere that makes you believe that another world is possible, then it is at the WSF.[84]

Another affirmed these statements: "Oxfam believes this is a unique occasion to mobilize, share and feel a part of a global movement of people."[85] Concretely, Oxfam has co-sponsored workshops and has lent its high-profile name to issues and campaigns, such as those on trade and arms control at the 2004 WSF.[86]

In a similar way, Jubilee South members also see the social forums as a valuable opportunity to strengthen their global and regional partnerships with others, exchange information on debt campaigns with allies around the world, and work toward a common analysis among a wide range of interested actors which can lead to coordinated strategies and transnational action. Toward those ends, not only do they organize numerous workshops for their own members, but they also co-sponsor and participate in larger seminars during the forums. For example, at the third WSF, Jubilee South joined other organizations in coordinating a seminar called Strategies Addressing the Illegitimacy of the Debt: Popular and Judicial Initiatives, Citizen Audits, Non-Payment and Other Alternatives.[87]

Turning now from sharing experiences and networking within co-sponsored seminars to the more ambitious work of campaigning, as the forum process has grown exponentially over just a few short years, it comes as little surprise that anti-debt networks would choose to launch their campaigns within the space of the WSF itself. The forum has therefore become a crucial site – perhaps *the* crucial site – for the follow-up networks to J2000 and individual member organizations to launch their campaigns. Jubilee South used the space of the forum to plan, promote, and then kick off their campaign in 2000 for an International People's Tribunal on the Debt. They did so by holding initial planning workshops on external financial debt, trade, and ecological debt at the first WSF. Through these events and others they forged a coalition among Jubilee South, Jubilee USA, the American Association of Jurists, the Committee for the Abolition of Third World Debt, the World Council of Churches, Kairos-Canada, the World March of Women, and Seattle-based Ustawi.[88] Continuing their coordination throughout the year, they returned to the WSF in 2002 with the goal of deepening understanding among activists as to the origins and outcomes of external debt across the globe by launching the Tribunal in the space of the forum, on 1–2 February 2002. The first three debt tribunal sessions were held there, wherein some 5,000 activists directly participated, making this the largest such public hearing on debt ever convened. This campaign culminated in a concluding session in Washington, DC. Jubilee South activists and their partners have coordinated ongoing campaigning on these issues at subsequent forums, in which the goal remains a genuine "jubilee" where the entire debt will be erased.

Oxfam promotes its own campaigns in the spaces of the forum as well and, as stated earlier, lends its name and support to others' campaigns to draw greater attention to those issues. Oxfam has hosted WSF seminars and strategy sessions as part of a campaign against the WTO investment treaty, and instead has given its support to the Jubilee Framework by calling for a new international convention within the UN to balance investor privileges and responsibilities. It has further participated at the social forums in joint calls and campaigns for mobilization against the WTO Cancun meetings. These campaigns entail pressuring home governments through media activism and other nationally focused actions which nonetheless are coordinated transnationally, during and between the WSFs. In these efforts it has sought to build the broadest possible alliances among those participating in the forums, including social movements, trade unions, and industrial representatives from the South.[89] Finally, in perhaps the most well-publicized – and controversial, which will be discussed below – campaign launch yet at the WSF, Oxfam joined a coalition of over 100 NGOs to debut the GCAP at the fifth WSF in Porto Alegre on 27 January 2005. Over 10,000 people and considerable media watched as coalition members, including Oxfam representatives, presented President Lula with the campaign's white band.

There are two additional ways in which both Jubilee South and GCAP members have cooperated in order to deepen and broaden the WSF process and the network of networks: through helping to found the WSF and participating in its coordination as part of the IC, and by working to spread the social forum process to the regional, national, and local levels. Anti-debt campaigners from J2000 were seminal in conceiving the WSF and have continued to be important shapers via the IC. In 1999, on the eve of the millennium year that would bring J2000 to an end, anti-debt campaigners including Oxfam, Fifty Years Is Enough, and Focus on the Global South were among a small group who first coordinated meetings and counter-summits against the World Economic Forum. This group would eventually help plan the first WSF the following year.[90] These same anti-debt groups were invited, along with the newly formed Asian, African, and Latin American Jubilee South networks, to be among the first members of the WSF IC, which came together between the first and second WSFs in order to advise and assist the Brazilian Organizing Committee – now called the Secretariat – with organizing the annual forum.[91]

Indeed, participation in this council, which meets a few times a year, is *in itself* transnational collective action. For this rather ad hoc collective of several dozen activists representing a variety of organizations works to institutionalize and diffuse the WSF as a permanent global process, or space, for dialogue, debate, and coordinating action from the global to the local levels. In a more informal way, as well, IC members have developed relationships over the years which deepen and broaden understanding of issues and campaigns in various parts of the world, cross-fertilization of ideas, friendships and solidarity, and ultimately collaborative efforts. The IC therefore can be seen as a microcosm for what happens much more broadly in the spaces of the WSFs themselves: that is, networking and strengthening alliances, both within one's own network and across networks; coordinating toward launching campaigns in the space of the forums; and diffusing the social forum process to all political levels.

Regarding the latter, outside of the IC we also see anti-debt groups taking the initiative to spread the social forum process. Jubilee South-Latin America plays key coordinating roles in all of the macro-regional social forums being organized in its region – including those of the Americas, the Pan-Amazon, the Caribbean, and the sixth, polycentric WSF in Caracas, Venezuela, in January 2006.[92] Furthermore, Jubilee South and Jubilee South Africa helped to organize a three-day Durban Social Forum which was held parallel to the World Conference Against Racism in August 2001. There they linked debt to racism, by framing the former as just another means of exerting control over Africa, and therefore calling for a dismantling not just of the institutions that keep poor countries indebted, but of "the global system of oppression and exploitation." Reflecting their frame-extending efforts, to build the citywide forum they networked broadly with social movements representing those who are excluded from effective political participation as well as precarious workers. Jubilee South regards spaces such as these local social forums as necessary building blocks toward constructing, first, a South African Social Forum and, eventually, "similar formations the length and breadth of the continent to be part of the growing and strengthening World Social Forum."[93] Likewise, the Asia-Pacific branch of Jubilee South has been working toward similar goals in its part of the world: In late October 2001 it held its regional committee meeting in tandem with the Asian Peoples' Solidarity Forum of plenaries and protest marches, in order to participate in discussions on the military dimensions of neoliberal globalization and to help coordinate upcoming protests around the World Economic Forum regional meeting scheduled for Hong Kong.[94]

Oxfam and other members of the GCAP have been equally active in regional, national, and local social forums. Since the beginning of the ESF process, the European-based Oxfam affiliates have regularly attended the European preparatory assembly meetings in addition to being well represented on large ESF panels. At the most recent ESF in London, Oxfam, among others, promoted the UK's Make Poverty History campaign. At the national level, Novib helped bring together what was likely the broadest domestic coalition in the Netherlands' recent history for the Dutch Social Forum held in December 2004. Oxfam is also active beyond Europe. For example, representatives have participated in forums throughout the Americas, including the Social Forum of the Americas in Quito in August 2004.

Terrain of competition over nature of forum and future global network

The above demonstrates the ways in which the GCAP and Jubilee South members' actions have been cooperative and complementary in both constituting and promoting the WSF process. These efforts should be kept in mind, and, further, should not seem diminished, by our turning to address the third theme of our analysis, that of the WSF as a terrain of competition. Through their distinctive actions, networks attempt consciously or not to mold the forum in an image more like themselves. The outcome of this struggle is bound to have a significant impact not only on the WSF itself but also on any transnational network of networks that may arise.

With regard to Jubilee South, three themes stand out, reflecting this network's composition and character. First, they emphasize building social forums at the local level, as we saw in their participation in Durban, which demonstrates their dedication to a bottom-up organizational approach. This is done in order to support local struggles and construct transnational campaigns and consensus strategies with strong local roots, so as to empower those who are most closely suffering the effects of debt and SAPs. Hence, those who emphasize the importance of the WSF as a transnational vehicle for forging a united global movement may find Jubilee South's insistence on deepening and spreading the social forum process locally to be a frustratingly slow strategy. This leads to a related second point, which is that through Jubilee's work in the spaces of the social forums at every level they seek first and foremost to dialogue, coordinate with, and build solidarity among activists sharing the common identity of citizens living under the threatening, precarious rule of transnational creditors. Therefore, some NGOs who are accustomed to speaking on behalf of, or taking the lead in, debt coalitions may consider Jubilee South to foment exclusionism. They may further regard the new network as a hostile competitor to their leadership, expertise, and thus more "professional" campaigns.

A final point was illustrated in Jubilee South's networking and campaigning at the WSF, as well as in Africa, Asia, and the Americas, which is to some extent a rebuttal to accusations of their being an exclusionist network: that is, their efforts to forge broad alliances of reciprocal solidarity among people struggling against distinct facets of neoliberal globalization, from racism and militarism to debt and SAPs. They therefore are seeking to build a bottom-up, multi-issue network of networks based first upon identity solidarity but then linked, through reciprocity, to other struggles viewed as interconnected. This is done with the goal of multi-sector, structural transformation. This project is to emerge organically, from the grassroots up, through the ever greater articulation of struggles, and it intends to be revolutionary. That said, they also work within what Martin Khor called a transitional paradigm, making pragmatic alliances toward and tactical gains on reformist measures. Yet throughout they seek to develop a popular consensus strategy and movement toward global transformation. Some within the forums may feel threatened by the transformative changes demanded by Jubilee South, as well as by the forceful, defiant tone in which they demand them, nonetheless.

Indeed, those who find Jubilee South too strident or extreme take refuge in the GCAP. The latter's activities have been more ambiguous in the spaces of the forum. While it is clear that this campaign's lead organizations, such as Oxfam, have a long-term and enthusiastic commitment to global change in favor of alleviating poverty and misery, and an equally strong commitment to building the social forum process and what they term a "global civil society," the network's actions move the forum toward a more reformist paradigm and top-down, advocacy network model. This is witnessed in a number of ways, but perhaps most spectacularly – and controversially – in their choice to launch the GCAP at the WSF featuring the Brazilian head of state as their "star guest."

The WSF Charter repeatedly stresses that the forum is an exclusive space for nongovernmental actors, and thereby tries to keep at bay the divisiveness of party politics or the dangers that would likely result from opening the space to elected officials. This rule is enshrined in no less than three of the Charter's fourteen points. Point five states that the forum "brings together and interlinks *only organizations and movements of civil society* from all the countries in the world." Point eight further clarifies that the forum "is a plural, diversified, non-confessional, *non-governmental and non-party* context." Finally, number nine reiterates: "Neither *party representations* nor military organizations shall participate in the Forum." But at the same time, that very point introduces no small ambiguity by continuing: "*Government leaders and members of legislatures* who accept the commitments of this Charter *may be invited to participate in a personal capacity.*"[95]

One can draw the conclusion from the last about-turn either that activists should be able to dialogue informally with representatives of government, or at the very least that elected officials should not be barred from participating by virtue of the fact that they are in office. But, in either case, publicly showcasing Lula in a prime-time slot and venue at the WSF to help launch an anti-poverty campaign goes well beyond either of these interpretations of the Charter's spirit. No president of a country – and certainly not one as high profile as Lula was at the height of his popularity in early 2005 – can participate in a "personal" capacity. He was rather invited *as* president of Brazil, *as* head of the pro-poor Workers' Party, and as the dubious "our man in Davos."

One of the staunchest defenders of the WSF Charter's prudent wisdom is also one of its framers, Chico Whitaker. He expressed dismay at this highly publicized, governmental–NGO venture. Undoubtedly his concerns were not with Lula per se, but rather with who would come next. When Lula is invited to participate, how can the increasingly popular Venezuelan President Hugo Chavez then be denied a platform? And where will this slippery slope take us next? Indeed, inviting both of these heads of state to the WSF in 2005 created "huge problems," lamented Whitaker. Those who planned these events seemed to have conveniently forgotten about the WSF Charter. Yet the forum founder doubts whether the GCAP's hitching its campaign wagon to Lula's young star will help the struggle in the long run. This is precisely why the admonitions against including such volatile star material are embedded in the Charter. Given the Brazilian government's recent corruption scandal, in addition to mounting disillusionment with the slow pace of reforms, Whitaker's concerns have proven prescient. While the short-term pay-out of capturing media attention may have benefited the campaign, this elite-driven, top-down reformist approach threatens to "hijack," in the words of Whitaker, the very forum process, and turn the WSF into something more familiar to the mainstream participants: an NGO, a political party, or a social movement organization.[96]

A final way that the GCAP's supporters shape the forum is at an existential level. Oxfam and the Ford Foundation are the WSF's leading financial patrons. Both have distinguished themselves as loyal and enthusiastic supporters of the forum since the beginning. The Netherlands' Oxfam also administers a joint Oxfam International Fund dedicated to it. In 2004, their total support came to €550,000. With these funds they underwrite the WSF operating structure as well as specific events, providing both financial and content-related support.[97] So while there is little evidence that these generous funders attempt to influence the shape of the forum, informal concern was expressed by some to the WSF IC during a discussion over whether to allow the next WSF to be hosted in Chavez-run Venezuela. But this concern did not seem to bear upon the ultimately affirmative decision or upon the budget for the 2006 event. Still, the risk, and indeed possibility, is there, and could play a crucial and largely hidden role in steering the WSF along a reformist, NGO-style path. Risks such as these are some of the reasons why the Indian organizers of the 2004 WSF decided to refuse private foundation funds such as those offered by Ford. This is both an ongoing debate and a permanent risk, the outcome of which will have concrete, though difficult to assess, effects on the WSF, and the network of networks more broadly.

4   Our World Is Not For Sale

In Chapter 3 we learned about the many ways in which activists are resisting, critiquing, and advocating alternatives to transnational structures – that is, the practices, norms, rules, laws, and institutions – pertaining to poor-country debt. We also saw that many of these activists argue that the structural violences stemming from debt are exacerbated by the Bretton Woods institutions' SAPs, which countries are forced to accept as a condition for both additional loans and debt reduction. And directly related to this chapter's focus on the struggle against neoliberal trade agreements, we further learned that two of the three networks that came out of Jubilee 2000, those of Jubilee South and the Global Call to Action Against Poverty, have extended the framing of their demands out from debt cancellation to encompass trade justice.

In order to achieve what activists consider to be a more just global trade regime, a number of the anti-debt organizations have joined up with a broad range of other groups to forge Our World Is Not For Sale (OWINFS), which has quickly emerged as the key transnational network fighting neoliberal globalization manifested in international trade agreements. This vast and loosely coordinated network of NGOs, think-tanks, social movements, networks, and individuals consists of some seventy national level campaigns as well as several international networks. Its membership embodies today's activist credo of "unity in diversity": It includes numerous research and advocacy centers and networks such as the Bangkok-based Focus on the Global South, Food First, and the Asia-Pacific Research Network; citizen watchdog organizations like the Council of Canadians, Public Citizen, and its Global Trade Watch; workers' and peasants' networks, including Via Campesina, the World Forum of Fisherpeople, and Public Services International; environmental parties and federations, including Friends of the Earth International; and national umbrella organizations such as the Korean People's Action against the Korea–Japan Free Trade Agreement and the World Trade Organization (KOPA).

Those involved in this network argue that recent global, regional, and bilateral trade agreements are posing serious threats to democracy, human rights, and the environment while promising little to poor nations by way of release from the traps of debt and uneven development. They therefore share the immediate goals of at the very least diminishing the scope of the trade negotiations and at best derailing them entirely, as well as a longer-term strategy of replacing the current neoliberal trade regime with one based on democratic accountability, social justice, and environmental sustainability. Since its formation under the OWINFS banner following the Seattle WTO ministerial in late 1999, network members continue to target the WTO, but have also turned their collective attention to the Free Trade Area of the Americas (FTAA), the Africa Growth and Opportunity Act (AGOA), the Asia-Pacific Economic Cooperation (APEC), the Plan Puebla Panama (PPP), the Central American Free Trade Agreement (CAFTA), and the proliferating bilateral agreements. Recognizing the wide repercussions of these trade agreements and reflecting the diverse interests of its constituent members, OWINFS's concerns include not only trade and invest-ment regimes, but also agriculture, war, and terrorism.

Broad change processes: the WTO and regional trade agreements

We begin our analysis of why and how local activists eventually shifted to the transnational level to contest this second important facet of neoliberal globaliza-tion by overviewing broad changes and triggers in the realm of international trade that have sparked autonomous contention across the globe. The WTO was founded in 1995 and has come to be viewed by many activists as the "third pillar" of the Bretton Woods system.[1] Formerly the GATT, which was charged with reducing certain tariffs and setting broad trade principles, this organization has grown more powerful in each successive trade meeting since the 1986 Uruguay Round. While most critics of the emerging neoliberal trading regime do not deny that international commerce can positively contribute to economic development and quality of life, their vehement protests against the WTO center on what they perceive to be a strong bias toward corporations at the expense of democratic processes and principles. They argue that under the WTO corporate rights largely trump international human and labor rights and environmental agreements, in addition to domestic laws judged by closed tribunals to impede the free flow of trade and investment. In just one example of the WTO's reach and priorities, India has been ordered to change its constitution that guarantees access to low-cost generic drugs for its people, effectively ruling in favor of protecting the profits of foreign drug companies over the health of the Indian populace.[2]

The WTO's rules, as well as those of other regional trade agreements like the NAFTA, the CAFTA, the FTAA, and the EU's Maastricht Treaty, are strikingly similar to the policies of the SAPs and, activists argue, have produced the same results in both Northern and Southern countries. For liberalization has not necessarily led to increased economic growth or development.[3] In addition, the deregulation of investment and banking called for by these agreements has brought greater instability, allowing for the reckless lending and currency specu-lation that precipitated the Asian financial crises of 1997–8 as well as others in Argentina, Brazil, Mexico, Turkey, and Russia.

These new trade regimes are further criticized for eroding the agricultural self-sufficiency of small farmers and indigenous communities. Activists blame the agreements for dislocating millions throughout Latin America, Asia, and Africa by corporate takeovers of land for upscale export crops and the construction of giant dam and other energy projects. Economist Martin Khor of the Third World Network (TWN), a long-time investigator of the harm done to poor countries by economic globalization, has concluded that these agreements "threaten to stop developing countries from industrializing, upgrading technology, developing local industries, protecting small farmers, achieving food security, and fulfilling health and medicinal needs."[4] They also appear to limit a community's ability to sanction unethical behavior abroad. Referring to the successful economic boycott of apartheid South Africa that was won partly through legislation passed at local and regional levels in foreign countries, the IFG concludes that "if such [trade] rules had been in place twenty years ago, Nelson Mandela would likely still be in jail."[5]

Activists have not been alone in their growing concern and criticisms of these agreements. Southern governments are becoming increasingly frustrated that the promises made to entice them to back a stronger WTO have been largely unfulfilled by the North. A few officials have joined with activists in denouncing *this* "free trade" as not free at all, but rather as having exacted too high a price and for too long delivered too little for too many in the South. This is the main reason for the WTO and the FTAA negotiations stalling since the Seattle WTO ministerial in 1999. The crux of this critique is that, rather than "free trade," what the wealthy countries led by the US and EU are promoting is in fact neo-mercantilism, which protects their own domestic markets while aggressively promoting their corporations' interests abroad by ramming through liberalization agreements in investments, services, and government procurement contracts with other countries, especially in the Global South. This is all done, say critics, with a neocolonial, paternalistic approach and with an attitude of: "we know best what is good for you – free trade, investment rules to enable our corporations to take over your economic space, and with some preferences for your exports, mostly commodities that we need – but not in competition with our own producers, but at the expense of other developing countries."[6]

Why, one might wonder, do the trade rounds continue if so many of the world's nations have gotten such an ostensibly raw deal? Here is where the structural violence addressed in this chapter, that of trade agreements, is deeply entwined with the violence of debt elucidated in the previous one. The structural relationship between debt and free trade is reflected in the prevailing development paradigm of recent decades. This now conventional wisdom holds that a country must produce for export in order to achieve economic growth and earn the hard currency necessary to meet its debt obligations. In order to trade abroad, barriers must come down, and so poor countries have had little choice but to sign on to the only trade deals on offer and hope for the best. As it turned out, the promised quid pro quo which enticed debt-burdened nations to expand the GATT into the WTO in the first place – that of rich countries lowering tariffs on agricultural and other key imports in exchange for developing countries liberalizing investments, services, and government procurement – has not gone so well for much of the South.

With this growing realization comes increased resistance on the part of frustrated governments to make further concessions. When the ideational structures of the development paradigm can no longer maintain poor-country compliance with the free trade regime, debt must be wielded as a blunt instrument. It then becomes a means of leverage for wealthier countries to force nations to drop their opposition, and thus coercively manufacture the consensus that is needed to move forward in negotiations. A recent report by the development agency ActionAid, entitled "Divide and Rule: The EU and the US Response to Developing-Country Alliances at the WTO," chronicles the bribery, bullying, arm-twisting, threats, and blackmail that wealthy countries have reportedly used in attempts to break the nascent alliances among developing countries within the WTO. Chief among these subversive tactics are threats to cut aid budgets and to block necessary loans and debt relief to poor countries. These tactics are said to go back to the mid-1980s, but have intensified in recent years in response to growing opposition. In just a few examples, Tanzanian and Kenyan officials reported being threatened just prior to Cancun with the cancellation of market access preferences for their key exports if they persisted in defending their own country's interests in the upcoming round. And Brazil and India, as leaders of the Group of Twenty (G20) which surfaced during the 2001 Doha Ministerial to collectively push for the agricultural question to be placed front and center, have been singled out – in the words of the report – for "particularly vicious treatment."[7]

Localized actors are key to founding OWINFS: Focus on the Global South and the Council of Canadians

From this brief overview of the wide-ranging criticisms of the WTO, we can better understand why it has come to be considered the third pillar which, in addition to the World Bank and IMF, props up neoliberalism's globalizing rule. It also helps us to see why varied groups – from those suffering under SAPs, debt, land evictions, and loss of markets to those struggling for workers' rights, environmental protection, and democracy at the national and local levels – could eventually come to identify in each other common allies being harmed by and therefore resisting the same transnational target. But for this attribution to take place, leading to the solidarity necessary for sustained transnational coordination, prior actions were needed. Specifically, "protest entrepreneurs" – to use Tarrow and della Porta's term – had to *perceive* that it was necessary to shift to the transnational level of contention, and therefore reach out and successfully broker ties, diffuse information, and frame their appeals in such a way that would resonate widely. This would result in a collective shift and refining of objects and claims toward the WTO, regional, and bilateral trade agreements, and the trade ministers and governments who negotiate in the name of their countries' citizens.

Given the vastness of the OWINFS network, in order to get a sense of how these mechanisms work in specific contexts it is perhaps most useful to trace this process within two of the network's founding organizations, Focus on the Global South (Focus) and the Council of Canadians (COC). They were chosen as illustrative cases because of what they have in common as well as how they differ. They both were key in founding OWINFS, and continue to be two of its most active coordinating members. Yet they also differ markedly: One is Northern based, began with narrow demands for governmental policy reform to defend national sovereignty and interests, and therefore reoriented rather belatedly and reluctantly toward transnational collective action and mass mobilization; whereas the other is Southern based, but was oriented from the beginning toward a transnational focus and agenda, and has therefore long been a leading voice providing critical analysis in a number of transnational struggles, specifically against debt, SAPs, militarization, neocolonialism, and war. It has constantly sought to frame-extend among issues, groups, and regions of the globe toward evolving a transformative frame for critique and collective action against neoliberal rule.

The two illustrations further differ in the levels at which their scale shift has taken place. In the case of Focus, organizers conceived of their new entity from the outset at the macro-regional, and thus transnational, level. While its individual members had been involved in a number of prior local, national, and transnational groups, Focus was a consciously transnational actor. Its initiators therefore set out to broker ties and diffuse information toward building transnational solidarity and collective action from the start. The COC is perhaps a more typical case of an organization's scale shift process, which brought it first from its localized beginnings to a national organization, then a macro-regional one, and finally one participating in global networks. Tracing its trajectory therefore illustrates these two cycles of scale shift: the first one from localized contention to forging itself as a national campaign; and then again reaching out across its borders to collectively initiate a second cycle of scale shift mechanisms, by linking up with seasoned actors first around North America to fight NAFTA and then transnationally. This is witnessed in the COC's becoming a participant in the IFG, then the anti-MAI, and again the Seattle anti-WTO network, which would finally mature into OWINFS.

Transnational "focus" assumes key brokerage, diffusion, and framing roles among economic, political, and environmental domains

Throughout the 1980s and 1990s, popular movements, organizations, and research centers emerged in response to chronic problems and new threats in the Global South: worsening debt, severe economic crises, and the growing involvement of the World Bank and TNCs ostensibly to help solve these problems, the ongoing inequalities in power and wealth both between the industrialized North and the developing countries and within poor countries themselves, the dismal failure to strike out upon a successful road to development, and the problems of corruption and lack of popular participation in domestic politics. One of the most influential and versatile of these new organizations has been Focus on the Global South. Walden Bello, co-founder of Focus and today a key broker in OWINFS in addition to a number of other networks, began to track as early as the 1970s the emerging development model being articulated by US–World Bank-funded projects in his native Philippines and across Asia. A social scientist formally trained and politically active at home as well as in the US and Latin America, Bello observed that the model prioritized the entry and increased involvement into national economies of TNCs as well as export-oriented growth. He drew the parallel conclusion that the levels of analysis, of popular response, and of alternatives must also be transnational in scope. "Examining World Bank development models and other patterns of domination," recalls Bello, "made me increasingly aware that these couldn't simply be challenged at the national level." Therefore, when Bello and his associates founded Focus, they chose to locate their research center in Bangkok in order to facilitate this macro-regional perspective.[8]

From the beginning the Focus founders saw their role not solely as researchers but equally as activist-brokers and information disseminators working to foment struggle encompassing multiple levels, objects, and claims. "Although we started from Asian and Pacific issues, our horizons were always the global patterns of domination and resistance. ... [For] whether it was a question of opposing the US military, or the World Bank or the IMF or multinational corporations, it was crucial to begin creating cross-regional links."[9] Bello, along with Focus's co-director Kamal Malhotra from India and other Thai scholars such as Suthy Prasartsert, quickly initiated ties with likeminded Korean and Japanese intellectuals.

In addition to this proactive brokering with other Asian critical scholars, Bello was also able to act as the key nodal point for relational diffusion based on his considerable global contacts. In this role, he and Focus shared information and analysis through his pre-existing connections with pro-democracy groups in the Philippines, with student activists with whom Bello was acquainted from his studies in the US in the 1960s, and with transnational NGOs, such as Food First, Oxfam, and Greenpeace, in which he had been active. With a staff that now numbers about two dozen, Focus has also become an important conductor of non-relational diffusion through its web-based and print publications and communications, made available via its website.[10] Focus members research and then publish on-line and in print on a wide range of interrelated facets of globalization. These include free trade agreements, security issues – especially revolving around US military and political dominance in Asia-Pacific and its local–global connections – citizens' potential for enhancing democratization as well as the danger of organizations being coopted, and ideologies such as Islamic revivalism and other forms of religious fundamentalism.

Through its ambitious brokerage and diffusion roles, Focus's framing of the issues, targets, and potential solutions has made a strong imprint on OWINFS, in addition to the other networks in which it plays similar roles. Specifically, Bello and his colleagues' synthesizing analysis of economics, politics, and ecology from the local to the global levels has helped many to see how their own struggles interrelate with others'.[11] They insist that the economic logic of global corporations, the WTO, and other regional trade agreements is inextricably bound up with US military dominance, which in turn is having devastating environmental effects, particularly in the Global South. This analysis, which has come to be adopted as the prevailing discourse within OWINFS and enjoys considerable prominence in other networks as well and in the spaces of the WSF and regional forums, constructs a web of targets and interlinked claims against the WTO, the free trade agreements, the Bretton Woods institutions, and American elite and military interests. According to Bello's analysis, these entities are responsible for causing great structural violence in the Global South. He particularly derides the WTO as:

> an opaque, unrepresentative and undemocratic organization driven by a free-trade ideology which, wherever its recipes – liberalization, privatization, deregulation – have been applied over the past twenty years to re-engineer Third World economies, has generated only greater poverty and inequality. That's the first point: implementation of neo-liberal dogmas leads to great suffering. Secondly, the WTO is not an independent body but a representative of American state and corporate interests.[12]

In order to disseminate their critical analysis, Focus scholars undertake "capacity-building" education and consulting for Southern governments, national NGOs, and grassroots organizations who call upon Focus's considerable technical and analytical expertise to help them reach decisions or plan campaigns around free trade negotiations. In these roles as broker and diffuser of information, their framing strategy can be characterized in terms of both bridging and, most crucially, extension. First, Focus scholars have sought to forge or strengthen links with others who already hold similar views. But, second, they have also constantly worked to extend the boundaries of primary frameworks, both their own and those with whom they seek ties. It is interesting to note that in practice Focus's frame extension endeavors seem not to be solely uni-directional, which is the way frame extension has been commonly portrayed in social movement literature.[13] Theirs are rather considerably more dynamic and co-constitutive efforts, consisting of back-and-forth information flows via relational and non-relational diffusion channels and brokered ties to movements, NGOs, and other research organizations.

Finally, its broad perspective and framing of the issues has also positioned Focus as a key broker of ties between anti-corporate globalization activists and the re-emergent peace movements that have sprung up in the wake of the US's war on terror and lead-up to the attacks on Iraq. In his characteristic "bridging" analysis that promotes broad-based action, Bello asserted, "We need to understand how the two connect – which also means trying to bring together two different movements." Toward those ends, Focus has organized international conferences on finance, trade, and military issues and has spearheaded international days of protests and popular campaigns, much of this organization taking place within the General Assembly of the Anti-War Movement which Focus helped initiate in the space of the social forums. In these, as in all of their endeavors, they consciously "work to bring together the global movements."[14]

Nationalist Canadians go global (and more local) in brokering ties to fight NAFTA

Now let's go back and pick up a second strand of the OWINFS network, the Council of Canadians. The COC began as a very different sort of group than Focus on the Global South: Whereas Focus shot out of the gate with a transnational perspective and agenda and therefore ready to broker ties internationally, the COC emerged as a decidedly inward-looking group, drawing a defensive line of demarcation at the national border. In the mid-1980s, a number of Canadian intellectuals grew alarmed over reforms introduced by Brian Mulroney's government that paved the way for a free trade deal with the US. Perceiving these as threats to Canada's cultural, political, and economic sovereignty, the COC was formed as a government and corporate watchdog organization, and Maude Barlow was elected its chair.

Their defensive nationalism proved to be a successful initial tool for mobilizing and brokering broad-based ties among their fellow citizens. Early protests and activities included dropping a maple leaf flag onto the deck of a US icebreaker that had illegally entered Canadian waters, and protesting the selling off of Canadian companies to the Americans. The COC organized a counter "Maple Leaf Summit" in tandem with Mulroney's official meeting with Ronald Reagan. This parallel event brought together representatives of labor, the environment, indigenous people, women, farmers, pensioners, students, the poor, and religious communities from across Canada to form a "Pro-Canada Network" in opposition to free trade. In the late 1980s, this network (which was later renamed the Solidarity Network) led the fight against the US–Canada Free Trade Agreement and soon followed up with campaigns to block deregulation and cuts in social spending.

In these early years the COC were self-described "progressive Canadian nationalists," meaning that, "throughout these battles, the Council proudly carried the banner of Canadian sovereignty and pressured governments ... to live up to their responsibility to protect the rights of citizens."[15] Therefore, in their brokering of national ties, the COC's main framing strategy was that of amplifying longstanding values that were heralded as particularly Canadian and in need of defending, and then contrasting these with popular stereotypes of the US. Theirs were more evolved, human, and civilized values than those of the hunched behemoth to the South. "Living next to the biggest superpower in the world," they reminded their elected officials, "our ancestors rejected the American narrative of 'survival of the fittest' and instead built a nation-state forged on the Canadian narrative of 'sharing for survival.'" The original mandate of the COC flowed from this heightened contrast with their lowbrow neighbor, and was to promote "the right of Canadians to continue to have a distinctive and progressive political culture." In appealing to traditional, national values widely perceived as under threat, while at the same time amplifying the stereotypical belief of the American leviathan, the COC was successful in brokering ties that led to attribution of similarity, solidarity, and coordinated action based upon a shared Canadian identity and the defense of national sovereignty.[16]

Yet it was the campaign against the impending NAFTA that spurred the COC to sprout both deeper roots and taller branches. In the lead-up to the NAFTA fight, this group of intellectuals felt the need to reach out to the grassroots. They therefore launched a nationwide, participatory process called the "Citizens' Agenda." Through this they sought to outline a popular vision and action plan to bring economic, social, and environmental decision-making back under democratic control. It was a resounding recruitment success in that the COC membership swelled to some 100,000 activists. Yet ironically, in its metamorphosis from scholarly collective to popular movement, the COC also began to frame its struggle in less exclusively nationalist terms, stressing that citizen rights should not be conceived of solely as the domain of Canadians, but were rather due to "all the peoples of the earth" equally. In a similar vein, brokering relations with Quebecois spurred the COC to change the name of its "pro-Canada" campaign to that of "Action Canada Network," a process which put the network members, recalls Barlow, "through a major re-think of the concept of nationalism."[17]

The International Forum on Globalization emerges as key space for facilitating the scale shift process

From the brief overviews above of the COC and Focus, we begin to glimpse the possibility – but certainly not the inevitability – of how and why the geographically and ideologically disparate organizations that would eventually forge the OWINFS network would recognize the others' struggle as sufficiently interconnected or similar to warrant solidarity and collective action. What were needed were forerunning actions and campaigns throughout the 1990s that would bring such groups into greater contact. The first were the anti-NAFTA initiatives sprouting up around North America and the second was the creation of the IFG. The fight to stop NAFTA forced the COC to reach out across North America and into Mexico, leading to two important meetings: the Canadian–Mexican *encuentro* with civil society representatives in Mexico City in 1991 and, two years later, the formation of the IFG. The latter began drawing intellectuals from around North America and beyond to discuss the various facets of contemporary globalization and alternatives to it. And as we will see below, this group proved to be key in spearheading the campaign to defeat the MAI as well as in planning the Seattle WTO protests, out of which OWINFS would emerge.

The IFG – in which the COC has played a prominent role and of which Barlow has been a director – quickly became a catalyst and nodal point for anti-neoliberal debate and scholarship, solidarity building among activists, and transnational coordinated action. The San Francisco-based Foundation for Deep Ecology (FDP) conceived of, sponsored, and initially hosted the IFG, recognizing that in the wake of NAFTA, the WTO, and the European Common Market, the Foundation's own goals of preserving diverse ecosystems could no longer be achieved within either national or sectoral parameters. The FDP observed:

> something new was afoot: a global juggernaut that profoundly and permanently affected all of our most important interests. There was little point in working to save a watershed or forest, or stop a horrific dam, or to establish new regulatory controls on development, if powerful new global bureaucracies could overrule these gains.[18]

The foundation therefore decided to gather together scholar-activists who were making a name for themselves at home or further a field in these related areas, but who had been working largely in isolation from one another. The FDP's Jerry Mander and Debi Barker coordinated the first meeting, and went on to become IFG president and executive director, respectively. This forum began with about three dozen members but quickly expanded to around sixty coming from some two dozen countries. Since its inception this forum was a brokerage site for the "who's who" of anti-corporate scholar-activists: The COC's Barlow and Focus's Bello were brought together, in addition to TWN's Khor, Vandana Shiva, also of TWN and the Research Foundation for Science, Technology and Ecology, Lori Wallach of Public Citizen/Global Trade Watch, John Cavanagh of the Institute for Policy Studies, Helena Norberg-Hodge of the International Society for Ecology and Culture, David Korten of People Centered Development Forum, and Mark Ritchie of the Institute for Agriculture and Trade Policy, among many others. In addition to providing an important transnational brokerage site, these first meetings reinforced scholar-activists' sentiments that the level of analysis, critique, and, crucially, collective action needed to be transnational: "It quickly became evident to all participants," remembers one of them, "that working in isolation within individual countries was not sufficient for battling such a global monolith. Coordinated efforts were crucial."[19]

Indeed, the IFG meetings provided a much-needed venue for the cross-fertilization of ideas and for a perception to emerge among this core group that one another's concerns and targets were similar enough to warrant common action. This made possible an ambitious and broad program that entailed collaborative research and public education via relational and non-relational diffusion, lobbying of power centers, and brokering and strengthening of ties toward transnational mobilization. In this vein, IFG members have held numerous teach-ins throughout the Americas and Europe. Along with the organizations that they represent, they have convened strategy meetings, participated in networks, and launched campaigns and popular actions.

IFG's first major transnational collective action: the anti-MAI campaign

The first of these was the campaign to defeat the MAI in 1998. Two years prior, TWN's Khor informed other IFG members about a secretive global investment treaty that was apparently near ratification among the twenty-nine OECD countries, which he had learned about from sources in Geneva. IFG members began demanding information about this treaty, and finally the COC obtained a copy and diffused it over the worldwide web to other members of the IFG network. Thus was born the first successful, transnational internet campaign to defeat an international treaty. IFG members moved rapidly to broker relations among seventy labor, environmental, and citizens' groups. From that they concluded they were in a position of strength – or at least sufficient credibility – to request a meeting with official MAI negotiators at the OECD headquarters in Paris. Their consensus demand was for a one-year moratorium on the treaty so that they could hold public meetings and educate their own governments as to its potential negative ramifications. When this was denied, the network members returned home to embark on a multi-pronged strategy of grassroots organizing, on-line activism through posting petitions to sign, and lobbying government ministries through these petitions as well as in person.

They established broad coalitions in their own countries among all sectors that would be affected by the treaty, amounting to "thousands of small campaigns working in concert, but not directed from on high."[20] While coalition members included major organizations such as Greenpeace and the World Wildlife Fund, the great majority of groups signing the on-line petitions against the MAI were nationally based organizations.[21] The more well-funded and better-staffed groups provided research and then disseminated this information via listserves, including the STOP-MAI list organized in Australia, the Washington, DC-based Public Citizen's MAI-Not list, and another of the same name administered from Ottawa.[22] By coordinating the listserves and maintaining informational websites, these organizations became central nodes of both relational and non-relational diffusion.

Through these sites IFG members were rather successful in frame-bridging within, and frame-extending among, sectors. They cross-referenced other websites of those participating in the campaign and provided secondary analysis on related issues and concrete suggestions for how to get involved. The same analytical pieces were often posted on numerous sites. Local groups accessed and adapted these resources for their own purposes, amplifying those issues that most concerned them. These websites also helped mobilize "desktop activists" by posting contact information of government representatives and the media, to whom they could then send opinion e-mails. One researcher described this flexible anti-MAI network as a "new species" that "shifts its focus comfortably between the local, the national, and the global, from issues in one national jurisdiction to another, and from issue-area to issue-area."[23]

This new species of network that was spawned from the IFG synergized the talents of researchers with those of cultural activists around the globe and utilized the internet to disseminate these resources and then diffuse them through national coalitions that would then adapt them for their own use. They were thereby able to creatively and successfully extend the frames among diverse sectors and geographical regions and articulate a powerful belief and value amplification that the MAI was an affront to national sovereignty in the cherished areas of culture, the natural environment, and social services. They therefore framed their grievances and claims largely in terms of cultural and societal protection from an overbearing economic threat. This seems to be a key factor in their eventual success, in that activists were able to "frame the public message long before governments did, and so, by sending the first 'take' on the issue into the public arena, set the conditions for winning."[24] Crucially, they were able to pressure and educate their own governments, convincing cultural, environmental, and health ministers that this treaty – which activists derided as "a global charter of rights and freedoms for transnational corporations" and as "NAFTA on steroids" – would constrict their ability to regulate and legislate in these areas. Campaigners persuaded their ministries that by signing the agreement governments would be abdicating effective sovereignty over these areas. Specifically, they warned that the treaty, which would set the terms of foreign direct investment, allowed corporations to sue all levels of government for "future losses of profits" caused by laws protecting consumers, the environment, public health, or local culture. These laws would therefore be challenged in courts and forced to be rescinded.

Their tactics worked. Governmental members demanded more and more exemptions from the MAI, totaling some 1,300 and paralyzing the talks. The European Parliament passed a resolution urging member governments to reject the treaty. Last-ditch efforts to salvage it failed. OECD Secretary-General Donald Johnston lamented that the impasse was due to an effective "disinformation" campaign waged by global activists. If it was disinformation, then the French government, among others, was duped by it. It was the first to withdraw from the talks, signaling the treaty's defeat, and issued a report praising the well-researched and well-presented material of the anti-MAI campaign when compared with that disseminated by the OECD itself.[25]

The COC's Barlow and Tony Clarke reflected on the significance of this campaign in terms of the globalizing terrain of contention upon which non-state and state actors alike now find themselves:

> Until this time, groups fighting free trade and economic globalization had been nation-state-based; they had come together only as loose coalitions, to cooperate temporarily on a common project. The anti-MAI campaign, however, was fundamentally different. Because they were abandoned by their own governments, which had bought the rhetoric on investment liberalization lock, stock, and barrel, workers, environmentalists, and citizen advocacy groups had to create a movement outside their nation-state

boundaries, one that was based in cyberspace and undergirded by a common set of values and beliefs.[26]

As the campaign progressed and the networking grew more extensive, a consensus emerged around situating the MAI within a larger struggle against "corporate rule" and "neoliberalism." Hence, the MAI, and the campaign against it, came to be seen not as a one-time endeavor, but rather as part of a larger project requiring ongoing, coordinated, transnational effort.

Next stop: Seattle, and the WTO ministerial

From their expanded perspective and their fear that the battle was not won for good, a new and even more formidable target was soon spotted on the horizon, that of the WTO and its upcoming ministerial meeting in Seattle. For the "free trade agreement" is akin to a cat with nine lives (which is currently on about its fourth): What appeared to be road kill in front of the OECD headquarters was about to bound again, this time through the streets of the neoliberal boomtown Seattle. Activists accurately foresaw that the WTO was to be the avenue upon which the defeated MAI would be reborn.[27] As it turned out, the resurrected MAI/WTO would not be left to roam as it wished about Seattle. The broad and deep diffusion channels that had been established to challenge the MAI were used to great effect in organizing for the mobilization against the Millennium Summit in late 1999, which would entail marches and mass actions, public lectures and debates, and NGO tribunals. The tens of thousands who turned up represented at least 700 NGOs and social movements, predominantly from the northwestern United States and Canada but also from across the country and around the globe. The international presence seemed greatly due to mobilizing efforts on the part of IFG members in their regions.[28]

IFG helps launch a transnational network in Seattle: Opposed to the WTO/People for Fair Trade

Little reframing effort was needed to mobilize the existing network, since the core issues of concern in the MAI – those of erosion of sovereignty in the areas of culture, the environment, and social services – were just as apparent in the WTO. All that was needed was a shift in the object or locus of blame from the defeated MAI to the ascendant WTO. This educative reorientation had already begun on the part of IFG members months prior, through posting analyses on their websites and diffusing them over listserves. Yet the shift in target from the narrower MAI to the more expansive WTO did offer new opportunities for forging broader alliances via mutual frame extension, since the new trade negotiations encompassed additional areas of concern. These included the removal of trade barriers and subsidies in agriculture, the forced import of genetically modified organisms (GMOs), the strengthening of corporate intellectual property rights, a considerable opening of the global service sector in areas of education, health care, culture, and water, the requirement of governments to tender contracts on the global market, and weakening legislation against corporate concentration of ownership.

The network that emerged out of the IFG and the anti-MAI struggle there-fore played a crucial, though by no means exclusive, role in planning and carrying off the weeklong activities.[29] Within this network, Public Citizen was particularly instrumental in initiating planning and coordination. In activities that complemented the Seattle Jubilee 2000 campaigners' efforts we learned about in Chapter 3, Washington, DC-based Mike Dolan of Public Citizen and the Citizens' Trade Campaign[30] teamed up with local Public Citizen activist Sally Soriano to mobilize and create information to disseminate among community activists and to help coordinate many of the events. And, consistent with what we saw among Jubilee activists, locals took great ownership in the planning process and the event itself, a "localizing the global" phenomenon that seems necessary for mass demonstrations or for gatherings of the network of networks to take place, be they in Chiapas, Washington, DC, Genoa, Porto Alegre, or Mumbai. Demonstrating both the breadth and the autonomy of the popular dissent on the ground, the first planning meeting in February 1999 organized by Public Citizen drew dozens of seasoned local activists, including, recalls one, "Earth First!ers, organic farmers, labor representatives, academicians, university students, puppet makers, gay and lesbian activists, peace workers, and ... anar-chists, from Seattle; the list went on and on."[31]

Although a shared desire to protest the WTO existed among these diverse grassroots and nationally focused activists alike, the main brokerage challenge was to arrive at a common stance that would lead to maximum participation in the planned events. The on-site steering committee led by Soriano wanted a strong statement of "NO to the WTO," while major organizations within the network – namely Citizens' Trade Campaign, Public Citizen, and the AFL–CIO – preferred a more circumscribed position advocating reform. A creative agreement-to-disagree was eventually struck, which established dual framing tracks of the collective demands that nearly everyone could get on board for: Ian Murray suggested this "high tech compromise" of launching two campaigns, one calling itself the Network Opposed to the WTO (i.e. the abolitionists), the other the People for Fair Trade (the reformers); yet both would share a website called peopleforfairtrade.org and a phone number 1-877-STOPWTO. This clever compromise allowed "the radicals and the moderates [to] share the same office but be free to express their different views via custom-printed materials. Computer technology at its most egalitarian."[32] This was another example of the much-acclaimed "unity in diversity," as good as it gets. This rather schizophrenic network managed to develop a consensus statement of "No New Round-Turn Around" leading up to WTO week, and posted it on their website, inviting others to sign on. In a short time, some 1,500 organizations did so. In this way the website served as a brokerage space for literally any individual or organiza-tion with an internet connection and the ability to read English to participate in this coordinated global campaign against the WTO.

IFG help launch second transnational network in Seattle: indymedia

In addition to spearheading the People for Fair Trade/Network Opposed to the WTO, IFG member Public Citizen also involved itself in another network which came to fruition in Seattle and which would spread to every corner of the globe, that of indymedia. The initial group was comprised of "techies" and "culture jammers" such as Free Speech TV, Paper Tiger TV, Fairness and Accuracy in Reporting, Adbusters, Direct Action Network, and a few organizations – like Public Citizen – that could raise money. What brought them together was a shared concern for the need to develop the means for an activist-generated and focused, alternative media. Having experimented throughout the 1990s, in Seattle this group was finally able to realize its powerful potential in an innovation that would truly revolutionize information diffusion and brokerage from that day forward.

The web-based independent media, or "indymedia," as it quickly became known, provided what activists herald as more democratic, accurate, and sympathetic coverage of their protest events, campaigns, and issues of concern. In many cases, indymedia provides the only public record at all that a protest or campaign has even taken place. This experiment, borne out of necessity, was launched in Seattle to widely disseminate news and analysis from the perspective of, and largely created by, activists themselves. All week long, self-styled indymedia journalists uploaded text, audio, and video footage reporting on a full range of activities from the teach-ins to the marches to the direct action. They also publicized critical analysis by activist-scholars on the negative policies and rulings of the WTO.

In addition to the innovative coverage and participation, indymedia profoundly democratized and rendered interactive this form of media by using a Linux-based, open-publishing code on their website, created and provided to them by an Australian technology collective only a day before the website was launched. To carry this whole project off, 500 mostly volunteer reporters, technicians, and photographers staffed the Seattle indymedia center (IMC). The website was resoundingly successful at reaching a wide audience: It reportedly received 1.5 million virtual visitors that week. Locally, for those lacking internet access, indymedia published a daily newspaper throughout the events as well as broadcast audio segments on local radio.

This form of media has mushroomed from that day forward. Today, there are nearly 150 collectively run websites across the United States and Canada, Europe, Latin America, Oceania, Africa, and East, West, and South Asia. Indymedia has therefore become a truly global space for non-relational diffusion of information as well as for virtually brokering ties so that activists can "meet," discuss, and build toward mass mobilization. The sites therefore entail a number of framing strategies, from bridging among activists working on the same issues, to extending the frames among complementary issues, to initiating the curious web-surfer into an entirely new and transformative frame.[33]

What was won in the Battle of Seattle

Returning to the role of the IFG during WTO week, as an organization it was heavily present, disseminating literature, sponsoring public debates, hosting a Food and Agriculture Day and a Corporation Day, and holding packed teach-ins where thousands came to hear speakers from all over the world. One local attendee reflected on the success of these IFG events, saying,

> Friday night's "The Impacts of Economic Globalization" was the hottest ticket in town. The same was true on Saturday, when the topic branched out to include forests, rivers, and oceans as well as labor rights, biotechnology, global finance, and corporate power.[34]

These IFG-sponsored events denouncing the myriad ills of neoliberalism employed a number of frame-aligning strategies. First, they appealed to the values of popular sovereignty, human rights, diversity, environmental steward-ship, and nonviolence. Second, they amplified beliefs about the seriousness of the problems facing all of humanity, the locus of causality, the efficacy of collec-tive transnational action, and the need for people to mobilize. Third, IFG members extended a number of popular frames, connecting one area of concern to another. In doing so, they helped thousands of activists and interested attendees to better connect the dots between complex issues, and to attribute interconnectedness and similarity among each other's struggles, leading to recip-rocal solidarity and collective action.

While they were not the sole or even the main cause for the WTO talks' grinding to a halt, the Seattle protests did have a discernible impact, both concrete and symbolic. First, in terms of their tangible effects, the mass marches, street blockades, and sit-ins *did* prevent some delegates from getting to their scheduled events and – perhaps more importantly – to each other's hotel rooms, where key agreements are hammered out before they are brought to the main body.[35] Second, the protestors in the streets, who were Americans joined by allies from around the world, seemed to embolden many Southern delegates to stand their ground in opposition to what they felt to be an undemocratic, pressure-filled, and biased process that has not delivered real benefits to their countries. COC's Barlow, for example, was told by the trade secretary from Papua New Guinea, "The people who demonstrated basically represent the world's silent majority."[36] This new fighting spirit has been sustained, as Public Citizen activists claim that at subsequent WTO negotiations, when the US tries to apply pressure to developing countries' ministers to accept a concession, they invoke the word "Seattle" as a defensive reminder that many Americans don't even want the agreement, so why should they?[37]

Third, Seattle was, in the words of writer-activist Naomi Klein, both a "coming out party for a global resistance movement" and a demonstration of the "globalization of hope."[38] It was therefore critical in (re)awakening the belief that together change is possible. Reflected one long-time UK activist, "Seattle was the point which showed that ordinary campaigners and trade unionists could get together. You look back now and Seattle was very small [compared to later mobilizations] but because there was so little before that, it's like even the smallest molehills are big when you're on a plain."[39] One of the reasons why Seattle did inspire such hope among activists the world over is very much related to its location and the nationality of many of the protestors. While massive street demonstrations against neoliberal institutions had already occurred in Asia and Europe – 75,000 protested the IMF and World Bank meeting in Berlin more than a decade earlier in 1988, and 130,000 marched in defiance of the Asia-Pacific Economic Cooperation (APEC) in Manila in 1996[40] – one organizer concluded:

> Seattle was a huge turning point, and not that there hadn't been work done before, … but to suddenly see that in the heart of where all of these policies were emanating from, that there was dissent *there*, I think lit a match, that the whole world just thought, "oh my God, if the *Americans* are doing it, we really have a shot at this, we've really got a chance!" … Suddenly the *Wall Street Journal* is writing about this, the *Washington Post*, the *New York Times*, and whether we like it or not in a world where the US essentially calls the shots, if the papers of the US are writing about it, then finally something exists as a political issue. So I feel like Seattle is really crucial in … opening up that connection between the North and the South. Seattle was what brought all of those struggles into people's living rooms and is what then allowed for the space to kind of continue building on that.[41]

IFG help launch third transnational network in Seattle: Our World Is Not For Sale

Finally, as touched upon by Klein and as the previous analysis has shown, Seattle was a crucial event in the emerging networks' shift in scale to include sustained, transnational coordination and campaigning on a number of issues. It represented a dramatic surfacing of the myriad, submerged connections that had been forged in the months and years prior to that watershed event. In addition to helping birth indymedia and the WTO week planning coalition, out of these processes also came the most ambitious and sustained transnational network fighting neoliberal trade agreements wherever they appear, that of OWINFS. For the network that grew up around the IFG, debuted in the anti-MAI struggle and then bore the creatively ambivalent moniker the Network Opposed to the WTO/People for Free Trade going into Seattle, emerged post-Seattle bigger, stronger, and with a clearer collective vision that allowed these activists to give themselves one name: "Our World Is Not For Sale: WTO – Shrink or Sink!" This was the title of its second international "sign-on" statement, and the name stuck.

Groups officially launched their sign-on campaigning network three months after Seattle at a protest press conference staged during the WTO-sponsored NGO Symposium in July 2001 in Geneva. There the OWINFS signatories denounced the symposium and its claims to open space to dialogue with "civil society" as a publicity stunt on the part of the tarnished international trade organ. They then laid out their eleven-point demands to significantly curtail the WTO's scope and to stop any new trade round until developing countries' existing grievances were met.[42] These provide a broad and concrete foundation upon which all of their campaigning is organized.

OWINFS's broad claims against the WTO target

This platform consensus statement calls for no more WTO expansion, the protection of basic social rights and services and environmental sustainability, and limits on corporate patenting of seeds and medicine so as to safeguard communities' collective rights and health. It furthermore expresses opposition to patenting of life forms, to the Agreement of Agriculture so as to instead promote food as a basic human right, and to the WTO Trade Related Investment Measures (TRIMs) agreement. The platform also calls for halting investment liberalization, promoting "fair trade" through recognizing and expanding special and differential rights for Southern countries, prioritizing social rights and the environment, and democratizing decision-making in trade negotiations. Finally, it demands a replacement of the WTO dispute settlement system with procedures it deems more democratic and just, emphasizing workers' and producers' rights and local and national sovereignty, a prerequisite of which is the complete annulment of poor-country debt so as to reallocate funds to poverty eradication and development initiatives. They frame their arguments throughout in terms of working toward a more sustainable, just, and democratic system.

The network's website reinforces scale shift mechanisms

Beyond occasional press conferences at large activist meetings, the public face and entry point for this post-Seattle network is its website, ourworldisnotforsale.org. Maintained by volunteers from participating organizations, this "network of networks" acts as a virtual hub for local and national groups to share information and develop coordinated actions toward the goal, in its own words, "of reshaping the corporate-dominated trade agenda to support human rights, environmental sustainability and democratic principles."[43] The website contains position statements, news updates, analysis of globalization issues, event announcements, links to participating organizations, and information on how to become involved in their campaigns. Network participants also reach decisions about joint action through a consensus process that takes place in a "members-only" space on the website, in addition to conference calls and international meetings.

The OWINFS website therefore plays a powerful role in both non-relational and relational diffusion of information. It encourages the attribution and the maintenance of interconnectedness or similarity among geographically dispersed and differently focused organizations through its frame-extending analyses of globalization issues, and thus reinforces identity and reciprocal solidarity among its diverse membership. It further plays a non-relational diffusion and brokerage role by familiarizing new visitors to the site with popular movements, campaigns, and NGOs, and helping to steer them toward getting involved by providing contact information. Finally, by letting members post their own stories of struggle, it encourages emulation of tactics and actions among groups.

Transnational collective action: campaigns target WTO and a whole lot more

With regard to campaigning, as stated above, the network's coordinated action is centered around its eleven-point consensus statement. Thus, OWINFS campaigns address a wide range of issues, objects, and claims, namely agriculture, Cancun, GATS, investment, TRIPs, WTO, regional trade (specifically the FTAA, APEC, AGOA, and PPP), as well as war and terrorism. Organizations with experience in one of these areas tend to take the lead in devising and coordinating a specific campaign, often centered around an upcoming trade meeting, which can then be voluntarily joined by other network members.

These campaigns often entail, first, capacity building and outreach in areas which are threatened by bilateral or regional trade agreements; second, coordinated lobbying of national governments to strengthen domestic laws and to diminish the scope of WTO rules; third, sending delegates to advise and lobby WTO negotiators in Geneva; fourth, organizing press conferences and other smaller actions to pressure governments; fifth, developing position statements that other NGOs may endorse, such as the ones leading up to and coming out of Seattle; and, sixth, mobilizing by first disseminating calls for action and then organizing mass protest events at international trade meetings.

An example of a member organization devising a campaign that is then joined by others from the network is Friends of the Earth International (FOEI) spearheading a global "Bite Back: WTO Hands off Our Food" initiative. This is also illustrative of the tremendous solidarity among diverse networks today, in that FOEI is the largest network in the world defending the environment from the harm caused in part by neoliberal policies today, and is also an active member in OWINFS. Further evidence of this solidarity can be found in the diversity of OWINFS members signing on to FOEI's Bite Back campaign, which include ActionAid Alliance, Public Citizen, Public Services International, the International Gender and Trade Network, Confédération Paysanne, and the Research Foundation for Science, Technology, and Ecology. These organizations have joined FOEI in circulating a global petition which argues that "the WTO should not undermine the sovereign right of any country to protect its citizens and the environment from Genetically Modified (GM) foods and crops." The petition gathered about 100,000 signatures from ninety countries and over 500 organizations representing nearly 50 million people. It was recently hand-delivered to the WTO headquarters by OWINFS members, who creatively designated the building a "bio-hazard" area in order to make their point.[44]

IFG's role within OWINFS of diffusion and frame extension toward a global interpretive frame

Throughout, the IFG can be considered the brain trust of OWINFS. It continues to play a crucial, non-relational diffusion role as a major publisher of critical analysis on neoliberal globalization as well as alternatives to the prevailing paradigm and policies. This collective of public scholars has debated, reached consensus, and then disseminated a common analysis of both the problems of neoliberalism and potential alternatives, which is largely consistent with OWINFS's platform. Viewed from the perspective of their framing strategies, these common texts work to extend frames from one issue into another, in order to offer a consensus, transformative frame of alternatives to neoliberalism which are "more localized, democratic, and ecologically viable economic forms."[45] This emergent, transformative frame is both domain specific as well as global interpretive. Regarding the former, the IFG has developed and published alternative policies on food and agriculture, the environment, water, technology, and indigenous peoples. Nonetheless, these domain-specific alternatives taken together add up to a novel, global interpretive frame.

IFG scholars have published and then organized popular debates around this transformative frame, which is delineated in their *Alternatives to Economic Globalization: A Better World Is Possible.*[46] This work, translated into a number of languages, was the result of a three-year consensus process of ten IFG members. Moving from non-relational to relational diffusion and interaction, IFG members have organized local book readings and panels at global meetings such as the WSF in order to discuss and share this global transformative frame. The publication has also become the basis upon which to organize meetings in every region of the globe to advance dialogue, gain feedback, attempt to adapt local initiatives from the report, revise and expand their analysis, and work toward a global consensus on transformative alternatives to neoliberalism. The first of these seminars was held in Santiago in April 2004, bringing together leaders of popular movements, government officials, scholars, NGO representatives, and community members to dialogue. The IFG furthermore held a panel and launch of their book's second edition at the WSF in Porto Alegre in January 2005. For those who cannot participate in person in these popular consultations, the IFG provides on its website the possibility for groups or individuals to contact the forum with their comments, as well as to obtain information on how to participate in implementing these alternatives in their local area.[47]

The ongoing strategic game of cat and mouse between OWINFS and free trade promoters

This network has shown tremendous dexterity in what is clearly a complex, obtuse, and rapidly changing terrain of the emergent neoliberal trade regime as it seeks to spread and establish itself. In the few short years since Seattle these actors have demonstrated a dogged ability to, first, find out what governments are hatching to try to push this "free" trade agenda forward; second, to diffuse this information through the network in order to deepen awareness; third, to discuss and arrive at a consensus analysis; fourth, to expand their targets and broker relations so as to strengthen the network where it is needed to confront those new targets; fifth, to adjust or develop new campaigns accordingly; and, finally, to strengthen the coordination among these campaigns. If the free trade agreement can be compared to a cat, then the OWINFS network has become a crazed yet crafty swarm of mice giving reverse chase in this game. Below we will briefly track this post-Seattle tit for tat.

Post-Seattle and post-September 11: a "Fortress WTO" meets in Doha

After the battle in Seattle, the WTO promoters decided to hold their next minis-terial in a more "hospitable" environment in fall 2001: the kingdom of Qatar. OWINFS responded creatively to this challenge of confronting the WTO in a country where protest action is severely restricted. Focus, the IFG, COC, Public Citizen, FOIE, the Via Campesina, the World Forum on Fisherpeoples, and the Arab NGO Network for Development developed a three-pronged strategy, which included: first, local and national educational events targeting the public and policymakers to be held simultaneously with the meetings; second, a parallel summit on neoliberal globalization and the WTO planned in Beirut in order to provide a brokerage space for local and regional activist organizations to come together and strengthen regional and global ties; and, third, two protest *flotillas*, one coming from Mumbai and another from Jordan, of several hundred activists to descend on Doha by sea. In the wake of the September 11 attacks and even stricter security measures at the Qatar meetings and around the Middle East, OWINFS members held an emergency meeting in early December in Brussels to analyze the current environment for activism and to take steps to ensure that their coalitions formed to resist trade agreements would not be lost. Vowing that the mobilization would continue, they nevertheless decided they had to scale down their upcoming efforts. The Beirut parallel summit and the *flotilla* were cancelled, while the educational mobilizations took place as planned, as did protests in more than sixty countries around the world.[48]

The Cancun mobilization

By the following year, the anti-WTO forces were again ready to confront the WTO with massive action on the ground. In the run-up to the fifth ministerial, to be held in Cancun in mid-September 2003, network members organized seminars and held preparatory meetings at the WSF, where they were able to build a large coalition that yielded a considerable international turn-out.[49] In Cancun, OWINFS joined up with Mexican popular movements in calling for a Worldwide Day of Action Against Corporate Globalization and War on September 13. Network members urged groups and individuals to plan solidarity events on that day. They also helped bring thousands of protestors to the week's meetings in southern Mexico. In this campaign, as in their others, OWINFS strove to frame opposition to the WTO as one of a "basket" of broad-ranging issues, and thus encourage attribution of interconnectedness among diverse groups leading to reciprocal solidarity and coordinated action. Their frame extension efforts are evident in the network's call to action: "These September actions to derail the WTO will kick off a powerful autumn campaign of action for peace and justice, involving major mobilizations for immigrant rights, against the Free Trade Area of the Americas, and against militarism and occupation."[50]

Wealthy countries change course again in the wake of Cancun

The angry protests in the streets mirrored the mounting frustration within the talks themselves. Ultimately the G20, led by Brazil, India, and China, held their ground and the meetings stalled without an agreement.[51] With two of the last three meetings breaking down, the WTO looked to be especially vulnerable. Activists cheered, while in Cancun's wake wealthy countries changed their strategy, on the one hand, to more aggressively pursuing regional and bilateral trade agreements and, on the other, to attempting to break the unity of the G20. In this environment, forging regional agreements became more important on the US and EU agendas, though these have also been foundering for similar reasons to the WTO breakdown.

At the same time, the pressure tactics to break the G20 met with only limited success: Tanzania and Zimbabwe joined the group, while Thailand and the Philippines held up and stayed the course. But ultimately what pushed the EU and US to tack in a different direction was Brazil and India failing to crumble under what has been described as a kind of good-cop, bad-cop routine, with each assuming their usual roles. One Asian trade representative put it wryly: "The EU might be digging your grave but will be smiling at you. The US will dig the grave, but with a grave face."[52] Rich countries have recently turned from this routine to one of bribes and sweet-talk, in the form of creating the so-called Five Interested Parties (FIPs). The FIPs resulted from an effort to revive the current trade round at a mini-ministerial meeting on 14 May 2004 during the OECD meetings in Paris, in which the US, EU, and Australia invited Brazil and India, among others, to give their input into the WTO framework on agriculture.[53] This has proved to be a more successful approach: A few weeks later, behind closed doors in Geneva at the WTO General Council meeting in July, this small group agreed to restart the negotiations.

OWINFS reassesses shifting terrain and develops multi-pronged strategy

Through all this the OWINFS mice-army have been running to keep atop this shape-shifting neoliberal trade regime. In spaces of transnational meetings like the WSFs and regional social forums, as well as in the transnational meetings the network holds independently, existing members have brokered new relations among various levels of actors in order to deepen and broaden the network and help to make these various campaigns aware of each other. In these shared spaces they have also been debating toward developing a common critique. Through these efforts, they have been able to establish a loose coordination framework among the various campaigns and participants in the network at all levels.

With regard to the first point, through their discussions toward deciphering the US and European change in strategy since Cancun, network members have recognized that both the regional and global trade agreements operate from the same agenda. The Transnational Institute's Brid Brennan noted:

> In the meetings organized [at the WSF], there was a lot of interaction and a kind of a coming together of various [strands, and] a kind of convergence on strategy, that it's not a case of only paying attention to WTO and not paying attention to regional trade agreements and vice versa.[54]

Second, through these face-to-face encounters, OWINFS activists have developed a consensus critique decrying both the Five Interested Parties negotiations and the broader decision-making powers assumed by the WTO Geneva General Council. They view the FIPs as a clearly divisive effort to resurrect the WTO while lopping off the leadership of the G20. In a similar vein, the so-called July agreement of the WTO General Council is seen as a manipulation of WTO procedures, which resumed the Doha agenda behind closed doors at headquarters rather than having these issues properly discussed at the upcoming ministerial in Hong Kong. "There's a strong feeling," observes Brennan, "that through this mechanism at the general council, especially the Northern powers within the WTO are getting the WTO up and running again and in a way sidestepping more open processes of discussion and debate."[55]

The OWINFS has therefore agreed to a multi-pronged strategy, decentralized in its development and execution but with loose coordination among actors and campaigns at these intermittent meetings. It is based, first, upon strengthening national campaigns to keep countries united in the G20 and especially to put pressure on India and Brazil to withdraw from the FIPs, in addition to supporting national-level groups to fight bilateral and regional trade deals wherever they crop up. A second strand of the strategy is to continue lobbying in Geneva, but also to monitor more closely the WTO General Council, and toward that end to forge stronger alliances with local activists there. Third, OWINFS activists are gearing up for the next ministerial meeting in Hong Kong in December 2005 by building a broad-based national coalition with ties to both region-wide mobilization and global support. Fourth, the network continues to strengthen North–South exchanges, mutual learning, and alliances, toward reconstructing solidarity based on both identity and reciprocity. Each will be briefly examined below.

Strengthening and coordinating among national campaigns

Strengthening national campaigns has become a primary aim of the network. Network members are especially focusing on capacity building and brokering ties in regions threatened by bilateral or regional trade agreements. This is a task they deem even more complex than coordinating the fight against the WTO, but one that is equally necessary in today's decentralizing environment.[56] Network members realized that national campaigns are the most well placed to monitor the changes in policy as well as to pressure governments, and therefore information dissemination and coordination among them is crucial.[57] Via Campesina members in India and Brazil, for example, were the first to inform the OWINFS network of its governments' "caving in" to the FIPs and thus the revival of the WTO trade round talks. One of the most immediate and important goals for the network as a whole has therefore become persuading these two nations to pull out of the FIPs negotiations and refocus their energies on building a united front within the G20, and, beyond that, among the middle-range developing countries' Group of Thirty-three (G33) and the larger Group of Ninety (G90), which includes the least developed countries. So while this is the most urgent priority of the network overall, this challenge falls mainly to the Indian and Brazilian social movements, who have the most leverage in pressuring their trade negotiators to, in the words of one campaigner, "put weight on their negotiators to back off this trap."[58]

Indians did just that at the March 2005 meeting in New Delhi of the G20. While the latter reiterated their demands of rich nations to eliminate all export subsidies in agriculture within five years' time, around fifty farmers' organizations, social movements, and NGOs from across India held a parallel meeting where they proposed their own "People's Agenda" to the G20 representatives.[59] This they symbolically delivered to the prime minister's office. To reinforce their collective position, some 30,000 farmers rallied and marched on the parliament building, calling for agriculture to be taken out of the WTO. They therefore pushed their own government to go further in its demands *vis-à-vis* the WTO and to represent not only its national elites' economic interests but rather those of small peasants across the South in confrontation with agribusinesses of the North, and thus preserve the right of national food sovereignty for all peoples.[60]

Another example of national campaigns mobilizing to defeat trade agreements in ways they deem most appropriate for their targeted audience can be seen in the US-based lobby against the CAFTA. The Washington, DC-based Interfaith Working Group on Trade and Investment is comprised of some three dozen religious institutions, some of the most active being Church World Service, National Council of Churches USA, United Methodist Church, Lutheran World Relief, Presbyterian Church (USA Washington Office), United Church of Christ, American Friends Service Committee, Mennonite Central Committee, Maryknoll Office of Global Concerns, and the Columban Office. Framing their argument in terms of justice, Christian charity, and defense of human rights and the environment, their appeal states, "It is abundantly clear that the passage of CAFTA will not advance human rights, contribute to sustainable development or the reduction of poverty in Central America. Rather, CAFTA will increase discrimination against those who are economically poor and vulnerable."[61] Here we see activists' making the connection between structural poverty and terms of trade, and thus one of the many examples of spillover between the Jubilee anti-debt networks and the efforts to reform or defeat multilateral trade agreements.

Lobbying, monitoring, and brokering ties in Geneva

A second prong of the OWINFS's strategy centers on the WTO headquarters in Geneva. For a number of years, network members have developed lobbying strategies to target individual government delegations. But with the July agreement at the General Council, which OWINFS members viewed as unfairly concentrating decision-making power, they realized they must also keep a watchful eye on Council activities themselves. Toward these ends, the network has recently decided to step up efforts to broker greater local ties with activist groups in the city of Geneva. This is a first step toward coordinating more effective mass actions on the ground there, and thus to tap into those resources that already exist in order to maintain oversight and popular pressure.[62]

Gearing up for the Hong Kong WTO ministerial

A third objective has been preparing for and launching a broad-based mobilization around the December 2005 WTO meeting in Hong Kong. Here OWINFS members were seeking to replicate the successful combined strategy at Cancun, which was strong local participation coupled with significant mobilization internationally and good coordination between the two. With this "inside and outside strategy," they aimed once again to derail the ministerial.[63] The network held two major international coordination meetings in 2005 around Hong Kong, one at the WSF in Porto Alegre and a second in the Asian city itself. Both sought to develop their two-level strategy by, first, strengthening the Hong Kong coordinating committee; second, building region-wide ties; and, third, reinforcing their relations with transnational actors planning simultaneous mobilizations. Regarding the first point, in late February the Hong Kong-based People's Alliance Against the WTO (HKPA) hosted in Kowloon some 250 people from twenty-three countries and more than 110 organizations, including trade unions, peasant groups, migrants, and environmentalists. The meetings began with a general overview and debate within working groups divided by sectors, and was then followed by strategy meetings for the upcoming mobilizations. They also created transnational working groups on the program, outreach, media, actions and mobilization, and finance and documentation, and were able to reach consensus on their action plan.

In their discussions, important parallels were drawn among regions on the "race to the bottom" they see as occurring all over the world, first from North to South and now, increasingly, from South to *further* South, so to speak. Au Loong from the host organization commented that the corporate logic today reasons:

"In manufacturing, why go to Southeast Asia and not China? In South Korea and Taiwan wages are higher and they have trade unions." Another remarked: "There is an expanding process of takeover of production in the South by corporations of the North – but workers in the North also suffer due to the unfair competition and because most subsidies go to corporations, not them."[64] Parallels such as these help to frame the source of harm and thus the target of claims as the same among those present, regardless of where in the world one is struggling. These efforts also promote and reinforce attribution of similarity and thus identity-based solidarity among diverse workers.

Regarding the second point noted above of strengthening regional ties in the lead-up to Hong Kong, Focus on the Global South has recently begun to move beyond its primary role of generating and diffusing analysis and information by attempting to broker alliances toward mass mobilization against regional trade agreements in Asia, and thus to emulate the popular efforts against the FTAA in Latin America. The Hong Kong WTO thus provided a good opportunity for Focus to begin such efforts.[65] Finally, regarding strengthening global ties for the upcoming ministerial, we see evidence of considerable cross-over in recent meetings held in Asia and in South America. Numerous activists from Europe and the Americas attended the Hong Kong planning meeting, just as members of the Hong Kong coordinating committee went to Porto Alegre to participate in strategy and networking meetings of OWINFS at the 2005 WSF.[66]

South–North information exchange and solidarity building

Fourth and finally, the OWINFS network members continue to strengthen their ties between South and North, through face-to-face meetings at the WSFs and elsewhere, wherein mutual learning takes place. This in turn helps deepen their understanding and analysis as to the sources of shared threat or suffering, from which more effective national and regional campaigns can be crafted which support one another's causes. The overall effect is attribution of similarity and/ or interconnectedness of struggles, toward what some activists believe to be a necessary rethinking and reconstructing of solidarity based upon shared identity or reciprocity at the interregional level:

> We see the WSF process as a major impulse to rethinking everything, but in particular … we feel that especially North–South solidarity has to be rethought and reinvented and has to keep pace also in a sense with the globalized reality. … The point is that we really need to go beyond them and reinvent them in line with real changes in strategies, paradigms, trends.[67]

A good example of these mechanisms which help strengthen bi-regional solidarity toward collective action is in the relationship among Latin American and European members of OWINFS. In meetings planned within the social forums as well as in their own encounters, such as one held in May 2004 in Guadalajara sponsored by Latin American movements with some assistance from Europeans, the themes of trade liberalization and the role of European TNCs in Latin America were very strongly brought to the attention of European activists. In Guadalajara they organized panels divided by Latin American region addressing the role of the EU and European corporations in each. The encounters are true occasions to listen and learn for many Europeans present. One commented, "This was really just amazing, the commonality of analysis, experience, pinpointing common European TNCs. All of this [critique] now is much more advanced in Latin America than it is in Europe. ... I think there's still a very fragmented notion of Europe's role in the South, [from] the Europe side."[68]

This new understanding gained from these sorts of encounters in turn shapes the work of European-wide networks themselves, such as the Seattle to Brussels network. The latter, which participates in OWINFS, has recently developed its own strategy to stay abreast of EU negotiations. This includes pressuring the trade commissioners and ongoing coordination with activists doing the same in Geneva. It also monitors regional trade agreements such as the EU–Mercosur negotiations, which have been reopened, in addition to the economic partnership agreements with Africa and the Caribbean.[69]

Europeans also came away from these encounters with the idea of bringing that more holistic analysis back to Europe to challenge activists there. They therefore organized similar panels at the ESF the following autumn. From those panels and discussions came the decision to form a bi-regional network, called the Europe–Latin America Network, focused specifically on fighting the regional trade agreements and launching coordinated campaigns. This joint effort is motivated by a vision of "not anymore just Europeans on their own thinking about what can we do to respond to Latin America. ... We're challenged by Latin Americans about what can we do *about Europe*."[70] In this they have strengthened their ties with the Latin American Hemispheric Social Alliance and with a number of others in the region to continue to gain a more comprehensive understanding of their own governments' and corporations' actions in Latin America, with which they can then better address the question of Europe in Latin America today.

The picture that is emerging for Europeans is not one that many would readily accept, but relates to what Brennan has called for: namely the need to rethink and reconstruct solidarity in light of the current global reality. For the composite image of Europe in the Americas today is a far different one than that based on the popular North–South solidarity of the 1980s. At that time, even most European governments could have been perceived as allies in the struggles against dictatorship and for a restoration of democracy, especially given the framework of bilateral cooperation aid aimed at strengthening these nascent democracies which followed. The debate in Europe therefore has largely remained stuck within the realm of tinkering with cooperation policy and aid on the part of development agencies and organizations. Members of the OWINFS network, however, through their candid discussions with their Southern partners are coming to the realization that

There's a whole other kind of policy regime working and being accelerated and being driven by corporations, and so we really need to catch up with that. … Today the role of Europe in relation to the South has changed drastically. A free trade agenda is being aggressively pursued and this is also changing very much the basis on which we would continue to develop solidarity.[71]

So while there still seems to be a place for individual-, organizational-, and even national-level solidarity, a number of European activists are realizing that there needs to be a shift up from these levels to a solidarity that is *bi-regional*, in the sense that they must listen to and work much more closely with partners in Latin America in order to determine the priorities of solidarity in a globalizing world.[72] This shift to the macro-regional level also reflects the reality of Europe as a growing bloc overshadowing the state in the realm of foreign economic and political policy, as well as a similar, though more uneven and nascent, process being forged by both state and non-state actors in South America.

This new "movement-based, people-driven" solidarity seems genuinely reciprocal in that many Europeans in the OWINFS network feel strongly that through the experiences of learning and then providing solidarity to Latin Americans to fight EU trade policy, Europeans also become more informed and thus effective in their own struggles against *this* Europe that they feel is being foisted upon them. The recent EU Bolkenstein directive on public services, for example, was more than reminiscent of the WTO and regional trade agreements that Latin Americans are fighting. Public opinion was mobilized against it, and OWINFS activists in Europe were able to draw the connections between the two policies. The same can be said for the popular campaign for the *Non* vote in France in 2005, which defeated the EU constitution in a referendum and was widely perceived among European activists as a win for their side. These sorts of experiences in Europe help also to sensitize the population to what is happening under the trade agreements in the Global South. It becomes the European activists' task, then, to frame-bridge between the two regions, in the attempt to build widespread attribution of interconnectedness among Europeans and Latin Americans, toward reciprocal solidarity.[73]

Analysis based on conceptual continua

Let us now draw out more precisely the composition and the character of this network, through the analytical lens of our six conceptual continua of proximity to the problem, affective response, solidarity, network model, operational paradigm, and claims. OWINFS is in itself a vast network of networks, comprised of myriad groups from across the world with different organizational structures and emphases. The two illustrative examples in this chapter, those of Focus and the COC, bear witness to some of this diversity comprising OWINFS, while others mentioned throughout – the Via Campesina, the Hemispheric Social Alliance, and the Hong Kong-based People's Alliance Against the WTO, to name a few –

clearly demonstrate its broadly and deeply webbed nature. In comparing the scale shift process of Focus and COC, we can discern that their core members became active based on a personal experience of problems they wished to address, and similarly a sense of suffering or threat to their country, in the case of the COC, and to their region, in that of Focus. Solidarity within these organizations therefore began largely by identifying with others sharing a similar fate as oneself: For the COC it was the Canadian identity threatened by the changes brought on through opening to the US via the NAFTA; while for Focus's members it was a shared fate among Asians – and people from Southern countries more abstractly – of suffering under the emerging so-called development policies, which in practice tightened World Bank and foreign TNC control over poor countries' economies and reinforced the US's neocolonialist aspirations for political and military dominance of the globe.

Both of these earlier network models were hybrids between first-generation NGO advocacy and second-generation direct activism social justice. Each began with a first-generation structure and formation, centered around lead individuals or organizations who brokered a strategic coalition among likeminded activists. The COC bore the additional NGO advocacy traits of tight issue and goal framing in order to create a strong organizational identity, which eventually had to be loosened as they brokered wider ties with Quebecois and then others around North America to fight the NAFTA. On the issues of claims and paradigms, the COC also started out within a limited scope of policy change, targeting domestic politicians with clear reform goals and demands.

But as the Council matured and was confronted with the expanding of the US–Canadian agreement to the NAFTA, it began to adopt features of a direct activism social justice network: Instead of a one-time strategic campaign, Council members realized that this would be an ongoing battle with a continuous protest calendar. They furthermore expanded their membership through a popular consultation to set their agenda. In the process, they transformed themselves into a mass protest organization, brokering ties and diffusing information across diverse networks, and increasingly utilizing internet technology for these purposes. The position that the COC eventually evolved into *vis-à-vis* a broadening scope of claims is where Focus on the Global South began: The latter has from its inception attempted to broker wide ties across diverse networks to promote its broad social justice agenda. Furthermore, reflecting a paradigm of global structural transformation, Focus actively brokered relations with diverse social justice groups, calling for – though never embodying – mass mobilization across a wide spectrum of issues and domains, and targeting a diversity of actors and institutions of neoliberal rule.

This evolution away from a strictly NGO advocacy model and toward a hybrid, embodying key features of direct activism social justice, becomes more apparent at higher levels of coordination against the trade agreements. While the IFG is structured as a collective of leading intellectuals representing mostly NGOs and think-tanks from around the globe, it is *not* a representative body that takes binding decisions on behalf of these groups. Further, the IFG has articulated a paradigm that places global structural transformation in all sectors where neoliberal rule has gained a foothold at the center of its discussions and coordinated efforts. Although the first campaign launched by this group, to defeat the MAI and prevent its resurfacing in the Seattle WTO, was perhaps by necessity circumscribed, reformist, crisis intervention, as the network has matured into the OWINFS its capacity and aspirations have greatly increased. It has broadened its timelines so that its campaigns and paradigms are able to become less reactive and reformist.

Here it is useful to recall the experience of one of IFG's senior scholars, Khor, that although he is often forced by circumstances to work within the reformist paradigm of making globalization less painful, his vision and allegiance belong to the transformational paradigm. He therefore advises that campaigners work to infuse the latter into the former in a kind of transitional, evolutionary strategy. Beginning with the anti-MAI and WTO Seattle actions, these were so many fires that volunteers scurried desperately to put out. These treaties were accurately perceived as dangerous externalities requiring an immediate response from a nascent collective; in that sense, then, they *were* crisis intervention, out of sheer necessity.

Yet even in their most reactive mode, they have displayed glimmers of potential capacity that stretches beyond reaction, crisis intervention, and reform advocacy. Even in these earliest transnational efforts we can see features of direct activism social justice. The anti-MAI effort, for example, was widely heralded as a "new species" of campaign that successfully utilized technological infrastructure to expand its network and actions while shifting facilely among different levels, targets, and sites. The same can be said for the Seattle coalition, not to mention the indymedia movement that network participants helped to create and which is the very embodiment of the second-generation model. But while IFG members have played key initial brokerage roles in anti-free trade networks, these networks quickly became polycentric and distributed among self-organized, smaller groups and campaigns formed based on affinity ties. The development of these efforts further demonstrates how communication among the smallest units of the network has been greatly enhanced thanks to the internet, turning this web of ties into "hyper-organizations." Given the diffuseness of this network built upon interconnections among smaller, affinity-based collectives, its stability did not – and indeed probably could not – depend upon constructing a strong organizational identity. Unlike the efforts we saw with the Jubilee 2000 campaign in Chapter 3, these forerunning campaigns to OWINFS developed an organizational code of inclusive diversity, creating a dense network of weaker ties which helped ease fracture lines and cooperation. This fact was thrown into sharp relief with the high-tech compromise of the bifurcated Seattle network which nonetheless shared scarce resources.

Furthermore, membership was less about "signing up and paying up" and much more about opting in and showing up to the mass demonstrations, first in Seattle and since then at numerous high-profile protests around the globe. And although both the anti-MAI and the Seattle coalitions could be considered strategic campaigns, they soon were viewed by those involved as just two coordination points along a proliferating, permanent, and multi-pronged path of struggle against free trade agreements at all levels. Hence, no group in particular has been able to "switch off" this mass movement. Also, as the core activists grew more adept at framing their collective message, bridging has become less difficult – or costly, as they say – across diverse networks and issues. As they have broadened their claims and expanded their paradigm, they have also enlarged their targets from the OECD governments to include all governments participating in the trade negotiations, as well as the international trading organization itself and regional entities like it. Corporations and the Bretton Woods institutions have also been cited as accomplices, as has the US military as the tool of American global domination.

Seattle, then, was a crucial turning point from first-generation to second-generation networks in many ways, not least as the site of the rebirth of mass protest, especially in the US, and of personal involvement in direct action as a goal in itself. This trend toward becoming a direct activism social justice network was nearly completed with the emergence of OWINFS post-Seattle. While initially formed as a hybrid model, in that conscious efforts were made to broker strategic coalitions and provide support for groups fighting trade agreements wherever they spring up, since then it has shifted toward a more polycentric, distributed structure, best captured by the phrase a "network of networks." As with its preceding collective efforts, those taking the lead on specific OWINFS campaigns come together based on affinity ties, experience, and rootedness in a particular region. The network's multi-level, multi-pronged approach signifies a clear understanding among those involved that their struggle is an ongoing, and perhaps permanent, one against a labyrinthine trade regime, and therefore their targets must also be flexible, ranging from numerous governmental ministries to the trade bodies themselves. The organizational ethos is inclusive and inviting of diversity, and is therefore a dense network of ties, some of which are rather weak, while others are quite strong. The multiple campaigns running simultaneously mean that groups and individuals opt in or out as they can or wish to. Furthermore, membership itself is open, comprised of diverse social justice actors, and oriented toward a hybrid of mass activism complemented by targeted, elite lobbying. Decision-making and agenda-setting are based on consultations and consensus via the web, as well as face-to-face meetings, and therefore the campaigns are difficult to switch off. Given the use of the internet and the decentralized network structure, brokerage costs are relatively low.

With regard to the network's operational paradigm, the sum total of its frame extension among diverse actors plus the proliferation of campaigning issues amounts to a domain-specific paradigm of structural transformation of the neoliberal trade agenda. In its stead it proposes trade rules that would prioritize human rights, environmental sustainability, and democratic principles. Yet the fact that this network is also comprised of groups and networks whose primary focus is *not* trade but rather lies in other related domains – for example the environment, the peasantry, debt, and women's rights – is evidence that those involved are cognizant of how this particular facet of neoliberal globalization interlinks with others. It further signifies a deeper understanding that the one must be transformed alongside the others. Therefore, consistent with Chapter 3's Jubilee South, while OWINFS takes aim at a particular domain, it does so with a clear recognition that trade justice is only one piece of a multi-pronged, mass-based strategy for global transformation. In this regard, its paradigm could be seen as a transitional one in support of a larger transformational agenda.

Finally, reflecting on network solidarity, we can see that, first, building solidarity among such diverse groups becomes more difficult and labor intensive the further the network is expanded. Difficulties arise with distance. As the proximity to the problems faced by others – and thus one's affective response to those threats – becomes more remote, the solidarity evoked tends to be more abstract. Stimulating and maintaining solidarity then grows more costly in that greater efforts must go into drawing parallels between groups and their struggles in order to arrive at attribution of, if not similarity, then at least interconnectedness, and thus produce a solidarity based upon either identity or at least reciprocity.

Yet these challenges are being overcome to a considerable degree, mainly along two parallel and largely complementary tracks. First, identity-based solidarity is being fostered among formerly unconnected groups who are struggling against a similar threat or harm. When brought into contact with others suffering from the same sorts of problems, it is not difficult to attribute similarity to the other, no matter how geographically or culturally distant they are. These activists recognize that, despite their differences, they share a similar fate, and thus identity-based solidarity at the transnational level emerges.

A second track to overcoming these challenges lies in reciprocal solidarity. As the networks grow more complex and opportunities for dialogue, exchange of information, and dynamic frame extension become more abundant for activists at the national, macro-regional, and transnational level, more and more individuals and groups are attributing a connection between their own problems and those of others. They are empathizing with the others' suffering, and giving and receiving reciprocal solidarity as a result. OWINFS is comprised of these two types of solidarity, which bind the network together in interconnected circles of identity and reciprocity.

Involvement with the WSF: strengthening the network and reinforcing the shift to the transnational level

We can now analyze this network's involvement with the WSF, beginning with the ways in which OWINFS has been strengthened and its scale shift to the transnational level reinforced. As was discussed above, network members have utilized the world and regional social forums to hold transnational meetings that have served a number of purposes. First, these are spaces in which to bring formerly unconnected actors together, thus brokering relations among new allies. They further serve as opportunities to share (i.e. diffuse) information and to discuss openly toward reaching deeper understanding. And in the process relationships are established or strengthened between Southern and Northern activists and, as Brennan has pointed out, transnational solidarity is "rethought and reinvented," based upon shared identity and/or reciprocity. All of this relational groundwork in the spaces of the forums is a prelude to what comes next: developing a common critique, concrete campaigns, and a coordination framework among network participants at all levels. Finally, meetings have therefore been crucial in building capacity both for national campaigns – which have recently become a priority to OWINFS – as well as for transnational coordinated action – as we saw, for example, with the Hong Kong Coordinating Committee attending meetings at the 2005 WSF in Porto Alegre.[74] All of these features work to both deepen and broaden the network in its fight against the proliferating trade agreements.

The forum as a space for encounter and building toward one global network

Let us turn now to the second theme, that of the social forum as a place for encountering others beyond one's group, network, and issue area, which in turn helps foster rejuvenation, learning, cooperative action, solidarity, and construction of a "network of networks." We find evidence of this in three kinds of activities: in building broad mobilizations around major trade meetings, in members' participation in the WSF IC, and in consultations over the IFG's evolving document *Alternatives to Economic Globalization*. With regard to building broad-based mobilizations, in the run-up to Cancun OWINFS members organized some six different seminars at the WSF in addition to holding a press conference to raise awareness of their campaign.[75] Likewise, in preparation for the APEC meetings in Korea as well as the Hong Kong ministerial in 2005, KOPA initiated a call for an "Asian Peoples' and Social Movements Assembly Against War and Neoliberal Globalization" at the fifth WSF. Endorsed by Focus on the Global South, in addition to a number of trade unions, peasants groups, women's organizations, and peace and justice groups from around the region, the assembly sought not only to mobilize for the upcoming events. It further aimed to unite and coordinate Asian-wide struggles and strengthen regional solidarity so as to then be able to contribute to the broader transnational resistance against neoliberalism and war. The assembly stated:

> We, the Asian people, have fought long and hard against neoliberal global-ization and war, against military threat, discrimination and oppression. However, we must now strive further ahead. With evidences of neoliberal economic integration and imperialist threat looming ahead of us, and also with the APEC Ministerial (Korea) and the WTO Ministerial (Hong Kong) scheduled to be held in Asia, Asian movements must, more now than ever, strengthen our voice and stand in the forefront.[76]

Next, just as KOPA, joined by Focus and others, initiated at the Asia-wide level, OWINFS members have been attempting to build consensus among the larger "network of networks" transnationally within the WSF. This is seen, first, in the significant participation of OWINFS organizations in the WSF IC and, second, in the book launch and consultation process at the forums on the IFG's *Alternatives to Economic Globalization*. As witnessed with the Jubilee network actors previously, participation in the WSF council embodies various forms of transnational collective action: OWINFS members come together with a group of several dozen activists in order to institutionalize and diffuse the WSF as a permanent global process and a space for dialogue, debate, solidarity promotion, and coordinating action. And again, the IC is a microcosm – though not a representative one – of the larger WSF event itself, in that these meetings have become a space for encounter and discussion which often leads to greater solidarity and coordinated action among networks that are present there. This is especially true in the case of OWINFS, since its members are heavily represented: the IFG, Focus, the COC, Public Citizen, and TWN are all members of this coordinating body.

A second way that network members attempt to build consensus among the larger network of networks transnationally is through their holding open discussions of the IFG's alternative proposal for neoliberal globalization. Their consensus document, which forms the basis of the OWINFS network's global transformative vision, calls for a re-embedding of the economy back into societies which are to be decentralized, environmentally sustainable, and democratic in nature. At these public discussions, network members promote dialogue, gather feedback, and hear stories on local alternatives in action, with which they have then revised and expanded their analysis. IFG has recently published an amended edition that it presents to others as a tentative, global consensus on transformative alternatives to neoliberalism.

A terrain of competition over the nature of the forum and future global network

We can now examine how the forum is a space of not only cooperation, as just demonstrated, but also of competition, where network actions shape the forum in the image of themselves. Again, this competition is important because its trajectory will impact not only the forum itself but also any global movement that is growing out of it. Since OWINFS has perhaps the largest collective presence on the WSF IC and participates fully in the forum events, its actions leave a strong imprint upon the social forum process. The previous section detailed ways that were largely facilitative and consensus building. Below I will highlight two activities in which OWINFS members have participated that, in contrast, have created some tension. These are the SMA, which issues a call to mobilization at the close of each forum, and the Porto Alegre Manifesto, which was released by nineteen intellectuals at the end of the WSF 2005.

The SMA and its calls for mobilization have to some extent arisen out of skepticism or frustration with the non-deliberative, non-hierarchical design of the WSF as stipulated in its Charter. Indeed, the backlash against the conception of the WSF as a space in which no final document could be issued in the name of the forum was immediate. This defiance has become institutionalized in the SMA, which sprang up alongside the first WSF. This ad hoc grouping entails preparatory meetings during the social forums and a volunteer committee charged with synthesizing this information and then drafting a final call to action for the upcoming year.[77] This document is then presented to thousands of activists and summarily agreed to by a "consensus" round of applause in a final assembly which takes place at the forum's close. Further, a contact group of promoters has come together to attempt to sustain this coordination over the course of the year and to help build a Social Movements International Network (SMIN): that is, a global network of networks. The contact group maintains the SMIN website, which in turn displays links to members' web pages. These include OWINFS-affiliated organizations, among them Focus on the Global South, the Hemispheric Social Alliance/Continental Campaign against the FTAA, and Via Campesina, as well as more nationally based struggles including Indian Dalits' rights and hunger-striking Palestinian prisoners. The first call for mobilization at the end of WSF 2001 declared:

> Social forces from around the world have gathered here at the World Social Forum in Porto Alegre. Unions and NGOs, movements and organizations, intellectuals and artists, together we are building a great alliance to create a new society, different from the dominant logic wherein the free-market and money are considered the only measure of worth.[78]

There they committed themselves to coordinate and participate in global mobilizations against the WEF, the WTO and FTAA, the World Bank, IMF, and Asian Development Bank, and the G8, as well as for specific days of action in favor of peasant farmers' and women's rights. In each subsequent year, as participation in the call-drafting process becomes more diffuse, the list of targets and events grows longer. The most striking change has been the prominent place dedicated to mobilizations against the US war on terror, its military bases, and militarism and US imperialism in general. This has encouraged considerable issue spillover and frame extension.

The 2005 call is emblematic both of this proliferation of issues as well as of spillover and frame extension. Entitled "Call from Social Movements for Mobilizations Against the War, Neoliberalism and Exclusion: Another World is Possible,"[79] it is a veritable laundry list of demands reflecting those movements that showed up and made their case for inclusion. There are nearly thirty entries appearing on the "agenda of struggles," including campaigns to cancel Southern debt, end US warmongering, halt free trade agreements, back the World March of Women's global campaign, protect socially marginalized groups, stop EU military support in Latin America, promote food safety, sovereignty, agrarian reform, environmental sustainability, and the peasantry, fight against GMOs and TNCs, support Palestinian rights and Israeli peace activists, impose UN sanctions against Israel, condemn the US embargo against Cuba, defend the rights of migrants and refugees, protect children, support students, public education, and public health and thus counter privatization of these services, and defend communication freedom.

While the call demonstrates the considerable diversity of issues and actors that are being brought together within the SMA, some question the impact of this lengthy document on collective mobilization or the construction of a single transnational movement. On the one hand, the SMA's calling for days of mobilization against the war can be credited with helping to mobilize tens of millions, most notably on 15 February 2003. To a lesser extent, this listing of diverse issues and campaigns in a single call to mobilization is arguably a small step toward frame extension of one issue into another – with the spillover issues of war and militarism into existing campaigns being the most obvious example. These efforts may encourage attribution of interconnectedness and reciprocal solidarity. Yet on the other hand, from this participant observer's standpoint, the actual process of the preparatory meetings and the final declarative assembly look much like the horse-trading and haggling that occur over a platform of a political party or social movement organization. The more well-staffed and professional organizations – including leftist parties and state-funded NGOs – thrive in this sort of bureaucratic environment and have therefore taken the lead in these assemblies. By claiming to be open to all, the assembly process instead seems to mask as much as it reinforces existing disparities in resources and expertise among activist groupings themselves.

Just as this assembly has potentially both positive and negative effects on mobilization and the construction of a single network of networks, it has a similarly ambivalent impact on the WSF itself. On the positive side, it responds to a widely felt need among many activists to be able to deepen their ties toward coordinated transnational action. As one ATTAC member noted:

> If people end up feeling … that they can't come here in order to actually deepen a process and come out of here enriched, more enriched and in a different way than they did last year, [or] use this place in order to strategize and move forward; if it ends up becoming just … a festival, … a celebration: Celebration is wonderful but we're not happy with celebration alone. We need something more. So I guess that's why we're seeing these networks emerging now. … They are corresponding to needs.[30]

Yet the increasingly prominent place that the SMA has assumed within the global and regional forums, in addition to its declaration issued at the forums' end, has created a backlash among those who feel that it threatens the integrity of the social forum as a space. As early as 2002, WSF founder Whitaker began to address the clamor for a final document. He defended the WSF as

> a process and not an event or a new international organization directed by the leaders of a substitutive "unique-monolithic thought," which would be fatal to the Forum itself. It is also necessary … to see to it that the conferences

don't end up with guiding syntheses, voted by their respective audiences, or that they do not prevail over the workshops. ... The biggest challenge for the organizers of the World Social Forum does not consist in defining new and better *contents* that could lead to even more concrete proposals, but to guarantee the *continuity* of the form the Forum was given ... in which the means are determinant for the aim to be reached. ... What is most important is to ensure that that new paradigm of political transforming action, created by the World Social Forum, is not absorbed by the "old models."[81]

The old models that the forum founders were wary of – the hierarchical political party, social movement organization, trade union, or socialist international – have not gone away, but instead tend to be replicated in, among other places, the SMA. In recent years Whitaker and other WSF "constitutionalists" have grown increasingly vocal against this development. In 2003, in an open letter entitled "Forum: Space or Movement?," Whitaker defended at length the forum as a space. In the face of what he interpreted as a "positive crisis" confronting the WSF, he stressed as fundamental the preservation of the forum as a space and the need to resist mounting pressures to convert it into a social movement. He averred that to allow this to happen would be self-sabotage, for it would discard what he and other social forum founders believed to be the most crucial political innovation of recent years, "the power of the free horizontal articulation." They credit this method for the popularity of the Porto Alegre forums as well as the surge in mobilizing against the WTO and the war on terror. Whitaker thus implored his fellow activists to recognize the constitutive value of the horizontal social articulation in the ongoing struggle toward creating the much heralded other possible world.

Whitaker furthermore singled out a number of practices, present from the beginning but gaining strength, that he felt threatened the WSF's open character. Intensifying his earlier critique, he denounced efforts to lead or direct the actions of all those present through the issuing of a de facto final document at the close of the forum by the SMA. Pointing out that this practice runs counter to the WSF charter, he accused social movement actors of attempting to subsume the forum itself within their own mobilization strategies and steer it toward their more narrow objectives, and in the process fomenting competition, the need for representatives, and, inevitably, exclusions. He concluded by warning:

> Those who want to transform it into a movement will end up, if they succeed, by working against our common cause, whether they are aware or not of what they are doing, whether they are movements or political parties, and however important, strategically urgent and legitimate their objectives might be. They will be effectively acting against themselves and against all of us. They will be hindering and suffocating its own source of life. ... In fact, a great challenge emerges, in my opinion, for the continuity of the Forum process, and for the fulfillment of its vocation of "incubator" of more and more movements and initiatives: to multiply such "spaces" worldwide –

genuinely open and free, without drawing the attention only to specific proposals. We must hope that nobody, however inadvertently, contributes to drive the Forum to a closing process until it disappears as an open space.[82]

These tensions and concerns have not been resolved. On the contrary, they appear to grow stronger with each successive WSF. A similar development has arisen within the ESF, which further strains relations among the original WSF framers and a number of European-based organizations representing some of the most influential transnational organizations and networks. A further effort very much like the SMA and its final Call emerged at the 2005 WSF, where a small group of well-known scholar-activists, among them Focus's Walden Bello, took it upon themselves to issue a manifesto.[83] From a nearby hotel lobby on the last day of the summit, eighteen men and one woman called a press conference to unveil their twelve-point program, the "Porto Alegre Manifesto." With the aim of "giv[ing] sense and direction to the construction of another, different world," they offered "these fundamental points to the scrutiny of actors and social movements of all countries," and invited the approximately 120,000 to sign on to their program.[84]

This group of nineteen, or G19, as they were quickly labeled, divided their blueprint into the three themes of economics, peace and justice, and democracy. In it they called for Southern debt cancellation, an international tax imposed on financial transactions, the eradication of corporate tax havens, the enforcement of workers' rights worldwide, fair trade prioritizing social and cultural rights instead of "free" trade agreements which only expand the rights of corporations, food security through safeguarding peasant agriculture, banning the patenting of knowledge on living things and the privatization of the global commons and especially water, legal protections against all forms of discrimination for all peoples, halting environmental devastation and global warming through promoting alternative development, closing all foreign military bases and withdrawing troops unless under UN mandate, protecting the right to information through laws against media concentration and promoting press freedom and alternative media, and reforming international institutions in line with the UN Universal Declaration of Human Rights, and placing the World Bank, IMF, and WTO under UN control.[85]

One of its signatories, Ignacio Ramonet of *Le Monde diplomatique* and ATTAC, proclaimed, "Now, nobody can say that we have no programme. Now we have the Porto Alegre Consensus and we are sure – we're confident – that the great majority of the people of the Forum will agree with this proposal."[86] They made the further assurance that, despite what it might look like, they were not attempting to change the WSF's methodology or challenge its charter, but simply to focus debate and encourage international cooperation toward building a global movement. Reactions ranged from constructive criticism to restrained hostility. One of those who found it to be somewhat useful was the South African scholar-activist Patrick Bond. While welcoming certain points, he criticized a number of others as insufficiently clear and not embedded in concrete struggles.

He instead advised the intellectuals to allow these sorts of integrated proposals to emerge from transnational sectoral forums and networks, a process – he reminded the G19 in case they had forgotten – that is already underway.[87]

Others did not engage the manifesto on its merits, but instead dismissed it outright due to the manner in which this "consensus" was reached and then presented. Indymedia journalists quite rightly termed it "a bold break with the concept of the WSF as a horizontal, open space." This, of course, was not lost on the WSF founders Candido Grzybowski and Chico Whitaker. Grzybowski was in fact invited to sign on, but refused. This was not because he disagreed with its content, which he characterized as "perfect" and, further, with which he believed that the majority of the WSF attendants would concur. He rather stated:

> What kills this proposal is the method with which it was created and presented. It goes against the very spirit of the Forum. Here, all proposals are equally important and not only that of a group of intellectuals, even when they are very significant persons. … It was a political mistake because it did not follow the agreed method and it could even generate a rejection by the grassroots of the Forum.[88]

Both tried to play down the incident, at least publicly, framing it as just one proposal among hundreds of others. Whitaker averred that "it does not generate consensus," and instead encouraged the authors to post it on the "Proposals Wall" within the official WSF alongside the others.[89] Though it is difficult to gauge how this was received by the larger "network of networks," Grzybowski's comments are probably shared by many. One activist echoed the sentiment in a frank manner: "It is just the same old 'celebrities' who cannot swallow being part of the masses they once led."[90]

Returning to this chapter's focus, the OWINFS network: Bello's participation in the G19 should not be conflated with the network overall. And to their credit, the manifesto-writers stated publicly that the document is merely the summation of their personal opinions, and is anyway a proposal for discussion, not a final decree. That said, Ramonet in particular sounded rather confident that the small group had divined and distilled the larger "consensus" into a twelve-point program, thus sending a mixed message. Even their more sympathetic critics, such as Bond, intimate that the manifesto does not adequately capture their concerns or those of the largest movements. When one adds in the testier response of the WSF founders, it becomes apparent that the criticisms leveled against the G19 manifesto are the same as those against the obviously larger and more inclusive SMA and its calls to mobilization. Both give the impression – especially to outsiders – of being final documents, although many of their authors would deny this. These sorts of initiatives will therefore continue to be met with denunciations of attempting to speak on behalf of the WSF or a "network of networks" as a whole. Wittingly or not, these attempts move the forum further in the direction of a political party and its platform, or of a social

movement and its agenda, and thus foreclose the "potentialities of the non-hierarchical space."

This debate cannot be settled here. It is a crucial, unavoidable, and possibly
intractable one for transnational activists today. If a creative compromise – or
consensus, if you will – is not found, it will likely greatly alter the social forum
process and perhaps splinter the emergent network of networks along horizontal
versus vertical lines; indeed there are signs that both are already underway.
Whatever the outcome, these are, in a larger sense, instances of the tensions
created when some of the most resource-rich individuals and social movements,
such as members who comprise the OWINFS, collectively innovate in – or
ambiguously close to – the space of the social forums.

5   Via Campesina

Via Campesina (VC) means the Peasant Way or Peasant Road. It is a global network of small and medium farmers, agricultural workers, fisherpeople, and rural organizations, including women's and indigenous agricultural groups, claiming to represent over 15 percent of the world's population, or 400 million individuals spread across five continents.[1] VC is not only the largest rural-based network to have emerged in many decades, but is also the most massive single organization resisting neoliberal globalization today, and particularly the emerging "free" trade regime. As we learned in Chapter 4, the VC has been a crucial member of the OWINFS umbrella network fighting these trade agreements wherever they are proposed. Both as a part of that network and in its own right, the VC contributes a unique perspective to the critique of neoliberalism in that it struggles to preserve and revalorize "peasant ways" of life and identities while at the same time proposing alternative and popularly conceived "peasant roads" to sustainable development, where the peasantry would be a vital socioeconomic class. This network therefore simultaneously engages in multiple and related struggles for both redistribution *and* recognition: for land reform, food sovereignty and safety, dignified rural work, alternative economic development, environmental sustainability, local self-reliance, democratization, and equal rights and respect for rural people and peasants, women, and ethnic minorities. Further, given these diverse and bivalent claims, we can also see why VC members would undertake collective action with all of the networks studied in this work, and with many more comprising the larger network of networks.

The fact that such a vast number of rural and often marginalized people – North and South, East and West – could be unified under a single banner is on the surface astonishing. This becomes more explainable, however, when we realize that the contemporary conditions facing small farmers and rural people the world over have become more and more homogeneous in recent decades, largely due to the changes brought about by the spread of neoliberal policies. In the context of many rural communities, these changes are experienced as suffering, and can thus be characterized as structural violence of neoliberal rule. Let us here touch upon two of these broad changes which have triggered – and indeed continue to spark – localized action across the globe among individuals and groups who would eventually forge themselves into the VC, those of increasing landlessness and the related privatization of the commons.

Broad change processes and triggers: landlessness and privatization of the commons exacerbated by SAPs and the GATT/WTO

Indian scientist and environmental activist Vandana Shiva recently decried, "Global free trade in food and agriculture is the biggest refugee creation program in the world." She continued: "It is equivalent to the ethnic cleansing of the poor, the peasantry, and small farmers of the Third World."[2] Following directly from the analysis in Chapter 4 dealing with the violence of WTO and regional free trade agreements and the localized contention they ignite, in this chapter we focus more closely on one key effect of the emerging trade regime, which is the existential threat posed to small farmers and their communities, North and South. Largely through the lobbying efforts of US corporations, and against the mounting protests of small farmers, agriculture was brought into the GATT/WTO negotiations in 1995. A harbinger of what many Third World peasants felt of this development could be found in the reaction in southern Mexico to the NAFTA. This agreement required the break-up of traditional communal lands in what many believed to be preparation for their buy-up by agro-businesses, and was the central grievance decried by the Zapatista rebellion on 1 January 1994, the day the treaty came into effect.[3] The spread and codification of such agreements on a global scale in the form of the GATT and subsequent WTO in the early 1990s are broadly cited by farmers as the main motivator for their banding together into the Via Campesina.[4]

The greater concentration in land ownership that was widely expected to come about under the neoliberal trade agreements would have significant global ramifications, in that approximately half of the world's population are small farmers producing for themselves and for local markets. Historically, when masses of people in the Global South have been displaced from their land, the impact unfortunately hasn't felt much like progress for those affected. Large-scale displacements create a panoply of socioeconomic and cultural ills in poor countries with no ready solutions: hunger, poverty, unemployment, mass migration and crowding into cities, environmental depletion, health crises, devaluing of cultures and jeopardizing of communities, leading to social disintegration, rising tensions, and, at times, open conflict. In citing one recent statistic on this regressive "development," the UN's Food and Agricultural Organization (FAO) reports that hunger has been rising steadily since the early 1990s, and 14 million children die every year from diseases caused by hunger, reversing trends from the two decades prior. These negative indicators in human development are coinciding with the spread of SAPs and the neoliberal trade pacts, and activists draw a clear line of causation between the two. They are not, however, alone in their critical analysis: The United Nations Environment Program (UNEP), for example,

has blamed "modern agriculture ... [as] one of the major threats to the indigenous and local communities as well as to biodiversity, healthy ecosystems, and
food security."[5] The FAO concurs, estimating that three-quarters of the world's
crop diversity has been destroyed as a consequence.

These troubling trends toward human and environmental impoverishment
are often masked by the growth-oriented jargon of neoliberalism, which
measures an economy's health and development in terms of its rise in gross
domestic product (GDP). However, because corporate economic activity is
counted in the country where it is produced (i.e. India or Brazil), *not* where its
profits are being spent (that is, the US or Europe) or stashed (i.e. in tax havens in
Jersey, UK, or Delaware, US), a growing GDP often contributes to a largely
invisible growth – from the perspective of neoliberalism – in hunger, landlessness
and joblessness, pollution, human insecurity, and suffering. These concurrent
trends have been identified in many countries, including Thailand, the
Philippines, Bolivia, and Brazil. To illustrate, in the 1970s Brazil began growing
soybeans for export as feed for wealthy countries' animals. At the same time –
and critical scholars say largely as a consequence – Brazil's hungry leaped from
an estimated one-third to two-thirds of the entire population. As more and more
peasant farmland was lost to the production of soybean for export, the yields in
Brazil's staple foods, like rice, have dropped significantly. When asked what
Northerners could do to support Brazil's poor, one leading Brazilian activist from
the MST scolded, "stop buying soya to feed your mad cows."[6]

The mounting struggle to halt the concentration of land is also connected to
the fight to preserve the commons. Much of the earth's water, forests, air, land,
and seeds has traditionally been held in common, as have been cultural products
and, more recently, the so-called modern commons of government public
services. But under recent agreements, the commons have increasingly become
tradable commodities. Fresh water, the new "blue gold," is being bought up by
Bechtel, Vivendi, and, prior to its bankruptcy, Enron.[7] The bulk of the traditional commons still remaining is found in indigenous communities. These
groups are feeling more and more threatened by corporate encroachment of
their land, minerals, forests, and rivers, as well as their knowledge and steward-
ship of seeds and plants, and even, according to a number of indigenous
accounts, their own blood and genes.[8] Global agricultural and pharmaceutical
corporations like Monsanto, Novartis, Aventis, and DuPont travel the earth in
search of traditional knowledge and medicinal plant species which they can
then patent and claim sole ownership to their production and sale. This is now a
legal practice under the new trade rules, but is quite reasonably deemed
"biopiracy" by the original stewards. Furthermore, under the proposed GATS
negotiations, which has become one of the main sticking points in the WTO
talks, the "modern commons" of "health care, elder care, child care, water
purification and delivery, education, prisons, domestic rail and air transportation,
public broadcasting, parks, museums, and cultural institutions, social security and
welfare programs, and public works" would all be fair game for corporate
takeover.[9]

Neoliberal globalization in trade agreements and SAPs similarly impacting rural areas, sparking localized contention

Due to the above trends, small farmers and rural people in many parts of the world are experiencing similar upheavals in their everyday lives. One VC scholar-activist expressed this mounting shared perception, which is sparking localized contention and, simultaneously, the realization that pressure to implement these neoliberal policies is increasingly emanating from transnational actors and institutions:

> With the implementation of structural adjustment programmes, regional trade agreements and the World Trade Organization Agreement on Agriculture, rural landscapes are undergoing rapid and profound change as national governments redefine agricultural policies and legislation to facilitate integration into an international market-driven economy. Existing agricultural and marketing structures are being dismantled while new agrarian laws aimed at restructuring land tenure, land use and marketing systems are being promulgated to increase production for export, industrialize and further liberalize the agricultural sector.[10]

Let us now begin to trace how these global trends triggered widespread but unconnected contention at the local level, which would eventually reach across borders to forge a mammoth network coordinating sustained, transnational action. We will do so by exploring the by now familiar mechanisms that constitute the scale shift process. Similarly to what was done in the previous chapter on OWINFS, these mechanisms will be tracked across three of VC's most active constituent organizations, those of the Brazilian Movimento dos Sem Terra, the Indian Karnataka State Farmers' Association, and the French Confédération Paysanne. What we will see is that, in spite of their rootedness in distinct locales, cultures, and histories, each followed a similar trajectory from dispersed, localized contention against immediate threats and suffering to a shift in scale, first to the national level and ultimately to the transnational level of contention.

We will also see that these two scale shifts – from the local to the national and then from the national to the global – transpired through the same mechanisms: Each group contained "protest entrepreneurs" who brokered relations and diffused information initially within their own borders and then across them. Their efforts strengthened the attribution of similarity among farmers leading to solidarity based on the identity of peasant endangered by neoliberal policies. Protest entrepreneurs facilitated this attribution by, first, successfully adapting and employing cultural and regional symbols to frame externally imposed changes as threats to their identities as peasants and rural people. Second, they used these frames to encourage, interpret, valorize, and legitimize their own active resistance and that of others with whom they identified.

Next, as farmers moved from disparate local contention to greater national coordination, their collective claims-making, objects, and framing strategies were also broadened. Finally, we will see that despite their considerable efforts to urge their own governments to reverse neoliberal policies and to support sustainable, small-scale agriculture, those mobilizing eventually concluded that the sources of their suffering – and hence both the objects of their claims and indeed their allies – needed to be sought at the transnational level. In their shift in scale from statewide organizations to one global network, we will see that the identity of peasant injured or threatened by neoliberalism has proven to be as potent a basis for attribution of similarity and solidarity at the transnational level as it was in the national and local settings. This identity has shown its ability to transcend – while not erasing – differences among small farmers and rural people in their unique locales and to provide a strong foundation for commonality among them, which motivates and sustains their concerted transnational coordination.

What has just been said about the constancy of identity-based solidarity across national and transnational levels can be stated more generally in terms of all of the mechanisms constituting scale shift: For in addition to depicting three important strands of the VC's genesis, each of these national movements below illustrates how the mechanisms that constitute scale shift hold not only in the process from the national to the transnational, but equally in the evolution from localized contention to national-level coordinated action. This process, therefore, should more accurately be envisioned as encompassing hundreds of simulta-neous and entwined processes occurring among farmers the world over. This is because, as action is triggered locally, groups often go through their own scale shift process from the local to the national. And as we will see below, often just as their scale shift to the national level has solidified and they emerge as strong regional or statewide political players, they nonetheless came to realize that their objectives could not be met at that level. This realization set off another spiral of the scale shift process, similar in its mechanisms to the previous one, but this time from the national to the transnational level.

This is not to say that all individuals or groups pass through identical, linear processes from local to national and then from national to transnational. Certainly, once a network has been initiated at either level, newcomers can enter the cycle at any point. An example of this is found when individuals or nascent collectives jump immediately from the local level of contention to the transna-tional, therefore bypassing the national level entirely, when they sign up to a VC campaign on the internet or show up at an anti-WTO demonstration in a major city. But to reiterate, what *is* demonstrated herein is the widespread consistency across diverse collective actors, in, first, their shift from the local to the national, and then their subsequent collective efforts to shift the scale to the global by forging the VC as a transnational network.

Scale shift from the local to the national I: Brazil's Movimento dos Sem Terra

The Movimento dos Trabalhadores Rurais Sem Terra is more popularly referred to in its abbreviated form of Movimento dos Sem Terra (MST), or "landless movement." The MST is a mass-based squatters' movement known as "land reform from below." It arose in a nexus of stagnating industrialization in the late 1970s that confined rural youth to the countryside rather than providing factory jobs in the city as before, coupled with the rising number of strikes and other protests against the military dictatorship. It also owes much to the dissemination of liberation theology in the 1960s and 1970s among activist Catholic priests. Liberation theologians denounced Brazil's deep inequalities and grinding poverty and provided material and moral support – and, in some cases, leadership – for poor people's struggles. In this environment, land occupations cropped up in all agricultural areas of the country. While not spontaneous and instead planned by local activists, there was little if any contact, and no coordination, among these groups.[11]

This began to change at the end of the 1970s, when the Catholic Church's Pastoral Land Commission (CPT) – the only non-state body with a capillary system allowed under Brazil's military regime – started networking among Christians working with the rural poor.[12] The CPT thereby played broker to local leaders of land seizures and other religious activists by hosting national-level meetings. At these encounters, precious information was swapped and ties were established, which led quickly to the emulation of tactics, the attribution of similarity and thus identity-based solidarity, and attempts to shift claims, objects, and collective action from the local to the national level. Remembers MST spokesman João Stedile, who was invited to these first meetings:

> The farmers talked things over, in their own way: "How do you do it in the North-East?" "How do you do it in the North?" Slowly, we realized we were facing the same problems, and attempting the same solutions. Throughout 1983 and 1984 we held big debates about how to build an organization that would spread the struggle for land – and above all, one that could transform these localized conflicts into a major battle for agrarian reform.[13]

These debates were informed by the experience gained from peasant organizing and from the ever bolder land occupations, largely spurred on and justified in terms of liberation theology. This framing amplified Christian values of fraternal love and peasant moral economy in order to legitimize the land occupations and agrarian reform in general.[14] An example of this can be found in the most successful initial occupation which immediately preceded the MST's establishment, that at Natalino Crossing. Carter describes the dynamic religious framing on the part of Catholic activists, which was readily taken up and adapted by the thousands of peasants camped there, the great majority of which already belonged to a Christian association:

> During Natalino's first months, the parish of Ronda Alta, aided with CPT subsidies, invested great efforts in consciousness-raising at the camp. Guided by theology of liberation, this entailed an important re-working of religious symbols, discourse, prayers and music, most of which was assimilated in a

few weeks. The pedagogical experience took its cues from Paulo Freire's critical method, while seeking to animate a constant dialogue, notably in small discussion groups. In this way, the landless chose to re-design the cross that occupied the camp's center space and came to identify themselves with the Israelites' Exodus from Egypt and their quest for the Promised Land.[15]

Despite the preponderance of Catholic imagery and clergy in the nascent movement, at its founding meeting in late 1984 MST members decided to launch the movement independent of both political parties and the Church. This, they reasoned, would be the only way to build an organization free of external political hierarchies, whims, and pressure. They also agreed that the movement had to be mass-based, nonviolent, and framed in terms of national law and rights. Specifically, Brazil's rural landless were demanding their constitutional right as citizens to land reform.[16]

The peasants of Brazil were not alone in their growing assertiveness for land. Throughout the 1980s and 1990s, agrarian movements were coalescing across the continent against changes brought about by neoliberal reforms, forging the Coordinadora Latinoamericana de Organizaciones del Campo (CLOC) and the Asociación de Organizaciones Campesinas Centroamericanas para la Cooperación y el Desarrollo (ASOCODE). In addition, study tours, youth exchange programs, capacity building, and women-to-women ties were begun between farmers' associations in North and South America.[17] Perhaps as a result of both these increased continental ties as well as the MST founders' decision to establish their organization independent of the Catholic Church, over time the MST's *mística* has expanded from an exclusively Christian frame to include more explicitly anti-imperialist and pan-Latin American symbolism while still rooted in Brazilian folklore. This change is illustrated in a land occupation that took place in 1999 in the Zona da Mata and was described as follows by participant observers:

> This first assembly [on the squatted land] consisted almost entirely of *mística* – the moral boosting, quasi-religious communal ceremony at the heart of the MST culture, involving songs and chants. One slogan proclaimed: "Che, Mumbi, Antonio Conselheiro na luta pela terra, somos todos companheiros," invoking Che Guevara, an icon of the movement, and two northeastern revolutionaries: Zumbi, a Brazilian slave who headed a revolt in the sixteenth century, setting up a *quilombo* known as Palmares, which lasted 95 years, and Antonio Conselheiro, a mystic who led a rebellion among the rural poor in the nineteenth century and set up a quasi-communist community of Canudos. "We are all comrades in the struggle for land," affirms the slogan.[18]

This dynamic and powerful mystique has helped to sustain MST activists through the physical and mental stress that accompany occupation and holding of settlements, evasion and false promises on the part of Brazil's government, slander campaigns through the media, military threats and siege, mass beatings, humiliating evictions, and secret abductions, torture, and murder of their members. In spite of this considerable repression geared toward silencing and demobilizing the struggle, the plight of Brazil's 4 million landless families can no longer be ignored. In recent years considerable support and recognition has grown among the populace that something must be done to address this widespread problem. And, thanks to the dedication of some 20,000 trained activists and the solidarity of trade unions and churches, hundreds of thousands of landless families have marched in protest and participated in write-in campaigns demanding land. Most significantly, more than 350,000 families have occupied, held, and gained legal title to over 80,000 square miles of under-utilized farmland. They have then transformed it into collective agricultural communities complete with shelter, schools, clinics, cooperative stores, and places for worship and meetings. Within these new communities, families have raised a new generation of activists, who have worked to make the settlements more environmentally sustainable and democratic. These communities have also inspired experiments across South America and in urban neighborhoods, as well as the Movimento dos Sem Teto, or the movement of those without roofs in Brazil's urban *favelas*.[19]

Yet their growing numbers, concerted efforts, and broad alliance and solidarity building were checked by neoliberal reforms that the Brazilian government initiated in 1989 and accelerated over the next decade, quashing hopes of any significant land redistribution. Instead, the reforms brought with them both the entry of international capital and the application of the "North American model" into Brazilian agriculture. And consistent with what transpired in North America the decade prior, these developments led to an even greater concentration of land in fewer – and in the Brazilian case often foreign – hands, and to agricultural trade being more and more controlled by giant agro-corporations. Hence poverty and landlessness grew just as the public sector was rendered less able to provide assistance through neoliberal cutbacks.

According to VC accounts, so too grew the repression, criminalization, and defamation of the MST. In this frustrating and increasingly hostile political environment, activists realized that they needed to broaden their movement. While continuing to squat land as the only immediate palliative for hunger, homelessness, and unemployment, at their 2000 meeting they jointly realized the imperative "to confront the neoliberal programme itself." With this decision, they set out to chart a transitional strategy that would sustain direct action to address immediate needs and to demonstrate the necessity of national land reform, while at the same time broadening their objects and claims to encompass structural transformation across a number of related sectors which impact rural lives. To do so, they began by extending their frame from solely an appeal to their own government for land redistribution, to include a more broad-based struggle against TNCs, especially in the areas of milk production and genetically modified seeds. The latter concerns were framed in terms of posing a dire threat to Brazil's national food sovereignty.[20] MST coordinator Stedile attributes this need for a shift in strategy to the growing homogenizing conditions and threats posed by neoliberal globalization, and specifically foreign corporations. And, importantly, for the scale shift process to move forward, the Brazilians were increasingly coming to perceive these conditions, threats, and targets of neoliberal globalization as shared by peasants beyond their own borders, a realization that could serve as the basis for attribution of similarity leading to identity-based solidarity and transnational coordinated action among peasants the world over:

> As long as capitalism meant only industrialization, those who worked on the land limited their struggle to the local level. But as the realities of neoliberal internationalization have been imposed on us, we've begun to hear stories from farmers in the Philippines, Malaysia, South Africa, Mexico, France, all facing the same problems – and the same exploiters. The Indians are up against Monsanto, just as we are in Brazil, and Mexico, and France. It's the same handful of companies – seven groups, in total, worldwide – that monopolize agricultural trade, and control research and biotechnology, and are tightening their ownership of the planet's seeds. The new phase of capitalism has itself created the conditions for farmers to unite against the neoliberal model.[21]

Scale shift from the local to the national II: India's Karnataka State Farmers' Association

Another mass-based peasant organization that would follow a similar trajectory and arrive at the same conclusion as the MST is the Karnataka Rajya Raitha Sangha or, in English, the Karnataka State Farmers' Association (KRRS). Let us now trace this second key member of the VC from its localized beginnings through establishing itself as a formidable actor in nationwide politics to its decision to begin reaching out for allies in the struggle against neoliberalism beyond its borders. The KRRS's membership, like popular organizations in many parts of the world, is difficult to assess since it keeps no official count, but it is estimated at around 10 million.

Founded in 1980, the association grew out of earlier struggles agitating for greater political representation and against the urban bias of development policies. But since that time, it has come to take the lead in brokering relations both among peasants and across diverse sectors of Indian society. In the former role it helped forge a national network called the Indian Farmers' Union, while in the latter it brokered relations not only among agriculturalists but also environmental and citizens' groups and left intellectuals to form a nationwide movement for ecological sovereignty. This broad-based movement coalesced in response to IMF austerity measures introduced in the early 1990s that abruptly reversed the Nehruvian socialist-developmentalist trend. Austerity was compounded with trade liberalization under the GATT and subsequently WTO, which threatened Indian small farmers' interests and recently won rights. These measures, which included the severing of fertilizer subsidies, had the cumulative impact of dashing farmers' and environmentalists' hopes for ecological sovereignty afforded them by the Indian Patent Act of 1970, which now had to be over-turned in line with the new GATT/WTO rules.[22] Out of these struggles has grown the Joint Action Forum of Indian People against the WTO, wherein KRRS helps to bring tribals, anti-dam, women's, and fisherfolk activists from across India together in the struggle against a common perceived threat.[23]

Reflecting this early realization of the considerable impact of external forces on domestic politics, this forum's central concerns – which are also shared by the KRRS – include not only demands specific to India but those of a transnational nature as well, and calls not only for distributive justice but for recognition as well: In addition to issues of land reform, agricultural subsidies, GMOs, and trade liberalization via the WTO, the KRRS and many of its Indian allies are also working to preserve and protect local and national cultures, to promote autonomy, and to abolish the caste-system and patriarchal structures.[24]

Like the MST, the KRRS has been astute at drawing on powerful cultural traditions and images to frame its anti-neoliberal struggle. In the Indian context, this translates into invoking Mahatma Gandhi's experiments in village-level, autonomous, and decentralized politics of self-sufficiency as well as his confrontational civil disobedience tactics. Both were key ingredients in the Gandhian struggle against colonialism and for national sovereignty, including as a prime facet food security. And both have become central to this modern Gandhian revival in the form of the KRRS. But like the "Christ-*cum*-Che" mystique of their South American allies, KRRS activists also syncretize their philosophical-religious frame with a neo-Marxist analysis of the periphery's dependency on and exploitation by the wealthy core states.[25] They therefore conjoin Gandhian praxis with Marxist communism, anarchist autonomism, and radical democracy in their efforts to bring about Gandhi's ideal of the village republic. The latter is seen as a holistic organization based upon "direct democracy, on economic and political autonomy, on self-reliance, on the participation of all members of the community in decision-making about the affairs that affect them." They further strive to create consultative processes among villages when decisions must be taken whose consequences will have effects beyond the local community. Mirroring this ideal, the KRRS organizational model comprises the village unit, the sub-district, district, and state-level bodies.[26]

As a Gandhian organization, the KRRS is also committed to nonviolent struggle. But theirs is a muscular and media-grabbing form of civil disobedience designed to evoke the memory of Gandhi's assertive challenge against the colonial masters and their affront to Indian sovereignty, culture, and values. This well-framed direct action, along with their alliance building with other farmers' and civic organizations around India, awarded them some early wins. Protests against the GATT proposals were launched on Gandhi's birthday, on 2 October 1991. These were followed with a national convention brokered by the KRRS and others among farmers' groups exactly one year later, where they began to strategize collectively. They chose as their first transnational target the agro-corporation Cargill. KRRS members raided its offices in Bangalore in late

December 1992, setting papers and seed samples aflame. To some Western and especially American minds accustomed to private property being revered as a sacred cow, so to speak, this tactic may be decried as the violence of thugs and vandals. But in the Indian context, these acts were steeped in anti-colonial history, for they mimicked the Gandhian-led raiding and burning of imported cloth over a half-century earlier.[27] The KRRS pressed on with their campaign against Cargill the following year with another invasion of its seed warehouse in Bellary, forcing the unit to close its operations.

Several months later farmers organized a rally and procession in coalition with other community groups from Dandi to Kandla in the western state of Gujarat, where Cargill had planned to conduct salt mining. The march, beginning on 31 August 1993 and ending on 27 September at the salt fields owned by the foreign multinational, was an intentional replay of the Dandi salt march led by Gandhi decades prior, marking the launch of the Quit India movement that would explode into a nationwide struggle. These actions, crafted to draw a clear connection in Indian hearts and minds between the anti-British struggle and that of the present-day anti-neoliberal one, undoubtedly contributed to Cargill's withdrawal from its salt operations in Gujarat.[28]

Another claim framed within the rubric of Gandhian anti-colonialism and sovereignty and used in campaigns against Cargill, other TNCs and the neoliberal trade agreements in general is the call for food security, which has for decades constituted an important element of Indian nationalism and culture. Being self-sufficient in food production is seen as a pillar of national independence, economic development, and justice for many Indians. The KRRS have therefore increasingly ensconced their campaigns in terms of the defense of India's food security. A first example of this can be found in their efforts to ward off the arrival of multinational fast food chains. In 1996 their first campaign was launched against Kentucky Fried Chicken. Employing the tactic used against Cargill – and indeed foreshadowing the French Confédération Paysanne's dismantling of a McDonalds, to be detailed in the section that immediately follows – KRRS activists destroyed the chicken chain restaurant, justifying the act in terms of championing Gandhi's virtues of nonviolent vegetarianism and doing so on the holiday commemorating his assassination. Another example came three years later, which would be emulated in France, Brazil, and elsewhere: As subsistence farmers felt increasingly threatened by a combination of creeping consumerism, pressure toward export-oriented agricultural production, and the foreign patenting of their seeds, KRRS began a campaign called Operation Cremation Monsanto. According to KRRS, Monsanto had been running trials of genetically modified cottonseeds without farmers' consent across five Indian states for months. When the locals realized that the seeds they had been given were GMOs, they called in the KRRS for backup. Together they mobilized thousands to occupy these fields, pull up the crops, and torch them.[29]

And like their other major actions, this campaign was launched with a concerted effort to communicate clearly their demands and reasons for action. Furthermore, reflecting their long-held understanding of the domestic–transnational link, they also appealed to others throughout the world to do the same. An open letter announcing the campaign's launch is illustrative in that it shows the KRRS's realization that India's food sovereignty is inextricably bound up with powerful global entities – namely the WTO and TNCs – as well as with the outcomes of related struggles that must be waged in, and increasingly coordinated among, all parts of the globe:

> The campaign will run under the following slogans: "Stop genetic engineering," "No patents on life," "Cremate Monsanto," "Bury the WTO," along with a more specific message for all those who have invested in Monsanto: "You should rather take your money out before we reduce it to ashes."
>
> We know that stopping biotechnology in India will not be of much help to us if it continues in other countries, since the threats that it poses do not stop at the borders. We also think that the kind of actions that will be going on in India have the potential not only to kick those corporate killers out of our country; If we play our cards right at a global level and co-ordinate our work, these actions can also pose a major challenge to the survival of these corporations in the stock markets. ... For these reasons, we are making an international call for direct action against Monsanto and the rest of the biotech gang. This call for action will hopefully inspire all the people who are already doing brilliant work against biotech, and many others who so far have not been very active on the issue, to join hands in a quick, effective worldwide effort.[30]

Scale shift from the local to the national III: France's Confédération Paysanne

Now let's go back to trace a third VC founding member's shift in scale from its localized beginnings through establishing itself as a major national movement, to arriving at the realization of the need to go global, at which point it would help initiate another scale shift process, this time to establishing the VC as a transnational peasant network. Though unique in many ways, France's Confédération Paysanne (CP), like the MST and the KRRS, is an agrarian organization very much rooted in a distinct place and culture. And also consistent with their Brazilian and Indian allies, movement entrepreneurs within the French confederation have drawn on cultural and regional symbols to evocatively frame externally imposed changes as imminent threats to traditional ways of life and to the food sovereignty of their nation.

The confederation grew out of a decade-long struggle beginning in the early 1970s to stop the national government from converting the Larzac Plateau in southern France into a practice ground for NATO tanks. Local sheep farmers who were prepared to defend their communities' way of life drew support from the anti-war student movement, some of whom, like the young José Bové, resettled on the plateau to take up what could aptly be called resistance farming. This nascent alliance of youthful, back-to-the-earth pacifists and stubbornly autonomous peasants together developed creative, participatory actions: With volunteer help, they constructed a traditional sheep barn made of stone on land deemed by the military to be a no-build zone, carving its walls with messages in many tongues of peace and resistance. A small band of them also marched to Paris and encamped under the Eiffel Tower. These media-grabbing campaigns, along with successful outreach and solidarity to industrial workers across France – often in the material form of cheese and meat gifted to strikers – won the Larzac movement widespread solidarity and recognition among the French populace, which was a key factor in the government's eventual acquiescence to its demands. When the newly elected Mitterrand government conceded victory after a decade of stealth struggle, a strong rural movement with wide national ties and support had been forged.[31]

The CP's roots, and leadership, stem directly from the Larzac struggle. Throughout the 1980s, small and medium farmers in France were facing increasingly similar conditions as elsewhere with regard to the corporatization of agriculture brought on by neoliberal reforms. Their individual concerns had thus grown more generalized and existential: Instead of defending one swath of land and one community's livelihood from government expropriation as the Larzac activists had done, fighting for one's very existence as a small farmer became a pressing concern all across their nation. For these reasons, in 1987 two peasant organizations, the Fédération Nationale des Syndicats Paysans (FNSP) and the Confédération Nationale des Syndicats de Travailleurs Paysans (CNSTP), merged to form the Confédération Paysanne.[32]

The nascent CP derided the neoliberal model of agriculture on a number of grounds. First, it tended to concentrate ownership and control of the farming system in the hands of a few multinationals, leading to the loss of self-employment on the part of small farmers. Furthermore, corporations prioritize low labor costs while they maximize export-oriented production, which CP charged was causing increased unemployment in the countryside and decreased national food security. Finally, they argued that giant agri-businesses – which perhaps not coincidentally were often American – show little regard for environmental sustainability and food quality, the latter allegation having particular weight in a country that takes great pride in its culinary legacy. The CP therefore made a savvy appeal, as one observer put it, to the time-held "French tradition of anti-Americanism in which the French countryside, food, national agricultural heritage and the related pride have figured prominently."[33] The resonance of their nationalist frame was further magnified by the fear pervading Europe over recent outbreaks of mad cow disease and foot and mouth, salmonella, meat poisoned with benzodioxin, and the widely suspected dangers of GMOs.

Similar to the decisions taken by Brazil's MST, the CP strove to maintain autonomy from both the religious right and the socialist left parties. On the one hand, the confederation took care that its rhetoric did not reinforce, and could not easily be manipulated by, right wing parties who had traditionally maneuvered European farmers' movements in a religious, nationalistic, and protectionist direction. On the other hand, many rural people had come to feel betrayed by the left's traditionally urban, anti-peasant bias as well as the socialist government's neoliberal reforms. Confederation activists therefore created a path – a *rue paysanne* or *via campesina*, if you will – independent of parties in order to articulate an agricultural strategy that addressed both the socioeconomic and the cultural harms they were confronting, by revalorizing and defending small farmers' interests, rights, livelihoods, and identities in and of themselves. Specifically, they declared their commitment to practicing and developing sustainable methods of agriculture that upheld workers' rights, protected the environment, and produced healthy food.[34] Yet this cautionary stance toward political parties does not at all mean that they have shied away from active engagement in formal politics. Since its inception in the late 1980s, the confederation has grown to some 40,000 members who have elected their own candidates in considerable numbers to the Chambres d'Agriculture in many French *départements*.

In addition to its electoral successes, the CP has also won governmental concessions both at the national and European levels through mass action that translated into considerable political pressure. In the late 1980s, it led a national boycott campaign which protected veal farmers from having to use growth hormones on their calves in order to compete against imports. It first won restrictions from the French agricultural ministry and eventually an EU-wide ban on their use. In 1996, the US challenged and successfully gained a WTO ruling against this ban. With the international trade body finding in its favor, the Americans demanded that its hormone-treated beef be allowed entry into the EU market. But popular opinion – influenced both by fear and by the campaigns waged by CP activists in coalitions with environmental and consumer groups – convinced the European Parliament to hold firm to its position. The US then returned to the WTO court (of a sort) to gain a ruling to impose 100 percent retaliatory tariffs on a range of EU products. Roquefort cheese – the bread and butter of Larzac's economic livelihood – was one of them. The US's retaliation, plus the widespread response it produced, would propel CP national secretary Bové to the forefront of the anti-corporate struggle, to become some latter-day Don Quixote tilting his weapon (in this case a tractor) at neoliberal globalization's windmills pervading the landscape, today symbolized by the Golden Arches.

Bové and the CP decided that, in symbolic protest of the US/WTO trade sanctions, they would dismantle the McDonald's fast-food outlet under construction in the nearby village of Millau. This was therefore no spontaneous looting riot, and, as for *sabotage*, it was a decidedly circumspect and low-key action. The confederation had negotiated in advance with the town officials over the extent of the destruction they would undertake. When the day arrived, ten sheep farmers carried off an orderly, festive, and public disemboweling of the dreaded Millau McDonald's, trailing the slain enemy's innards behind their tractors to the amusement of a small local crowd.[35] Little did they know – though they surely hoped – that this action would catapult the French peasant association to the vanguard of the anti-neoliberal struggle. Yet just as the event garnered tremendous international attention and solidarity for the small farmers' plight, it also provided an ambiguous symbol that others would attempt to frame toward their own ends. Bové, speaking on behalf of the CP, worked the media in order to assure that the event was framed by them, not others. He schooled his global audience that:

> Everyone understood why – the symbolism was so strong. It was for proper food against *malbouffe*, agricultural workers against multinationals. ... The extreme Right and other nationalists tried to make out it was anti-Americanism, but the vast majority understood it was no such thing. It was a protest against a form of food production that wants to dominate the world. I saw the international support for us building up, after my arrest, watching TV in prison. Lots of American farmers and environmentalists sent in cheques.[36]

Despite Bové's considerable media prowess, some nonetheless viewed the event as a theatrical tantrum on the part of spoiled European farmers in the face of America's justified tit for tat: "If you won't eat our beef, why should we eat your cheese, after all?" The CP replied to its critics by depicting the action as just one in an ongoing struggle against neoliberal globalization. They downplayed their own short-term economic losses caused by the sanctions and instead cast the tariffs as an attack on European citizens' long and hard-won ban on beef hormones, be they from domestic *or* international sources. Furthermore, and similarly to the Indian KRRS, they framed the WTO ruling and US actions as part of a more general assault on the French nation's sovereignty over what they produce, trade, and consume. The CP's efforts to paint the attack on the Millau McDonald's in these broader terms seemed to have been successfully communicated, if judged by the outpouring of positive press coverage and popular support in the farmers' defense. The trial of Bové and the nine others which took place in late June 2000 was turned into a carnival of solidarity and resistance. More than 100,000 young people, unionists, peasants, and other leftist activists flocked from around France and much further away to take part in what the CP hailed as "Seattle on the Tarn."

This French peasants' explicit connection to Seattle, and their frame-extending their actions to be construed as an attack on the neoliberal project itself, were not lost on the CP's antagonists, either. In this regard, one could say that the Millau McDonalds affair was also a success if judged not only by the sympathetic response it received, but also by the antipathy and expressed worry it sparked among neoliberal globalizers. A *Wall Street Journal* editorial on the peasants' tactics and trial and their broader ramifications is worth a close reading for these reasons. "Globalization went on trial in southern France last weekend," the *Journal* pronounced, "alongside 10 vandals who pillaged a McDonald's restaurant there, led by the now famous Bové," revealing that it had interpreted the PC's actions in the way that they had intended them.[37] The paper rhetorically threw up its hands and asked, "How did we get here?" The *Journal's* blame-placing as to who brought us to these dark days where neoliberal heretics are celebrated as folk heroes in village festivals is instructive, in that it serves as a textual benchmark to gauge the extent to which activists have been able to call *back* into question issues, policies, and assumptions that just a few years earlier had been deemed settled by "consensus." The hostility with which the paper treats French society and government is apparent: The French media and Prime Minister Jospin are blamed for "lionizing" Bové and calling his fight "just." Yet it saves its worst tongue-lashing for its own: In tracing a direct lineage from Seattle to Millau, the *Wall Street Journal* singles out US President Bill Clinton for taking the finger out of what seemed to be the impervious dam of the Washington Consensus. By first "inviting [them] to sit at the table" and then "allowing his union friends and others to run riot in Seattle," the *Journal* warned, "Mr. Clinton has unleashed a force that will be hard to control."[38]

The editorial further expressed shock and outrage over the peasants' casual contempt of private property, as well as their government's *laissez-faire* and even enabling behavior that allowed this affront to gain a supportive audience:

> The 10 accused do not contest the fact that they willfully attacked the fast-food outlet, causing more than $100,000 of damage. Mr. Bové's two-day trial in the picturesque southern town of Millau, site of his attack last August, turned into a carnival as thrill-seekers converged on it from all corners of France and the world. The Transport Ministry saw fit to make extra trains available to transport every troublemaker who wanted to attend the "happening." The army was then pressed into service to maintain order. Friday night, an anti-globalization concert attracted 45,000 to Millau.

The *Journal* continued in its "this-*cannot*-be-happening" tone, depicting Millau as if it were located on a planet far to the left of Manhattan: "At the Bové trial, print press and television reporters almost stopped using the word *saccager*, to sack," it exclaimed. "Rather, they adopted the defense's more sanitized term of *démonter*, to disassemble." The business daily was further distressed by the resounding portrayal of Bové as a French Robin Hood, and rather cheered on the embattled prosecutor Marty's attempt to locate the peasants' tactics along a continuum that ended in terrorist acts: "Brava, Madame Marty!" In the end, however, justice was turned on its head in this flipside world so very different from the one the *Wall Street Journal* thrives in: "Prosecutors recommended a slap on the wrist for the vandals, while globalization was found guilty of heinous crimes – as charged by the vandals."

If the Millau ordeal was an other-worldly experience for the pro-business US daily, Bové himself was equally far-out: "Bakunin-quoting former hippie," the paper sniped – in an apparent attempt at an insult that falls somewhat flat outside the intellectually straitjacketed world of the *Wall Street Journal* – who anyway "only became a farmer in 1975 as a *political act*." Nevertheless, this self-styled, anarcho-hippie peasant was a man to be feared: His light sentence of eighteen months' probation was interpreted as a "moral victory" by the nervous press, which was surmised to likely boost his political profile even further. Wondering aloud who leaked the political elites' playbook, the paper opined that this clever peasant "Bové has shown that he understands how to manipulate symbols, fears and public opinion. ... The world [trans.: *Wall Street Journal* subscribers] should realize that it must from now on learn how to deal with this French child of Seattle."

At once lionized and notorious, CP's Bové has indeed become a *cause célèbre*. He has been interviewed on CBS's *Sixty Minutes* and appeared as a questioner in the televised French presidential debate, and was widely rumored to be running for the post himself. And in a marked departure from the tone of the *Wall Street Journal* editorial, some neoliberalizers have grudgingly decided to play nice as well. Bové was recently christened one of "fifty new stars of Europe" by *Business Week*. Yet since leadership, hierarchy, and representation are all seen as problematic at best and abhorrent at worst among many contemporary activists, more than a few have grumbled at Bové's apparent spokesman-like behavior. This criticism, however, seems not wholly warranted. For rather than speaking for others, he tends to use his celebrity to extend frames among issues and, hence, shines the media spotlight on related struggles against neoliberalism. The CP frontman has brought the press along on a number of GMO crop-pulls around the world, to a demonstration with Palestinian farmers in the Occupied Territories, to the comfortable office of Kofi Annan appealing for UN recognition of food sovereignty as a basic human right, and to the jungles of Chiapas exchanging pipes with another media darling, the Ejército Zapatista de Liberación Nacional's (EZLN) Subcomandante Marcos, thereby showing solidarity with the indigenous struggle against the NAFTA and for democratic rights.

In fact, a good part of Bové's wide-ranging support can be attributed to his and the CP's active engagement with a number of transnational networks, the Via Campesina being the most prominent. As longtime VC activist and scholar Desmarais observed at the outpouring of solidarity at the Millau trial, "The Confédération Paysanne was extremely adept at capturing the interest of the growing anti-globalization movements and using its links to the Via Campesina ... other social movements and NGOs around the world to publicize and garner support for its actions."[39] And, as we will see below, the French CP was a key broker not only among European farmers, but also with many around the Americas, the Middle East, and Asia. These transnational contacts on the part of the CP – in addition to the MST's exchanges with other peasant groups throughout the Americas and the KRRS's global call for actions against biotech TNCs and the WTO mentioned above – all point to a second scale shift process underway. In this higher-level process, these and other national groups would forge themselves into a transnational network able to launch sustained collective action. We can now begin to examine this second scale shift process, which would lead to the founding and flourishing of the VC.

Agriculture brought into the GATT sparks widespread realization of the need to organize globally

As was evidenced in peasant organizations in rural Brazil, in the Indian state of Karnataka, and on the Larzac Plateau, most VC members have long histories of activism that began at the grassroots level. But as decisions that profoundly effect rural peoples regarding food and agriculture have become more and more removed to higher levels of governance, farmers and rural workers have been forced to follow suit, often converging first into national umbrella organizations, then regional ones, and finally forging themselves into their own transnational network. Therefore, just as diverse, small farmers' groups established themselves as popular national organizations able to garner widespread support for their cause within and across sectors, they found themselves in a changing domestic political terrain. Here, elected leaders were increasingly unable, unwilling, or both, to address their concerns or safeguard their interests. This shift in the locus of policymaking was thrown into sharpest relief when agriculture was brought into the GATT negotiations, against the calls of small farmers the world over. This triggered the widespread conclusion that peasants needed to "go global" themselves in order to strategize together and to speak loudly with one voice. As a founding member of the VC explained:

> The Via Campesina emerged in explicit rejection of neoliberal agricultural policies and as a direct response to the fact that the concerns, needs and interests of people who actually work the land and produce the world's food were excluded in the GATT negotiations on agriculture. Peasants and small-scale farmers in the North and South were determined to work together on the urgent task of developing alternatives to neoliberalism and to make their voices heard in future deliberations on agriculture and food.[40]

Brokerage and diffusion lead to object and claims shift, attribution of similarity and solidarity, and nascent, intra-regional coordination

As agricultural policymaking receded from the national domain, farmers' groups began increasingly to broker ties with one another and diffuse information, first macro-regionally, and eventually across continents. From the European side, the French CP played a particularly active brokerage role. European peasant groups realized the need to set up a structure at the macro-regional level capable of countering the interests of the large corporations that they saw dominating EU agricultural policy. French farmers therefore brokered ties with other nationally based European groups to hold meetings aimed at developing their own reform proposal for the EU Common Agricultural Policy (CAP). Out of these meetings grew the Coordination Paysanne Européene (CPE). Established in 1986 and comprised of eighteen organizations from eleven countries, the CPE has offices in Brussels whose representatives regularly take part in EU hearings, and are now on the Agricultural Advisory Committee of the European Commission. To fulfill its mission of coordinating the positions and actions of member organizations, the CPE organizes mass actions and public awareness campaigns in coordination with other groups and networks, supports exchanges between farmer organizations, and organizes study trips and European-wide seminars. It further publishes documents on various issues related to European and global agricultural policy and diffuses this information to its members, as well as to a number of other associations lobbying at the macro-regional and transnational levels.[41]

Meanwhile, farmers across the Americas had set in motion a similar regionalization process. As noted in the previous section analyzing the Brazilian MST, nationally based agrarian organizations had established ties through study tours, youth exchanges, and women's committees beginning in the 1970s. These exchanges allowed for those involved to commonly search for their "place" in a neoliberalizing world, to swap stories and organizing tactics, and to consider prospects for joint action.[42] In the 1990s, Canadian, US, and Mexican farming organizations came together to fight the NAFTA, while regional associations such as ASOCODE and CLOC formed to further develop their common analysis and front against neoliberal trade agreements and policies.[43] Through these face-to-face encounters, friendships and trust were developed and a good deal of similarity was attributed among peasant youth, women, and men across the Americas. A joint committee established between Canadian and Nicaraguan farming women, for example, detailed their emerging sense of reciprocal and/or identity-based solidarity in this way:

> Solidarity with Nicaraguan agricultural producers ... means that Canadians must identify in concrete terms not only how we can support them in pursuing the revolutionary agenda for social justice there but, just as importantly, how that agenda can be pursued with farming people here in Canada and how Nicaraguans can support us as well. ... Solidarity is a two-way street. It demands that both parties reach an understanding and respect for each other's struggles and alternatives. The concept and concrete expressions of solidarity are closely connected to that of *partnership*. There can be no partnership between unequals. True partners in mutual projects will make equal contribution in terms of giving, avoiding the giver/receiver model of charity. Partnership is the mutual exchange of experiences, skills and resources for mutual benefit.[44]

Interregional ties are brokered, encouraging attribution of similarity and solidarity toward greater transnational coordinated action

In addition to their role as broker of European-wide relations, French farmers had also for some time been making informal connections among peasant groups beyond Europe. Even prior to the CP's formation, the CNSTP had reached out to organizations in North and South America, including the US's National Family Farm Coalition (NFFC), the Nicaraguan Unión Nacional de Agricultores y Ganaderos (UNAG), the Peruvian Confederación Campesina del Peru, and the Mexican Unión Nacional de Organizaciones Regionales Campesinas Autónomas (UNORCA). These initial encounters provided the opportunity for attribution of similarity toward identity-based solidarity, as French peasants learned how their counterparts in the Americas were also negatively impacted by Europe's CAP. Out of these brokered relationships was born the commitment to form a commission to strengthen their solidarity toward eventual joint action, called Solidarité et Luttes Paysannes Internationales (SLPI).[45]

The Nicaraguan UNAG reciprocated by inviting representatives of farm organizations from around the Americas and Europe to their second national congress in April 1992, where this joint analysis, search for commonalities, and identity-based solidarity could be deepened. At the meeting, representatives pledged to formalize their international links in order to realize coordinated global action. In the declaration that followed they identified their shared object as neoliberal policies embodied particularly in the GATT, which they blamed for constraining and impoverishing farmers to the point of extinction while enriching TNCs. In order to redress this collective existential threat, they demanded full participation in intergovernmental negotiations on agriculture.[46]

Transnational scale shift formalized: the founding of the VC

UNAG had for a number of years worked with the Dutch NGO Paulo Freire Stichting (PFS), from whom they sought assistance in planning the follow-up transnational meeting. This "help" would prove to be problematic, in that following the 1992 gathering, the PFS had begun to plan an agenda for the next meeting quite divergent from that discussed by the farmers in Nicaragua. Simultaneously, the peasant coordinating committee that was selected at that meeting, comprised of representatives from the CPE, ASOCODE and the Canadian National Farmers' Union (NFU), was preparing an agenda that would implement the forceful call of the Managua declaration: to found an international peasant movement to articulate and collectively mobilize for an alternative development model.

These two agendas clashed rather spectacularly in Mons, Belgium, several months later. There, the PFS unveiled to its audience of forty-six peasant organizations the "Via Campesina" as in international forum for farmers to access funding for research and policy development. The farmers present, having already undertaken considerable information-sharing, solidarity building, and planning of their own, balked at what they saw as a clear misrepresentation of their expressed will in Managua. They instead seized the opportunity to found the VC with a more militant agenda and autonomous character.[47] Desmarais describes the peasant revolt, one could say, that marked VC's launch:

> The farm leaders gathered together in Mons wanted complete control over the content and process of the conference. A struggle for power and position ensued between a key group of farm leaders and the NGO responsible for convening the conference; tension and conflict escalated to the point where the NGO representative walked out of the meeting. Farm leaders essentially

took over the meeting, proceeded to discuss what they felt were the most critical issues and collectively defined the purpose, structure and ways of working of the newly formed international peasant and farm movement, the Via Campesina. The conflict with the NGO also forced peasant leaders to contemplate their future work and relations with NGOs.[48]

VC's independence and autonomy stem from the history of NGOs speaking on peasants' behalf

This conflict with the PFS spelt a difficult birth for the VC, but was characteristic of the history of relations between many rural organizations and foreign NGOs.[49] For decades prior, nationally based and transnational development organizations and research institutes were deemed by themselves and donor governments to be the spokespeople for small farmers on a range of issues including food, agriculture, and rural development. This unappointed position stemmed from their roles as funders, service providers, and program managers. Given the great disparities in resources and the divergences in goals and work styles, these relationships were often marked by inequality, paternalism, power struggles, misunderstandings, and disappointments. Some farmers felt taken advantage of by NGOs in their efforts to win funds that were then channeled to meet their own needs rather than those of their peasant "partners." Others felt exploited as research objects for publications that produced no real returns to the peasants themselves. Still others who were politically organizing averred that development and research NGOs undermined their groups' cohesion and internal functioning in a number of ways: by manipulating members with the lure of financial resources, bypassing internal decision-making and selection processes, failing to accept the role of supporter rather than director, and thus speaking on behalf of peasant groups who could readily represent themselves, if given the opportunity to do so.[50] These paternalistic tendencies were transposed and replicated on the international level, as hand-picked peasants were often trotted out for photo-ops to publicize and legitimize NGO programs or were invited to participate in discussions where the agenda had already been delimited to policy research or reform.

Given this history of relations, what transpired with the PFS at the VC's founding meeting only served to reinforce for those present the need to establish themselves as a completely autonomous peasant movement. Consistent with what we saw at the national level with the Brazilian MST and the French CP, the groups that comprise the VC asserted their new transnational network's independence from political parties and religious organizations. But in addition they also declared their autonomy from NGOs. Only peasants', farmers', rural women's, and indigenous organizations, they decreed, could join the VC. Indeed, from the outset, clearly distinguishing themselves from those who have long claimed to represent them – be they NGOs, political parties, churches, or other large farmers' organizations such as the International Federation of Agricultural Producers[51] – was seen as paramount.

The need to forge a unified peasant voice and movement is spurred by a perceived existential threat

This demand for autonomy stems both from their experience of being voiceless in debates on agriculture and rural development, and from a dawning perception that, as peasants in a neoliberalizing world, they have been thrust into an existential battle against a formidable and shared threat. A VC leader from the Basque country, Paul Nicholson, has stated:

> To date, in all the global debates on agrarian policy, the peasant movement has been absent; we have not had a voice. The main reason for the very existence of the Via Campesina is to be the voice and to speak out for the creation of a more just society. ... What is involved here is [a threat to] our regional identity and our traditions around food and our own regional economy. ... The Via Campesina must defend the "peasant way" of rural peoples.[52]

In their consensus declaration at their third international conference held in Bangalore, VC farmers further elucidated the perceived biopolitical stakes of their struggle against neoliberal trade policies, and the vanguard role they see themselves playing, as follows:

> The imposition of the WTO and regional trade agreements is destroying our livelihoods, our cultures and the natural environment. We cannot, and we will not, tolerate the injustice and destruction these policies are causing. Our struggle is historic, dynamic and uncompromising. ... This is a peasant struggle for all humankind.[53]

This collective perception of being both endangered and unheard – by governments, international institutions, and the NGOs which have long claimed to speak on their behalf – has produced a strong united position against the neoliberal agricultural policies of the WTO and regional free trade agreements and for articulating an alternative development model where peasants and their produce have pride of place. VC's three central demands are therefore that food and agricultural issues should be taken out of the WTO and other trade talks, that life forms such as seeds, plants, and animals should not be allowed to be patented, and that people's right to food sovereignty should be recognized as fundamental.[54] Through popular education, mass mobilization, direct action, and lobbying of governments, it proposes concrete local, national, and international reforms toward these ends. In addition, the VC strives to continue to build solidarity and a united position among small farmers and rural people, facilitate communication, and democratize its internal processes. In order to do so, it is redressing power imbalances by encouraging participation and leadership of rural women and Southerners. Finally, it seeks to organize more widespread and effective collective action by forging ties and launching joint campaigns across sectors and through strategic alliances with NGOs – yet on the peasants' terms. But throughout, the VC remains necessarily rooted in the local. Each of these points will be addressed below.

VC continues to broker ties with other peasant groups to expand and institutionalize the network

In just a decade of existence VC has spread to nearly ninety countries, and today is coordinated by a fourteen-member international council composed of regional representatives, half of whom are women, from organizations including the MST, CPE, KRRS, UNORCA, ASOCODE, NFU, the Federation of Peasant Organizations of Indonesia, the Belize Association of Producers Organization, the Asociación Nacional de Agricultores Pequeñas (ANAP) of Cuba, the Windward Islands Farmers' Association, and the Chilean Asociación Nacional de Mujeres Rurales e Indígenas.[55] While the CPE was the network's operative secretary for the first three years, in 1996 an international secretariat was set up in Tegucigalpa, Honduras, along with regional coordinating committees throughout the Americas, the Caribbean, Asia, and Europe. African representatives participate in VC conferences, but have decided to organize and consolidate on the continental level first before joining the VC formally.[56]

Framing evokes democracy, stewardship, rights, sovereignty, and security

Though diverse and mammoth, the VC has managed to build a consensus platform independent of the particular local, national, or regional struggles of its members. Its first and central demand is for fundamental agrarian reform in each country that "would democratize the land – both as a basis for political democracy, and for building an agriculture of another kind."[57] Through their discussions, VC members have come to frame an ideal relationship to the land that amplifies Asian and indigenous beliefs and values. They have therefore collectively eschewed a Western framing of the redistribution of land to be owned by small farmers as private property. Instead they have embraced an idea of farmers as guardians of land, practicing ecologically and community-sustainable methods during the time they are entrusted with it. As Stedile reflected:

> It's not enough to argue that if you work the land, you have proprietary rights over it. The Vietnamese and Indian farmers have contributed a lot to our debates on this. They have a different view of agriculture, and of nature – one that we've tried to synthesize in Via Campesina.[58]

Second, they argue that every group of people and every country has the right to produce their own food, and on this basis strongly oppose the WTO and similar regional trade agreements. In direct contradiction to the WTO's core principle *vis-à-vis* agriculture of "the right to export," the VC demands that each country must have the right and responsibility to develop its own agricultural policies that prioritize the health and wellbeing of the people, environment, and culture. This is the heart of its notion of "food sovereignty."[59]

Third, VC activists assert that seeds are the common property of humankind. Although not opposed to all forms of biotechnology, they rather argue that these developments must be democratized, being made readily available to all who need them rather than to a few who would profit from them. The old saying of "whoever controls the seed, controls the farmer"[60] is taken to be even more totalizing in the contemporary environment of global corporate monopolies and genetic mutations of their means of production than it was in the past. This ownership of seeds is also framed in terms of human and national security, demanding that the health and safety concerns of society as a whole be given priority in this matter.

The nature of transnational collective action

VC undertake an array of activities to realize the demands called for in their consensus platform. They petition, lobby, and advise governments to adopt their positions. They have sent sizable delegations to all major meetings where agriculture and trade are discussed, making their first international appearance at the Global Assembly on Food Security in Quebec City in 1995. Next came the World Food Summit in Rome in 1996, where they challenged the FAO to formally recognize them by granting official delegate status, a request that was denied.[61] In addition to attempting to gain a voice inside these meetings, they are increasingly mobilizing outside in the streets, linking up with local and transnational activists into mass demonstrations as well as nonviolent direct action at these forums. Their first such outing was just a few months after the network's founding, when over 5,000 European, North American, Latin American, Japanese, and Indian farmers marched on the GATT meeting in Geneva.[62] And given that their main target is the WTO, VC have been a conspicuous presence at their ministerials. In Seattle, for example, the CP's Bové made a rousing speech in front of a downtown McDonald's wherein he lambasted Monsanto, bovine growth hormones, and Roundup-ready soybeans. After passing around contraband Roquefort cheese to the crowd, they did a repeat performance of Millau, breaking windows and urging the stunned patrons and employees inside to join them in the streets.[63]

Beyond this inside–outside approach around intergovernmental meetings on agriculture, the network has established and promotes two significant and more autonomous actions. The first is an International Day of Peasant and Farmers' Struggle on April 17. The day commemorates a massacre of Brazilian landless peasants on that date in 1996. In memoriam, each year they invite other sectors of civil society to join them in protest against neoliberalism and in favor of alternatives. In 2004, April 17 was observed by hundreds of thousands carrying out self-organized, public actions in over two dozen countries around the world. Furthermore, VC has also helped to launch a major initiative called the World

Forum on Agrarian Reform (FMRA). It is conceived as a space of dialogue, exchange, and proposal development on how agrarian reform can promote food security and sovereignty, human rights, world economic development, environmental protection, peace, and democracy. Held for the first time in early December 2004 in Spain, its goal is to initiate a dialogue among peasant farmers, indigenous and fisherfolk organizations, researchers and NGO representatives, consumer and environmental groups, as well as government and the private sector.[64]

Promoting internal dialogue, diffusion, and exchange of information to address power disparities

The VC has taken a number of steps toward strengthening communication, democratizing its internal processes, and redressing and even reversing traditional power relationships among its members. First, its decision-making process is a bottom-up, often arduous procedure of multi-level consultation. Democratically chosen representatives from its seven regions are the VC nodal points of power, and are given their mandate to speak on behalf of the others at the VC international coordinating commission only after extensive dialogue. These delegates first hold preparatory regional meetings before attending the international conference and women's assembly held every three or four years, where they debate and chart the direction, policies, and overall strategy of the network. But throughout, the rationale of VC leadership is to support the efforts of those at the local and national levels, rather than to decree from above.[65]

Second, the VC has supplemented its face-to-face conferences and regional gatherings with communication over the internet. Its website posts updates of actions and events, chronicles past campaigns, and provides information about their ongoing collective efforts as well as on how to get involved. It further entails position platforms, declarations, and critical analysis, chronicles the VC's international meetings, conferences, news coverage, and press releases, and provides links to member organizations in four languages. Finally, the network has recently added a more interactive component where VC members can share information and plan campaigns.[66]

The content of its website, as well as its guiding platform, indicates that VC's pledge to "build unity within the diversity of organizations" is being achieved to a considerable extent. So much so that farmer organizations from the Global North have found themselves in the unusual position of being behind the learning curve. The president of the Wisconsin-based Family Farm Defenders, a VC member, recently commented on this role reversal, echoing the Brazilian Stedile's reflections above:

> We in the North must make a profound change in ourselves; in how we view ourselves as small family farmers. ... We seem to be caught in a trap of always becoming larger and more efficient. We must view agriculture from the eyes of a peasant; from the eyes of our compatriots in the South. Their

history is one of having lost their land and their livelihood, but from these ashes they were able to rebuild through sound agricultural production models that are successful. For example, we can look toward the cooperative model in Cuba and Brazil (ANAP and MST). We can see that another world is possible through the eyes of these dignified people. ... Those of us in the North can take courage from our counterparts in the South – especially the women – and we need to join with them to reclaim the dignity of agriculture.[67]

Indeed, women have assumed an increasingly important role within the VC. At its second international conference the network began to address the issue of gender more systematically, since participation by female delegates had remained flat at about 20 percent. After a long and heated debate forced by the women present, the conference members agreed to adopt concrete steps toward increasing women's participation and gender equality. They agreed to form a special committee, which has become a key space for women to organize. They quickly developed it into a women's commission, wherein they hold meetings, share experiences, forge greater solidarity, develop leadership capacity, and together analyze the VC positions. Out of this process have come initiatives that integrate the issues of environment, food sovereignty, and development policy with a gender analysis. They have further sought outside funding to hold a series of workshops for women at the regional level, entitled "Peasant Women on the Frontiers of Food Sovereignty," in order to increase their participation in the struggle at large and in the VC in particular at all levels. While these efforts have been most successful in Latin America, organizing and workshops also began among Asian women as well in the late 1990s. They continue to meet separately as a group prior to or between major VC international meetings, including holding an international women's assembly preceding the VC's third international conference in India in 2000.[68] Realizing that there is still much to be done, they continue to frame-extend between the VC's three main demands and the struggle for gender equality. In doing so they have pushed the network to commit to struggle against both neoliberalism and patriarchy, and thus for women's economic autonomy, gender equality, and the eradication of all forms of violence.[69]

Through dialoging openly about difficult issues, allowing for individual and group initiative, and adapting as a network, VC seems to be successfully managing another potentially divisive conflict, one that would pit Northern farmers against their Southern counterparts. Over the years of learning about and participating in each other's struggles, trust building, analysis, debate, and collective transnational action, VC members have come to view the fundamental conflict not as one between North and South, but rather as between two competing and contrary models of development: neoliberal, corporate-driven agriculture based on profit-making and the ever greater concentration of productive resources versus their own models based on a "rediscovered ethic of development," and built upon and organized by the efforts of small-scale agriculturists.[70]

Bové reflects on this remarkable North–South synthesis, reached through tremendous attribution of similarity and identity-based solidarity:

> We're all agreed on the three main points – food sovereignty, food safety, patenting. For the people of the South, food sovereignty means the right to protect themselves against imports. For us, it means fighting against export aid and against intensive farming. There's no contradiction there at all. We can stage an action in one part of the world without in any way jeopardizing the interests of the peasants elsewhere, whether it's uprooting genetically modified soya plants with the Landless Movement in Brazil, as we did last January [during the WSF 2002], or demonstrating with the Indian farmers in Bangalore, or pulling up GM rice with them when they came to France, or protesting with the peasants and the Zapatistas in Mexico – effectively, our demands are the same. Of course there are different points of view in Via Campesina – it's the exchange of opinions and experiences that makes it such a fantastic network for training and debate. It's a real farmers' International, a living example of a new relationship between North and South.[71]

Articulating an alternative paradigm with bivalent claims of recognition and redistribution

At the VC's third international conference, held in Bangalore, India, in October 2000, this "farmers' international" approved a holistic, alternative agrarian strategy. Their program calls for land redistribution based on the notion that the earth should belong to those who work it. They proposed a new vision of access to land as one of peasants' survival and of valorizing rural cultures. At the same time, and reflecting the impact of the women's commission, they urged that steps must be taken to safeguard against patriarchal land tenure systems. The farmers defended the principle of social ownership of land and called on governments to adopt various strategies that support small agriculturalists. The overall agro-industrial complex, they concluded, should be controlled by small farmers and rural workers.

The platform then went on to promote the concept of national food sovereignty, and call for export controls that would safeguard this fundamental form of sovereignty to assure that everyone gets fed at home. In addition, they demanded a number of social rights, including the rights to free public education, social security, free and publicly developed improvements to infrastructure and agriculture that are also safe for workers and the environment, and public and democratic access to water supplies. They then listed a number of principles, including among them the rights to work, care for the land, produce food first and foremost, preserve the environment and protect water, refuse to pay national debt, avoid "predatory monoculture," resist policies imposed by the World Bank and TNCs, and fight for and defend gender and racial equality.[72]

Taken together, the VC's consensus platform outlining agrarian reform strategies can be seen as a transformative frame to neoliberal globalization that is founded upon the claims of small farmers for both recognition and redistribution. While firmly rooted in their domain of agriculture and rural societies, the platform does not remain exclusively so. Rather, it extends the framing of their struggle in order to build the broad coalitions necessary to transform all aspects of society:

> The struggle for the implementation of land reform cannot be cloaked as a peasants' exclusive need or banner, *but as a social solution for the whole of society's problems*. From this perspective, it would become viable if it were inserted as a claim, a platform of struggle for wide popular sectors in our countries. We, as peasants alone, will not conquer land reform and rural changes. We have to propose changes in agriculture, in the land ownership and in rural development processes, *as part of a wide popular project for our peoples, where there would be a new economic, social and political order*.[73]

Brokering strategic ties across sectors and with NGOs to advance their alternative project

This frame extension reflects both a realization of the need to seek allies in the struggle against neoliberalism, and their cautious confidence in their collective identity and power as a transnational peasants' network. While still maintaining that the VC must be an all-peasants and rural organization, they are nevertheless building their own coalitions or joining existing campaigns across the spectrum of resistance to neoliberal globalization. In 2000, the VC amended their internal guidelines for alliance building and transnational relations by stating:

> The Via Campesina has succeeded in establishing itself as an important global voice for peasant and small-scale farmers in less than a decade of work. ... In order to build on those gains and become a more effective force, it is imperative to continue to build strategic working relations with others who support our agenda and to effect changes in the international institutions and agencies which are currently destroying peasant agriculture.[74]

They realized that NGOs could complement the VC's mass mobilization capacities with expertise in lobbying, research, and fundraising. They therefore cautiously began to reach out to carefully chosen NGOs who wanted to partner with the mass-based peasant movement on the latter's terms. Earliest efforts in this area were to allow for a parallel NGO forum at the VC's second international conference in Tlaxcala, Mexico, where NGOs could network with others like themselves and observe the peasants' proceedings. This was a measured response to NGOs' keen interest in the fledgling network and was done in the hopes of educating potential partners on how they could *support* – not lead – their cause. This partial opening to NGOs yielded some positive results, in that the ten participating organizations – among them the Transnational Institute and Oxfam-Solidarité – in the end pledged to stand aside and let the peasants lead, to assist only when asked, and to work to create more opportunities for mass-based organizations in the future. This meeting bore further fruit in a summer 1997 meeting between mostly European-based NGOs and VC leaders to attempt to establish a code of principles for eventual collaboration that respected the VC's go-slow approach.[75]

This cautious *rapprochement* has not been without its historic challenges: Some NGOs balked at being consigned to a "parallel" space, calling this move unnecessary and even divisive, since in their view the struggle was a common one, wherein all "partners" are equal and should therefore be seated around the table. Some of these same groups that deny and resent the distinction and thus refuse to participate under VC's conditions have gone on to organize their own meetings for peasant groups, which the VC consider divisive themselves. In late 1996 the network refused to sign on to an NGO declaration at the World Food Summit that they believed didn't accurately reflect their experience or take into consideration peasant voices, a move that further drove a wedge between them and some NGOs.[76]

With this ambiguous relationship between NGOs and the VC, it is not surprising that the latter's first outings against the WTO – such as that at the Geneva ministerial in May 1998 – were done in a loose alliance with the anarchistic Peoples' Global Action. Yet while there, individuals made ties with NGO activists from the anti-MAI coalition, which soon launched its dual campaigns in the lead-up to Seattle. The VC, meanwhile, was making its own preparations for the WTO meeting, where farmers from around the Americas and beyond were to converge with many others for the "Battle in Seattle." They came to the WTO ministerial to press for their core demand of "food out of the WTO"; yet they also had a broader agenda in Seattle:

> The Via Campesina adopted its "globalize the struggle, globalize the hope" strategy; it forged links with a number of key NGOs, and consolidated alliances with other sectors in efforts to build a worldwide movement to develop alternatives to the neo-liberal model advocated by the WTO. The Via Campesina conscientiously focused work with a number of strategically selected NGOs and social movements who share common ideologies and similar visions for social change.[77]

They therefore came away with much stronger ties to those of the newly emerging OWINFS network, joining up with Focus on the Global South, the Council of Canadians, Public Citizen, Friends of the Earth International, and many others, and three months later were party to the network's founding.[78] The VC continue to actively participate in OWINFS, being crucial in organizing the mass protests at events like the Cancun WTO ministerial meeting and raising funds to bring thousands of peasants and indigenous people to these actions. Their demands at Cancun were "no" to export monocultures, the destruction of traditional farming, the introduction of GMOs, the industrialization of agriculture, and corporate piracy. During the event, VC organized a parallel International

Peasant and Indigenous Forum as well as nonviolent direct action and street demonstrations around the meeting site, and opened dialogue spaces with youth who came to demonstrate. Indicating their collective strength, after the meetings in Cancun broke down, the president of the EU's Agricultural Council invited VC to dialogue.

As a further step in their strategy for building transnational alliances, the farmers' network joined forces in late 1999 with an international human rights group, the Food and Information Action Network (FIAN) to launch the Global Campaign for Agrarian Reform. Organizing under the banner of "food, land and freedom," the campaign is composed of fact-finding missions, person-to-person exchanges to learn about each others' struggles, letter-writing campaigns, public seminars, lobbying of governments and intergovernmental institutions, the setting up of an emergency network to spotlight human rights abuses against peasant activists, and direct action such as mobilizations and land occupations across Asia, the Americas, and Europe.[79] Coordinating with VC members on the ground, this campaign has sent a mission to Argentina to investigate alleged violations of human rights of rural and indigenous workers and then submit a report to the UN, issued a public statement urging the World Bank to abandon its programs of market-based land reforms, and organized a global protest letter-writing campaign targeting President Mbeki to support the landless of South Africa. In the summer of 2002, the VC–FIAM coalition participated in and then issued public statements following the World Summit on Sustainable Development in Johannesburg, denouncing the propensity to blame the poor for environmental degradation, and instead pointed the finger at the IMF and World Bank SAPs.

The VC as a "glocal" network

Through all of these actions as a "global" network, the VC members – just as we saw at the onset of this chapter with the MST, the KRRS, and the CP – remain consciously and necessarily rooted in local places, and thus the VC is perhaps more aptly termed a "glocal" network.[80] Its alternative model of development based on agrarian reform seeks to amplify and revalorize local, traditional knowledge, while combining it with appropriate innovations. Examples of this hybrid development model abound in many locales where VC activists have won the space in which to experiment. And in a reversal of hundreds of years of power relations, peasant groups are now becoming confident enough to prevail upon interested scholars with the peasants' own research agenda, encouraging them to spend time with farmers' organizations at the regional and local levels to examine how their various issues, plans of actions, and proposed alternatives are developed in response to the globalization of agriculture.[81]

Even when the VC are mobilizing "globally," the fact that they *are* farmers and rural people means that the vast majority cannot travel to attend demonstrations in Seattle, Cancun, or Rome:

We are rooted in the places where we live and grow our food. The other side, the corporate world, is globally mobile. This is a big difficulty for us. But our way of approaching it is not to become globally mobile ourselves, which is impossible. We can't move our gardens around the world. Nor do we want to. The way in which we've approached this is to recognize there are people like us everywhere in the world who are farming people, who are rooted, culturally rooted, in their places. And what we need to do is build bridges of solidarity with each other which respect that unique place each of us has in our own community, in our own country. These bridges will unite us on those issues or in those places where we have to meet at a global level.[82]

The farmers' main form of global mobilizing, then, consists of staging local actions which are transnationally coordinated to coincide with others carried off by network allies around the globe. In just one example, every April 17 groups of Hondurans, Brazilians, Belgians, Italians, Indonesians, Indians, Filipinos, and many others hold local or national-level demonstrations or marches, plan direct nonviolent action, do media work, organize conferences, or set up meetings with policymakers. And as members of the most powerful and prolific peasant network on the globe, their individual actions are imbued with a growing confidence that comes from knowing that they are no longer voiceless and alone. Desmarais notes: "As its organizations engage in collective action within their national boundaries, they do so with the knowledge that they are connected to the actions of organizations of men and women half a world away."[83] Four hundred million of them, at last count.

Analysis based on conceptual continua

Now that we have traced the VC's scale shift process, let us turn our attention to its composition and character, analyzed through the framework of proximity to the problem, affective response, solidarity, network model, paradigm, and claims. The effects of SAPs, the WTO, and other trade agreements were strikingly similar among small farmers and their rural communities in many parts of the world, as land tenure systems have been restructured toward increased production for imports, industrialization, and liberalization of the agricultural sector. These changes have led to greater land concentration and privatization of the commons. Both have come to be viewed by many peasants as posing an existential threat to their livelihood, cultures, and natural environment.

This close fusing of immediate proximity to the problem, personally felt suffering and existential threat among peasant farmers provides a firm foundation upon which identity solidarity has been forged. The robustness of this threatened identity and its attendant group solidarity was exemplified in the three domestic-level organizations of the Brazilian MST, the Indian KRRS, and the French CP. Although each draws upon distinct cultural imagery and meanings to mobilize its constituency and frame its struggle for its domestic audiences, the underlying identity of peasant has nevertheless proved strongly resonant across cultural, linguistic, and geographic distances, in the process binding diverse farmer and rural groups together into the transnational VC. Furthermore, due to the peasantry's shared history of being (mis)represented by a paternalistic church, state, party, union, or most recently NGO, the farmers who founded the VC resolved to create an exclusively peasant and rural network.

This means that the VC is an identity-solidarity network in its purest form. Based on its members' history of unequal relationships, it has rejected ties with those who would attribute "worthiness" to their plight and thus lend paternalistic "help" based on altruistic solidarity. The VC furthermore has only recently entered into alliances based upon the mutual granting of reciprocal solidarity to those in interconnected struggles, after carefully vetting its potential partners to assure respect for its autonomy and that it would be valued as an equal. This deeply felt desire for recognition as an equal and autonomous actor and for local peasant voices to be heard in the transnational arena has deeply marked the organizational design of this network, beginning with its founding as an all-peasant organization. Yet, as with previous networks studied, this egalitarian and autonomous ethos does not mean that the VC can be clearly characterized as either first-generation NGO advocacy or second-generation, direct activism social justice. Instead, it is a highly effective hybrid of the two, which has moved away from the first-generation model and toward the second, but has retained certain characteristics of the earlier mode that it deems useful. Perhaps given that the very identity of peasant is widely considered anachronistic, the VC defies easy categorization as a contemporary transnational network.

On the one hand, in key respects the VC is the antithesis of a first-generation network: No one will be allowed to advocate on the peasants' behalf, and there-fore NGOs are permitted to play only an outsider's supportive role, never a central one, in the network itself. The VC is instead structured as a bottom-up, mass-activism, multi-issue network. Highly sensitive to concentrations of and disparities in power, its decision-making structure is distributed and flows from the grassroots up through the national and regional levels. Macro-regional hubs are the nodal points of the network. Preparatory regional meetings are held in the VC's seven regions, where representatives – divided equally among men and women – give their consent to their representatives only after extensive discus-sions. These representatives comprise the network's international coordinating commission; yet one of its primary duties is to support efforts of those at the local and national levels, rather than to decree from above. Finally, it holds inter-national conferences and women's assemblies where members debate and chart the network's direction, policies, and overall strategy.

Traditional concentrations of power and privilege have been further addressed and diffused through the establishment of the women's commission to increase participation and infuse a gender analysis into the VC platform. In addition, North–South disparities are broached through honest dialogue and searching out a common platform of food sovereignty, safety, and anti-patenting. While this consensus platform gives the VC actions coherence and defines their transnational campaigns, they realize that these goals will be achieved through concrete national and local initiatives that will vary depending on the context, and thus members are encouraged to adapt or devise policies as they see fit.

Furthermore, while certain peasant organizations did play key brokerage roles in its early formation such as the European CPE, the Central American ASOCODE, and the Canadian NFU, brokerage costs have become considerably lower over time. As the network has gained momentum and an international reputation, outreach to other farmers' groups based on affinity ties have helped to swell the network to its current size of approximately 400 million members. This brokerage and ongoing diffusion have been greatly facilitated through the use of internet communication. Specifically, the worldwide web enhances their distribution of information, allows for discussion forums, and facilitates mobilizing.

Another unambiguous, second-generation feature of the VC is its network capacity. Far beyond simply reform advocacy or crisis intervention, the VC is at the forefront among transnational networks today in its capacity for mass protest, especially in transnationally coordinated mobilizations which nonetheless target national governments. They have also been increasingly present at protests on the transnational level, especially against the WTO and regional trade agreements. But beyond the capacity to flex their mobilization muscles, the VC has likely done more to revalorize the role of the peasant in contemporary societies and struggles than any other movement in history. A final second-generation feature is their breadth of targets: While national governments remain central objects of mobilization and lobbying, they are targeted in order to effect changes among more remote bodies, including the WTO, regional and bilateral trade agreements, the EU CAP, the World Bank and IMF, and the FAO; that is, wherever decisions are taken that will impact food, agriculture, trade, and patenting laws.

The above has shown many ways in which the VC is incontrovertibly operating within a second-generation model. Now let us highlight those areas in which this network is either ambiguous or has retained features seen as first generation, beginning with mobilization tactics. While their campaigns, especially those surrounding the WTO and other "free" trade agreements, could be viewed as permanent and therefore difficult for any one lead organization to "switch off," and while local and national groups are encouraged to devise their own campaigns and tactics based on their shared platform, the VC's campaigns *are* strategically organized. Through their well-defined decision-making apparatus, their international commission can and does develop campaigns both on the network's behalf as well as in coalition with others, as we saw for example with OWINFS and FIAN.

Furthermore, the VC has a sharp inside/outside bifurcation due to its membership criteria, which makes its scale and diffusion both first and second generation. While among those who meet its criteria of bona fide peasants and/ or rural organizations it has greatly expanded through technology networks as well as face-to-face forums, the scale of the network for "outsiders" is limited to brokered coalitions with carefully selected allies. Diffusion, likewise, is two-pronged: its pledge to "build unity within the diversity of organizations" reflects considerable diversity among peasants and rural peoples the world over. And yet from an outsider's perspective and when compared with some other transnational activist networks, the VC seems relatively homogeneous.

There is a final incongruity when analyzing the VC from within this first-generation/second-generation framework, regarding its network stability. Most first-generation networks develop fracture lines due to laborious issue and goal framing and attempts to create a strong organizational identity, whereas second-generation networks are seen as creating a dense web of weak ties through their code of inclusive diversity. The VC therefore is first generation with regard to its clear framing of issues and identity, yet it lacks discernable fracture lines. On the contrary, its collective identity as an all-peasant, transnational network and its framing of issues and goals give the network a stability rivaled by few others.

Finally, with regard to the nature and scope of its claims, and thus its operational paradigm, the VC once again veers toward a second-generation model. Its first and central demand of agrarian reform is fundamentally domain specific. And yet it surpasses both what is normally conceived of as policy reform and the domain of agriculture alone. The VC's aim is to "democratize the land," which would form a new basis for political democracy and for building an agriculture of a different kind based upon a reciprocal relationship between humans and the environment. It sees its program not as simply reforming its own sector or class, but "as a social solution for the whole of society's problems ... [and] as part of a wide popular project for our peoples, where there would be a new economic, social and political order ... for all of humankind."[84]

In a kind of transitional paradigm toward achieving the above strategy of multi-sector structural transformation, the VC has devised campaigns and joined with others to promote a number of shorter-term objectives and reforms, targeting both national governments and international bodies such as the WTO. These include promoting social ownership of land, imposing national export controls to protect food sovereignty and guard against domestic hunger and malnutrition, resisting policies imposed by the World Bank and TNCs, ensuring the rights to free public education, social security, government improvements to infrastructure and agriculture, access to water supplies, and the abrogation of national debt payments, and instead fighting for gender and racial equality. The VC's agrarian reform strategies can therefore be seen as a transformative frame to neoliberal globalization that is founded upon the claims of small farmers for both recognition and redistribution. These claims are bivalent in the sense of not only safeguarding peasants' economic survival but also valorizing rural peoples, cultures, and their ways of life. While firmly rooted in their domain of agriculture and rural societies, their claims do not, however, remain exclusively so. Instead they extend their struggle's frame in order to build the broad coalitions necessary to transform all aspects of society.

Involvement with the WSF: strengthening the network and reinforcing shift to the transnational level

Let us now take a closer look at the VC's involvement with the WSF. As we found in our two previous cases, the VC's participation has helped to build the network at all levels while at the same time reinforce its scale shift to the transnational. "From its start," reflected a network statement on the forum, "Via Campesina understands this process as being very important to strengthen our struggle at the international level against the neo-liberal policies."[85] VC has had a strong presence both inside the WSF as well as in the mobilizations that take place around it: The network's signature green farm caps and scarves, or *panuelos*, were ubiquitous in the crowds of the first Porto Alegre WSF in 2001, largely – though not solely – due to the Brazilian landless presence there. And the following year, an estimated 4,000 VC turned up from around the world.[86]

In these earliest social forums, the network held workshops on three main themes: GMOs, the WTO, and food sovereignty. The aim in these first workshops was simply to give voice to local and national farmer struggles in a transnational venue.[87] At subsequent forums, these themes and this aim continue to figure prominently: Peasants share experiences among themselves, which encourages attribution of similarity, identity-based solidarity, and emulation, and urges them forward together toward coordinated action. The latter has been focused on strategizing as a network to plan protests against the WTO and other regional trade bodies.[88]

In addition to workshops aimed at strengthening the network internally, the VC also uses the forum space to invite others to join in solidarity with its struggle. At the first WSF, for example, it issued an international call to action for the April 17 day of the peasant farmer. By the end of the week, more than 185 organizations had pledged their support.[89] Beyond the workshops and invitations to joint future actions, the network pulled off, both literally and figuratively, its first transnational, collective direct action as a mass movement at the second WSF. Over 1,000, mostly MST, joined by other VC activists, led an invasion of a controversial Monsanto biotech plant nearby, pulled up GMO soybean and corn crops – which are illegal in Brazil but for which the TNC had permission to experiment on that site – and squatted the compound. While this action nearly got the French farmers deported, at the same time it drew media attention and evoked an outpouring of solidarity for their transnational campaign – which was also being launched simultaneously in Rome – in defense of "peasant seeds" and to denounce what the VC call the "lie" of genetically modified seeds, which breed dependency of farmers on corporations.[90]

The forum as a space for encounter and building toward one global network

Turning now to the second theme, that of the social forum as a space of encounter which helps foster rejuvenation, learning, cooperative action, solidarity, and construction of a network of networks, we see evidence of this in, first, VC's participation on the WSF IC; second, their networking both within the IC and in the space of the forums to deepen alliances toward joint action; and, third, the opening of their *own* autonomous space within the forum itself. On the first point, VC members have from the beginning been involved in the design and oversight of the WSF process. The MST was one of eight founding members of the WSF Secretariat, while VC as a network has joined MST on the IC as well. Participation in the WSF IC has brought the peasant farmers into much closer contact and cooperation with a number of the largest networks mobilizing today, not only those whose main concerns are free trade agreements, but also environmentalists' and women's networks alike. The IC meetings therefore facilitate a good deal of spillover and reciprocal solidarity among formerly unconnected networks, while at the same time strengthening ties already made prior to the founding of the forum. Both encourage greater transnational coordinated action toward bringing a single network of networks closer into being.

For example, the VC sits on the WSF IC alongside its partner in the Global Campaign for Agrarian Reform, FIAN. This periodic contact has helped them plan how to jointly advance their campaign within the WSF itself: At the forums, they decided to promote exchanges of experiences on land struggles and debate over the ways that their campaign can support struggles at local, national, and transnational levels, especially targeting the World Bank. Other pre-existing relations, like those with OWINFS members, have also been reinforced through the forum process. TNI's representative on the IC, Brid Brennan, credits the WSF with providing opportunities for greater coordination between the two giant networks. She also now views the VC as being at the forefront of OWINFS, largely because of its mass-based groups at the national level which are able to keep their eye on their governments as well as apply popular pressure on them. It was VC members in India and Brazil, we should recall, who were the first to alert OWINFS to the "cave-in" of their governments in joining the FIPs, which jump-started the WTO in Geneva again.[91]

In addition to strengthening already existing coalitions, the WSF and the IC have encouraged relations toward joint action among those who had little, if any, previous contact. FOEI, which is also an IC member, credits the WSF with providing the opportunity to effectively link its environmental justice campaigns with those of the peasant farmers. Both the IC meetings and the social forums have allowed FOEI to build upon its informal contacts with the VC made at the earliest anti-Davos meetings. The environmentalists and the peasant farmers formalized their ties in a joint position paper drafted in 2001. They have continued to strengthen this relationship since then, to the point where in 2005 the two networks held a trade and agriculture event together at the forum. Furthermore, since both have a similar organizational structure that grants considerable autonomy to the local and national levels, they are striving to better calibrate their coordination by linking up directly at these levels, in addition to at the transnational one. Their aim is to continue dialoguing on their respective positions on the issues of trade, agriculture, and food sovereignty in order to identify where they overlap and can thus combine forces in joint campaigning.[92]

A last example can be found with the World March of Women (WMW). This transnational network fighting against poverty and patriarchy like FOEI cites the WSF and the IC as crucial opportunities to work more closely at the transnational level with farmers and rural people. WMW's Diane Matte feels that their collaboration especially reinforces the progress that women are making toward full participation within the WSF. At the same time, this relationship benefits the WMW network through educating them about the peasants' struggles and fostering an interconnectedness among them. It further enriches the emerging network of networks in that together they bring a broader feminist analysis to the construction of "another world."[93]

A final way that the VC's involvement with the WSF promotes encounter with others toward forging a network of networks is through its autonomous, International Via Campesina Space, first established at the WSF in India in 2004. Not only was this a place to build its own network and develop a common agenda for transnational action; it was also an attempt to bridge a schism that had emerged during the planning of the Indian forum. As a kind of compromise position, the VC set up an autonomous, third space near the official WSF grounds as well as the dissenting Mumbai Resistance event.[94] It was organized by VC members from Southeast and East Asia, who invited peasant organizations and fisherfolk as well as representatives of other social movements to join them in order to seize, in their words, "this opportunity after the victory in Cancun to strengthen our struggle against the neo-liberal policies and common agenda of action."[95]

Over the course of two days, those present in this neutral space shared experiences and opinions aimed at developing concrete action around a number of topics: first, the struggle for full recognition of peasant rights at the national and international levels, toward which end the VC presented and discussed its draft "Declaration of Peasant Rights"; second, how to strengthen the struggle for genuine land reform at the local, national, and international levels, especially against the World Bank, where the VC was joined by its campaigning partner FIAN to promote its Global Campaign on Agrarian Reform; third, the defense of seeds and the struggle against GMOs and patents; and, fourth, people's food sovereignty as a crucial concept in the struggle against the WTO, other multilateral trade agreements, and corporate agriculture in general. On this subject European farmers shared their proposal for "another agricultural policy" on the part of the EU. This autonomous event therefore helped peasants and other social movements move closer to a common agenda.[96]

A terrain of competition over the nature of the forum and future global network

We can now elucidate how the forum is a space of competitive action where networks mold the forum – and by extension the network of networks – in the image of themselves. In Chapter 4 we already learned about VC members' participation in the controversial Social Movements Assembly and its calls to mobilization. Here we will focus on two additional activities: those of direct mass action in the space of the social forum, and efforts to organize autonomous forums. The latter occur both at the WSF, as in Mumbai, and in thematic forums which are at once linked with but also independent from the WSF itself.

The VC, like OWINFS, is a close approximation of a mass, direct activism social justice network that is also a complete WSF insider. Through its media-grabbing direct activism, as we saw above in the Monsanto plant invasion, the VC pushes many WSF organizers and attendees outside of their comfort zone by unsettling the space from its routine of discussion and cultural bazaar to one of confrontational, transgressive action as well. The legal controversy that the Monsanto action created forced WSF organizers as well as Brazilian government officials to choose a side: Would they defend the forum as an incubator for this sort of assertive protest, or would they rather support Monsanto's argument of being "a victim of an aggressive movement that puts the rights to freedom of movement and to private property at risk" and called on the local authorities for a "quick reaction ... to restore order"?[97]

This forced WSF organizers into a difficult position, given that the first WSFs were largely funded and supported by the Brazilian Workers' Party (PT), in power at the time in Porto Alegre. The maneuvering to get a stay on the depor-tation order against Bové and other European peasants likely strained relations among Brazilian organizers, their close allies in power, and Brazil's most powerful mass movement, the MST. Other groups, particularly those affiliated with the PGA, as we will see in Chapter 6, also try to make the forum a space for spontaneous direct action, and run into similar confrontations with the less mili-tant elements present. The Indian KRRS, which was active especially in the earliest years of the PGA, has been perhaps the most critical VC member of the social forums, and refused to participate in the first Asian Social Forum in 2003 due to it being an alleged NGO-driven process in India.[98]

This tension, I would argue, is a healthy dynamic for the forum's collective identity, both at the transnational level and as it fans out to regional, national, and local forums. The popularity of the mass marches accompanying each world and regional forum attests to the widely felt desire to not just talk or even to plan future campaigns, but to *act together now*, as one diverse network of networks. If the VC continues to organize direct action not only for its own members, but to invite everyone to join in its escapades, this would likely be met with a groundswell of positive responses. This is especially true among the young people who predominate at the forums, but whose energy is largely dissipated by the unimaginative, lecture-style meetings which unfortunately comprise much of the forum's organized events.

Another activity on the part of the VC that has created some tension, but which again seems rather positive, is its establishing autonomous spaces. As described above, this has taken the form of a neutral site within the forum, that of the International Via Campesina Space in Mumbai. Again, the aim is not only to strengthen the network internally; it is also to bridge the schism that developed around the WSF India and to bring together peasants and fisherfolk as well as other social movements to learn from each other toward building a common analysis, reciprocal solidarity, transnational alliances, and coordinated action. But beyond the WSF, the VC's World Forum on Agrarian Reform in 2004 in Spain was conceived as a thematic forum in the spirit of the WSF

Charter of Principles. The spreading of the forum model of open spaces to deepen debate and link up transnationally has been an explicit goal of the WSF organizers from the beginning. In addition to the macro-regional forums held in Europe, the Pan-Amazon, the Americas, Africa, and the Mediterranean, organizers also, in theory, promote thematic forums as well. Yet to date, only three such forums have been recognized on the WSF website, those on democracy, human rights, war, and drug trafficking held in Cartagena, Colombia in June 2003, on the issue of Palestine held in Ramallah in December 2002, and on the Argentine economic crisis held in that country in August 2002.

It is therefore somewhat incongruous that the VC would explicitly frame their World Forum on Agrarian Reform as in the spirit of the WSF, yet there was no such acknowledgment on the part of the WSF organizers. This may also have something to do with tensions surrounding the VC's ongoing request – shared by some others – to hold the WSF every two years instead of annually, so that networks such as theirs could organize their own international meetings or forums rooted in their main theme during the off-year. Others who are active in macro-regional forums have also proposed a similar pattern. In doing so, the VC voice a common complaint that they do not have enough resources to be present at the WSF en masse every year, attend IC planning meetings wherever in the world they are held two to three times a year, and still adequately prepare for their own thematic or regional forums. Those in favor of maintaining the annual WSF, especially on the Brazilian Committee, counter that if these networks or organizations have enough resources to plan their own major event in the off-year, they have sufficient resources to attend the annual WSF. This request so far has been a dead letter in the rather mercurial decision-making apparatus of the IC and Brazilian Committee; yet if the sentiment grows among IC members, and particularly among mass-based groups whose collective absence at the WSF would be felt, this could force a change of the WSF to a bi-annual calendar.

The effect of such a shift is difficult to forecast, both for the forum itself and for the development of a global network of networks. While the Brazilians are naturally protective of their invention and seem to believe that momentum would be lost if the WSF went to a bi-annual schedule, this outcome is not a foregone conclusion. On the contrary, it is possible that encouraging the decentralization of the forum process, whereby either regionally based or thematic solidarity, alliances, and action could be better planned – may in fact give more richness, purpose, and direction to the transnational meetings when they do occur. Recalling the South African activist Patrick Bond's reminder to the G19 Manifesto drafters, would it not be better to allow thematic proposals to emerge from sectoral forums and networks, rather than hastily attempt a synthesis at the transnational level? Perhaps efforts such as the G19 Manifesto and the SMA are premature but natural responses to the need to lend some order and direction to an environment marked by too much diversity and not enough bottom-up consensus building. While certainly the G19, the SMA, and the WSF are each different political animals, there is a sense among the VC and many others that the blueprints for another possible world – as well as the forces necessary to carry it into existence – must come out of identity-based solidarity groups whose daily experience is the battleground against neoliberal globalization, and is thus also the litmus test for the network of networks' successes and failures. These are not to be one but multiple blueprints, rooted in sectors and regions of the world, that can then be linked to each other through encounter, discussion, attribution of interconnectedness and reciprocal solidarity, and finally coordinated action. This is likely the best antidote to the rash, and increasingly popular, efforts on the part of many within the WSF and the ESF to assume, or force, a supposed "consensus."

6 Zapatista-inspired Peoples' Global Action

We turn our attention finally to the Peoples' Global Action (PGA), whose adherents have been closely linked with those of Chapter 5, the Via Campesina. PGA is an organized network of direct action, urban and rural collectives and grassroots movements for autonomy and against capitalism. Inspired by the 1994 Zapatista uprising against the Mexican state and its neoliberal reforms, this network grew out of the Zapatista's intercontinental *encuentros*, formed to share information and coordinate action toward the goal of building one global network "against neoliberalism and for humanity." There are now PGA affiliated groups across Europe, the Americas, and Asia, but given the nature and fluidity of the network their total numbers greatly fluctuate and are therefore difficult to estimate. What makes these disparate groups and individuals part of one transnational network is their subscribing to a set of militant, anti-capitalist, and anarchistic principles and taking action accordingly. These actions have been wide ranging and remarkably innovative, and include internet-diffused calls to action for global protests, international activist caravans, street reclaiming, indymedia and convergence centers. They further entail direct action to counter official meetings that range from pacifist and playful through defensive to combative and angry: As part of the activist "swarm," PGAers don carnival costumes and march in samba bands, suit up in padded white overalls to take baton blows and break through barriers, and dress in black with faces concealed in order to carry out more "projectile" tactics.

The PGA seeks to approximate a rhizomatic web of affinity-based, autonomous, direct action groups who are philosophically averse to hierarchical structures, centralized leadership, and spokespersons representing the network. This group therefore comes the closest to the ideal type of a second-generation direct action network of all the networks studied in this work. But these very characteristics seem to also create the most difficulty for sustaining transnational coordination. The PGA is rather characterized by spikes of organizational activity and mass mobilization around large-scale events such as WTO and G8 meetings, in addition to the world and regional social forums, toward which PGAers have assumed an assertive position of engaged critics. Finally, examining this second-generation network brings into focus most clearly four main tensions inherent in the so-called network of networks and its approximate microcosm of the social forums, namely: hierarchical versus distributed power (i.e. the "vertical vs. horizontal" debate); the age paradox, in which youth comprise the obvious majority both in the streets and at the social forums but are largely absent from positions of "leadership" or "authority" either on public stages or behind the scenes on quasi-official councils, committees, or assemblies; bureaucratic forms of contestation versus transgressive direct action; and, finally, anti-neoliberalism versus anti-capitalism.

All of these supposed dichotomies reveal the fundamental questions confronting activists today, and over which it is nearly impossible to reach "consensus," namely: "Which way forward to what world? And is there only one best way (and one best world)? And if not, are different ways and different worlds complementary or contradictory? And how exactly do you know that?" Given that the PGA is a horizontal, youthful, anti-capitalist, direct action network, it is no wonder that its adherents are met with a mix of trepidation, bewilderment, hope, and devotion by their more senior comrades in the struggle against neoliberal globalization or capitalism. This reception is not unlike the one that greeted their immediate forbears and source of inspiration, the Zapatistas, where our examination of the scale shift process must begin.

Discrimination, rights violations, and land disputes spark localized resistance in rural Mexico

The roots of the PGA can be traced directly to the Ejército Zapatista de Liberación Nacional (EZLN).[1] Although the cultural and spatial distance between Mexico's rural rebels and the young urban anarchists that largely comprise the PGA is considerable, the Zapatistas are both the ideological inspiration for and the concrete brokers of the PGA's founding, and therefore it is important to spend some time elucidating the localized roots of this rebellion. The Zapatistas emerged in 1983 in the resource-rich but dirt-poor state of Chiapas in southeastern Mexico, where nearly 70 percent of the largely indigenous population are malnourished and infant mortality is double that of Mexico's national average. The EZLN itself grew out of *campesino* groups who had banded together across the state in the 1970s against discrimination of indigenous peoples and in defense of agrarian reforms and workers' rights. Not unlike what we saw in the Larzac region of France, which would spawn the CP, these indigenous *campesinos* were joined by leftist students and intellectuals from the Mexico City uprisings and the repression that followed of the late 1960s. And also similar to the CP's José Bové, one of these urban scholars who sought refuge in the countryside went on to become the group's iconic spokesman, Subcomandante Insurgente Marcos. As land disputes intensified, the EZLN emerged as a self-defense force against the growing intimidation and violence by the armed security groups of the cattle ranchers. Although the post-revolution Mexican Constitution affirmed the right to land reform in its Article 27, legal recourse was effectively precluded by chronic electoral fraud, bribery, intimidation, and disenfranchisement of indigenous voters. These disputes grew even more intractable throughout the 1980s and early 1990s.

NAFTA triggers a Zapatista armed uprising

So while these indigenous peasants had been waging a long struggle for their rights to land and to equal treatment under Mexican law, the straw that broke the *chiapanecos*' back – and which triggered the ELZN and its supporters into local rebellion, framed in first national and then transnational terms – was the NAFTA among the US, Mexico, and Canada. The Zapatistas feared this agreement as a mortal threat to the very identity and existence of the indigenous communities in the region, and, indeed, across Mexico. NAFTA required substantial changes to domestic law. First, the already barebones support that the government provided to small farmers would be cut further. Second, the price for their maize would fall and they would lose their internal market, as cheap corn – often genetically modified – would flood Mexico from *el norte*. Third, and just as significant, there was the reform of Article 27 of the Mexican Constitution, which removed the legal right of *ejidos*, or communally held land, and therefore erased the sole legal mechanism by which property could be redistributed in a manner appropriate to indigenous cultures. Finally, this foreclosing of the possibility of agrarian reform augured the scattering of the community, to search for jobs in the *maquiladoras* of the border region or to join the masses of unemployed in the shantytowns that swelled the outskirts of Mexico's metropolises.[2]

In the face of what were perceived as existential threats precipitated by the NAFTA, the Zapatista communities realized the need to generalize their struggle to the nationwide level. They therefore voted for armed uprising as a final resort, expecting either to spark a widespread rebellion or to be crushed by the Mexican army soon after. In the early hours of New Year's Day 1994, just as the continental trade deal was to come into effect, EZLN fighters occupied the Mexican army barracks throughout Chiapas, stormed the prison in Altamirano, setting free over 150 prisoners, took over five city halls, including San Cristóbal de las Casas, and captured the main radio station broadcasting from Ocosingo. Via the radio and from the balconies of the occupied municipal halls, the previously obscure rebels proclaimed their insurrection, reading out their "declaration of war" against the Mexican state as well as promulgating a set of revolutionary laws.[3]

What could have been perceived as a quaint throwback to the neo-Marxist liberation movements of the 1970s nevertheless struck a deep chord in Mexico, across the continent, and soon throughout the world. In appealing first and foremost to Mexicans, the EZLN declaration invoked the revolutionary hero Emiliano Zapata and his uprising for *tierra y libertad* – land and liberty – that led to the post-revolution agrarian reform laws. They called on their fellow citizens to, first, recognize their struggle for sovereignty and against oppression as legitimate under the embattled constitution and, second, to join them in this liberation struggle "for work, land, housing, food, healthcare, education, independence, freedom, democracy, justice and peace," toward "forming a government of our country that is free and democratic."[4] In their appeal to indigenous Latin Americans, the EZLN traced their lineage back through five centuries of anti-colonialism and resistance by indigenous peasants to hold land in common. They further reached out to the international community by declaring themselves subject to the Geneva Accords and asking NGOs and the International Red Cross to monitor their conflict with the Mexican army.

The EZLN linking the revolt to NAFTA evokes transnational solidarity

While their main audience was clearly a domestic one and only secondarily international, the EZLN's timing of the uprising as a symbolic protest against an international free trade agreement was sufficient to quench a global thirst for someone, somewhere, to say, "Enough." It was as if the Zapatistas' pained cry of "*Ya Basta!*" rising from the most marginal corner of the continent shattered the protective silence that had encased the *pensamiento único* of neoliberalism in its ascendancy, which proclaimed no alternative to the market and to (this) globalization. "The naming of the intolerable is itself hope. ... With their uprising the Zapatistas named an old enemy in new clothing – neoliberal globalization. Their rebel yell: 'Ya Basta!' (Enough!) announced the *end* of the end of history."[5]

Their call met with an almost instantaneous response of identification and gratitude from across the globe. Marcos reflected:

> When we rose up against the government, we began to receive displays of solidarity and sympathy not only from Mexicans, but from people in Chile, Argentina, Canada, the United States, and Central America. They told us that the uprising represents something that they wanted to say, and now they have found the words to say it, each in his or her respective country. I believe the fallacious notion of the end of history has finally been destroyed.[6]

What accounts for the Zapatista uprising's tremendous resonance? At its most basic, the rebellion was like a match dropped on a parched terrain that was ready to burn. As we have seen throughout the previous chapters, resistance to neoliberal policy reforms had been building both across the Americas and worldwide throughout the early 1990s. And 1994 seemed to be a particularly hot year: At home, Mexicans suffered the crash of the *peso* and the painful economic and social repercussions that followed. The multi-sector, cross-border alliances of labor, environmentalists, small farmers, human rights activists, and citizens groups that had formed to fight the NAFTA had not been victorious, but neither had they demobilized, and thus they were looking for an outlet to continue their struggle. Anarcho-environmentalists and peasants alike were bringing back direct, non-violent action to the urban streets and countryside from the US and the UK to India and Brazil. Furthermore, IMF riots against debt and structural adjustment scattered across the developing world surged in 1994, along with general strikes – the highest number recorded in any year of the twentieth century.

Second, precisely because alliances and solidarity networks had already been established and strengthened through the new technology of the internet, the news of the Zapatista uprising was able to be diffused quickly and broadly to all those in struggle across the globe. Yet as important as this virtual communication web was fast becoming, the first word of the uprising went out through relational diffusion channels, from tourists – some worried, some exhilarated – to their embassies, families, and travel agents. Furthermore, one student's cell phone call to CNN brought incredulous journalists to investigate and then send the first feeds out over the wire to newspapers, radio, and television.[7]

EZLN and supporters are actively framing and diffusing news of their struggle

Yet the Zapatistas, who had declared war and decreed revolutionary laws from the balconies of taken-over municipal buildings, immediately went to work framing the message themselves, faxing these texts and all further communiqués to a wide range of press outlets. In addition, while Mexico City's *La Jornada* provided the most steady coverage among mainstream press sources in print and on the web, with time Mexican civic and solidarity organizations which sprung up around the Zapatistas – namely the Frente Zapatista de Liberación Nacional (FZLN), the Enlace Civil and the Congreso Nacional Indígena – became increasingly "internet savvy." In a short time, they took the lead in framing the struggle.

One important local source of support with broad-ranging, relational diffusion channels were indigenous groups that had first come together to struggle for public services and against state repression. These collectivities had also been networking for over a decade with others around the Americas, meeting in Ecuador in 1990 and again in Mexico in 1993 for Continental Encounters of Indigenous Peoples. Upon the Zapatista uprising, one of the hosting organizations of the Mexican encounter located in San Cristóbal sent out a call through its coordinating commission asking for indigenous witnesses to come to Chiapas as observers.[8]

Another key set of relational diffusion actors were locally based NGOs who gathered and condensed firsthand information and then diffused it through their larger domestic and international networks. These included the Catholic Bishops of Chiapas, the Canadian Inter-Church Committee on Human Rights in Latin America, Amnesty International, and Human Rights Watch. Their larger networks, in turn, had both relational and non-relational access to the national, continental, and eventually transnational web of already-existing listserves, newsgroups, and websites. These tapped into anti-NAFTA activists, Latin American peace and solidarity groups, and environmental, human rights, and anti-debt e-networks, such as PeaceNet conferences, the Mexico-L, Native-L, and Centam-L listserves, and UseNet newsgroups. The Ya Basta! website established by Justin Paulson and one at the University of Texas in Austin by Harry Cleaver were crucial in pooling news and analysis and in providing their own sympathetic take on the uprising and its broader meaning and ramifications. Others, like the Latin American Data Base at the University of New Mexico and the Institute for Agriculture and Trade Policy, began compiling and then issuing regular news briefings, while still other institutes duplicated and uploaded this information on their own sites. The worldwide web fed into more traditional means of diffusing leftist news, such as local and national papers, journals, and radio programs.

Diverse diffusion channels and frame amplification lead to attribution and solidarity

Through all of these diffusion channels, activists within and beyond Mexico's borders were able to quickly gain information as well as analysis that began to amplify the anti-NAFTA, and more broadly anti-neoliberal, character of the Chiapas uprising. This in turn fostered attribution of worthiness, interconnectedness, and similarity toward solidarity among a wide range of individuals and groups. The resulting outpouring of sympathy, empathy, and identification with their plight, as well as the condemnation and calls for restraint heaped upon the Mexican government, had the immediate effect of shining a collective spotlight on the volatile region and thus preventing the military and police from cracking down with total impunity.[9]

Responsive rebels amplify framing and shift objects and claims toward neoliberalism

A third factor in comprehending the resonance of the EZLN uprising was the leadership's sensitivity and responsiveness to their foreign well-wishers. Perhaps taking a cue from their empathetic web analysts, the Zapatistas quickly reframed their appeals and targets away from the almost exclusively domestic arena of their Declaration of War. They began to more explicitly acknowledge their new international allies in a shared struggle arrayed against a collective enemy. The rebels were in this regard emboldened in their targeting neoliberalism as the source of wide-ranging political, social, economic, and cultural violences suffered across the world, a term that had been in use since the 1970s among activists:[10]

> Re-named "neoliberalism," the historic crime of the concentration of privileges, wealth and impunities, democratizes misery and hopelessness. A new world-war is waged, but now against the entire humanity. ... With the name of "globalization" they describe this modern war which assassinates and forgets. ... A new lie is sold to us as history. The lie about the victory of neoliberalism. ... Instead of humanity, it offers us stock market value indexes, instead of dignity it offers us globalization of misery, instead of hope it offers us emptiness, instead of life it offers us the international of terror.[11]

A Zapatista solidarity website reflected on – and reinforced – their successful frame amplification as follows:

One of the most striking aspects of the Zapatista movement has been the ability to provoke an understanding of common struggle among diverse peoples around the world. In the context of the unusually homogenous character of capitalist policies throughout the North and the South, the Chiapas uprising has united diverse grassroots movements within Mexico and internationally around the recognition of a common enemy – inspiring a collective Ya Basta! from all the victims of international capital. The Zapatistas see themselves as a simple fragment in this kaleidoscope of the exploited people of the earth.[12]

One of the more creative ways that the EZLN has communicated this message is via Subcomandante Marcos's magical realist alter ego, *Durito* the beetle. This witty little bug has become appreciated for his cutting soundbites against neoliberalism. The underlying message is always that neoliberalism is self-destructive, inherently unstable, relentlessly ruthless and anti-human, and therefore evokes progressive resistance everywhere.[13] Declaring that NAFTA is the "death sentence" for the indigenous people of Chiapas, Marcos *qua* Durito has expanded the frame from a local struggle for autonomy and land rights to a global fight against neoliberalism, and, beyond that, against all manifestations of exclusion.

In this way, with the homogenization of neoliberal policies around the world, Chiapas has come to be framed as a "representative" space, both a no place and an everyplace, while its inhabitants, the Zapatistas, are seen as an everyman and everywoman who struggle against *this* globalization. In their framing, too, neoliberalism is equated with all forms of structural violence: "To this recognition of the omnipresence of neoliberalism is added the evidence of diverse forms of violence that are essential to it: the violence of unemployment, of impunity, of racism, of competition."[14]

> Zapatista communiqués repeatedly highlight[ed] the reality of deepening inequalities and concentration of wealth in fewer and fewer hands, the deterioration of social services and cuts in food subsidies leading to increased marginalisation and hunger. The neoliberal model equally represents a systematic attack on worker's rights, social and environmental standards and on the functioning of democracy through regional free-trade treaties such as NAFTA, the European Union, APEC (Asia Pacific) and Mercosur (South America). Finally, they highlight[ed] the increasing domination over the world of a small group of countries and transnational corporations. Globalisation is indeed the new colonialism.[15]

This generalization of neoliberalism as global public enemy number one has greatly promoted the attribution of similarity among diverse struggles. It has prompted discussions and analyses linking NAFTA to the neoliberal policies pursued in the US from the Reagan to the Clinton administrations, similarities between these and Thatcherism in the UK, the changes occurring under the EU

Maastricht Treaty throughout Europe, and the World Bank and IMF SAPs across the debt-ridden developing world.[16] Through this conscious frame amplification that allowed for tremendous frame extension on the part of Marcos and the information brokers on the internet, they were able to bridge what had first emerged as a purely Mexican conflict into an extremely broad one, encompassing virtually all others in struggle against neoliberal and exclusionary policies across the globe.[17]

Zapatismo as a global transformative project of localized action linked by reciprocal solidarity

Fourth and finally, what accounted for the EZLN's resonance was the dynamic, co-constitutive nature of *zapatismo* itself. *Zapatismo* quickly became a project that everyone was encouraged to learn about, engage in, emulate, and adapt to their own situation. Whether via the internet's "virtual" Zapatista community, through activists' traveling to Chiapas as observers, or as "revolutionary tourists" (to use the anguished government's term) participating in the *encuentros* to be discussed in detail later on in the chapter, "practicing *zapatismo* at home" through emulative innovation became *de rigueur* for rebel supporters. Activists have become considerably involved in shaping this alternative mode of organizing, struggling and living *contra* neoliberalism and for "a world that can hold all worlds," in the words of Marcos. It has become a global transformative frame that is constantly evolving and distinct in every locale where it is practiced.

Zapatismo is a heady mix of poetry, inspiration, active resistance, local autonomy, radical pluralism and inclusivity, horizontality and dispersed power, servant-leadership, and communication. It furthermore champions the local and the marginal while recasting internationalism and solidarity in terms of a deep recognition of mutually dependent, webbed relations based on reciprocity and acknowledged dignity among diverse peoples. Each of these features will be touched on below. First, regarding its poetic inspiration, Subcomandante Marcos has characterized *zapatismo* and the emerging network of networks that has grown up around it as an "International of Hope," which is a concept that has had tremendous emotive appeal:

> Into this chapter of history entered the Zapatistas, masked people the colour of the earth, women wearing multi-coloured clothes, some carrying makeshift weapons, and all speaking a quite different language of resistance – of land, poetry, indigenous culture, diversity, ecology, dignity. ... The inspiration, the poetry, and the hope that run deep in the hearts of the Zapatistas [were] contagious, and the tale of the unlikely army found its way in to the hearts and minds of activists around the world for whom hope had become a rare commodity.[18]

Zapatismo is also unapologetically militant. After all, it is an army that declared war on the Mexican state and decreed revolutionary laws – albeit one whose soldiers explicitly long for the day when they no longer have to be an army, and which rather openly acknowledges that its soldiers are often "armed" with fake or unloaded guns. The Zapatistas welcome other militants into a more generalized struggle, inviting them to take a stand in what Marcos has called World War Four, between neoliberalism and dignified existences.[19] Therefore, while nonviolent struggle – seen as non-harm to human beings, animals, and the planet – is a virtue and a general practice in *zapatismo*, the decisions made by those in struggle as to the appropriate tactics for their own situation are respected. Also following the EZLN's example, while leaders can engage in negotiation with the state, it is commonly understood that mass mobilization, autonomous action, withdrawing consent and actively resisting being ruled are the surest ways to overturn neoliberalism and all forms of oppression.

Indeed, the centrality of withdrawing consent to be governed and experimenting with self-organization and collective rule is apparent in *zapatismo*. The examples set by the more than thirty autonomous "liberated zones" across Chiapas, which are run by mass assemblies and which strive to challenge all forms of oppression, to be self-sufficient, and yet to be networked with the others, are seen as models in this regard. In these liberated zones is also manifested *zapatismo*'s idea of power: They eschew seizing power or taking over the state, and, rather, work to break power up among autonomous communities so that each can wield it for themselves. This is their idea of waging a "low intensity revolution" that transforms society from the bottom up, eroding the legitimacy of the state – and, in the contemporary situation, weakening the global governance structures that have come to wield ever greater power over local lives.

Also embodied in the mass assemblies that make collective decisions in the autonomous villages is the circumscribed role of leadership in *zapatismo*. They downplay the idea of a vanguard, and rather have developed a philosophy of *mandando obediciendo* – leading by obeying the will of the community. But while this may be put into practice in Chiapas, it is sometimes difficult to reconcile their stated philosophy with the international image of the EZLN, which is dominated by the charismatic Marcos. Whether *el sub* is in fact leading by obeying or just leading the old-fashioned way, what is undeniable is that *zapatismo* places heavy emphasis on communication, be it in the village assembly or the global solidarity network: It aspires to direct forms of democracy where everyone participates in discussions and decision-making, and where leaders listen. Communication and listening mean that there is no preordained path to revolution, and no exceptionally enlightened leaders. Marcos's exceptional oratory skills notwithstanding, he is certainly no Fidel Castro, and *zapatismo* no Cuban Revolution. Marcos was appointed chief military leader by the Zapatista's Clandestine Indigenous Revolutionary Committee (CCRI in its Spanish acronym), an all-indigenous command group that, one assumes, has the power to remove him from that post if its members so desire.[20] The title itself – that of *sub*comandante – implies subordination to a higher authority, which is that of the community. In any case, *zapatismo* is an explicitly contingent, communicative, and communitarian process, and the *process* itself must embody the ends that they seek.

Zapatismo therefore champions multiple paths to liberation with dignity, captured in the motto "One No and Many Yeses." The "No" is against neoliberalism, and the "Yeses" are the "many worlds" that can fit into one world. In this regard, radical plurality, inclusivity, and respect of difference are all virtues. Finally, though *zapatismo* arose in the most marginal of places, the philosophy seeks to let all of these margins speak. In doing so, it is not at all a "retreat to localism," but rather constantly reaches out from one's own isolation to build toward a new conception of both internationalism and of solidarity.[21]

> The Zapatistas ... [along with] many peasant and campesino movements in this situation have demonstrated an increasingly effective ability to frame the terms of the debate such that they, too, are in favour of moving forward into a "globalized" world – albeit of a different kind. The Zapatista struggle in particular advances the very notions of autonomy, collective action, and dignity that are denied under neoliberalism.[22]

In their organizing of popular *consultas* with Mexican civil society and then continental and intercontinental *encuentros* with foreign activists, the Zapatistas demonstrate a new kind of internationalism, one that is deeply respectful of and mutually dependent on the autonomous struggles of others. As Paulson has observed:

> The Zapatistas know full well, as do most of their supporters, that the struggle isn't just about Chiapas or Mexico; they know that whether they stand or fall will depend on events around the world, just as what happens in Mexico can have a profound effect on the spread or collapse of neoliberalism as a global strategy. Is there any significant meaning to a "struggle at home" when neoliberalism has placed internationalism back on the agenda, both for capitalism and those opposed to it (if they hope to have any effect)?[23]

Zapatismo seeks to network these struggles by fostering a new kind of international solidarity. It is one that attempts to blur the line between attribution of interconnectedness and of similarity, based on a sense of interconnectivity, mutual dependence, and identification among struggles against neoliberalism and for other possible worlds that nonetheless maintain their autonomous character. "In this way, the concept of solidarity itself was redefined – no longer as a relation between those who have and don't have, between those who know and don't know, but instead as a common journey."[24] The solidarity of *zapatismo* therefore encourages people to make their own revolutions in places and manners relevant to them but in identification with and recognition of the mutual dependence upon the outcomes of struggles elsewhere. In this way we can see how the Zapatistas

> conceive[d] the scope of its movement to reach well outside Chiapas, understanding that it is fighting against the momentum of global capital as well as

the national state, and fighting *alongside* other movements similarly disaffected or with similar goals. Thus while … globalization does not lead to the inevitable end of the peasantry or of peasant-based struggles, it does lead to a "globalized" solidarity between these and other struggles against neoliberalism.[25]

This resistance on the part of indigenous peasants demanding rights and recognition recalls Chapter 5 on the Via Campesina, who themselves defy the developmentalist assumptions of both capitalism and communism of the peasantry as a backward, inefficient, and thus disappearing class. As mentioned above, through *zapatismo* an omnipresent neoliberalism has come to be blamed for diverse forms of structural violence, ranging from material violences of the denial of economic and social rights, to racism and all forms of discrimination and exclusion based on difference. The claims made by the Zapatistas are therefore bivalent, reflecting both a social politics of equality and hence claims for redistribution, but, equally important and not reducible to the first set, those of the cultural politics of difference and thus claims for recognition.

The latter are reflected in the fundamental importance of *dignity* to the Zapatista struggle. This was a lesson that the indigenous inhabitants of Chiapas taught to the urban vanguard aspirants who arrived in their lands spouting Marxist rhetoric, viewing the indigenous as an exploited people undifferentiated in any meaningful way from themselves as workers or students. Marcos recalls his metamorphosis from initial frustration through ideational crisis and, eventually, to an educational reckoning. By abandoning the presumptuous vanguard role of guiding the locals along the correct revolutionary path, he instead learned to listen to their grievances: of exploitation, yes, but *also* of humiliation and racism, and of being erased as unique peoples and cultures from history.

Recalled Marcos:

> It's very difficult when you have a theoretical scheme that explains the whole of a society and then you arrive in that society and you realise that your scheme explains nothing. It's difficult to accept; to recognise that you have dedicated all your life to a project, and that this project is fundamentally warped.[26]

But through listening and re-education, what Marcos calls the "Indianization" of the Zapatistas began, which eventually led to the transformative politics not only of emancipation but also of dignity, which would resonate across the world as *zapatismo*:

> The idea of a more just world, of everything that was socialism in broad brushstrokes, but redirected, enriched with humanitarian elements, ethics, morals, more than simply indigenous. Suddenly the revolution transformed itself into something essentially moral. Ethical. More than the redistribution of the wealth or the expropriation of the means of production, the revolution began to be the possibility for a human being to have a space for

dignity. ... The revolution would be the guarantee for dignity, so that it might be respected.[27]

This concept of dignity comes up repeatedly in *zapatismo* parlance. To them it means the right and the act of defining and defending one's individual and group identity. This is not, however, in isolation from, but rather in communication with others whose identities are also respected and recognized. To the Zapatistas, dignity is not an abstract ideal but instead a necessary *practice* for becoming fully human, a practice that makes an ethical revolution possible: "Dignity cannot be studied: you live it or it dies. It aches inside you and teaches you how to walk."[28]

A transnational Zapatista solidarity network emerges

In the immediate aftermath of their New Year's Day uprising, concrete actions of solidarity took the form of huge demonstrations in Mexico as well as smaller manifestations in front of embassies across the US and Canada. Human rights, Latin American peace and solidarity, and indigenous groups soon sent witnesses to monitor the struggle and prevent repression by the Mexican forces. As the "virtual" solidarity network continued to widen – and along with it the framing of neoliberalism as a common enemy and *zapatismo* as a common project – solidarity played a "boomerang" role: A nascent Zapatista solidarity network began pressuring from outside the Mexican government to uphold the human rights of the indigenous population and for greater democratization. As the support infrastructure grew more sophisticated from the ground up to the global level, activists were better able to monitor the army's activities and publicize human rights abuses.[29]

While news and analysis of the uprising continued to be diffused, the Zapatistas attracted wider support from outside of North America, mainly from two very different sorts of groups: rural peasant and indigenous organizations from the South, and urban anarchists from the North. Peasant movements, including the Brazilian MST and the Indian KRRS, along with other members of the Via Campesina, could rather easily frame-bridge to the Chiapas peasant uprising and attribute similarity with their own situation and struggle. This successful bridging was exemplified in VC's issuing one of only two press releases in their first year of existence in support of the Zapatista struggle.[30] Yet significant attribution of *something* – be it worthiness, interconnectedness, or even similarity – also came from European collectives of anarchists, autonomists, environmentalists, and anti-capitalists, such as the UK's Earth First! and its spin-off Reclaim the Streets, and the Italian *operaista* Ya Basta! and Tute Bianche, or White Overalls. Virtual *zapatismo* also inspired media activists and culture-jammers who would go on to pioneer "hacktivism" and indymedia.[31] Noted activists themselves in some disbelief:

> These two groups, the natural resource-based movements – the indigenous, the farmers – of the South, and the post-industrial marginalized of the

North, have somehow recognized [with] one another a shared enemy – global capital. Suddenly, the "blue indians" and the real Indians [*sic*] are speaking the same language.[32]

Brokered spaces of *encuentros* foster solidarity and commitment to found a transnational network

The space that was opened to give them the opportunity to speak and to develop a shared language that is *zapatismo* was, first of all, the virtual spaces of the list-serves, described above; but, second and just as important, it was in the face-to-face *encuentros* called for and brokered by the Zapatistas themselves, and out of which the global network of the PGA could be formed. As a collective of *zapatismo*-inspired activists put it:

> It was the poetic communiqués and powerful stories that trickled from the Zapatista autonomous zones in the Chiapas jungle onto the relatively new medium of the internet which told of their suffering, their struggles, their mythologies, that began to weave an electronic fabric of struggle in the mid-nineties. This web of connections between diverse groups gave birth to a series of face-to-face international gatherings – the Zapatista Encuentros – which soon grew to become the roaring, unstoppable torrent of movements for life and dignity and against capital that are emerging across the world.[33]

Marking the two-year anniversary of the uprising, in January 1996 the EZLN proffered the First Declaration of La Realidad. This declaration, sent through its considerable diffusion channels, called on activists around the world to form a "bridge" among themselves by self-organizing continental *encuentros* in the spring, as preparatory meetings for an Intercontinental Encounter for Humanity and Against Neoliberalism to be held in Chiapas that summer. In this regard, the Zapatistas were playing both non-relational brokers by calling for groups to self-organize into continental meetings, and relational ones by hosting the American and then intercontinental meetings themselves in Chiapas. Their call drew an enthusiastic response: outside of the Americas, Zapatista supporters organized three other continental encounters in Berlin, Tokyo, and Sydney.[34] The EZLN cast a wide net by framing their invitation in the broadest possible terms:

- To all who struggle for human values of democracy, liberty and justice.
- To all who force themselves to resist the world crime known as "Neoliberalism" and aim for humanity and hope to be better, [and] to be synonymous of the future.
- To all individuals, groups, collectives, movements, social, civic and political organizations, neighborhood associations, cooperatives, all the lefts known and to be known; non-governmental organizations, groups in solidarity with struggles of the world people, bands, tribes, intellectuals, indigenous people, students, musicians, workers, artists, teachers, peasants, cultural groups,

youth movements, alternative communication media, ecologists, tenants, lesbians, homosexuals, feminists, pacifists.

- To all human beings without a home, without land, without work, without food, without health, without education, without freedom, without justice, without independence, without democracy, without peace, without tomorrow.
- To all who, with no matter to colors, race or borders, make of hope a weapon and a shield.[35]

Around three thousand activists took Marcos up on his invitation and made their way to the muddy backwater of Chiapas to participate in the EZLN-brokered encounter, or *intergaláctica*. Over the week of 27 July through 4 August 1996, activists from forty-three countries representing fifty-five nationalities shared position papers, analysis, stories, and arguments – as best they could in a dozen languages – on the topics of politics, society, economics, culture, and gender, scattered across five autonomous communities, which in *zapatismo*-speak are called *aguascalientes*. Though most of those in attendance were young and European – German autonomists, Italian Ya Basta! and Rifondazione Comunista party members, Basque fighters, ecologists, and Spanish trade unionists – the meeting also attracted Brazilian MST and Workers' Party representatives, retired guerilla fighters from around the Americas, a Cuban delegation, plus leftist intellectuals and artists like Eduardo Galeano, Alain Touraine, and the political rock band Rage Against the Machine.[36]

In the discussions, one long-time chronicler of the EZLN, John Ross, detected a distinction between Northern and Southern conceptions of autonomy. The Europeans tended to view it as an *autonom*, a squat, a fringe space, at the edge of society – and, one might add, at times a space made out of choice to *remove* oneself from mainstream society;[37] while South Americans were fighting not only for autonomy but also for *inclusion* in their societies, because their marginal place – not chosen but *given* by centuries of racism, colonization, and poverty – was threatening not only their autonomy but their very existence. Such mutual discoveries had a profound effect on many present, for they foreshadowed the formidable obstacles to forging a truly united and sustained transnational resistance network. At the same time, such mutual discovery brought them a small step closer to such a "network of networks" becoming a reality, through face-to-face solidarity building that would lead to future experiments in coordination and mobilization as the PGA. Remembers one activist who was there:

> They invited people for an international gathering of the very first of the type. ... Thousand[s of] people went to the jungle, in the mud and everything. It was really great [because] ... we saw how all these networks that we developed over the e-mail became human. And then we rode that, and from there, we went to Seattle. ... I see a very clear connection: Chiapas in '96 in the jungle, Spain in '97. ... We started working and talking about the WTO and everything there, and then we had Seattle.[38]

This week of encounter culminated in a shared commitment to build a transnational resistance network. In the Second Declaration of La Realidad, those present pledged to forge "a collective network of all our particular struggles and resistances, an intercontinental network of resistance against neoliberalism, an intercontinental network of resistance for humanity." This innovative network, which is the direct forerunner of the PGA, was not to have an "organizing structure; it has no central head or decision maker; it has no central command or hierarchies. We are the network, all of us who resist."[39]

The PGA forerunner RICA organizes the second *intergaláctica* in Spain

In calling for the formation of an intercontinental network of resistance, the Zapatistas not only took care to propose a network of people, but also had given some thought as to *how* activists would actually be linked together. They therefore proposed an alternative communication network, which would mirror and facilitate the ideal web of struggles that they wanted to create. As a result of the meetings, efforts bloomed over the internet as well as in other mediums toward creating this Intercontinental Network of Alternative Communication, bearing the Spanish acronym of RICA, imagined by the Zapatistas.[40] A number of new listserves were created to build this network, for example the EZLN-it in Italian and the Jovenes & Jovenes-d for Spanish-speaking youth.[41]

Through these and the preexisting listserves, European members immediately got to work on brokering a second intercontinental encounter, this time on their side of the Atlantic. Spanish groups working under the umbrella Mesa de Madrid hosted the event from 26 July to 2 August 1997. Emulating the Chiapas intercontinental's five autonomous *aguascalientes*, the Spanish organizers located the same number of squatted or communal spaces around Madrid, Aragon, and Andalucia to hold the roundtables. Also, like the first *intergaláctica*, the second attracted thousands from some fifty countries. While many were, again, young and European, there also were participants from Brazilian, Indian, and Indonesian peasant associations representing the VC, Nigerians fighting Shell Oil, Tuaregs from the Sahara, Bolivian workers, and two Zapatistas.[42]

The stated purpose of the meeting was to focus on the struggles themselves, with the central objective of continuing to build this network of resistance to which they committed in Chiapas. The method was to exchange ideas and experiences on new forms of struggles against neoliberalism and new ways of doing politics, centered on the bivalent themes of North–South relations, culture, education and information, women and patriarchy, land and ecology, and marginalization. Like the first *encuentro*, the follow-up had a profound impact on many who attended, making "real" their virtual ties and in the process strengthening the attribution of interconnectedness of struggles against the common target of neoliberalism, leading to reciprocal solidarity among disparate groups and individuals. Here are one European activist's reflections on the experience:

With two others from the UK I had traveled down south to Andalucia where a local community had squatted a farm. ... Our group was to discuss the struggle for the land. With me were delegates from the Karnataka State Farmers Association, Indonesia's land reform struggle, the landless peasant movement Sem Terra from Brazil, Bolivian mine-workers, Ogoni people from Nigeria, Gorlbeen anti-nuclear activists – to name but a few. We had come together to build networks, to listen, to share and most of all to look at how we could resist together the onslaught of neoliberalism. ... As teams of translators gave meaning to the voices of the voiceless I began to realise that our struggles which at first appeared so different *were intricately linked*. In spite of the cultural and language differences between us I made friends. A week later representatives of hundreds of groups had committed themselves to taking action together.[43]

Scale shift is consolidated with the establishment of PGA: an analysis of the network composition and character

At this encounter these activists developed a more tangible consensus statement on how to construct a permanent network of people and organizations to communicate and coordinate resistance and action. Reaching this consensus at the second *intergaláctica* served to consolidate this network's shift to the transnational level. As we examine their founding statement, we can at the same time begin our analysis of the composition and character of this emerging transnational activist network that would become the PGA.

What is most striking about the consensus document is that, of all the groups studied herein, the PGA most closely embodies a second-generation, direct activism social justice network. Regarding its formation, as we have traced up until this point, the network grew up both in the face-to-face brokered spaces of the *encuentros* and on the listserves that preceded and followed them. This means that rather than key NGOs strategically brokering relations around a pre-established agenda – as we saw in previous chapters in Oxfam's seminal role in Jubilee 2000 or in the Paulo Freire Stichting's thwarted efforts to found the VC as a research network – the PGA forged itself largely through affinity ties among individuals and collectives who prize autonomy and direct action. Together they developed a consensus to launch a permanent campaign "against neoliberalism and for humanity," in the words of their Zapatista muse, Marcos. Given these militant roots coupled with the broad scope of their claims, the network was, from the beginning, organized to foment mass activism around multiple issues.

How they planned to go about it was by crafting a polycentric, leaderless, inclusive, and distributed network structure. Here it is useful to remember Bennett's depiction of second-generation network's organizational model *being* the network ideology, for this is largely accurate *vis-à-vis* the PGA.[44] Indeed, the PGA is often referred to by those who adopt its moniker as nothing but a mechanism or a tool for communication toward promoting coordinated action.[45] As a tool or a mechanism, second-generation networks attempt to embody and facilitate the goals of personal involvement in direct action through establishing communication among groups in a "hyper-organization" with diverse and evolving political goals and campaigns.

These features are all present in the PGA consensus statement. They explicitly patterned their new network on the worldwide web, to be comprised of organized nodes which would connect them into a horizontal structure without a specific center. These nodes are to send and receive information with the capacity to organize common action, and are to encourage the free flow and distribution of information, connectivity, mutual support, and complete equality among all members. But while their organizational model and practice to a large extent *are* their ideology, these activists also identified more tangible goals, demonstrating the scope of their claims as a diverse social justice movement. Their main collective purpose, according to their initial statement, is to combat all forms of oppression, degradation, and destruction of the person and of distinct peoples, while "simultaneously constructing a new world that can contain all worlds: those of today and also those of the future."

With regard to diffusion, membership, and network stability, in their statement they recognized the need to build their network at the local, regional, national, and international levels in order to grow into their goal of one global network for humanity and against neoliberalism. They acknowledged, however, the current imbalances within their network – both virtual and in the face-to-face encounters. So while the PGA had begun in Europe and the Americas, they sought to encourage participation of social movements in Asia, Africa, East Europe, and Oceania. Furthermore, they recognized that many were already mobilizing against neoliberalism across the world, and therefore they needed to build relations with these other actors, promoting creative mixing, while at the same time maintaining their autonomy. This latter point, coupled with their expressed desire to affirm and strengthen the autonomy of each PGA affiliated group at every step of the network-building process, reveals an important feature of their perceived network stability. For in this regard they believe that their collective integrity, as well as that of others, is guaranteed not through an "anything goes" or an "everyone welcome" attitude, which could be the excess of an organizational code which places no limits on inclusive diversity. Instead – and this is perhaps the only feature that the PGA shares with a first-generation advocacy network – a good deal of autonomy was seen as necessary both within the network as well as among allies in order to maintain some network cohesion and a distinct identity, and thus stability.

Turning now to the emerging network's mobilization tactics and targets, participants at the second *intergaláctica* decided on concrete initiatives for the near future. Each collective was to build the web at their local level while working together on a campaign of coordinated action against upcoming meetings of the WTO in Geneva in March 1998 and at the official summit to be held in May 1998. But beyond targeting the trade organization – and reflecting its broad scope of bivalent claims – this emerging network also identified a range of targets for future campaigns: all regional trade agreements, the European

Maastricht Treaty, Northern imperialism, TNCs, and in particular Shell, Nestle, Nike, and Siemens, climate change, political prisoners, patriarchy, GMOs, and the Schengen Treaty's policy on immigrants.[46]

In reaching this consensus at the second *intergaláctica* and consolidating their shift to the transnational level, there were also other, less perceptible but portentous, shifts occurring within the emergent network. These will be taken up in greater detail later in the chapter in the discussion of identity and solidarity; but here it is just important to point out that, while aspiring to be diverse and global, the organizers of the second international *encuentro*, along with those in attendance, were again overwhelmingly young, urban Europeans. So although Southern activists, including two EZLN representatives, were present in Spain, in a real sense this meeting marked three crucial shifts with regard to taking the lead in coordinating this emergent network: from Latin America to Europe, from rural to urban, and from older to younger. While *zapatismo* was still the guiding force, the *Zapatistas* were no longer so. At the conclusion of the meeting, Ross observed: "The Intergalactica had gotten away from the Zapatistas. They were no longer the reason for the gathering, and although everyone faithfully sang the Zapatista hymn, when it came time to chant 'Todos Somos Marcos!' radical feminists refused."[47]

In the months that followed the Spanish encounter, those activists who had agreed to found the PGA got to work on planning for the upcoming WTO protests and simultaneously kicking off their network, which they did at a conference and series of roundtables from 18 to 27 February 1998.[48] Despite the shift noted above toward young, urban Europeans gaining momentum, the diffusion of their message among diverse activists as well as their organizational code of inclusive diversity (but within certain limits) was still broad ranging: Over 300 delegates from seventy-one countries participated in PGA's founding. In addition to direct action anti-capitalist, autonomist, and ecology groups from around Europe like the UK's Reclaim the Streets and Ya Basta!, those present included peasant and fisherfolk organizations from India, the Philippines, Brazil, Estonia, Norway, Honduras, France, Spain, Switzerland, Bangladesh, Senegal, Mozambique, Togo, Peru, Bolivia, and Colombia, many of whom were part of the VC. Indigenous peoples like Ogoni, Maori, Mayan, Aymara, U'wa, and others also signed on, including representatives from the Zapatista support group FZLN. So did educators fighting against privatization in Argentina, women organizing in the sweatshops of Mexico, Bangladesh, El Salvador, and Nicaragua, and other women's rights activists, as well as anti-nuclear and peace activists, defenders of workers' rights in Ukraine and South Korea, anti-NAFTA groups from the United States, Canadian postal workers, environmentalists and animal rights activists, and those fighting racism, discrimination, and employment precariousness.[49]

In the lead-up to this founding meeting, activists had drafted and circulated via the web a manifesto which expanded upon the declaration of the second *intergaláctica*. At Geneva, they reached a consensus on this new document, which entailed a "manifesto" centering on economic globalization and taking aim at the WTO especially, a set of hallmarks, and organizational principles. Regarding the first point, the manifesto clarified the network's objects and claims by overviewing globalization's harmful effects, ranging across the exploitation of labor, gender oppression, threats to indigenous people's survival, oppression of ethnic minorities, harm to nature, agriculture, and cultural diversity, biased knowledge production and technology, distorted educational systems, militarization, and migration and discrimination. They ended their manifesto as they began, by naming the enemy as economic globalization and reinforcing their proximate target of the WTO, but also delineating, *zapatismo*-style, a positive vision of how to build an alternative together:

> The need has become urgent for concerted action to dismantle the illegitimate world governing system which combines transnational capital, nation-states, international financial institutions and trade agreements. Only a global alliance of peoples' movements, respecting autonomy and facilitating action-oriented resistance, can defeat this emerging globalised monster. If impoverishment of populations is the agenda of neo-liberalism, direct empowerment of the peoples through constructive direct action and civil disobedience will be the programme of the Peoples' Global Action against "Free" Trade and the WTO.
>
> We assert our will to struggle as peoples against all forms of oppression. But we do not only fight the wrongs imposed on us. We are also committed to building a new world. We are together as human beings and communities, our unity deeply rooted in diversity. Together we shape a vision of a just world and begin to build that true prosperity which comes from human empowerment, natural bounty, diversity, dignity and freedom.[50]

Second, the founding groups also reached a consensus on five hallmarks, which would become the ideational glue that adheres individuals and collectives to the network. In so doing, they gave the PGA a minimal, and doubtless necessary, identity, showing once again that even in those networks that epitomize so-called second-generation direct activism, there are limits to inclusion and diversity, and hence there needs to be some consensual *content* to ideology, beyond simply ideology *as* network model. The hallmarks, which they revisit at their international meetings, state the network's opposition to capitalism, imperialism, and feudalism, and to trade agreements, institutions, and governments that promote destructive globalization, patriarchy, racism, and religious fundamentalism, while they affirm human dignity. To advance their hallmarks, they choose confrontation over persuasion or lobbying of governments. Their methods therefore entail direct action, civil disobedience, and active solidarity with other social movements. But while they are physically assertive, they advocate forms of resistance that respect life and people's rights.[51] They further seek local alternatives to overcoming global capitalism, based on decentralization and autonomy.

Third, in their organizational principles, the PGA explicitly eschew the term "organization" or "NGO" and rather call their network "an instrument of inspiration, coordination, and international projection of struggles against global capitalism and neoliberalism and for indigenous and cultural preservation." They therefore have no membership *per se*, yet maintain a secretariat as well as "contact points" for each region of the world. These contact groups or individuals disseminate information and coordinate conferences. They have also established a support group to do fundraising. Volunteers from the network maintain the PGA website and coordinate separate e-mail lists. They share information via postings to their website and listserves and face to face at conferences and protests.[52]

In laying down their set of hallmarks and organizational principles, the Zapatista-inspired PGA sought to clearly distinguish themselves from first-generation and some hybrid networks led by NGOs that often reflect a reformist agenda. Instead, both the content of their hallmarks and their organizational design entail bivalent claims against capitalism and all forms of domination and aim at transforming these oppressive structures through loosely coordinated, yet autonomous, direct action. Although not stated as such, it appears that their multiple targets and campaigns are conceived of within a transitional paradigm that never loses sight of the transformative goals.

Given their explicit anti-capitalism, prioritizing of confrontational tactics, and decentralized coordination, the PGA founders – unlike the Via Campesina – did not need to ban NGOs from participating outright: Their paradigm, tactics, and organizational structure rendered the network both unpalatable and uncooptable for most professional NGOs working to counter some facet of neoliberalism. We will look at this prickly relationship in more detail when we examine the PGA's critical inside/outside stance *vis-à-vis* the WSF and regional forums. But in order to better understand both the PGA's appeal to younger activists and the controversy they provoke among their targets, the media, and many activists engaged in more contained forms of protest and persuasion, let us first examine the PGA tactics in greater detail.

Innovative tactics demonstrate a capacity for mass mobilization and commitment to direct action

As a transnational network, PGAers have been responsible for developing a number of popular tactics emphasizing creative direct action, ranging from high-tech and global to low-tech and localized, from "fluffy" to "spiky," and others in between. Each demonstrates this network's capacity to mobilize a diverse array of activists. These tactics include the internet-diffused calls to action for global protests, international activist caravans, street reclaiming, and indymedia and convergence centers. They further entail direct action and civil disobedience at street protests that fall along the so-called "fluffy" versus "spiky" continuum: that is, from pacifist and playful through defensive to combative and angry. As part of the activist "swarm" of official meetings, diverse PGAers break off into autonomous blocs that can include a "pink bloc," who create a carnival atmosphere by combining outrageous costumes with samba marching bands; a "white bloc," who don padded white overalls to absorb baton blows and attempt to break through police barriers; and a "black bloc," who dress to intimidate and carry out "projectile" tactics that range from throwing stones through windows, to tossing Molotov cocktails at the police, to hurling their bodies over barricades and into the "red zone," all in an effort to physically shut down official meetings. Each of these tactics will be detailed briefly below.

Calls to global days of action

At their founding meeting, the PGA agreed to issue a call for a global day of decentralized actions of nonviolent civil disobedience and in the construction of local alternatives to protest against the upcoming WTO meetings. This second WTO ministerial, to be held in mid-May 1998, was to be a "50 Years of GATT" celebration at its Geneva headquarters. The nascent PGA called on activists to crash that party. To publicize and coordinate the day of action and encourage emulation and diffusion of the protests, PGA established a press group from different regions to centralize information, keep the network informed about protests by posting them on the website and over various listserves, and contact the press. This would be the first of many such calls that members would put out from then on, sparking a series of mass mobilizations that would see consider- able autonomous but coordinated action across the globe, in addition to creativity in direct action tactics.[53]

PGA's first call to action against the WTO was answered by tens of thou- sands. In more than sixty actions on all continents, groups autonomously organized marches, mass street demonstrations, and parties throughout the month of May. Ten thousand activists converged on the Geneva WTO headquarters. Beyond Europe, dozens of initiatives were carried off throughout Latin America and Asia. Tens of thousands of Brazilian landless, Filipino fisherfolk, and indige- nous Maori from New Zealand marched on and rallied in their capital cities. Korean unions called a general strike.[54] The largest protests were undertaken in India, where the KRRS helped launch a series of nationwide actions beginning on May Day that would mobilize an estimated half a million through the course of the month around demands for their government's immediate withdrawal from the WTO.[55] This "global call" tactic is now emulated by many other networks, including ATTAC, the SMA, activists of the GAAWM, and the VC. The latter's calls for a global day of action in support of peasants have in turn been supported and distributed by the PGA themselves.

Caravans of solidarity and resistance

The Indian KRRS was also vitally important to another innovation of the PGA network, that of the peoples' caravans.[56] At the PGA founding meeting, the KRRS proposed the idea for an Intercontinental Caravan of Solidarity and Resistance which would cross Europe in protest against the G8. Together with several hundred European PGAers, 450 Southern activists – mostly KRRS but also others from India, Mexico, Colombia, Brazil, Pakistan, Bangladesh, and Nepal who were also part of the VC – traveled through nine European countries over the course of a month, culminating in a "Global Day of Action Against Financial Centers" and a "Carnival against Capitalism" at the G8 Summit in Cologne, Germany, on 18 June 1999.[57] Throughout that month, eleven busloads of activists participated in 63 direct actions, 85 public meetings, 38 farm visits, and 30 parties. Along the way they held angry protests at the WTO building on Lake Geneva, Cargill's offices, and the NATO headquarters in Brussels; the KRRS joined with the CP and Bové to uproot a field of genetically modified rice; and they ended their tour with a "laugh parade" at the G8 Summit.[58] The caravans' arrival in Cologne coincided with considerable coordinated action in over 100 cities in forty-one countries.

Reflecting on the purpose of this caravan and the possibilities for South–North mutual learning, identification, and action, one KRRS activist stated:

> We want to say to the G8 leaders: "We do not want your charity, we do not want your loans." Those in the North have to understand our struggle and realize it is also part of their own. Everywhere the richer are getting richer, the poor are getting poorer, and the environment is being plundered. Whether in the North or South, we face the same future. We see the European farmers also being affected by "free trade" policies. Just as Europe exported its development model to the rest of the world, now it is our turn to bring an alternative development model to you.[59]

Street reclaiming

Meanwhile, at the G8 Summit in Birmingham held in the two days prior to the WTO meeting, as Jubilee 2000 ringed the conference site, a Reclaim the Streets event hosted about 8,000 partygoers. Reclaim the Streets originated as an Earth First! campaign launched in Britain in 1995. Their first initiative in an urban environment combined direct nonviolent action and massive civil disobedience with a carnival atmosphere to "reclaim the streets" from cars and for people. The action entails physically blocking a street – often by crashing two old cars into each other – and then quickly securing the space with scaffolding, furniture, and/or webs of string. A sound system is erected, refreshments are provided, and a dance party is started to attract passersby. Sometimes it entails the use of giant people and/or puppets which hide beneath their skirts another ecological tactic, that of "guerrilla gardening": In the street party version of it, shrouded activists jack-hammer the pavement and hastily drop in a tree, recently "liberated" from a suburban-sprawl lawn.[60] Street reclaiming would be repeated the following June in the City of London, yielding some 10,000 street reclaimers in a "Carnival Against Capitalism," while others gathered in Cologne to protest the G8 meeting there. Street reclaiming has now taken on a life of its own, entering the repertoire of direct, non-violent action – though often entailing some property theft, defacement, and destruction – and becoming a popular activity especially across the Global North.[61]

Zapatista-inspired indymedia

As noted earlier, another significant innovation inspired by the Zapatistas and brought to fruition by the "virtual *zapatismo*" support network that grew up around them is independent media, or indymedia. In 1997 Subcomandante Marcos's video communiqué found its way to the Freeing the Media Conference in New York; in it he called for an independent media that would become "a knot of resistance against the lie."[62] In the audience were activists who would soon come together to form the first indymedia center during the Battle in Seattle in late November 1999. One of them was Jeff Perlstein, who noted: "In the independent and activist media world, there was a lot of discussion about networking, the need for us to have a powerful, vibrant network, as a true alternative to the corporation's network – a people's network."[63] Just weeks before the project was to be launched, Perlstein traveled to Austin, Texas, for the Public Grassroots Media Conference. There he met up with seasoned alternative-media activist groups like Paper Tiger and Free Speech TV, who pledged their help. He also encountered Austin-based Acción Zapatista, who were able to infuse *zapatismo* into the Seattle initiative. As it turned out,

> [Acción Zapatista] provid[ed] a lot of the ideological framework, a lot of input on the process and the importance of process and how the Zapatistas have put that at the forefront, and also a reclaiming of space and keeping this decentralized network, and this whole idea of "one no and many yeses," that we all can come together in these movements from one unified "no" ... to global capital, to confront power from above, but that the model and the process [have] to have ways for people to express their different yeses, their different identities. ... So the whole project really accelerated then.[64]

Over the course of the week of protests, the *zapatismo*-influenced Seattle IMC created a website that received 1.5 million hits and sent 100 videographers into the streets to chronicle the stories of activists themselves, the escalating protests and the violent police crackdown, the public hearings that condemned this behavior, as well as the jail solidarity. The space itself, a donated storefront in downtown Seattle, was also crucial: When a curfew was imposed on the city, the IMC media-activists, being in the heart of the "no-protest zone," were detained and essentially trapped in the center overnight.

It is perhaps ironic that in the process of constructing this largely virtual, web-based initiative, what is vitally important to the rapid growth of indymedia is the work of local activists, the face-to-face encounters, and the experience of being physically in the protest milieu. As one media activist describes it:

> Although we are all linked now by this website, Indymedia.org, there's a real emphasis on the physical spaces, because one of the whole points is to reclaim space for ourselves, for people to interact and to come together and dialogue and exchange, and that that can happen in the virtual realm, but

most powerfully happens when we're face-to-face, so these physical locations are linked by this virtual connection.[65]

Indeed, wherever a PGA call for action has been directed, an indymedia center and website have usually sprung up to support it. While the PGA has no official membership, indymedia activists tend to be more aligned with the anarchist principles of the PGA than with other activist networks present at street protests, and it is therefore in this informal way that indymedia can be considered a PGA "tactic." Often these centers, as we saw in Seattle, face threats, intimidation, and sometimes outright seizure by government authorities. In October 2004, for example, the US Justice Department, in apparent collaboration with the Italian and Swiss governments, persuaded the UK authorities to seize hard drives from two indymedia servers, which temporarily downed twenty websites across Europe, South America, and the US. In response, indymedia issued a declaration condemning this type of action and calling on activists to sign on to support free speech.[66]

Convergence centers as experiments in village-based solidarity

A related autonomous space that has sprung up alongside the PGA global days of action – and suffers similar treatment by the authorities as the IMCs – is the convergence center. In Washington, Philadelphia, London, Gothenburg, and Genoa, police have raided these centers, often confiscating food, medical supplies, and activists' belongings, while destroying props, banners, and costumes. These centers are seen as subversive perhaps because they are framed in terms of temporary, autonomous spaces, outside of the cash economy, and rather an experiment in village-based solidarity:

> A convergence centre [is] a gathering site for people to come together, learn new skills, meet new allies, hold incredibly long meetings, and together, make plans for the upcoming actions. A convergence centre can be little more than a space in which to gather, or it can be a highly coordinated community centre, offering information to folks from out of town, helping to find accommodation, hosting cultural events, trainings, spokescouncil meetings,[67] health clinics, art-, puppet- and banner-making.[68]

Activist swarm

As touched on earlier, in answering the first PGA global call to action thousands of activists converged on Geneva in the first of many "swarms" on WTO headquarters. This swarm included teach-ins, silent processions, direct action, marches against unemployment and exclusion, obstruction of transnational businesses on "Peoples' Trade Day," and bicycle caravans.[69] The swarm label was coined by the conservative US think-tank Rand Corporation to describe the Zapatista insurgency, as well as the support networks and affinity groups it has spawned both over the internet and in large-scale protests, like the Direct Action Network and the black bloc tactics in Seattle.[70] The term has since been appropriated by anarchists and other activists to describe their own organizational mode. Its characteristics include a spreading and self-regulated movement based on intercommunicating smaller units, an emphasis on localized knowledge, information, relations, and action, and creative randomness that comes through decentralization.[71]

The direct action tactics that comprise these swarms have often been characterized as either "fluffy" – that is, playful, theatrical, carnivalesque, and non-violent – or "spiky" – that is, defensive or offensive tactics that engage the police and attempt to physically disrupt and stop the official proceedings. Rather than a sharp dichotomy, fluffy to spiky is best seen as a continuum of tactics and views on engagement. While these divergent positions continue to spark heated debate, tensions, and splits among anarchists, and although the PGA is committed to non-harm of individuals and other living things, there is at the same time a general acceptance of "diversity of tactics" among them. In order to respect this diversity and still be able to collectively swarm the same meetings, these activists have organized themselves into distinct blocs, comprised of smaller affinity groups with agreed-upon protest routes and actions, who still often maintain limited coordination and identification with other blocs. As one member of the White Overalls Movement Building Libertarian Effective Struggles (WOMBLES) put it:

> Our movement is highly diverse, with people from across the social spectrum getting involved. So, therefore, should our events be organised in a way that accommodates and respects this diversity. Let the "fluffies" be fluffy, let the "spikeys" be spiky, and let's make room for everything else in between, physically as well as tactically.[72]

Although the blocs can go by different "colors," the most common are pink, white, and black.[73] Each will be overviewed below.

Pink bloc: tactical frivolity of carnival costumes and marching bands

As we saw in previous discussions of street reclaiming and caravans, "carnival" is a recurrent theme in PGA's repertoire of contention.[74] The pink bloc evolved from the more localized Reclaim the Streets parties as a way of taking that carnivalesque show on the road. For many, the carnival symbolizes both the means and the end that they seek: an immediate, joyful, anarchic revolution of contemporary society. "Carnival and rebellion have identical goals: to invert the social order with joyous abandon and celebrate our indestructible lust for life. Carnival breaks down the barriers of capital, and releases the creativity of each individual."[75]

Individual creativity is in abundance in groups like the UK's Tactical Frivolity. This group of women create pink and silver carnival costumes and props in order to bring glamour, humor, and femininity to what oftentimes devolves into a *macho* test of strength at street demos. "Glam it up girls. Pink is power," muses one of the seamstresses. Capturing the essence of Tactical Frivolity's pacifist strategy, she continues, "Wearing pink in threatening situations changes everything. It calms the anarchists and the cops. You change minds much faster by celebration and smashing peoples' sense of reality."[76] Costume-clad revelers have combined creative forces with bands such as the Rhythms of Resistance (ROR) to form their pink blocs. ROR emerged in the lead-up to the Prague IMF and World Bank demonstrations, and is perhaps the most well known of the drumming groups and marching bands that have sprung up around the world and which now form their own "international network of percussive resistance to the march of capitalism." Drawing on Brazilian samba and Bahian Afro bloc drumming, these groups effectively provide the soundtrack to the anti-capitalist resistance actions.[77] The celebratory atmosphere created within the pink bloc allows for people of all ages and physical abilities to take part in anti-capitalist actions, without, as ROR says, "getting locked into a dialectic of escalating physical force between young able bodied militants and the cops."

Yet others, such as the Seattle-based Infernal Noise Brigade (INB), veer toward the spiky end of the spectrum. Their color is not pink, but traditional anarchist black and red. Further, their rhythms are not meant to be peaceful, but rather "threatening," and therefore include not only carnival beats but also warrior rhythms. INB see themselves as providing "tactical psychological support" through a "propaganda of sound" and the waging of "psychological warfare."[78] Their mission statement (which seems consciously absurd) is:

> [to] strike fear and incomprehension in the minds of the powerful. Disrupt the dominant trance. Be calculatedly unpredictable and undermine the spectacle by introducing music of a disorienting or ecstatic nature into the sterile political discourse. Disrupt the stale dichotomy of leftist protest and police cliché. Facilitate the self-actualization of the mob. Be the dope propaganda.[79]

Perhaps not surprisingly, the fierce INB got gassed and attacked in Seattle. But so did the tactically frivolous pink bloc in Prague. It goes to show you never can tell.

White bloc: defensive tactics of Tute Bianche

Another, more defensive, tactical innovation of PGAers was developed in the streets of Europe, by the Italian Ya Basta!, embodied by their *Tute Bianche*. The Ya Basta! groups took their names from the Zapatista declaration of "Enough!," and came together in the squatted autonomous youth centers in Italian cities. Coalescing after the first intercontinental and helping to plan the second in Spain, their main purpose was to support the struggle in Chiapas, foment anti-neoliberal mobilization across Europe, and experiment with *zapatismo*. Their primary efforts have been in practicing civil and social disobedience around the issues of anti-capitalism, anti-racism, and anti-sexism and promoting a universally guaranteed basic income, global citizenship, and therefore the right to travel freely.[80] In support of the latter, many of these activists are involved in the No Borders network, No One Is Illegal initiatives, and the border camps that have been set up across Europe to challenge EU immigration policies.[81]

What they have become most known for, however, is their "white overalls," or *Tute Bianche*. The name originates from a statement made by police upon raiding a social center in Milan in 1994 and declaring the squatters to now be "ghosts." In response, they dressed all in white – in *"tute bianche"* – and rioted all night. From that time on, at the street protests called by the PGA in their global days of action – such as in Nice, Davos, Gothenburg, and Genoa – they carried this "consciously ridiculous" tactic forward to a carnivalesque extreme. Dressed in white overalls and padding themselves with foam, inner-tubes, cushions, construction helmets, and plastic shields, they confront police and attempt to push through barricades into the off-limits red zone, while protecting other protestors by taking the blows. In doing so they claim to be rejecting the violence–nonviolence (that is, fluffy vs. spiky) dichotomy, and are aware how their tactics can capture media attention by their doing the unexpected. *Zapatismo*, as they see it, calls for innovative engagement and experimentation in the now, such as the *tute bianche* tactic. In their view, "the Zapatista practice does not dream of a brave new world, it makes experiments in order to build many possible worlds. Thereby, *zapatismo* is not a theory, it is an indefinitely re-adaptable method."[82] As a direct act of support to the EZLN, they traveled to Mexico to escort them on their caravan to the capital city in early 2001. Ya Basta! and the Tute Bianche have inspired other groups around Europe, including in Spain, Finland, Belgium, and the UK WOMBLES.[83] After the unprecedented police violence at the Genoa G8 Summit in June 2001 – which in its most extreme moment resulted in the death of Carlo Giuliani – there was much debate as to whether the tactic could be sustained in the face of an all-out police attack. From these disagreements came the splinter group the Disobbedienti, as well as a shift by some to more assertive, black bloc tactics.

Black bloc: direct confrontation and projectile tactics

The black bloc, like the white and the pink, is not a single group but rather a changing cluster of activists who agree to use specific tactics during a particular action. Furthermore, the nature of the black bloc varies depending on the history of anarchism and struggle of those taking part. In general, a black bloc consists of anti-capitalists, autonomists, communists, anti-racists, anti-fascists, radical ecologists, and/or direct action groups from trade unions known as a "union flying squad." The name apparently was a label given by the media to black-clad, German *autonome* groups of anti-nuclear squatters in the 1980s. Their tactics and dress were appropriated by Love and Rage anarchists in North America during the first US Gulf War.[84] While resurfacing across Europe at street protests in Genoa, Prague, Gothenburg, and Thessalonica, among other cities, the black bloc came to the notice of the US press – and to notoriety – due to its appearance at the Battle in Seattle. Although, as elsewhere, the media attention paid to this bloc seems disproportionate to both its numbers and its actions. According to one local activist and writer, the bloc amounted to about fifty mostly young people, many of them women. Furthermore, despite the crim-inalization of (especially young) activists that is commonplace in media reporting of protests, most of the looting that occurred during Seattle week was not black bloc tactics, but rather Seattle's street gangs seizing a good opportunity.[85]

This bloc's tactics entail non-permitted marches, building and setting fire to barricades, stone- and Molotov cocktail-throwing, defending themselves and others from police beatings, locking arms to resist arrest, and "unarresting" activists from police captivity. Their "projectile reasoning" is meant to penetrate the red zone and disrupt meetings or bring them to a halt.[86] A final, and perhaps the most prevalent, tactic of this bloc is symbolic property destruction. In Seattle, the sum total of this vandalism was directed against what activists call "sweat-shop row": Niketown, the Gap, Old Navy, Banana Republic, Adidas, Nordstrom's, plus a Bank of America branch and Starbucks. Jeffrey St. Clair, of the leftist publication *Counterpunch*, describes the relatively minor acts of vandalism and window breaking as a kind of "Gulf of Tonkin" incident used by the police to justify their heavy and rather indiscriminant violence and the deci-sion to call in the National Guard.[87]

While generally tolerated by other anarchists under the "diversity of tactics" norm, black bloc tactics are denounced by many prominent activists as either naive or criminal, and in either case detrimental to the movement overall for they send the "wrong message." This argument is repeated often enough that it warrants some attention. Public denunciations almost always come from the most established NGOs or political parties, who are keen to seek dialogue with politicians and thus strive to be seen as credible professionals. In Seattle, for example, the Sierra Club's Carl Pope blamed anarchist "violence" for making NGOs such as his "look bad," while Global Exchange's Medea Benjamin and her affinity group, of sorts, used obstructionist tactics, but not to block the WTO meetings. They instead tried to prevent the looting of Niketown and the Gap, exclaiming to a *New York Times* reporter, "Where are the police? These anarchists should have been arrested."[88] Similarly, after Genoa the leaders of ATTAC France blamed anarchists for provoking the police. PGAers, for their part, claimed that the Italian government sent undercover police and fascists into the streets posing as black bloc, and that it was they who were responsible for much of the rioting that occurred. This is an allegation not unheard of in Italian history; yet, whatever the case, ATTAC's public pronouncements, especially in light of the police killing of Carlo Giuliani and their midnight raid, beatings, and mass arrests of young protestors sleeping in a school dormitory – drove a wedge between the ATTAC leadership and its younger members, and between ATTAC and the PGA in general.

These denunciations of black bloc tactics can be addressed in at least two ways. First, it is merely stating the obvious that a marginal grouping of young people cannot be held responsible for creating the media's fixation with violence or the wider culture's fascination with seeing and hearing about it. Therefore,

216 Peoples' Global Action

what some more staid activists see as a resolvable problem for "our movement" – that is, to purge black bloc tactics from the anti-neoliberal (*not* anti-capitalist) struggle – is perhaps upon closer evaluation a vexing contradiction of contemporary culture which is difficult to resolve through an avowedly more ethical, nonviolent stance. For in many media cultures today, as the saying goes, "if it bleeds in leads." When applied to mass political action, if there is not a fighting chance that there will be blood – nearly always that of the protesters, but no matter – there may be little coverage of the event at all. And on a rather practical note, it is the disruption, obstruction, and mayhem created in and around official meeting sights that contribute to their being canceled, not the permitted marches and ritualized "civil disobedience" allowed at safe distances from the center of power. Whatever symbolic value and long-term effects the latter tactics may have, they do not shut down meetings, nor can that even be a realistic goal, although they sometimes profess to this aspiration. This is not to say that shutting down a meeting a day early, as activists accomplished, for example, in Prague, has any *lasting* strategic value. It is only to point out that one forces a concrete change in one's adversaries' behavior or planned actions at the moment, while the other makes a symbolic showing that has an imperceptible, immediate impact on the adversary, but is thought to somehow cascade into a more serious change in the future, most likely through causing an educative shift in public opinion that will translate into political pressure.

A second point regarding violent tactics is that the acts of a few individuals – be they agents provocateurs or bona fide black bloc – cannot excuse either legally or ethically the indiscriminate violence and violations of civil rights on the part of the state and its agents. Nor do they justify the mass criminalization of the network of networks and of youth activism in particular. Both reactions on the part of the state and corporate press may in fact be having the reverse impact on young activists. Many have become radicalized by the indiscriminate police violence and through their growing perception of capitalism's structural violence, which goes largely unquestioned and unreported by the press. Some are, rather, pushing back and defending the black bloc tactics as largely in self-defense and in any case as miniscule in comparison to the violence caused by those they are revolting against. One activist who personally practices nonviolence and who has been involved with the anti-WEF mobilizations for a number of years commented:

> I have radicalized, and now I also feel that I am not willing to say we're gonna have a peaceful manifestation. If the same sort of media journalist – why do they ask *us* if we are gonna be peaceful or not? Why don't they go to Coca-Cola or to Nestle and ask them about *their* violence? It's really unfair.[89]

Rather than blaming the black bloc as divisive, irresponsible, or attention-grabbing thugs, a more constructive and dispassionate analysis searches out the organic relations between these young people's life experiences and the economic, political, social, and cultural institutions they are both products of and rebels against. One of the few sensitive analyses of contemporary anarchist violence in this direction is the work of scholar-activist Sian Sullivan.[90] Sullivan links the structural violence of late capitalism to personally and politically destructive practices, and focuses particularly on the effects of depression and anger as they manifest in drug abuse and self-cutting, as well as the more overtly political, violent confrontations with representations of state and capitalist violence (i.e. the cops) in street battles. The latter, Sullivan suggests, are cathartic and even psychologically – though not always physically – healthy for the activists who take part.

This is largely unexplored terrain by both scholars and many older activists who uneasily share the streets with these shadowy youth. The more "legitimate" activists and NGOs may in fact succeed in purging "violence" from "their movement." But they are naive to think that in doing so their adversaries will likewise lay down their multiple, subtle, but undeniably powerful weapons through which neoliberal structural violence is wielded. And in the process, they will alienate their young allies who suffer from the biopolitical power of capitalism in ways that older activists were partially shielded from in their youth, and therefore can only dimly empathize with from their current, relatively privileged, positions.

PGA as transnational network: an uncertain status and identity

Despite the PGA's considerable success in mobilizing hundreds of thousands to coordinated action through their internet calls, their innovative adaptations of *zapatismo*, and their creative protest tactics, the network participants are ambivalent as to their status and identity as a transnational network. In reality, PGA has gone largely inactive on the transnational level over the last few years. This they attribute to the nature of their groups – not NGOs with staff or budgets, but rather grassroots organizations and small collectives. The very fact that most of these groups *are* autonomist and grassroots means that local and national action remains their priority. Indeed, in recent years groups identified with the PGA have been involved in ongoing protests at the local and national level that have had considerable impact: PGA-linked peasant movements in Ecuador and Bolivia helped to topple unpopular administrations, while hundreds of thousands of PGA and VC affiliated Brazilian and Indian farmers have worked to shift their governments' positions on international trade closer to their own.

Yet, as these successes demonstrate, the growth of the VC as an exclusively peasant and rural organization has diminished mass-based and Southern participation in the PGA. The WSF and regional social forums provide further competition as a transnational space for encounter and networking that was once filled only by the Zapatista *encuentros*. Other large networks have appropriated their signature "call to action" tactic. As one activist at the European PGA conference in Belgrade commented: "The idea is to move beyond the Global Day of Action, which is in danger of becoming a tired cliché. ... The main point is the need for innovation. Either we begin to recreate ourselves, or the train will soon stall out."[91] Despite being the direct heir to the Zapatista *encuentros* and hence initially inspiring broad allegiance, in comparison with the social forums and networks like the VC, the PGA's skeletal design has so far proven too slight an edifice upon which to build a strong transnational network.

Furthermore, as this work has demonstrated throughout, there are real limitations to what kind of solidarity can be sustained among activists with vastly different experiences of threats or harms, affective responses to them, and identities. While the "real Indians" and the "blue Indians" that came together in the Zapatista *intergalácticas* undoubtedly experienced an emotional connection with many in those face-to-face encounters, it seems that their diversity was so great that little unity could be sustained even over the medium term. The so-called "real Indians" – be they KRRS farmers forging the VC or the *indios* of the Americas coming together into the Continental Encounters of Indigenous Peoples – have fused themselves into their own transnational networks based on a shared immediacy of the problem and personally felt suffering due to a common identity, which helps to evoke strong solidarity among them.

What remains of the PGA, then, seems largely, although not exclusively, the "blue Indians": young, urban, green, technologically connected anarcho-anti-capitalists wedded to their principles of autonomy, horizontality, and direct action and to the PGA as a mechanism, not an organization. Far from them lacking an identity, the above exploration of the pink, white, and black blocs demonstrates distinct identities and forms of activism among young people today, who nonetheless identify with each other across their respective "blocs." Further, Sullivan's participant research with those using black bloc tactics sheds much-needed light on a particular form of suffering which is often obscured by the glare of (post-)industrial societies. The depression, drug addiction, and self-mutilation witnessed among the most politically violent anarchists suggest that sensitive youth today indeed suffer, albeit in distinct ways from the "real Indians" they so greatly admire and with whom they have attempted to forge and maintain reciprocal solidarity ties.

Therefore, while it is undoubtedly different than either the Zapatistas or the young anarchists themselves had intended, the PGA has grown – or rather shrunk, with the possibility of gaining again on a firmer foundation – into a transnational network based on the attribution of similarity among its diverse adherents, leading to identity-based solidarity as anti-capitalist, anarchist youth. But while the PGA may have found its appropriate identity, it may still succumb to the usual pitfalls of attempting to form a transnational network on anti-hierarchical and autonomist principles. For example, from the beginning it has had trouble communicating and developing sustained working relations among adherents.[92] While a support group comprised of largely European-based volunteers assumed this coordinating role, others accused them of "taking too much the lead," a cardinal sin among this crowd. But as the Europeans have pulled back, others have yet to take their place in international coordination, which remains spotty.

Whether or not the PGA will be able to overcome the challenges of maintaining a transnational network based upon anarchist principles therefore remains to be seen. As one of the few purely second-generation direct action networks, its success or failure should be of interest to activists and scholars alike concerned with the relationship between a network's structure and its ability to sustain itself as a transnational collective actor. I have identified that the PGA is now, for all intents and purposes, comprised of young, urban anti-capitalists. Whether those remaining give up the Bakunin ghost of becoming the first Anarchist International where blue Indians and real Indians are collectively housed is unclear. But if they fail to acknowledge what they can never be they will miss this opportunity of – yes I am going to say it – *representing* and *organizing* who they actually *are*: deeply disillusioned young people who refuse to buy into the hollowed-out existence upon an increasingly unlivable planet that global capitalism has in store for them. They are further "heartbroken and furious" – and playful and daring – enough to put their bodies on the line to resist. The PGA should embrace the identity it has come to embody and organize upon that basis.

PGA and the WSF: strengthening the network and reinforcing the shift to the transnational level

This distilled identity – and the network it animates – has partially been forged through the PGA's contentious participation in the world and regional social forums. We will begin with analyzing how the PGA's engagement in the forum process has helped to strengthen the network from the local to the transnational levels, and thus encouraged its precarious scale shift. PGAers have been wary of the social forums from the beginning, not least because many view them as a hierarchical and reformist Johnny-come-lately that has sidelined the more authentically radical and horizontal PGA.[93] Despite their skepticism, in PGA meetings held in Barcelona, at the Strasbourg No Borders camp, and again at the PGA conference in Leiden, they evolved a "one foot in, and one foot out" stance *vis-à-vis* the social forums. The idea is to maintain a critical engagement while also promoting self-organized spaces where PGAers and others could still engage. They organized the first such autonomous space at the ESF in Florence in November 2002. The Italian Disobbedienti and radical trade union Cobas took the lead in what was called the Hub project. This model has taken root in the social forums and continues to become more ambitious and creative with each new experiment. As one participant-researcher observed, "The politics of autonomous space allow us to remain true to our own values, forms, and practices, while tactically intervening within the official forum to move out from our radical ghettos and simultaneously spark constructive change."[94] At the third ESF in London two years later, a local Dissent network came together around PGA principles to host the autonomous events. One of its participants called on activists

> to renew our vision of the forum itself, recognizing that our movements are too diverse, even contradictory, to be contained within a single space, however open it may be. This does not mean abandoning the process, but rather building on the London experience to recast the forum as a network of

interconnected, yet autonomous spaces converging across a single urban terrain at a particular point in time.[95]

As with the Italians organizing around the first Florence ESF, the Dissent network demonstrates concretely how the PGA is strengthened locally whenever a regional social forum or WSF is to be hosted. This strengthening occurs locally but in anticipation of welcoming international activists, and thus helps expand the network on that level too.

Other examples of PGA's active engagement in the social forums can be seen across the Americas and in Asia as well. The Latin American contact organization for PGA, the Confederación Nacional del Seguro Campesino of Ecuador (CONFEUNASSC), helped organize a Latin American Social Forum in spring 2004 while simultaneously hosting a regional PGA youth meeting. Furthermore, at the WSF in India that year, their "one foot in, one foot out" terms of engagement meant that while some PGAers attended the "official" forum, others took part in the parallel counter-forums to the WSF, those of Mumbai Resistance and the Peoples' Movements Encounter II. They as well had their own network meeting, where approximately forty activists came together to discuss how to move forward as a transnational network. Those present included the Bangladesh Krishok Federation of farmers, women, indigenous, and landless, the Serbian-based Drugaciji Svet je Moguc! (DSM!) coalition, the India Coordinating Committee of farmers' movements, the Narmada Bachao Andolan, the National and World Fishworkers' Forum, the Nepal Peasant Federation, and representatives of organizations from Argentina, Aotorea (New Zealand), South Africa, Europe, and North America.

Space for encounter, debate, and constructive cooperation toward building a network of networks

Since in the eyes of its adherents the PGA is not an organization with a set identity but rather a tool for coordinating among autonomous groups, their engagement in the social forums is by definition about encounter, dialogue, and concrete action in order to construct the network of networks, which again for them has been synonymous with building the PGA. This view that they *are* the network – or more precisely that they embody a network model that is struggling for hegemony in the spaces of the social forums against the "old models," and indeed against a hierarchical and reformist WSF itself – makes this engagement something of an existential battle every time. That said, in this section we will focus on the ways that the PGA attempt to positively "contaminate" the social forum process and other activists through their modeling the change they seek within the forums. In the final section that will follow, we will examine their more contentious attempts to shape the forum and the network overall.

Their constructive engagement in modeling behavior has been most apparent in their autonomous spaces running parallel to the official forum. This is seen most readily in the "Beyond ESF" events and those linked to them surrounding the London ESF in fall 2004. Partly fueled by their righteous anger toward the planning process, which was widely viewed as illegitimate and hijacked by the Socialist Workers' Party (SWP), the final straw came when the "ESF leadership" imposed compulsory affiliation fees.[96] The PGA's local Dissent network and especially the WOMBLES pulled out all the stops and largely upstaged the rather staid official ESF held at the showy Alexandra Palace. The local "dissenters" realized that many young people would be attending the forum, and therefore to not participate would be to pass up a key networking opportunity. They surmised that

> [since] every person has the potential for radicalization, both in thought and action, we want to organize events which promote, not only different (horizontal) ways of organization but rather, a radical, anti-authoritarian critique of the contemporary institutions of domination – and we consider the ESF as one of them.[97]

Despite falling out with the ESF coordinating committee, they did not pitch their parallel event as "anti-ESF," but, rather, *beyond* it spatially and politically. Their goal instead was to facilitate networking in an attempt to "contaminate by association the ESF with non-hierarchical practices." Beyond ESF was part of a larger web of activities that linked them to the indymedia center and the Laboratory of Insurrectionary Imagination, among others, scattered across London's Camden Center, Middlesex University, and the London School of Economics. While operating independently of the others, event organizers sought ways to coordinate and join in actions while still respecting their differences. In the end their events were heralded by many as the most vibrant and interesting on offer compared to the rather formulaic forum.

The program was based on the principles of self-organization, solidarity, autonomy, and direct action, and was billed as "five days and nights of anti-authoritarian ideas and action." It entailed workshops and assemblies to meet and to network for future events. Themes included autonomy, the No Borders network and migration issues, repression and social control, and precarious employment, as well as planning for the upcoming protests against the G8 in Scotland in summer 2005. In a tribute to both their localized UK roots in radical environmental groups as well as their inspiration from Chiapas, their two final themes were radical ecological space and "Zapatismo: ten years on."

The thrust of the parallel events was to promote the attribution of interconnectedness and build toward reciprocal solidarity among those attending:

> We see these as being diverse and common struggles to us all. Common because they exist in our global neighborhoods and at some point in our lives we are all involved in their consequences. Diverse because of their perceived separation from each other. As we have all come to find, every thing in life is connected. And by providing that connection, we can facilitate a consciousness that goes beyond the limitations of "single issue" struggles to creating ruptures in the orders of capitalism.[98]

Unlike the official forum, PGA-inspired events were free of charge, including complementary meals (of sometimes dubious origin, to be explained below) and solidarity housing in occupied social centers and venues squatted especially for participants. In addition to workshops, they also carried out joint actions in and near London. In a solidarity action coordinated with the No Borders camp and the French-based Sans Papiers, they occupied Waterloo station and took over passport control, allowing those coming from France to pass freely. They also held a spontaneous party on the underground to reclaim public transport, allowing for free travel and free food, provided by a Spanish collective whose main tactic appears to be shoplifting, Yo Mango (translation: "I swipe"). This "happening" ended with a street party where young activists danced along to Rhythms of Resistance at Victoria station, followed by a police crackdown.

WSF as terrain for contention and outright confrontation

Finally, let us examine how the forum is a space not only for constructive – though autonomous – engagement, as just demonstrated, but also one of confrontational competition. Here the PGA attempt to shape the forum, and by extension the network of networks, in the image of themselves: that is, into becoming more radically open, decentralized, horizontally connected, spontaneous, autonomous spaces of self-organized action, guided by visions of a world radically different from the current neoliberal order. PGAers see their attempts as a countermove to the trend within the social forums, which they perceive as centralizing around lead NGOs, social movement organizations, and political parties, who seek to reform the current global system or build a new "International," either of the reformist nature or the old communist kind.

The PGA's use of the forum as a terrain of confrontation is witnessed by their open denunciations of other groups' centralizing and reformist tendencies, the calls by some activists for a boycott, and their confrontational tactics in the forum spaces themselves. These more contentious acts highlight the tensions raised in the very beginning of this chapter, namely those between vertical and horizontal network formations, bureaucratic forms of contestation versus transgressive direct action, anti-neoliberalism versus anti-capitalism, and the "age paradox," where the majority of activists in the streets and at social forums are young, while those in positions of "leadership" are considerably older.

PGAers' denouncements of the WSF and regional forums have been ongoing, and center on allegations of the forums being insufficiently revolutionary or anti-capitalist and therefore hostile to more radical voices. They further accuse lead groups of desiring to influence and eventually seize state power rather than regarding the state as equally problematic to the capitalist structures with which it is enmeshed. A final criticism is leveled against what they see as premature and illegitimate attempts to channel the diversity of activists mobilizing today into a single vertical organization led by a few NGOs and leftist parties. Each of these critiques will be illustrated below.

The WOMBLES, for example, angrily dismissed the ESF, and by extension the WSF, as incapable of carrying off revolutionary change due to its acceptance of the hierarchical system and its reformist stance toward governmental structures. They further accused it of being a new "reformist International," and concluded:

> The ESF analysis criticizes neo-liberalism as an ideology promoted by the powerful of the world, and not capitalism as a whole, as a socio-economic system and an everyday relationship. Moreover, the ESF does not provide any comprehensive critique of other domination mechanisms like the nation state, which is directly connected with capital. As a result of this analysis, it promotes reformist demands by using symbolic (and not direct, material) pressure and it promotes a vague vision of a "democratic civil society".[99]

Furthermore, the PGA has leveled attacks against the WSF and ESF for compromising its "open space" character by cozying up to leftist politicians, and indeed violating the WSF's own rules by allowing participation of parties such as the Brazilian PT, the Italian Rifondazione Comunista, and, most controversially, the British Labour Party and the SWP. PGAers have warned anyone who would listen that this poses twin dangers of, first, political parties using the forums as a campaigning platform and a vehicle for recruiting members; and, second, and perhaps more harmful, lead organizations steering the forum in a reformist direction and silencing radical voices that would challenge the present state and capitalist institutions, due to their drive to present themselves *cum* forum as "a legitimate negotiator."[100]

The PGA have saved their most serious critiques for attempts by some lead organizations within the forum to create the Social Movements World Network through the Social Movements Assembly and its calls to mobilization. While not denying that greater coordination among social movements is desirable and indeed necessary to forge a "movement of movements," they strongly disagree with the way that the SMA has gone about doing so. The Brazilian CUT and PT and French ATTAC were particularly singled out as leading this charge to create a "new International" cloaked in the language of a horizontal network: "hierarchical, centralized, aspiring to represent the totality of the social movements just like the Internationals of the past – rather than a network."[101]

PGAers were equally incensed by once again being snubbed. To them, the SMA was only the most recent, reformist, and vertical attempt to recreate the wheel that is already spinning in the form of the PGA: One exasperated Argentinean lamented:

> The WSF does not have to create a network of the movements because *this network already exists*: we have been constructing this network over the last six or seven years. Certainly, this network is still not strong enough, but we have to build upon what already exists before we can create ONE institutionalized network under the WSF's control. ... Who wrote the statements of the

SMWN? Who decided how it is going to organize? And more important, who elected the Secretariat, or even decided that a Secretariat was needed? Certainly not the movement I belong to, or any of the movements in Argentina, or most of the movements of other countries, as far as I know. Did the piqueteros, the Bolivian cocalero peasants, European No Border activists, South-African Anti-Eviction campaigners, etc. discuss the issue? I would be surprised if they knew what I'm talking about. Grassroots activists of real social movements were simply not there at the meetings. And no substantial effort was made to make sure the initial proposal was available in advance, so that the movements could at least discuss it at home and send their opinions.[102]

He went on to pose a rather embarrassing question about network models: "If they now suddenly believe in horizontal organizing, why don't they start by reforming their own organizations?"[103] More to the point, he asked: "Why would the representatives of hierarchical organizations create a structure of coordinated networks, that is to say, a horizontal and decentralized one?"[104] A similarly chilly reception greeted the recent attempt to "orient" the network of networks toward the agenda of the Porto Alegre Manifesto issued by the so-called G19 of scholar-activists. At the 2005 WSF, PGAers joined others to plan and participate in the semi-autonomous *caracol intergaláctica*, which was held within the WSF youth camp and is said to have been one of the liveliest and most networked spots at the forum. It was there that they got wind of the G19 manifesto. In an open debate about the future of the WSF and power relations within it, the overall sentiment was that the G19 was attempting to seize the agenda from grassroots organizations.[105]

These sorts of trust-busting moves on the part of individuals or organizations more comfortable with "leading" have themselves led to some PGAers refusing to participate in the forums and further calling on others to join in the boycott. These public refusals have accompanied nearly every regional and world forum. For example, the KRRS accused the groups coordinating the Asian Social Forum as rushing the process in order to establish themselves as leaders of a movement that the KRRS say has developed without their participation in the first place. Instead they should have built the process organically based on grassroots movements, which would necessarily take more time.[106] A similarly defiant tone was struck by Brazilian anarchists in the lead-up to the second WSF, and again referenced the Zapatista *encuentro* process, which they see as the sole legitimate transnational network:

> We will not go to the World Social Forum. With us is the majority (or all) of the groups which have participated in the battles against the farce of 500 years, the global action days, … and the 2nd American Encuentro for Humanity and against Neoliberalism.[107]

They instead denounced the WSF process in Brazil as a ploy by the old left to usurp the anti-capitalist movement that they did not initiate and to channel it toward their reformist goals of national development, "humanizing" capitalism, and getting their parties into power as an "alternative."[108]

But beyond simply decrying these centralizing tendencies within the forums, PGAers have been keen to offer a positive vision for the constructive role they would like to see the forums play. Specifically, they call on the WSF coordinators to support existing transnational networks – the PGA prominently among them – in enhancing their functioning rather than attempting to build a new central structure in the form of the SMWN. They feel that the WSF could strengthen coordination among movements toward building a network of networks by facilitating voluntary and flexible coalitions, which will in turn allow each group at each level to decide how they will participate in that action.

> [T]his type of organization, through singular and temporary coalitions, ... allows for the articulation of heterogeneous movements without reducing them to a homogeneity, ... only this type of organization respects multiplicity, the most valuable thing that we have.[109]

Toward this end, PGAers suggest that the WSF could help each of the various nodes, or activist collectivities, to communicate with the others, through facilitating material solidarity of technology and funding resources from the North to the South, since many Southern activists do not have access to the internet or to translation of messages. Facilitating flows of information and supporting travel for poorer groups would, in their opinion, be the most tangible and helpful way of extending the network of networks on the part of the WSF organizers.[110]

Finally, the most forceful way that the PGA have confronted what they feel to be the forum's hierarchical and reformist tendencies is through what they do best: direct action. Some Brazilian anarchists registered their immediate concerns with what they saw as the closed planning process monopolized by the PT in the first WSF. Anarchists and ecologists affiliated with the PGA protested in that forum and the next, while indymedia activists wrote in their postings: "Porto Alegre isn't the social democratic paradise that the PT makes it out to be."[111] This confrontation came to a head in 2002. A large group of activists from the PGA affiliated Intergalactic Laboratory of Disobedience who were staying in the youth camp teamed up with young Brazilian anarchists to occupy the VIP room in protest of the top-down way that the Brazilian organizing committee allegedly functioned and of the elitist tendencies within the forum. According to PGAers, the PT called in riot police to evict them. But not before they effectively made their point: No such VIP room was scheduled the following year. This change emboldened the anarchists to continue launching such direct actions, in order to call attention through open confrontation to certain hypocrisies they saw growing in the forums.

The incongruities could not be more glaring than in the planning and execution of the London ESF. While most of the PGA's efforts were directed toward drawing energy away from the official ESF and into their dynamic autonomous spaces, they also coordinated one dramatic direct action in the official space of the forum. The WOMBLES, joined by others from Beyond ESF, chose to occupy a plenary to protest the cooptation of the London ESF by the Mayor of London Ken Livingstone, who was invited to speak on a panel entitled "Stop Fascism and the Far Right in Europe." About 200 people filled the hall just as it was about to begin, occupied the stage, and unfurled banners with slogans such as "Another World Is For Sale." They passed around the microphone, stating their complaints, which were many. They decried the lack of transparency, the lack of solidarity with the undocumented, and the exclusion of many from participating. They further denounced the hierarchical control of the forum by political parties, the police repression at the squatted social centers and harassment at the Beyond ESF events, and in general the "stage-managed" style of the forum, where big-name speakers lectured to audiences without any real interaction.

Displaying mostly "pink" carnival tactics, among them was a group called the Clandestine Insurgent Rebel Clown Army (CIRCA). Below is a conversation that took place between myself as a participant observer and "Clown no. 1," who I found with his feet up on the front table on the stage when I came into the hall:

Q: Can I ask you a couple questions?
A: Yes.
Q: What did you guys just do, and why are you here?
A: Well, I was tired and I came to sit at the front, and people think *I'm* the leader of the whole thing, and all I think is that the chairs should be in a big circle, and not in lines like this.
Q: Fair enough.
A: And that's *all* I want to say. Because I think the lines of chairs represent – and the people at the front – everybody thinks *I'm* important and they come and interview me. I'm just a normal person.
Q: I know, I know. So there wasn't any planning for this; it was just a spontaneous decision?
A: Yes. I was in the hall and I heard a loud noise, and I thought, "That must be *exciting* because everything else is so quiet and their voices are, *boring*, and" …
Q: Well alright. So what is your idea for a social forum: Would you like it to be different? Do you want something totally different?
A: I think it should be organized in a different way. It was organized by Ken Livingstone and from, you know, all the spaces I've been involved in have been self-organized. You know we should have squatted Alexandra Palace. We shouldn't have paid for it.
Q: How can we get this many people to communicate with each other, or is it just too big?
A: No, no, we should organize like a swarm – like a network.
Q: Can we all sit in a circle here, do you think? It would be a very thick circle.
A: We can have spokespersons from smaller circles. So this would be one small circle, and more small circles, and they come together and talk.
Q: Okay, do you have any plans to do this in the future?
A: Well, I'm a clown.

Q: You're a clown.
A: I'm a clown and I'm not, I'm quite forgetful and, you know, I'm in the army and I'm only a private.
Q: You're in the army?
A: I'm in the clown army.
Q: Can I have a [flyer]?
A: The Clandestine Insurgent Rebel Clown Army.
Q: Can I hire you for parties?
A: No, we don't – you can't hire us for parties. We don't do parties.
Q: Would you *volunteer* for a party?[112]

Scuffles, angry words, a quick exit, and arrests followed. "Debates once pitting activists against mainstream politicians and bureaucrats in the WTO, World Bank, and IMF now rage within the very heart of the Global Justice Movement itself," pronounced one scholar-activist.[113] The WOMBLES issued their own pointed explanation of the action and a scathing denunciation of the way it was received:

> Let us not forget the energy and anger and momentum of this "movement" came from the streets of Genoa, Prague, Nice, Evian, Gothenburg, where state forces were happy to teargas us, happy to break our bones as we slept in school buildings, happy to shoot us in the back as we ran away, happy to murder us in cold blood, the very same forces we now go to for funding to hold these Forums, the same forces that "welcome the anti-capitalists" (Jacques Chirac, Paris ESF). The same forces we allow to arrest and beat fellow ESF participants before our very eyes as we make political speeches from the stage under the watchful eye of government employees. The "movement of movements" unravels itself and reveals an empty space.[114]

It is rather ironic that the PGA's critiques – underscored by confrontational direct action – of the vertical tendencies within the social forums mirror those of the WSF Brazilian Committee. Whitaker's criticisms, for example, are leveled against many of the same actors – who also sit on the WSF IC – for strikingly similar reasons. Whitaker's passionate defense of the social forum as a space and his denunciations of the SMA overviewed in Chapter 4 differ perhaps only in that they were issued from the vantage point of an elite insider, rather than by a group of outsiders that is the PGA. Some PGAers dismiss the Brazilian organizing committee as "a bunch of people no one really knows" and the International Council as "so far a rubberstamp appointed by the [organizing committee] itself."[115] This is an unfortunate misreading of the internal politics of the social forum "leadership." From my own observations, I rather view the social forum as a space that is threatened, mainly by some within the IC itself and the related SMA. It may stand a chance of being defended if the PGA and the Brazilian committee were to recognize in one another their natural affinity ties and somehow join forces in maintaining and expanding the social forums as a horizontal, non-deliberative, radically open space and process.

This point can be illustrated by Whitaker's remarks at a recent IC meeting. There I observed him to be one of the few, and certainly the clearest, voices in defense of the social forum as a space. I also witnessed his obstructionist efforts against a mounting chorus from within the hodge-podge collective that is the IC who desire to hold "strategy" sessions and to expand their council. "What is the forum?" Whitaker asked rhetorically of those present:

> The objective is the same as an organization: It's to help us and make us more capable for changing the world. It is an *instrument*. ... The "strategy" is creating the most spaces of encounter, at the world level, the regional and the local, to struggle together. These [social forums] are moments in our struggles and the strategy is to repeat the process everywhere. We get to know each other and support each other and do things more efficiently. ... This is our strategy: connections, encounter is our strategy, the *mouvance* as they say in French. It is very dangerous to talk about this, to have "*our* strategy." There should be no themes decided here; it is the dynamic of encounter in which the themes are generated. [Our task] is to facilitate the connections.[116]

He further expressed a wary dismay over the discussion to expand the IC. The crux of his concern is that the organizations that have "occupied" and "hegemonized" spaces on the IC, as he puts it, are now calling to "democratize" the council. Yet this democratization will likely add groups that share the others' desire to make the IC an organizing committee that will lead the social forum "movement." This is dangerous, he avers, when organizations see their role not as extending the social forum process and improving communication among groups, but rather as charting the WSF-cum-network of networks' course by setting its strategy.

Whitaker shared a story to illustrate his commitment to forestalling this popular "rebellion" within the IC to turn the forum into a movement and themselves into its executive committee. His son asked him why he won't give up the social forum, given his advanced age and declining health. Whitaker answered that he has to defend the forum process from being "hijacked" by the seeming majority on the IC who act as if they are directing the network of networks, even though many of them represent NGOs and think-tanks comprised of professional staff and little else.[117] This is not to belittle their work, but simply to raise the question of on whose behalf this "strategy" will be made.

In my role as a participant-observer in these meetings, I was struck by the maturity (in age) of the IC members as well as by the "age paradox" apparent in this group. The only other person present who seemed to "get" what Whitaker said was, perhaps not coincidentally, also the youngest: the sole young activist in his twenties, who was there as an intern. What this impressionistic observation suggests is that if the WSF is to be preserved as a horizontal space aimed at coordinating among autonomous struggles and expanding the social forum process, as both the Brazilian founders had envisioned and the PGA actively promote,

I would humbly propose a two-pronged, radically ageist response. First, the "expansion" of the IC should be aimed at redressing the "age paradox" within the WSF and the network of networks at large, by inviting the youngest activists from social movements, organizations, and collectives to represent their groups there. Second, once the IC better reflects the youthful face of transnational activism today, only then should any discussion of "strategy" commence, with one important caveat: Those allowed to engage and reach consensus (no voting) on this portentous topic should be under the age of thirty and over seventy.[118] Thus, the age group with the greatest penchant and confidence to lead the network of networks would be effectively barred from doing so.

7 Concluding reflections on present and future scholarship and activism

The central focus of this work has been on the transnationalization of activism witnessed the world over in recent decades, which della Porta and Tarrow have called "the most dramatic change we see in the world of contentious politics." Specifically it has addressed the questions of why and how this shift to the global is taking place, what are the compositions and characters of these emerging activist networks, and what role the WSF has played in this transnationalizing process. The WSF slogan of "Another World Is Possible" reflects activists' collective desire to move beyond a neoliberal global order which is blamed for rising levels of poverty, inequality, environmental destruction, conflicts, corporate takeover of land and loss of the commons, and disillusionment with democratic institutions.

The main institutional drivers of neoliberalism's globalizing rule have been what activists call the "neoliberal triumvirate" of the World Bank, the IMF and the WTO. Among the largest networks coalescing to challenge this triumvirate and to construct another possible world are this book's case studies: Jubilee 2000 and its follow-up networks, the Via Campesina, Our World Is Not For Sale, and Peoples' Global Action. These four comprise the core of anti-neoliberal, global activism today, and that of the global left more broadly. Furthermore, as we have seen throughout this study, these networks have forged significant ties, launched joint campaigns, participated in mass protests, and initiated the social forum process with other networks whose main targets and concerns were not the neoliberal triumvirate. Chief among them are those promoting tax justice to aid developing countries, international peace, women's rights, and environmental sustainability. Thus, while tremendous diversity of opinion, issues, tactics, organizational models, goals, and paradigms exists across leftist activism today, this work has also demonstrated the growing overlap, cooperation, and even convergence around shared spaces, issues, campaigns, and alternative visions. This confluence, while still in its infancy, does lend support to the popular assertion that a single collective actor is emerging to counter neoliberal globalization/capitalism, which I have referred to throughout as the "network of networks." Stated more generally, this is the globalizing left at the cusp of the twenty-first century. Below I will reflect on my main findings in light of current and future scholarship and activism.

In light of scholarship on activism

Why and how activists shift scale

This research has addressed the dearth of empirical investigations to date, as was noted by Tarrow, Olesen, and Rosenau, into how and why activism is becoming transnational. It has done so by operationalizing and amending one of McAdam, Tarrow, and Tilly's hypothesized processes from their *Dynamics of Contention* work, that of scale shift. It has found that in spite of their considerable diversity, each of the four cases studied have followed a similar trajectory in going global. This work has specified a series of robust mechanisms that trace this scale shift to the transnational level of contention.

First, *broad change processes* and specific *triggers* of neoliberal policies, which I call structural violence, touch down to spark localized resistance across the globe. But based on frustration at the local and national levels in getting desired results, activists then recognize the need to seek allies as well as targets and solutions at the transnational level, in what I call the *realization of the need to "go global."* "Movement entrepreneurs" expand these nascent networks through *diffusion* of information via existing relationships as well as *brokerage* of ties with new actors or reinvigoration of those with former allies. Brokerage and diffusion can assume both *relational* (that is, face-to-face) and *non-relational* (i.e. broadcast media and internet) forms, and further require various *frame alignment* efforts, which continue throughout the scale shift process. This spurs a related *shift in objects and claims* among these existing or newly brokered umbrella groups *vis-à-vis* their targets – taking aim especially at the IMF, the World Bank, and the WTO, in addition to more specialized targeting of particular TNCs, regional trade agreements, and national governments.

As the network broadens, three types of *attribution* can occur for solidarity to be created, those of *worthiness* for distant issues and sufferers, *interconnectedness* with others whose struggles are seen as related to one's own, and *similarity* with activists sharing the same identity which is harmed or threatened by neoliberal change. These identities include peasant, debtor, indigenous person, precarious worker, and alienated youth. As was said, these three forms of attribution produce distinct kinds of *solidarity*, which will be taken up in the following section. Each solidarity path, nevertheless, leads to *transnational collective action*, thereby completing the scale shift process. But, finally, participation in a transnational network in turn informs, shapes, and re-energizes localized action, and hence the scale shift process should be understood as a dynamic loop.

In tracing why and how scale shift is occurring among activist networks, this work has engaged with various streams of scholarly literature. First and foremost was the *Dynamics of Contention* framework itself. In proposing this new approach, McAdam, Tarrow, and Tilly attempted to integrate the main strands of social movement theorizing into a cross-disciplinary, comprehensive approach to studying a broad range of contention, and have been heavily critiqued for doing so. The major criticisms seem to have clustered into a chorus of "It ain't broke, so don't fix it." Scholars, especially established ones, appear rather content to burrow down ever deeper into their chosen niche of the social movement scholarly enterprise. And while this sort of specialization has yielded a wealth of in-depth knowledge, it has come at the cost of a loss of leverage in our theories and concepts. The DOC's authors foresaw this entrenchment reaction when they averred that if their synthetic approach is to have a future it will be among graduate students and younger scholars in search of more flexible, dynamic, and generalizable tools for studying the "ongoing accomplishment of collective action."

So it was for me, and I have found it to be a fruitful endeavor. This integrative approach allows researchers to both explain and understand, or to step back and identify causes or mechanisms as well as to make sense of these mechanisms from the participants' perspectives. It therefore encourages us to conceive of activism as constituted by objective, or externally given, and subjective, or internally perceived, aspects. It further helps us to overcome the individualism vs. holism dichotomy by identifying cognitive, relational, and environmental mechanisms at play in what we are investigating. We are also urged to study actual practice and to elicit the interpretations of that practice from activists themselves, and thus to be both historically and empirically grounded. The DOC, in keeping with the pragmatic and pluralistic spirit of social movement scholarship, welcomes whatever research methods allow us to puzzle through these mechanisms. This middle-range approach strikes a realistic balance between the erasing of difference through theories that have too broad of a sweep and the particularism of descriptive case studies which find uniqueness at every turn. The DOC provides a flexible yet structured set of concepts and organizational frameworks with which to approach the research, and posits that these can be found across a wide range of contention in different combinations and outcomes.

Given that McAdam, Tarrow, and Tilly hypothesized mechanisms for three other processes that I had to set aside in my own research for lack of time, space, and resources, the DOC is still a largely untapped resource for future research into transnational activism. Most pressingly, the processes of *actor constitution*, *mobilization*, and *polarization* occurring within the emerging network of networks call out for scholarly attention. Yet these do not begin to exhaust the possibilities for conceptualizing processes, hypothesizing mechanisms, and then testing and amending them against comparative, empirical cases of collective action proliferating in the contemporary environment. That said, this approach seems equally well suited for historical studies.

We can now move from the broad research framework to the specific mechanisms that I corroborated or added to the scale shift process. In doing so, this work not only amended this particular DOC process, but simultaneously contributed to scholarship in a number of thematic areas, beginning with the concept of structural violence. While borrowing peace researcher Galtung's original term, I sought to make it more dynamic by introducing an Onufian constructivist notion of structure as social arrangements or stable patterns of rules, institutions, and unintended consequences leading to a particular form of rule. We could then view neoliberalism as a condition of rule where certain priv-ileged actors use rules to control and obtain advantages over others, via multilateral bodies, treaties, and policies. I also took methodological advice from Winchian philosophy and from cultural studies in holding that structures can be said to "exist" if sufficient actors act or behave in accordance with such rules or structures. I added the caveat that structures can also be identified when people are explicitly *reacting* to them, denouncing them for causing suffering, and collec-tively resisting them.

Subsuming the broad range of harms being blamed on neoliberal rule under the rubric of the *structural violence of neoliberal globalization,* and then casting these as *broad change processes* and *triggers* sparking localized protest and thus initiating the scale shift process, advances scholarship in three ways. First, it expands our explanatory power; second, it advances theory; and, third, it is consistent with the DOC approach overall.

With respect to the former, this move expands our explanation in that adding this umbrella mechanism and/or process plausibly answers the question of "why" activism is going global, not only the "how" questions that the subsequent mechanisms address. And in so doing, it also lends credence to the argument of the much-maligned "disorganization" and "deprivation" scholars, that suddenly imposed grievances and disruptions in social institutions can and do spark contention. Yet, once triggered, a series of further steps, or mechanisms, is needed for that localized protest to grow into transnational collective action, a process that this study delineates. Indeed, tracing the constituent mechanisms that constitute the scale shift process, beginning with the structural violence of neoliberalism but not ending there, answers the decades-long debate among social-psychological, structural-organizational, and constructionist-process theo-rists of social movements by saying, "All of the above."

Regarding the second claim, this addition strengthens theorizing on transna-tional networks today, in that subsuming the diverse grievances of localized activists under a single concept helps us identify a potentially powerful common-ality shared among all of them. It thus discovers the basis upon which reciprocal solidarity can be granted among distinct struggles that are nevertheless perceived to be interconnected, in that they share a common source of grievance, or enemy, and thus target. This attribution of interconnectedness leading to reciprocal soli-darity seems necessary for coordinated action across issues and identities. It further helps us to comprehend the underlying "we-ness" among WSF partici-pants, and also to grasp the basis upon which an emerging "network of networks" is being precariously and contentiously constructed.

Third and finally, construing neoliberal structural violence as broad change processes and triggers igniting the scale shift process is consistent with the overall DOC approach. This is because McAdam, Tarrow, and Tilly hypothesized change processes and triggers to be the initiators of a related process, that of *mobilization.* It is therefore a logical step to include it in the scale shift process as well, especially since it seems to provide a powerful commonality that propels activists to seek their targets, allies, and solutions at the transnational level in order to match neoliberal globalization. Much more research could be done in this area. Galtung's other forms of violence – direct and cultural – should be applied to the study of neoliberal globalization, and the interrelations among all three forms should be investigated. This is precisely because direct violence appears to be increasing now that cultural violence has failed to shore up the structural violence that exacerbates inequalities in wealth, resources, rights, and dignity both within and between societies.

This work makes another contribution to our explanation of the scale shift process by adding the cognitive mechanism of the *realization of the need to go global*. This mechanism captures the widespread frustration shared among activists today that their local and national politicians are increasingly unable or unwilling to redress their grievances, just as new threats and harms are surfacing from changes brought on by neoliberal globalization. This means that as so-called "movement entrepreneurs" frame their appeals, diffuse these through existing channels, and broker relations with new allies, they are doing so with the knowledge and aim that they must build alliances, locate their targets, and seek and frame solutions for their complex problems at the transnational level as well. Activists, therefore, first "think" globally before they "act" globally; yet "thinking globally" should not be conceived as some lofty, cosmopolitan, post-materialist higher consciousness, but rather as more mundane pragmatic realism brought on by frustrating experience.

Another further specification of McAdam, Tarrow, and Tilly's hypothesized mechanisms comes through my addition of both *relational* and *non-relational* paths for *diffusion* and *brokerage*, which was aided by Tarrow's own identification of non-relational diffusion in his amended model. In applying these two paths to diffusion and brokerage, I am recognizing the increasing prominence of internet technology in diffusing information to existing network members as well as in playing non-relational broker among formerly unconnected groups and individuals. This is witnessed, for example, by listserves which facilitate communication among previously unconnected activists who share similar interests, by calls for mobilization posted on websites and sent through listserves which spur people to turn up at mass protests, and by the provision of contact information on websites for those who want to get involved in a local or national group linked to a transnational network. These examples illustrate, further, how internet-based, non-relational brokerage is often a precursor to face-to-face, relational contacts at activist meetings and protests, just as already-existing relational bonds are strengthened by maintaining contact via internet technology.

As stated previously, part and parcel of diffusion and brokerage are *frame alignment* strategies, or portraying one's own activities, goals, and ideology as congruent with the interests, values, and beliefs of other non-affiliated individuals or groups. Very little research has been done to date on the obviously difficult task of framing at the transnational level, particularly of a comparative nature, as was noted by social movement scholar John McCarthy. My own work, which identifies various frame alignment strategies including *frame-bridging, amplification, extension,* and *transformation* across four transnationalizing networks, should be a welcomed contribution in this regard.

In particular, this research provides considerable evidence that transnational networks are attempting to evolve *global interpretive transformative frames*, which are nevertheless rooted in *specific domains*. It has, further, uncovered and traced the myriad ways in which these rather autonomous, transformative frames are becoming articulated with those of other networks. This is taking place, first, through activists launching joint campaigns. Second, it occurs by coming together in shared spaces of street protests, the WSF, regional, local, and thematic forums, its International Council, and in autonomous spaces linked to the forums. Third and finally, it is happening through efforts to forge a network of networks in, for example, the Social Movement Assembly. Despite these concerted efforts, this articulation process of creating one global interpretive, transformative frame is far from complete, and indeed may never come about. However, this work has shown a way that it may, in fact, be occurring in a genuine, bottom-up manner: that is, by these networks, first, devising their own transformative program rooted in their specific domain and, next, entering into relations – sometimes cooperative, other times conflictual – to attempt to articulate these frames into a coherent strategy for bringing about a world beyond neoliberalism or capitalism.

These findings therefore suggest that frame transformation should be thought of more broadly than it has usually been in extant social movement research. In classic works by Snow, Machalek, and Loflund, for example, it is commonly conceived of as individuals undergoing or experiencing a "conversion," entailing a radical transformation of consciousness. This emphasizes individual, psychological characteristics and focuses on the techniques that "recruiters" utilize to "hook" or "convert" their "target." By contrast, in the present study a global interpretive transformative frame is rendered more as an interactive, collective process in which a widening circle of activists engage. In this sense, constructing a global interpretive frame is a reasoned and principled expansion of awareness via group-level interactive processes of dialogue and debate, mutual learning, and joint action and reflection rather than a one-way cult-like technique that is applied to would-be targets. Additional sustained and engaged research tracking the actual processes of transformative framing both within and across networks is undoubtedly a fertile area of study.

Another two mechanisms that I identified as constitutive of the scale shift process follow closely on these framing strategies and are treated together because they co-occur: those of *objects and claims shift*. In the drive to articulate domain-specific transformative frames to address the myriad ills of neoliberal globalization, it becomes obvious that both the objects of claims as well as the nature of claims themselves should expand to include new targets and more sophisticated demands as activists enter the transnational level of contention. But, at the same time, object identification and claims-making become multi-layered in the sense that activists come to see the need to fight for change at all levels. Hence, as they shift "up," this does not mean that activists abandon targets or claims made at the local and national levels. It is rather that they develop a greater awareness as to how the various levels of governance are entwined, and therefore begin to conceive of strategies that address all appro-priate levels and actors. Given that my case studies are merely the tip of the iceberg when it comes to activism going global, there is ample room for others to investigate the expanding claims and targets of other transnationalizing networks today.

Another important amendment to the scale shift process suggested by this research was in underscoring the importance of solidarity to transnational coor-dinated action, in addition to specifying two additional paths to achieving it beyond *attribution of similarity* proposed by McAdam, Tarrow, and Tilly. Put simply, while the latter form of attribution is indeed a crucial mechanism toward forging transnational solidarity, it is insufficient in comprehending all significant ties that bind these networks. This is because activists also attribute *worthiness*, as we saw, for example, in the Jubilee 2000 campaign and its follow-up GCAP bestowed by Northern churchgoers and charities upon worthy recipients in the South. Activists further attribute *interconnectedness* among each other's struggles, such as those coming together within the giant OWINFS network. As we have seen throughout and as will be emphasized below, specifying these three attribution routes to solidarity aids in comprehending the complexity of solidarity itself, which in turn has concrete effects on the durability and the nature of activist networks. Therefore, while I concur with the DOC authors that attribution is a crucial mechanism mediating between learning about others' struggles and taking action, we must also acknowledge *that which attribution evokes* – that is, solidarity – which creates the affective bonds that make *transnational coordinated action* desirable.

With this latter mechanism, we come to the fruition of the scale shift process. This work has demonstrated the rich variety of transnational coordinated action undertaken by networks fighting various facets of neoliberal globalization. Much more empirical and theoretical work can be done in this area on related groups and networks coordinating such action. Descriptive, empirical work that cata-logues the expanding repertoires of contention as well as the links among the growing network of networks is warranted, as is greater abstraction into concepts and theories that will help us get an intellectual handle on the mammoth subject matter.

Finally, as was referenced in the above discussion on the shifting of objects and claims to encompass the transnational level but without abandoning the local and national, we can take this one step further: As I depicted in Figure 2 by arrows circling back from transnational to localized action, this research has demonstrated the ways in which participation in transnational networks loops back to impact local activism as well. Activists engaged in campaigns take initia-tive and ownership in bringing transnational networks "down to earth," so to speak. This work has therefore shown some of the ways in which activism is indeed going "glocal" and not just global, to use Robertson's term. Unstudied cases abound for the willing researcher to explore, as well as to theorize this rela-tionship among the three levels of action. Finally, while this work spotlights how participating in a transnational network has positively impacted and informed localized action, there are most probably negatives to this moving between levels as well, such as strains upon resources, conflicts in priorities, or the difficulties in translating transnational agendas into local settings, to name just a few. All deserve to be better explored.

Network composition and character

This work's second cluster of findings centers on tensions, conflicts, and uncertainties among activists as to the best way to move forward together, toward what goals, and through what organizational forms. The second analytical framework introduced in this study delineated six continuum concepts of network composition and character that help us better understand, first, what holds a transnational network together across time and space, and what creates fissures or causes complete ruptures in them; second, how transnational networks are structured today; and, third, how activists conceive of the problem as well as the solution. This framework devised herein aids in the systematic analysis of the different forms of solidarity shared among activists today, their network structures, and the scope and nature of their claims.

First, with regard to solidarity, I have identified a relationship among activists' *proximity to the problem*, *affective response*, and the *type of solidarity* evoked. Activists at a considerable *distance* from a threat tend to experience *sympathy* with others' suffering and, thus, if they choose to act, often do so based upon *altruistic solidarity*; whereas activists who *perceive a connection* between their struggle and that of others will likely feel *empathy* with another's plight as well as *remotely threatened* by the source of their suffering, and if they act it will be based on *reciprocal solidarity*. But finally, those activists who *immediately experience a threat or harm suffer personally*, and yet are not merely the passive recipients of the charitable, altruistic solidarity of distant others. For this work has shown that they are increasingly seeking connections, fostering solidarity relationships, and launching collective action with others who share the same threatened identity as themselves, albeit often with resources borrowed from, and relations facilitated by, NGOs granting altruistic solidarity. Thus, this work argues that *identity solidarity* forms the basis of many contemporary mass-based networks. This was witnessed most prominently in the Via Campesina peasants' and rural peoples' network, in Jubilee South, comprised of people living under debt and SAPs, and in the scaled-down PGA anarchist youth network. Yet, as these cases also showed, identity-based solidarity networks are often enhanced by relations with activist organizations with whom they empathize, perceive a connection, and, hence, grant reciprocal solidarity. These are oftentimes small collectives of experienced and committed activists who play key brokerage and diffusion roles in the emerging networks.

In summary, activist networks, especially complex transnational ones, are comprised of a mixture of the above solidarity forms, which are the complex, cognitive, and affective bonds that hold them together. But I have also found that it is these very differences in proximity to the problem, threat perceptions, experienced suffering, and the kinds of solidarity evoked that help explain divergences in perspectives on the problems themselves and their potential remedies. Grasping these differences can further aid us in comprehending variance in involvement and commitment to a cause. And finally, it is this considerable diversity that can create tensions, frustrations, and denouncements of paternalism on the one hand and radicalism on the other, which can strain a network to the point of rupture.

This leads to a related finding regarding the complex and shifting role of NGOs in contemporary networks. With altruistic solidarity increasingly eclipsed by solidarity based upon shared identity and reciprocity among connected struggles, the central place once held by the traditional NGO in earlier advocacy networks is increasingly being challenged. Therefore, while NGOs still play important roles in a number of networks resisting neoliberalism, they are no longer their sole initiators or directors. This work has corroborated Bennett's assertion that NGOs are finding themselves *embedded within* larger webs of activism growing up around them, a process which they have partially helped to initiate but which is now beyond their control.

This work has gone further still, to show that NGOs are not only increasingly hemmed in by a growing network surrounding them; they are also being shut out of certain networks altogether. This is done explicitly through "identity-group only" rules that forbid their participation, as we saw in the case of the Via Campesina. It is also achieved tacitly, by the relatively radical platform and tactical approach adopted by networks such as Jubilee South and the PGA, which make them unpalatable partners for most traditional NGOs. When confronted with this shifting terrain, NGOs are reacting in one of two ways. Some are adopting a new role of *supporter* of the emerging identity-based networks, and thus entering into coalitions based on listening, trust building, mutual respect, and reciprocal solidarity, as seen, for example, in the NGO partners of the Via Campesina. A second reaction is to fight to maintain their privileged position on the "civil society" heap, through distancing themselves from groups who advocate more transgressive tactics and claims or through attempts to banish radical elements from "our movement" altogether.

These tensions and exclusionary attempts were further probed and explained through examining group-level, relational features of contemporary *network models*, their *operational paradigms*, and the *nature of their claims*. Here we found that networks in which altruism plays a key role tend to be structured on the first-generation, NGO advocacy model and operate within a paradigm of *domain-specific policy reform*, whereas networks in which identity or reciprocal solidarity predominate fall along a continuum from a *hybrid model* to a pure, *second-generation, direct activism social justice network*. Additionally, the latter networks' operational paradigms tend to be *transitional*, with an eye toward *multi-sector, structural transformation*. Finally, while first-generation networks often advocate *economic redistribution* in the forms of charitable giving or economic relief, they may also call for *cultural recognition* or a *bivalent* mix of both. Likewise, those that are hybrids or tend toward second-generation direct action usually make bivalent claims that encompass both cultural recognition and economic redistribution.

These findings have considerable relevance for a number of streams of literature. First, solidarity, or a "new internationalism," has emerged as a central concern of social scientists in the wake of globalization. My findings shed direct light on the possibilities, and limitations, of transnational solidarity today. As alluded to above, the declining centrality of traditional NGOs brings with it the diminution of altruistic solidarity. This throws into question why solidarity movements and other distant issue networks based in this sort of solidarity continue to take pride of place in scholarship on transnational activism, as seen, for example, in recent works by Rucht, Olesen, and Rosenau. My work instead reinforces the more skeptical voices within social movement literature – ranging from resource mobilization scholars to those studying poor people's movements – who point out the risks that altruistic, "conscience constituents" can pose to their would-be beneficiaries, both through withdrawing support in rough times and by diverting rebellion into routinized forms of contention.

My work identifies and defends what is coming to replace altruism – namely identity solidarity – as the foundation upon which mass-based networks are actually being forged today. In doing so, I underscore what seems to be an obvious conclusion, but one that is often missed in vaguely optimistic or glowing depictions of "transnational civil society." Identity solidarity gives networks a cohesive strength difficult to construct in other ways. This is because the agency, and thus power, of these networks lies with those who have the dedication – and indeed the necessity – to make most sure that their grievances are redressed, for they are precisely the ones whose lives are impacted by the problem, and thus by their collective successes or failures.

In reaffirming the centrality of identity solidarity to global activist networks, I avoid both the reified "worker" category and the isolationist, in-group/out-group identity that is often feared and derided by scholars and, to a lesser extent, by activists. For the identities that comprise contemporary mass-based networks are not reducible to the Procrustean, Marxist proletariat or to Hardt and Negri's big church *multitude*. These identities are instead reminiscent of those conceptualized in the new social movement scholarship of Melucci and Touraine, as well as the post-Marxist work of Laclau and Mouffe. These theorists have recognized identities as being dynamic, contingent, contested, and socially constructed, and hence do not privilege or assume one to be more progressive or revolutionary than another. But that said, these identities, such as Southern debtor, peasant farmer, alienated urban youth, or precarious worker, are undeniably co-constituted with global capitalism. They have furthermore been (re)activated as political due to their being threatened in specific ways by neoliberal globalization touching down in concrete places all over the world.

This finding of the fundamental role of identity – in the plural – in activist networks also cuts against the grain of contemporary scholarship that has deemed a rather underspecified "reciprocal solidarity" to be pre-eminent and superior to other forms, calling it alternatively "mutual," "reciprocal," or "the new transnationalism." While I have shown that attributing interconnectedness among struggles, and thus reciprocal solidarity, often plays a crucial facilitating role in activist networks and coalitions today, and while this form of solidarity furthermore has the *potential* to bind an emerging "network of networks," it is largely a second-order solidarity form. What makes a mass-based, transnational network possible, I posit, is the first-order variety, identity solidarity, which melds together disparate groups and individuals fighting to uphold *their* rights and ways of life or preserve *their* immediate environment. If activists, like other homo sapiens, have to walk before they can run, then an aggrieved or threatened identity is what makes these networks "walk," while reciprocal solidarity may enable the *network* of networks to eventually "run."

Although I hold that this triple specification of solidarity moves us considerably closer to comprehending what binds networks together, there is still more work to be done. Future research should continue to explore cases that verify, falsify, or amend this tripartite conceptualization of solidarity. A more theoretically sophisticated line of inquiry could link the latter two manifestations of solidarity to Laclau and Mouffe's concept of a *chain of equivalence*. According to these theorists, activists must establish such a chain amongst themselves as nodal points in order to construct a new "common sense" in favor of radical and plural democracy, but without erasing their diversity or autonomy.

Turning now to the related finding on network models, this work has operationalized, recast, and extended Bennett's distinctions between two generations of activist networks. The first is characterized as a centralized, NGO-advocacy model of limited, policy-oriented campaigning aimed at governments. The second is a direct activism social justice network seen as polycentric and multi-issue, geared toward mass activism and diversely targeted campaigns proliferating via the internet, and therefore difficult for any group to switch off. As noted above, in using the two frameworks to analyze these contemporary activist networks, I found that the first-generation model is increasingly being superseded, although not exactly by a purely second-generation network. What is replacing the former is most often a hybrid mix of the two, but which tends toward the second-generation end of the spectrum. In fact, as illustrated by the case study of the PGA – which is the closest to a direct action social justice network one can find – a solely second-generation network is extremely difficult to sustain. My work therefore reconceives Bennett's models as ideal types, against which contemporary networks can be usefully analyzed and compared.

Furthermore, these findings extend our understanding of transnational networks by showing that each model carries with it strengths and weaknesses. While the PGA demonstrates the precariousness of a purely "horizontal" network, the Jubilee 2000 and its follow-on campaign GCAP exemplify the dangers of fracturing that relatively "vertical" networks can and do face. This is increasingly true now that more and more former "beneficiaries" demand to speak, strategize, and act for themselves within networks that purport to represent their interests. The hybrid models of OWINFS, Jubilee South, and the Via Campesina illustrate attempts to create innovative structures that strike a balance between organization and autonomy and between routinized politics and transgressive action. Negotiating this balance is an ongoing challenge faced by all contemporary transnational networks. Scholars and activists alike could learn from closer observation of and experimentation with achieving this balance, which is being sought by myriad groups around the world at every level. Furthermore, the relationship between network model and the sorts of actions in which they engage – such as was begun in my examination of network practices in the WSF – could benefit from more systematic attention and greater theorizing.

Next, my findings further contribute to areas of scholarship dealing with transnational networks' operational paradigms and claims-making. This work adds specificity to – just as it attempts to bridge – the age-old dialectic between reform and revolution; that is, between those who work within the current institutional framework to promote fairer rules of the game in specific domains and those who challenge and seek to transform the global structures that comprise neoliberal globalization/capitalism. It does so by turning scholar-activist Martin Khor's discussion of three operational paradigms into analytical categories with which to examine, compare, and contrast networks. Specifically, this work lends credence to Khor's pragmatic, evolutionary "third way" approach to activism. This approach attempts to infuse the revolutionary paradigm into the reformist one in a *transition*. Reforms are therefore conceived as steps along the way to transforming the global system.

With regard to working toward the second, transformative paradigm, Khor calls for evolution rather than revolution. My case studies have shown that *reformist, transitional*, and *transformational* are indeed useful categories for analyzing transnational networks, for they adequately capture the breadth of paradigms held by those seeking change today. This work has further found that networks tend to adopt Khor's transitional approach. And their doing so demonstrates the pragmatism of contemporary leftist politics, where flexible alliances are sought across a wide range of actors and issues. This was witnessed, for example, in Via Campesina members' launching campaigns and participating in mass actions with FIAN, Friends of the Earth International, the World March of Women, the PGA, and OWINFS, among others, which they would regard as necessary alliances toward achieving multi-sectoral, structural transformation.

The latter notwithstanding, this work also shows that considerable diversity, and thus divergences, does indeed persist along the strategic range from policy reform to structural transformation, and thus an analysis of where networks fall along this continuum helps us identify both points of convergence as well as contention among networks today. This sort of comparative analysis reveals the outer limits of the "inclusive diversity" mantra that prevails among many contemporary activists. And, finally, it is crucial to keep in mind that operational paradigms are dynamic and fluid constructs, and therefore individuals, organizations, networks, and indeed a network of networks are constantly engaged in action, reflection, study, dialogue, and debate with themselves and others along this continuum. This dialogic process forms and re-forms activists' views and their collective actions as to what they are fighting against and how to succeed in that struggle.

Let us go finally to this work's relevance for another, more recently identified dichotomy in social movement scholarship and practice, that of the social politics of equality vs. the cultural politics of difference. These cases have shown that transnational activist networks would largely consider this to be a false choice of either/or and, rather, treat these as both/and. My work further explains why this is so: Neoliberal globalization, at least in the short term, is making economic distribution even more skewed, while at the same time it seems to create or exacerbate "misrecognitions" in status. These structural violences, as I call them, range from economic harms of poverty and exploitation to cultural injuries of devaluing or threatening different ways of life and peoples. Activist claims reflect this broad range, and thus call for both economic redistribution and cultural recognition and protection.

This research has therefore drawn considerably on, and in the process has helped to advance, the work begun by Fraser in this regard. She has been dedicated to reconciling redistributive claims – which for over a century and a half have been paradigmatic for theorizing social justice – with what she and others call the newly ascendant "politics of recognition." My work therefore goes a considerable distance in exposing what seems to be a largely Northern preoccupation with a supposed polarization between the two. It further casts doubt on the assumption that identity politics has gained favor over that of redistribution in contemporary justice claims-making in the post-Cold War era. While this descriptive bifurcation has proven to be a useful analytic as I have treated it in this work, my empirical findings show that this is a dubious choice between the social politics of equality and the cultural politics of difference. Further research could take my findings of transnational networks' claims being bivalent in nature as a hypothesis to be tested in other cases. It could also, on the other hand, investigate those groups whose claims remain either one or the other, and theorize as to why that is so.

The role of the WSF in transnationalizing activism

My third set of findings revolves around the relationship between transnationalizing networks and the WSF process. Rather than one giving rise to the other, this work shows their co-constituted nature in three key ways. Namely, the forums are *fertile ground* to nourish and strengthen transnationalizing networks at all levels. They are, furthermore, *common ground* for activists to come together to network with others. But, finally, they are also a *battleground* for the future of the forum process, and for the global network of networks itself.

Regarding the first point, involvement in the forums both reinforces the networks' shift in scale to the transnational level and at the same time strengthens networks locally, nationally, and macro-regionally. This is achieved primarily through holding internal meetings and workshops in the space of the forums. These meetings serve a number of purposes: They provide brokerage sites that bring formerly unconnected actors together. They also serve as opportunities to diffuse information, hold discussions toward reaching a deeper understanding, establish or strengthen relationships toward identity and/or reciprocal solidarity, and develop a common critique. From there they can plan concrete campaigns and upcoming international conferences and protests. These internal meetings also allow network actors to develop capacity at both the national and transnational levels, while constructing a framework for coordination among network participants at all levels. Some also invite others to attend their meetings and join in their campaigns. Finally, those networks that employ direct action also use the forum to strengthen their network not only through dialogue, but also through action, and toward that end they plan and launch political activities in and around the forum spaces. All of these features work to both deepen and broaden the respective networks.

With regard to the second point, the social forums are a space for encounter, fostering rejuvenation, learning, cooperative action through joint campaigns, and the construction of a network of networks. We see evidence of this, first, in the considerable networking and strategizing undertaken across networks. This is aimed at strengthening global and regional partnerships, working toward a common analysis of complex problems and solutions, and coordinating action. Second, it is further witnessed by the enthusiastic participation of activists in founding the WSF, engaging in its coordination as part of the IC, and spreading the social forum process to the regional, national, and local levels. Finally, some networks organize their own autonomous spaces, which are connected to, but somewhat distinct from, the social forums. These facilitate encounter and mutual learning and build cooperative, autonomous practices and action. Each will be illustrated below by drawing examples from our cases.

Participants in follow-up campaigns to Jubilee 2000, such as Oxfam, credit the WSF with being a unique space to network and strategize toward coordinated action, and to restore hope and a feeling of being part of something much larger. Jubilee South and Via Campesina likewise see the forums as valuable opportunities to strengthen their global and regional partnerships, exchange information on campaigns, and work toward a common analysis that can lead to a coordinated global strategy. This translates into co-sponsoring workshops, endorsing others' campaigns, and launching campaigns of their own. Indeed, the WSF has become the prime site for J2000's follow-up campaigns and member organizations to do so: Jubilee South planned, promoted, and then kicked off their 2000 campaign for the International People's Tribunal on the Debt, while Oxfam joined with others to launch the GCAP in Porto Alegre in 2005. The Via Campesina have also used the forum space to jointly campaign with their partner FIAN on their Global Campaign on Agrarian Reform. Finally, activists attempt to build consensus among the larger "network of networks" transnationally in the space of the forums by hosting discussions of their platforms and proposals. This was undertaken, for example, by OWINFS's IFG on their book *Alternatives to Economic Globalization*. Here network members have promoted dialogue, gathered feedback, and heard stories about local alternatives in action, with which they have then revised and expanded their analysis.

Networks have also cooperated to deepen and broaden the WSF process and the network of networks by, first, helping to found the WSF, then participating in its coordination as part of the IC, and, finally, working to spread the social forum process to all levels. J2000, OWINFS, and Via Campesina members were all seminal in conceiving of and bringing to fruition the WSF. They have, further, maintained a presence in its coordination by participating in the IC. The latter has also proven to be fruitful for transnational collective action in and of itself, in that through the IC these networks attempt to institutionalize and diffuse the WSF as a permanent global process, while simultaneously developing relationships which deepen and broaden understanding of issues and campaigns, promote the cross-fertilization of ideas, friendships, and solidarity, and encourage collaborative efforts.

As IC members and on their own accord, networks are also coordinating macro-regional, national, and local social forums, as we saw in Jubilee South Latin America's role in the social forums of the Americas, the Pan-Amazon, the Caribbean, and the sixth polycentric WSF in Caracas. Another example is Jubilee South, in partnership with Jubilee South Africa and the Asia-Pacific branch of Jubilee South, who have been working to seed the social forum process locally, nationally, and macro-regionally in Africa and Asia. Oxfam and other members of the GCAP have also been active in these diffusion processes, especially at the European level through the ESF, but as well throughout the Americas and in national contexts. The same can be said for those affiliated with the PGA, albeit in more autonomous and challenging ways. Likewise, OWINFS members, including the Via Campesina, have been similarly active in building and diffusing the forum process. The latter has taken this a step further by planning a thematic forum, the World Forum on Agrarian Reform, modeled on the principles and practice of the WSF.

A final way that networks use the space to collaboratively build the network of networks is through organizing their own autonomous spaces, which are connected to, but still distinct from, the social forums. This was witnessed in the conciliatory International Via Campesina Space in Mumbai, and, with a more critical stance, the PGA's spaces such as the 2005 Beyond ESF events in London. Indeed, the PGA have tended to view the WSF as a hierarchical and reformist vehicle for building the network of networks, and thus as a rival to themselves. Because of this, they have been the most conscious about modeling in their autonomous spaces the change that they seek. This modeling combines decentralized and assertive practices with a defiant presence, and in doing so attempts to "contaminate" the forum and win adherents.

But, lastly, just as the social forum is collectively constituted by these networks, it is also increasingly contested and challenged by each of them to become more like the networks themselves in composition and character: that is, more "vertical," or centralized, routinized, and resembling an NGO, a social movement organization, or a political party; or more "horizontal," or radically open, decentralized, networked, spontaneous, autonomous spaces of self-organization and transgressive action. This work empirically shows four diverse networks and their constituent members struggling, through their practices, to define the forum – and by extension the emerging network of networks – in one or the other direction. Below I will briefly highlight the main ways that each network is doing so, beginning with the horizontalist actions of Jubilee South, Via Campesina, and the PGA, and then finishing with some verticalist initiatives on the part of members of the GCAP and OWINFS.

In the case of Jubilee South, three "horizontalist" themes stand out. First, they emphasize building the social forums at the local level, which demonstrates their dedication to a bottom-up organizational approach. Second, they prioritize dialogue, coordination, and solidarity building at the forums with activists who share the common identity of citizens living under the rule of transnational creditors. But, third, they also make efforts to forge broad alliances of reciprocal solidarity among people struggling against distinct facets of neoliberal globalization, ranging from racism and militarism to debt and SAPs. These three efforts combine to show that Jubilee South intends to build a bottom-up, multi-issue network of networks based, first, upon identity solidarity but then linked, through reciprocity, to other struggles viewed as interconnected. This is done with the goal of multi-sector, structural transformation.

The Via Campesina's actions within the forum also tend to move it toward a more horizontal design and a space for disruptive action. This is witnessed, first, in their coordinating transnational, direct action near the WSF, as when they occupied and pulled up crops at a Monsanto test site near Porto Alegre. Efforts such as these push some forum attendees and planners out of their comfort zones of routinized panel presentations and cultural fair, and into a space of confrontational, transgressive action. They thereby challenge the forum to be not only an incubator for future action, but also a facilitator of collective action here and now. A second way that the farmers' network prods the forum toward a second-generation, direct action social justice model is through their autonomous spaces, both inside and beyond the WSF. Their advocacy for holding the WSF every other year so as to allow time and resources for regional and thematic forums to be strengthened throws into question the optimistic belief that coherent, transnational coordination among networks is possible at this stage. It instead is a cautionary and probably realistic plea for more time and work to be done within networks, issue domains, and regions, before the potential of the WSF can be fully realized.

Finally, the PGA's actions have been the most provocative and direct in attempting to move the forum in a horizontalist and direct action direction. Their utilization of the forum as a terrain of confrontation is embodied in their frank denunciations of other groups' centralizing and reformist tendencies as well as in calls by some for an all-out boycott of the WSF. These highlight both the tensions between vertical and horizontal network formations and the related debate over anti-neoliberalism versus anti-capitalism. The PGA's use of the forum as a terrain of contention has even veered into open confrontation. This is through their assertive tactics wielded in the spaces of the forums themselves, such as squatting VIP areas and plenaries, in order to protest concentrations of power, alliances with state officials, the hierarchical and routinized format which features adult "experts" talking down to largely youthful audiences, and in general the marginalization of their and other voices within the forums. These confrontational tactics spotlight the tensions between bureaucratic forms of contestation and more transgressive direct action. They also highlight the "age paradox," where the majority of activists in the streets and at social forums are young, while those who assume positions of leadership are considerably older.

Now let us turn to the ways in which practices serve to push the forum in a more verticalist and routinized direction. A different set of activities, when compared with the above, has been found among GCAP members at the WSF. While the campaign's lead organizations, such as Oxfam, have a long-time commitment to global change in favor of alleviating poverty and misery, and are, furthermore, committed to building the social forum process and what they term a "global civil society," some of their actions move the forum toward a reformist paradigm and a top-down, advocacy network model. This is witnessed most obviously in their choice to launch the GCAP at the WSF and feature prominently the Brazilian head of state. This was a rather clear violation of the WSF Charter, which attempts to keep at bay the divisiveness of party politics or the dangers that would likely result from opening the space to elected officials. While the short-term benefit of added media attention may have helped the campaign, this elite-driven, reformist approach threatens the WSF with reverting to the more familiar organizing structures. Lastly, a heavy reliance on wealthy NGOs such as OXFAM as sources of funding could play a crucial and largely hidden role in molding the WSF along a reformist, NGO-style path. While little concrete evidence was found that such influence is being wielded, this was enough of a concern for the Indian organizers of the 2004 WSF to refuse private foundation funds. And this is part of the reason why the WSF is now in considerable debt. Hence, both accepting this sort of assistance as well as refusing it pose different risks and place different limitations on the forum process. Both, therefore, should be weighed and discussed in a transparent manner in the future.

Turning now to our last network, OWINFS, it must be underscored that their participation is not in the main "verticalist," and indeed Chapter 4 demonstrated the considerable degree to which it embodies a second-generation, direct action social justice model. Nevertheless, the prominent role played by some of its members, such as Focus on the Global South's Walden Bello, in the SMA calls to mobilization and the group of nineteen intellectuals issuing the Porto Alegre Manifesto illustrates centralizing tendencies that should be acknowledged. Both of these efforts arose out of skepticism or frustration with the non-deliberative and non-hierarchical design of the WSF as stipulated in its charter. They further reflect a positive and widely felt desire to deepen ties toward concrete, coordinated transnational action. To its considerable credit, the SMA through its annual call has helped mobilize millions of people into global days of action, such as the 15 February 2003 anti-war demonstrations. This illustrates that frame extension and issue spillover, leading to attribution of interconnectedness and reciprocal solidarity among diverse issues and actors, may be enhanced through the SMA. Likewise, the Porto Alegre Manifesto detailing the G19's twelve-point program arose from a similar impatience with the unruly diversity of the social forums. It was aimed at giving "sense and direction" to the masses gathered there, and as one in this group declared, "Now, nobody can say that we have no program." While the manifesto was undoubtedly a more coherent state-ment of principles than are the rambling calls negotiated in the spaces of the SMA, the former was met with less enthusiasm and more criticism, precisely because of the closed, elite method in which it was developed and delivered.

The broader critique leveled against both of these efforts is that they bring the "old models" of negotiating a political party platform or a social movement program back into the space of the forums, thus jeopardizing the still nascent experiment of the "free horizontal articulation" among struggles at the transna-tional level. These documents give the appearance that the WSF has leaders, that those leaders give direction to the masses, and that final statements detail these marching orders. These declarations are further seen as attempts by some (though certainly not all) of their propagators to absorb the WSF inside their own mobilizing dynamics, thus transforming it into a more familiar, hierarchical model. Though neither the SMA nor the G19 speak for everyone, they nonethe-less aspire to be the "consensus" of the whole.

Efforts such as these pose the danger of compelling forum attendees to be present at the SMA negotiations or to send representatives to speak on their behalf, so as to jockey for a position in the final "consensus" platform. They also encourage the formation of ideological cliques, which then vie with each other to craft the most compelling "manifesto." But instead of creating a genuine consensus from the ground up through the articulation of diverse, mass-based networks and struggles with one another, they foment a top-down, competitive process in which the most resourced, bureaucratized, and represented groups at the transnational meetings will dominate these platforms, and thus shape their final outcomes. All dissipate the "potentialities of the non-hierarchical space." Hence, for those who believe that only through new forms of organizing and interacting will we be able to construct this new world everyone talks about, these sorts of final proclamations, along with the practices that go into making them, are dangerously anathema.

Indeed, regarding the social forums as contested terrain is crucial, in that many WSF observers today believe that it is precisely the ways in which activists and their various organizations engage each other in and around the forums that will indelibly shape the "other possible world/s" beyond, or in spite of, neoliber-alism and capitalism. My work therefore speaks directly to the nascent research by scholar-activists on the WSF, such as that by de Angelis, Holloway, Sen and his colleagues, Patomäki and Teivainen, Hardt, Klein, Whitaker, Fisher, and Ponniah. They have each identified the paramount importance of *how* the social forum is being conceived and constituted, through practice. They have further focused on the rift between two competing conceptions of the forum, as either an *open space and process* or an *event*, the latter of which is more akin to the hierar-chical planning tendencies of the old left. As de Angelis noted:

> *How* struggles circulate, organise and are able to coordinate alternatives is the *key* question around which *an alternative* to capitalism as a mode of

> organising social production can emerge. … The alternative to capitalism … must manifest alternative *processes* of social production. The [social forum] might represent an important element in the constitution of this alternative.[1]

As I have argued throughout, the process and outcome of this contestation taking place among networks, when combined with their cooperative efforts within and around the WSF, will greatly impact not only the nature of the forum, but that of any network of networks that is in the process of becoming, as well as the "other possible world/s" activists are struggling to create. Participatory research should continue to empirically investigate and then theorize both the cooperative efforts as well as the conflictual and confrontational ones, in an effort to help activists think through the likely outcomes of their actions for the WSF, the network of networks overall, and the worlds that they want to make possible. Another strand of research could explore additional DOC processes by placing the WSF at the center of the analysis. Such research could identify the constituent mechanisms of the WSF *as* a process of *construction/appropriation of a mobilizing structure/space*. It could also operationalize the DOC's already hypothesized mechanisms that constitute *actor constitution*, by examining the role of the WSF in constructing a single network of networks, and building on what has been done herein.

In light of scholar-activism

We can now turn our attention from the exclusive focus on this work's findings for scholarship to that of scholar-activism. Just as I discovered that transnational activism and the WSF are co-constituted, so it is with activism and scholarship. In tracing my reflexive process of becoming a scholar-activist, I articulated how normative commitments, methodology, and political activism are mutually constructed. I did so by first positing that scholar-activism requires both explanation and understanding at the individual, relational, and structural levels, and proposed to reconcile these through *comprehending*, or taking up and grasping together. Comprehending, as I envision it, advises scholar-activists to hold off on committing to their research question, given that we have two audiences to whom our work must be credible and who bear differing criteria for what makes it so. The methods I used toward comprehending included adapting an extended-case method of semi-structured interviews and theory-driven participant observation in both physical and virtual fields sites, as well as scholarly and activist print and electronic literature reviews.

I next situated comprehension within participatory action research and, finally, introduced this approach to the sub-discipline of critical globalization studies as a way to address what some critical researchers see as weaknesses in current theorizing. Throughout this work, I demonstrated a conviction that *what* we study – that is, ontology – cannot be separated from *how* we study it – or our methodology. I therefore detailed the co-evolution of my three questions alongside the frameworks for analysis and research methods, showing this to be an engaged, organic process that reflectively spirals between the activist field and scholarly literature. The example of my research process could potentially help orient younger scholars in particular, who may feel themselves, as I did, to be adrift upon an endless sea of scholarship and activism.

To do this, I advocated finding one's own moral compass with which to navigate the scholar-activist through the fog and turbulent waters of this massive subject area that swirls around globalization and resistance to it. Specifically, I hope that my work encourages others to reflect on what it is that drives them to do their research and then to communicate that candidly. Since I tend to think that honesty makes for the best policy, I would encourage others to disclose why it is they are pursuing their own work. Whether this rumination makes it into the final publication or not is less important than discovering one's motivations for making certain choices. This discovery will undoubtedly change both the research process and the final product.

Beyond self-discovery, I am making an argument for ethical consistency, as well. I submit that our core values and motivations not only ought to inform the questions we choose to investigate, but also should determine *how* we relate to, study, and engage with actors or phenomena, if we are to remain consistent with these values. Said another way, our values should not be contradicted by the methodology we adopt as scholar-activists and should rather inform our approach. And when the process is made more reflective and consistent, the research product will surely be different than it would have been without bringing to light and scrutinizing our core values, assumptions, and motivations. I'd like to think it makes for more thoughtful and less assumptive work.

This research has further demonstrated the appropriateness of adopting PAR as a method for studying this sort of phenomenon. Again, PAR is informed by democratic values and treats activists as articulate and self-aware agents acting within and making history. The role of the scholar is therefore one of *accompaniment*, while the goal is to illuminate and clarify the interconnections and tensions that those involved would find salient. It is further to articulate a "common sense" that is considered authentic to the participants themselves, when judged in light of their own experiences. Although PAR has its shortcomings, as do all approaches, its strengths entail better access to research resources and informants, the level of trust and rapport one is able to establish, and the ability to support and accompany an organization or movement in its efforts for social change.

I further demonstrated the affinities between PAR and critical globalization studies, and then argued how participatory action can assist critical scholars concerned with the negative aspects of neoliberal globalization to overcome what Eschle and Maiguashca see as their sub-discipline's deficiencies. Both PAR and critical globalization share a commitment to reflexivity, historicism, decentering, interdisciplinarity, and to challenging and transforming hegemonic concentrations of power by giving voice to marginalized and emancipatory visions. Hence, by combining the two we can address critical globalization studies' theoretical weaknesses on both the scholarship side and the activist side:

that is, of being insufficiently conversant with the social movement literature in sociology and political science, and at the same time of not having enough of an empirical footing in the actual practices of activists themselves. I hope that my own empirical and theoretically informed research exemplifies how the one can be used to strengthen the other. I would therefore encourage other scholar-activists to continue to experiment with this cross-pollination, in what I consider to be a budding symposium research among scholars in the nascent field of critical globalization studies.

In light of activism

Let us now consider more directly this work's implications for activism, and namely for transnational networks themselves, for the WSF, and for the emergent network of networks. These implications go beyond my findings in an attempt to illuminate and clarify potential connections and thus avenues for greater joint action, as well as tensions that arise from certain actions within and between networks. This is consistent with the participatory action researcher's role as a sympathetic insider who *accompanies* activists with the aim of helping to articulate a "common sense" that may be considered authentic by many involved.

In order to be considered authentic, my comments must be based in the experiences and aspirations shared among those involved, which is an emerging "common sense" that comes from both fear and hope. This common sense underlies these networks, creates the minimal "we-ness" within the WSF, and makes an emergent network of networks possible. On the "fear" side, there is what I have called throughout the structural violences of neoliberal globalization and thus the desire, and even necessity, to ameliorate that suffering as well as to work to root out its causes. I have noticed this to be a common thread shared among networks mobilizing today, which has sparked localized contention in many places where neoliberal policies have touched down. It also provides the negative content for Laclau and Mouffe's *chain of equivalence* to be formed, if you will, of an increasingly recognized and shared source of threat and suffering, and thus a common target.

The fact that so many people who are personally suffering are coming together to resist but also to propose solutions means that strategy today is complex, pragmatic, and must be designed to meet people's immediate material and social needs, but at the same time with an eye toward transforming the processes that have created their suffering. This may explain the pragmatism of contemporary networks, which tend to operate within a transitional paradigm, as we have seen. If those who immediately suffer are the litmus test upon which success or failure is judged, then tactics and strategy must encompass both immediate relief and protection as well as long-term, structural transformation. Paradigms are therefore by necessity transitional between reform and revolution, where networks prioritize solutions based on meeting immediate human needs, but recognize that these are stop-gap measures that must move in the direction of longer-term, thoroughgoing transformation. Hence, in my comments below,

I recognize and respect the necessary pragmatism with which networks today operate, as well as their two-pronged strategies that combine short-term emergency measures as well as searching for long-term solutions through forging broad understanding and alliances.

Turning now to the "hope" side, a second common thread stitching together networks mobilizing today is that of a shared commitment to and aspiration for strengthening and reinvigorating democracy from the grassroots to the national to the transnational level, albeit in different ways. This flows from a widely shared grievance that local communities' and nations' decision-making processes and powers are being hijacked by the institutions, policies, actors, and effects of neoliberal globalization. This concern over an erosion of democracy is intertwined with the suffering mentioned above, in that many activists are finding that former channels and practices by which they could express and try to redress grievances are now closed off, while new grievances and threats are arising. Furthermore, as activists realize that decisions are being taken transnationally that seriously impact their everyday lives, they are demanding democratic decision-making at that level as well. They are also attempting to internalize their goal of deepening and broadening democracy, through self-critique and the implementation of changes within their own networks and organizations to become more inclusive, participatory, and horizontal in their decision-making practices. As they have created and become more invested in the social forum process, many are also experimenting with, learning from, and attempting to improve upon this autonomous space for encountering each other, mutually learning, building networks, and planning action. Most activists today therefore share the conviction that the greatest challenges facing humanity can best be met through a radical devolution and dispersion of decision-making power over all aspects of social life, coupled with transparent, democratic, and transnational decision-making bodies.

Hence, since democracy is arguably both the means and ends of the network of networks, it constitutes the main theme with which to reflect upon network practice. This also comprises the positive charge for Laclau and Mouffe's chain of equivalence to be ignited. It is, furthermore, consistent with the *content* of the struggle identified by those theorists two decades ago: that of striving for a radical and plural democracy as the left's global project. These two sides of the coin, of fear and hope, of a shared source of suffering and a common aspiration to overcome it through deeply democratic practices, are the negative and positive motivators that may interlink these networks into a united network of networks. These are the two currents of equivalence that do not require groups to sacrifice their diversity or their autonomy for the unity of the whole. The energy flowing through these linkages is solidarity, based first upon a shared identity, and then upon reciprocity among interconnected struggles. This, I think, is the "common sense" of the global left. It has also come to be my own normative project, as elaborated earlier in this work. It is therefore in this spirit that my closing comments are made *vis-à-vis* activism today.

Beginning with the follow-on campaigns to Jubilee South, the GCAP leadership would do well to reflect on their network's structure toward finding ways to democratize its practices by improving information and decision-making flows *from* the countries and organizations most effected by global trade, aid, and debt policies *to* the network's lead NGOs and celebrity spokespersons. More fundamentally, they should also rethink their roles atop this relatively hierarchical network as director and organizer, by contemplating the alternatives of facilitator, broker, frame translator, and information diffuser. These measures may help to avert a split of the network reminiscent of J2000, which may already be occurring in the wake of the recent Scotland G8 campaign.

Second, the GCAP's lead NGOs may benefit from a sober reflection regarding the basis upon which North–South solidarity can most successfully be cultivated on the issues of debt, trade, and aid. The GCAP has eschewed J2000's religious frame in favor of a kind of secular humanist message, therefore forgoing one of the few global, altruistic frames available today, that of Christian duty and charity. This is not to say that they should reappropriate the Jubilee imagery outright, but rather undertake a comparison between the emotional appeal – and the concrete response – that both campaigns have garnered, from various publics, media, and politicians. It strikes me that their current message that "it's not about charity, it's about justice" lacks the moral authority that accompanied the Judeo-Christian Jubilee year framing, and hence can demand very little of their wealthy audiences. Since the GCAP is the obvious heir to J2000, its members might want to explore ways of reviving the powerful imagery that they have passed over in favor of pop glamor and pathos.

Speaking of which, this star-studded campaign is clearly a double-edged sword. Planners should attempt to find ways of transitioning from their celebrity spokespeople to placing those who are suffering – and resisting – front and center. This is because the cost of free publicity that the celebrities attract today may prove to be too high years from now. If all the public hears is vague praise and congratulatory backslapping from Bono, Geldof, Oxfam, and the US's One campaigners greeting the G8's tepid pronouncement, they will assume that the good guys have indeed "won" on debt. What will happen in five or ten years from now when the issue comes once again to boiling point? Public opinion will recall the "victory" declared by the Irish rock-poverty NGO, shrug their shoulders, and say, "What more do these poor countries want? We forgave their debt back around the time of the Live 8 concert, and here they are back asking for another handout." *This* is the danger posed by overly polite celebrity spokespersons. Not only do they do little to solve the long-term structural problems that have created and perpetuate the debt and poverty of poor countries. More damaging still, they erode the base of support for such thoroughgoing change by creating a misinformation campaign as they rush to chalk up a "win" for our side in order to keep morale high, and to keep rubbing shoulders with political dignitaries.

Turning now to the Jubilee Framework which seeks to democratize the rules of the global financial architecture, it nonetheless occupies an uncomfortable position with respect to Jubilee South, as well as many other anti-debt campaigners. Its promoters realize that their framework likely must gain mass support if it is to be pushed onto the international agenda. Yet at the same time, it is doubtful whether such a plan for adjudicating debt can garner that support, given that many Southern groups have grown increasingly disillusioned with the G7 promises and are now calling for complete debt write-off as well as restitution. On the other hand, if Jubilee South activists were able to convince a few key governments to repudiate their debt, then maybe the Jubilee Framework would have its moment in the sun as a compromise measure. This contingency should be prepared for, especially because of the more basic question as to whether any such framework would in fact be implemented in the "just" and democratic way that its campaigners hope for, or whether it would simply become another mechanism for controlling debt-ridden countries dressed up as a new, pro-poor policy.

Moving on to Jubilee South, this network ought to continue strengthening internally based on identity solidarity, while forging transnational relationships of reciprocity and mutual respect, including with Northern-based think-tanks and NGOs. This is to be done on the condition that the latter recognize that those who have the most intimate experience with these complex problems should be the determining voice in setting the network's agenda and judging what is to be considered a "triumph." They also should continue to develop their domain-specific program and articulate it with other related networks, in joint campaigns and at the social forums. Toward these ends, Jubilee South could continue to put out feelers to former campaign partners from J2000 in the North, many of whom have belatedly expanded their own comprehension of debt to include related issues of global trade rules, enhanced development aid, agriculture policies, workers' rights, environmental degradation, and the arms trade. In this way they could more actively cultivate relations based on reciprocal solidarity with these groups, at least some of which have learned the hard lesson of the rift that tore apart J2000.

Furthermore, developing global campaigns that could have the broad appeal of GCAP and still remain true to Jubilee South's demands for structural transformation is undoubtedly an arduous task. But if the GCAP and the J2000 campaigns, moderate as they have been, taught us anything, it is that debt is indeed a concern that bridges the South and the North. A Southern-led initiative in this area, while not compromising its position, should attempt to maximize alliances and resources that can be gained from partnerships not only across the South, but with Europeans and North Americans as well. As referenced above in the discussion on the GCAP, a frame that worked well for the J2000 but which has been all but abandoned in the follow-on campaigns was the religious one. While this frame runs the risk of activating a "charitable" response and thus altruistic solidarity, the latter is – under certain conditions – better than no solidarity at all. Specifically, when introduced into a network whose decision-making structures are already built upon identity solidarity as well as reciprocal ties, the excesses and risks of charitable solidarity could likely be held in check.

In addition, religious conviction, at least for a minority of committed activists, runs beyond charity to more egalitarian, reciprocal, and even identity forms, and these should not be overlooked or discounted. These allies, along with their secular counterparts in the North, could attempt to frame Jubilee South's demands for retribution and, indeed, a revolution of sorts, into language that other audiences may find less threatening. These allies could act as gatekeepers who contemplate what their constituencies or broader publics are capable of doing on behalf of others. In this vein they could develop finite, reformist campaigns that complement, not contradict, Jubilee South's overall transformative program as part of a transitional paradigm and strategy. For even the most apolitical material support, such as funding for computers, internet connections, translation services, and travel funds, could greatly facilitate the overall effort. In a more political vein, targeted campaigns against specific governments or private lenders could also be of service for relieving the debt burden. The point is that there is no need to ask certain constituencies to sign on for the whole program. Yet well-coordinated, short-term campaigns that are "winnable" for those involved could positively feed into the transitional paradigm about which Martin Khor speaks and within which most transnational networks are forced to operate. The idea, then, is not to eschew or write off altruistic solidarity altogether, but rather to direct it toward ends that are congruent with, and overseen by, the Southern-led, mass-based network.

All of this requires lengthy, collective discussions on strategy, tactics, and targeted campaigns that support both. This should take place, first, among the Jubilee South identity-based partners, but then be expanded out to their allies granting reciprocal solidarity. The latter are in the best position to advise on how their message could be "packaged and sold" to various audiences. The religious frame, coupled with the vast networks of churches that were motivated to act by it, was largely positive for J2000 in helping them reach mass publics, politicians, and the mainstream press in a way that few campaigns have been able to do before or since. Hence, Jubilee South may want to think about a multi-pronged framing effort for future global campaigns in order to reach and mobilize different constituencies.

Certainly more dialogue and even joint strategizing between all of these anti-debt networks could be worthwhile, toward the goal of sketching out a transitional paradigm in which their work complements each other's, rather than competing with or being isolated from one another. The question remains whether campaigns such as the GCAP and Jubilee Framework can in fact be reconciled with Jubilee South's fundamental claim, which is that, on balance, the North owes a great debt to the South and that strategies must aim at making them pay. Jubilee South, for its part, may benefit from some of the expertise, resources, and contacts that the other two campaigns hold. But this can only come to pass if trust can be re-established. This could begin by lead NGOs who have for decades dominated advocacy networks on Third World debt adopting a supportive, rather than leadership, role.

Let us move on to our second issue and network, the neoliberal trade regime and OWINFS, who are fighting it. OWINFS's ongoing challenge is to maintain solidarity and consensus among a mammoth network comprised of such varying groups. This is made even more complex by the constantly changing trade environment in which they struggle, which now entails not only the WTO but also bilateral and macro-regional treaties requiring constant information-gathering, analysis, and the tailoring of appropriate responses and frames. Their main effort seems to be to continue to expand the network to all countries in order to strengthen the national-level campaigns, which they conclude is the level at which pressure can still be best exerted. This is witnessed, for example, in national-level organizations from Brazil to India, and Tanzania to Thailand maintaining a close watch on their governments and pushing them, through collective protest and lobbying, to represent them in trade talks. Strong campaigns at these levels, when coupled with better transnational information flows and coordination, may increase this network's response time and impact. Furthermore, strengthening their relationships and lobbying at the WTO headquarters in Geneva through enhancing ties with activist groups there can further boost their lobbying efforts and information-gathering capabilities.

Since OWINFS is comprised of a mix of both Southern and Northern mass movements and NGOs alike, it seems important to prioritize strengthening the leadership capacity of, and identity-based solidarity among, Southern mass-based groups. This requires the more resource-rich, Northern NGOs within the network to continue to "rethink and reinvent" North–South solidarity, as they have begun doing. This also entails reinventing their own organizations as brokers of relationships and diffusers of information, instead of lead organizations in a hierarchical movement. We have seen the beginnings of this rethinking in the examples of the Transnational Institute (TNI) brokering ties between European and Latin American activists. It is also exemplified in Focus on the Global South's recent efforts to move beyond their traditional brokerage and diffusion roles in order to take on the task of fomenting mass mobilization in Asia, and thus trying to emulate their network partners' work in the Americas around the FTAA. Throughout, these Northern NGOs need to serve as a bridge and an interpreter for their wider publics and politicians, seeking ways of translating the networks' transformative project into circumscribed, winnable campaigns in the Global North. Generating reciprocal solidarity is key to this task, as TNI is attempting to do by drawing parallels between the EU's pro-business internal policies and their foreign relations. And though surely complex, these need to be re-conceptualized and framed in terms of region-to-region relations, not simply the bilateral development aid packages of decades prior. Educating Europeans on the impact of EU policies abroad and attempting to harmonize demands for internal reforms with transnational transformation are all crucial for building these alliances.

Similarly to Jubilee South, the Via Campesina should continue strengthening internally based on identity solidarity while reaching out to forge transnational relationships of reciprocity with others in struggle. They should continue to prioritize mass-based organizations, but also, when it is deemed mutually beneficial, to network further with NGOs and think-tanks. They also should – and, I am confident, will – continue to develop their already sophisticated domain-specific program, while articulating this with other networks. Indeed, perhaps due to the marginal geographical and social location of the peasantry throughout history, the Via Campesina seem the most pragmatically attuned to the interdependence of the various struggles against neoliberal globalization and for other ways of living. They acknowledge that their project of democratizing the land needs to be inserted into popular struggles for a new economic, social, and political order to emerge domestically and then be articulated globally. This demonstrates a keen understanding of their interdependence with others, and therefore the need to foster reciprocal solidarity among struggles against neoliberalism/capitalism and all forms of exclusion today.

So although the VC recognize that their transformative vision will not come to fruition without the solidarity of others, it is important to underscore the pent-up potential of this massive movement, stemming from their numerical possibility and the current momentum to mobilize much of the world's people threatened by neoliberalism/capitalism. If, following Tilly, network strength equals "worthiness times unity times numbers times commitment," then the VC have got it all in spades.[2] This network could therefore potentially be the engine to push through real transformative changes on the global scale. The VC itself, as well as others, would do well to recognize this prospect, and perhaps to devise more ambitious, coordinated strategies with that in mind. Because, while seizing the factories was a good idea – and indeed continues to be in those parts of the world where factories still exist in critical numbers – we should recognize that occupying land may be equally effective, and perhaps more so in places where development is euphemistically called "uneven." And wherever one stands on the Marxist debate over revolutionary versus reactionary classes, the fact of the current matter is that the identity of the "peasant" has proved tenaciously resonant across cultural, linguistic, and geographic distances in forging strong solidarity bonds, in a way that "trade unionist," much less "worker," as of late has not. An important avenue for articulating diverse struggles that could place the VC as an "engine" for structural transformation is in the spaces of the social forums. Therefore, both in their experimentation with direct action – as we saw in their Monsanto crop-pulls – as well as in their autonomous spaces inside and beyond the social forum, they should experiment with ways of making this potentiality a reality, in dialogue and action, as a network and together with others.

Lastly, out of all the networks studied herein, the PGA seems to be the one most uncertain of its future as a transnational collective actor. Its failure to adapt to current conditions would be a loss to the emergent network of networks, and would pose a real danger to the social forum process as "space." This is due to its bona fides as the urban offspring of *zapatismo*, its brilliance in innovating tactics, and its role – which PGAers have been slow to embrace up to this point – as the only global youth network that embodies the anarchist, anti-consumerist, ecological, and anti-capitalist *zeitgeist* and *angst* of many young people today. In order not to squander its considerable potential, those who remain under the PGA banner ought to embrace its slimmed-down identity and to rebuild the network upon this basis. And since one of its hallmarks is opposition to all forms of fundamentalism, they would do well to consider that slavish adherence to a "pure" forum of horizontal articulation is also fundamentalism. If they are to survive and to thrive as the youth movement that is clearly their fate, then they ought to examine their own fundamentalist tendencies and to study the lessons of their former allies, the Via Campesina, as to how to organize a bottom-up, transnational, direct action network based in identity solidarity. The PGA should recognize – as have their more pragmatic *compañer@s* in the VC and indeed the EZLN – that there are innumerable degrees between the *x*- and the *y*-axis. They must consider what is being lost by refusing to move off – even a little – from the horizontal axis. That being said, they must also continue rattling their horizon-talist saber within and around and beyond the WSF, both in words and in actions (remember, you are winning). They should also seek other ways of engaging the social forum apparatus, as, for example, through an alliance with the WSF Brazilian committee, in order to defend and extend the WSF as a horizontal space and to inject a much-needed youthful voice into the WSF IC discussions.

If this self-conscious-to-a-fault network is able to overcome its self-policing against any form of organization and to embrace its identity, then it may actually be able to help realize the WSF's potential as a radical, open space. Without its concerted engagement along the lines detailed above, the forum is in serious danger of succumbing to the old models. In addition to shoring up the WSF as a space, it may also be able to follow in the footsteps of its farmer and rural allies by reaching out to forge alliances over finite campaigns. The VC is the most obvious candidate for this kind of coalition work, and in fact PGAers already endorse and promote the April 17 international day of the farmer. Yet given their diverse agenda, more sustained relations could also be forged with minimal difficulties with any number of transnational networks today, including OWINFS, Jubilee South, environmental groups like FOEI, feminist networks such as the World March of Women, and, when they are ready, indigenous networks as well. The mention of indigenous peoples brings up a final point for the PGA: As they hopefully move forward to embrace their identity as a radical youth network, they would do well to sustain and even strengthen reciprocal solidarity with those who helped them recover their dignity and taught them to walk, in the language of *zapatismo*. No longer simply admirers or "revolutionary tourists" off to commune with the rebel natives in the jungle, a more mature "blue Indian" network would have much to give, and get, from relationships with the "real" Indians. The Zapatistas should not be forgotten. Searching for concrete ways of expressing and developing this reciprocal solidarity ought to remain a central concern and inspiration of the PGA.

The above should provide sufficient evidence and food for thought as to the pressing need for further research by scholar-activists into the many facets and dimensions of this complex struggle against neoliberalism/capitalism and for another possible world. As this is still a work – and battle – in progress, and recalling the considerable cooperative efforts also underway among networks and within the WSF, I encourage others to continue to conduct empirically based investigations before rushing to declare the WSF a closed space of bureaucra-tized, reformist politics. As we have seen, the space is closing, and it is opening, and both efforts have their adherents and their rationales for pushing in either direction. It is the job of scholar-activists to continue to study this dialectic in an engaged manner, so as to highlight the potential points of convergence and tensions between groups, and to help think through the likely outcomes of particular courses of action. Throughout I have tended to favor those actions that maintain and expand the WSF as an open space for not only dialogue but also collective action. This is consistent with the pragmatic and democratic "common sense" of the emerging network of networks. It has, furthermore, never been tried on such a scale, which seems reason enough to experiment with the open space as far as it will take us.

Indeed, the open space for articulating democratic struggles seems to be the *zeitgeist* of contemporary leftist activism. As we have seen throughout, many networks are moving in the direction of bottom-up, mass-based models, where identity solidarity among those who personally suffer is the glue that holds them together as well as the fuel that powers them forward. But, further, we have seen how they are searching out allies who view the struggles against different violences of neoliberalism as interconnected, and thus are granting each other reciprocal solidarity. There is room, of course, for altruistic solidarity, although it should not be given the pride of place that it too often receives in much utopian thinking on "transnational civil society."

Finally, this work has also shown that networks have moved well beyond protest toward proposal. Many are developing global interpretive, transformative projects, based in their specific domains of debt eradication, SAPs, or the global trade regime, but broadening out in an attempt to address neoliberal globalization and/or capitalism in its entirety. These are pragmatic and contingent programs, and thus reflect activists' openness to dialogue, to learning from each other, and innovating together. These are also stealth projects of *evolution*, in the hopes of assuring that the revolution gets it right this time by addressing *both* material and ideational needs, or the social politics of equality and cultural politics of difference. This suggests the prospect that a single network of networks is in fact emerging. As noted above, this may be akin to what Laclau and Mouffe have called a chain of equivalence, or of articulating struggles together without erasing their diversity, toward building a radical and plural democratic movement. And this, I submit, provides the best chance for both alleviating the widespread suffering wrought by unrestrained neoliberal capitalism and for reinventing and revalorizing genuine democracy, based on the principles of horizontality, inclusion, and participation, in our age of globalization.

Appendixes

Appendix 1: The World Social Forum Charter of Principles[1]

The committee of Brazilian organizations that conceived of, and organized, the first World Social Forum, held in Porto Alegre from January 25th to 30th, 2001, after evaluating the results of that Forum and the expectations it raised, consider it necessary and legitimate to draw up a Charter of Principles to guide the continued pursuit of that initiative. While the principles contained in this Charter – to be respected by all those who wish to take part in the process and to organize new editions of the World Social Forum – are a consolidation of the decisions that presided over the holding of the Porto Alegre Forum and ensured its success, they extend the reach of those decisions and define orientations that flow from their logic.

1　The World Social Forum is an open meeting place for reflective thinking, democratic debate of ideas, formulation of proposals, free exchange of experiences and interlinking for effective action, by groups and movements of civil society that are opposed to neoliberalism and to domination of the world by capital and any form of imperialism, and are committed to building a planetary society directed towards fruitful relationships among Mankind and between it and the Earth.

2　The World Social Forum at Porto Alegre was an event localized in time and place. From now on, in the certainty proclaimed at Porto Alegre that "another world is possible", it becomes a permanent process of seeking and building alternatives, which cannot be reduced to the events supporting it.

3　The World Social Forum is a world process. All the meetings that are held as part of this process have an international dimension.

4　The alternatives proposed at the World Social Forum stand in opposition to a process of globalization commanded by the large multinational corporations and by the governments and international institutions at the service of those corporations' interests, with the complicity of national governments. They are designed to ensure that globalization in solidarity will prevail as a new stage in world history. This will respect universal human rights, and those of all citizens – men and women – of all nations and the environment and will rest on democratic international systems and institutions at the service of social justice, equality and the sovereignty of peoples.

5   The World Social Forum brings together and interlinks only organizations and movements of civil society from all the countries in the world, but intends neither to be a body representing world civil society.

6   The meetings of the World Social Forum do not deliberate on behalf of the World Social Forum as a body. No-one, therefore, will be authorized, on behalf of any of the editions of the Forum, to express positions claiming to be those of all its participants. The participants in the Forum shall not be called on to take decisions as a body, whether by vote or acclamation, on declarations or proposals for action that would commit all, or the majority, of them and that propose to be taken as establishing positions of the Forum as a body. It thus does not constitute a locus of power to be disputed by the participants in its meetings, nor does it intend to constitute the only option for interrelation and action by the organizations and movements that participate in it.

7   Nonetheless, organizations or groups of organizations that participate in the Forum's meetings must be assured the right, during such meetings, to deliberate on declarations or actions they may decide on, whether singly or in coordination with other participants. The World Social Forum undertakes to circulate such decisions widely by the means at its disposal, without directing, hierarchizing, censuring or restricting them, but as deliberations of the organizations or groups of organizations that made the decisions.

8   The World Social Forum is a plural, diversified, non-confessional, non-governmental and non-party context that, in a decentralized fashion, interrelates organizations and movements engaged in concrete action at levels from the local to the international to build another world.

9   The World Social Forum will always be a forum open to pluralism and to the diversity of activities and ways of engaging of the organizations and movements that decide to participate in it, as well as the diversity of genders, ethnicities, cultures, generations and physical capacities, providing they abide by this Charter of Principles. Neither party representations nor military organizations shall participate in the Forum. Government leaders and members of legislatures who accept the commitments of this Charter may be invited to participate in a personal capacity.

10   The World Social Forum is opposed to all totalitarian and reductionist views of economy, development and history and to the use of violence as a means of social control by the State. It upholds respect for Human Rights, the practices of real democracy, participatory democracy, peaceful relations, in equality and solidarity, among people, ethnicities, genders and peoples, and condemns all forms of domination and all subjection of one person by another.

11   As a forum for debate, the World Social Forum is a movement of ideas that prompts reflection, and the transparent circulation of the results of that reflection, on the mechanisms and instruments of domination by capital, on

means and actions to resist and overcome that domination, and on the alternatives proposed to solve the problems of exclusion and social inequality that the process of capitalist globalization with its racist, sexist and environmentally destructive dimensions is creating internationally and within countries.

12 As a framework for the exchange of experiences, the World Social Forum encourages understanding and mutual recognition among its participant organizations and movements, and places special value on the exchange among them, particularly on all that society is building to centre economic activity and political action on meeting the needs of people and respecting nature, in the present and for future generations.

13 As a context for interrelations, the World Social Forum seeks to strengthen and create new national and international links among organizations and movements of society, that – in both public and private life – will increase the capacity for non-violent social resistance to the process of dehumanization the world is undergoing and to the violence used by the State, and reinforce the humanizing measures being taken by the action of these movements and organizations.

14 The World Social Forum is a process that encourages its participant organizations and movements to situate their actions, from the local level to the national level and seeking active participation in international contexts, as issues of planetary citizenship, and to introduce onto the global agenda the change-inducing practices that they are experimenting in building a new world in solidarity.

APPROVED AND ADOPTED IN SÃO PAULO, ON APRIL 9, 2001, BY THE ORGANIZATIONS THAT MAKE UP THE WORLD SOCIAL FORUM ORGANIZING COMMITTEE, APPROVED WITH MODIFICATIONS BY THE WORLD SOCIAL FORUM INTERNATIONAL COUNCIL ON JUNE 10, 2001.

Appendix 2: List of interviews conducted by the author

I: Washington, DC, various dates

Name	Title and organization (date)
1 Mark Cimino	organizer, Washington, DC, Social Forum (07/24/02)
2 John Cavanagh	director, Institute for Policy Studies, Washington, DC (07/31/02 and follow-up e-mail correspondence, August 2002)
3 Timi Gerson	Global Trade Watch, Public Citizen, WSF IC (02/12/03)
4 Roxanne Lawson	American Friends Service Committee, WSF delegate
5 Stanley A. Gacek	AFL–CIO, Washington, DC (02/13/03)

II: European Social Forum, Florence, Italy, 7–10 November 2002

6 Hélène Bouneaud	Confédération Generale du Travail (CGT), France (11/07/02)	
7 Marina	Syndicat des Services Publiques and WMW, Switzerland	
8 Salvatore Ercolano	Instituto Universitario Orientale, Facultad Scienza Politica, Italy	
9 Caroli Albino	Rifondazione Comunista, Italy	
10 Roberta	women's activist, Italy	
11 Wolfgang Linke	Münchner Gewerkschaftslinke, Germany	
12 Pol de Vos	Anti-Imperialist League, Belgium (11/08/02)	
13 Constantin Cretu	Association Carpathian Genius, Romania	
14 Franco Cenacchi	businessman, Italy	
15 Valentina Conticelli	student, Italy	
16 Joy Knight	Revolution, Canada	
17 Angelika Lee	Collectif 44, Nantes, France	
18 Sophie Gosselin	student, Collectif 44, Nantes, France	
19 Nicolas Martino	Rifondazione Comunista, Italy	
20 no name given	Refugees Initiative Brandenburg, Germany	
21 no name given	activist, Poland (11/09/02)	
22 Andrew Baisley	Socialist Workers' Party, UK	
23 no name given	Socialist Workers' Party, UK (11/10/02)	
24 no name given	student, Sweden	
25 Chandra Ehm	student, Germany/Italy	
26 George Giannakopoulos	activist, Greece	

III: World Social Forum, Porto Alegre, Brazil, 23–28 January 2003

27 Antonio Cardoso	Workers' Party (PT), Rio Grande do Sul, Brazil (01/23/03)	
28 no name given	Comité Mercosur de Organizaciones de Trabajo Social (01/24/03)	

29 Dolmir Brutscher   Centro de Educacao e Assessoramento Popular (CEAP)
30 Jim Douglas   Ontario Secondary School Teachers' Federation,
                       Canada (01/25/03)
31 Katharin Ross   ATTAC Chile
32 Stephanie   ATTAC Chile
33 María Elena Martínez   executive director, CorpWatch, San Francisco
34 W.R. Varada Rajan   secretary, Center of Indian Trade Unions
35 no name given   anti-nuclear activist, Japan
36 Lucas Coelho   Central Directory of Students, Federal University, Minas
                       Gerais
37 no name given   Madre de la Plaza de Mayo, Linea Fundadora, Cucuey,
                       Argentina
38 no name given   GreenPeace International, WSF IC (01/26/03)
39 no name given   Rede Lilliput, Italy
40 Mie Asai   Peaceboat, Japan
41 Dada Suvedanda   Progressive Utilization Theory (PROUT), Brazil
                       (01/27/03)
42 Francisco "Chico" Whitaker   WSF OC, Brazilian Committee of Justice and
                       Peace
43 Fernando Vannier dos Santos Borges   student, Rio de Janeiro
44 Aldo Caliari   Rethinking Bretton Woods Project, Center of Concern,
                       Washington
45 no name given   WSF delegate
46 Juan Vicente   Catholic priest, Colomban Fathers, Chile (01/28/03)
47 Oya Sadaharu   founding member, ATTAC Japan
48 Dimi Mazzer   medical doctor, Brazil
49 Ouattara Diakalia   Forum National de Lutte Contre La Dette et la Pauvreté
50 Blandine Renaud   Centre International de Culture Populaire, Paris
51 Ali Hebshi   Clean Water Action, Pittsburgh Pennsylvania Social
                       Forum
52 Celine Porcheron   Pour un Monde de Saveurs, France
53 Nathalie Gregoris   Pour un Monde de Saveurs, France
54 Helena Tagesson   ATTAC Sweden
55 Jessie Sklair   British documentary filmmaker, São Paulo
56 Soren Ambrose   Fifty Years Is Enough Network, Washington, DC
57 Alison Marshall   Catholic Agency for Overseas Development, London

IV: European Social Forum, Paris, France, 12–16 November 2003

58 Hasan Bulut   ATTAC Stuttgart, Germany (11/12/03)
59 Albert Torrent   student, Catalunia
60 Guy   Fédération Syndicale Unifiée (FSU), France
61 Barbara Switzer   president, National Assembly of Women, UK
62 Garry   Socialist Workers' Party and Scottish Socialist Party
63 Denise

64   no name given   ATTAC Bergen, Norway
65   no name given   group of sixteen-year-old French students
66   Nicolas Quetelard   bicycle group, Lille, France
67   Francisco Florez   Movimiento Furiosos Ciclistas, Chile
68   Dominique Geneston   France
69   Ulrich Franz   trade unionist, Germany (11/13/03)
70   Peter Gustavsson   Socialist Youth, Sweden
71   Hélène Santeix
72   Panos Garganas   Stop the War Coalition, Greece
73   Daria de Vittor   Italian youth coordinator, Amnesty International
74   Elena Belleti   Italian youth coordinator, Amnesty International
75   Michele Tizzoni   human rights education coordinator, Piemonte, Italy
76   Beatrice Olocco   Amnesty International, Verona, Italy
77   Ilaria Giglioli   Amnesty International, Italy
78   Aldijana Sisic   regional campaigns coordinator, Europe, Amnesty
                        International
79   Barbara Lochner   student, Germany (11/14/03)
80   Christine Rehklan   student, Germany
81   Jaqcelin   student, Germany
82   Frida Jorup   Faltbiologerne, Sweden
83   Anders Agebjorn   Faltbiologerne, Sweden
84   Erika Hagegard   Faltbiologerne, Sweden
85   Phil Butland   ATTAC Stuttgart, Germany
86   Fabrizio Andriolo Italy
87   Ileana Petrini   Italy
88   Noel Douglas   Movement of the Imagination, Globalize Resistance
                        (11/15/03)
89   Aetzel Griffioen   Holland
90   no name given
91   Fabien Charbonnia   student, France
92   Sophie Pithon   student, France
93   Rosalie   green activist, Netherlands
94   Roosien   young activist, Netherlands
95   Ibai   young Basque worker
96   Caroline Mowatt   young activist, Catalunia
97   Walter Kanelutti   trade unionist, Austria (11/16/03)
98   Bernhard Kanelutti   militant, Austria
99   Ian Hood   Globalize Resistance, Scotland
100 Jon York   League for a Fifth International, London
101 Vladimir Marcus   Solidaires Unitaires Démocratiques – Postes
                        Telégrammes et Télécommunications (SUD PTT) trade
                        unionist, France
102 Barbara Rimml   ATTAC Switzerland, Potsdam, Germany (01/09/04)

V: European Social Forum, London, England, 15–17 October 2004

103 Matti Kohonen ATTAC, London School of Economics (10/15/04)
104 Chris Nineham Stop the War Coalition UK, SWP
105 Barbara Stocking director, Oxfam UK
106 no name given ATTAC Sweden
107 Martin Rochol Friends of the Earth Europe
108 no name given Friends of the Earth Europe
109 Ann Pettifor Jubilee Research (10/16/04)
110 Matyas Benyik president, ATTAC Hungary
111 Jacques Lefort Coordination Paysanne Européenne (CPE), France, and
Via Campesina
112 no name given Clandestine Insurgent Rebel Clown Army, clown 1
113 no name given Clandestine Insurgent Rebel Clown Army, clown 2, PGA
114 Idoya Cols Babels interpreter
115 Maddy Cooper Stop the War Coalition, Camden, SWP (10/17/04)
116 Liz Wheatley Stop the War Coalition, Camden, SWP
117 Gavin *Green Pepper* Magazine

VI: WSF IC and Commission meetings, Amsterdam and Utrecht, Netherlands, 28 March–2 April 2005

118 Teivo Teivainen (conversations with) Network Institute for Global
Democracy, WSF IC (03/28–04/02/05)
119 Francisco Whitaker (conversations with) WSF Organization Committee
120 Diane Matte coordinator, World March of Women and WSF IC
121 Brid Brennan Asia Program coordinator, Transnational Institute, WSF
IC (04/01/05)
122 Nicola Bullard (conversation with) Focus on the Global South and WSF IC
123 no name given Friends of the Earth International (04/02/05)
124 Jean-Pierre Beauvais (conversation with) ATTAC France, director-general,
Politis
125 Christophe Aguiton (conversation with) Euromarche and WSF IC

Appendix 3: Participant observation and interview sites

I: Events surrounding the spring 2002 meetings of the World Bank and IMF, Washington, DC, including anti-war protests, and follow-up events

1   Two Mobilization for Global Justice (MGJ) meetings to plan protests and educational events, March and April
2   Video presentation and discussion of Patrice Barrat's Globalization, Violence or Dialogue, sponsored by World Bank External Affairs Department, Civil Society Team, World Bank, 3 April
3   Teach-in to Unite the Fight for Peace and Global and Local Justice, MGJ and DC Anti-War Network, University of the District of Columbia, 13 April
4   Resisting Capitalist Globalization: Washington, DC, Canada, and Mexico, panel discussion, Anti-Capitalist Convergence, 17 April
5   From Engagement to Protest: A Public Forum on Citizens' Challenges to the World Bank, the Structural Adjustment Participatory Review Network (SAPRIN), the Development GAP, Fifty Years Is Enough Network, and International Rivers Network, 18–19 April
6   DC indymedia center Kick-off Unity Party and Multimedia Show, 18 April
7   Anti-oppression training, Ruckus Society and STARC Alliance, 19 April
8   Colombia Mobilization vigil to close the School of the Americas and lobby action, 19 April
9   Plenary panel: Kick-off to the Weekend of Global Justice, Colombia Mobilization, MGJ, Committee in Solidarity with the Palestinian People, and International ANSWER, 19 April
10   Meet and greet actions, in front of World Bank, 20 April
11   Rally and March for Global Justice/Stop the War Rally, March to the Capitol, and Rally on the Mall, 20 April
12   Festival of Hope and Resistance, Colombia Mobilization, 21 April
13   Protest against Arial Sharon, George Bush, and Racism, American Israel Public Affairs Committee (AIPAC) annual conference, ANSWER; SUSTAIN; Anti-Capitalist Bloc
14   .1K Race to the Bottom, theatrical protest at the regional meetings of the World Economic Forum, Washington, DC, MGJ and the National Campaign for Jobs and Income Support, 23 May
15   Meetings for planning actions for IMF/World Bank fall 2002 meetings, MGJ, 19 June and 31 July
16   Globalization: The Road to Johannesburg – What's at Stake?, a Public Briefing, International Forum on Globalization, 26 June

II: Washington, DC, Social Forum Working Group and preparatory meetings/MGJ Education Working Group

17   16 March 2002 meeting

18 25 April meeting
19 18 May meeting
20 22 June meeting
21 1 August meeting
22 8 August meeting

III: European Social Forum, Florence, Italy, 7–10 November 2002

23 Inauguration, Piazza Santa Croce, 6 November
24 From the EU Shaped by Neoliberal Globalization to the Europe of Alternatives, 7 November
25 The Role of Religions in the Critique of Globalization
26 Asia Window, 8 November
27 Student assembly
28 European demonstration against the war, 9 November
29 Social Movements Assembly, 10 November

IV: World Social Forum, Porto Alegre, Brazil, 23–28 January 2003

30 Second World Trade Union Forum, 23 January
31 WSF opening march and rally, 24 January
32 Against Militarization and War
33 Strategy Session on Monitoring/Confronting Transnational Corporations, 25 January
34 Parties, NGOs, and Social Movements – Different Political Logics?
35 Nonviolent Resistance and the Globalization Movements, 26 January
36 Asian Social Forum meeting, 27 January
37 Closing press conference

V: European Social Forum, Paris, Saint-Denis, Bobigny, Ivry-sur-Seine, France, 12–16 November 2003

38 The Women's Rights Assembly, 12 November
39 Against Global and Permanent War Plenary, 13 November
40 Amnesty International Workshop: The Role of Youth Activism in Creating Change
41 Strategy of Anti-Capitalist Movements: A Very Open Discussion
42 Anti-War Campaigning Assembly, 14 November
43 Jamming their Culture, Creating our Own: Summit of Anti-Capitalist Artists, 15 November
44 Protest March for a Europe of Social Rights in a World without War!
45 Assembly of Social Movements and Activists, 16 November

VI: European Social Forum, London, England, 15–17 October 2004

46 Building Locally, Link Globally, the Role and the Future of Local Social Forums in Europe, a meeting of the European Network of Local Social Forums, 15 October
47 Preparatory meeting for Assembly of Social Movements
48 The Plight of Roma/Gypsies and Travellers: What Are the Challenges for Europe?, 16 October
49 Stop Fascism and the Far Right in Europe
50 Assembly of Social Movements, 17 October
51 Closing march
52 ESF 2004 Observation Team meeting

VII: WSF IC and Commission meetings, Amsterdam and Utrecht, Netherlands, 28 March–2 April 2005:

53 Participant in meetings of the WSF Methodology, Content and Expansion Commission meetings, the Transnational Institute, Amsterdam, and Interchurch Organization for Development Cooperation (ICCO), Utrecht, 28–30 March
54 Observer at the WSF IC meeting, ICCO, Utrecht, 30 March–2 April

Notes

1 The globalization of neoliberalism and of activism: an introduction

1 Each of these institutions will be discussed in greater detail in the subsequent case study chapters.

2 These policies and their impacts will be examined in greater detail in subsequent chapters. For historic analyses of the rise of neoliberal globalization and the Washington Consensus, see, for example, Charles Tilly, "Foreword," in *Coalitions across Borders: Transnational Protest and the Neoliberal Order*, eds. Joe Bandy and Jackie Smith (Lanham, MD: Rowman & Littlefield, 2004), ix–xiv; Robert Cox, "A Perspective on Globalization," in *Globalization: Critical Reflections*, ed. James Mittelman (Boulder, CO: Lynne Rienner, 1996); Stephen Gill, "Globalization, Market Civilization, and Disciplinary Neoliberalism," *Millennium: Journal of International Studies* 24, no. 3 (1995): 399–423; Leslie Sklair, *Sociology of the Global System* (Baltimore, MD: Johns Hopkins University Press, 1995); and John Williamson, *The Progress of Policy Reform in Latin America* (Washington, DC: Institute for International Economics, 1990).

3 An exceptional, third avenue for neoliberalism's expansion has come in the form of executive orders imposed by an invading force on an occupied country: The Bremer Orders decreed by US military leaders in Iraq sought to achieve the rapid transformation of a once statist economy into what the *Economist* has called a "virtual free-trade zone" and "wish-list that foreign investors and donor agencies dream of." In *Economist*, "Let's All Go to the Yard Sale," *Economist* (25 September 2003): 62. See also Herbert Docena, "How the US Got Its Neo-Liberal Way in Iraq," *Asia Times Online*, 1 September 2005.

4 For overviews of the debates around globalization, see David Held *et al.*, "Introduction," in *Global Transformations: Politics, Economics and Culture* (Stanford, CA: Stanford University Press, 1999), 1–31; David Held and Anthony McGrew, eds., *The Global Transformations Reader: An Introduction to the Globalization Debate* (Cambridge: Polity Press, 2000); Frank J. Lechner and John Boli, *The Globalization Reader* (Oxford: Blackwell, 2000); James H. Mittelman, "Globalization: An Ascendant Paradigm?" *International Studies Perspectives* 3, no. 2 (2002): 1–14; and Mauro F. Guillén, "Is Globalization Civilizing, Destructive or Feeble? A Critique of Five Key Debates in the Social-Science Literature," *Annual Review of Sociology* 27 (2001): 235–60.

5 See James H. Mittelman, "Globalization: An Ascendant Paradigm"; and James H. Mittelman, "What Is a Critical Globalization Studies?," in *Critical Globalization Studies*, eds. Richard P. Appelbaum and William I. Robinson (London: Routledge, 2005), 19–32.

6 For works largely championing neoliberal globalization, see Jagdish Bhagwati, *In Defense of Globalization* (Oxford: Oxford University Press, 2004); Martin Wolf, *Why Globalization Works* (New Haven, CT: Yale University Press, 2004); Johan Norberg, *In Defense of Global Capitalism* (Washington, DC: Cato Institute, 2003); Dani Rodrik, *The New Global Economy and Developing Countries: Making Openness Work* (Washington, DC: Overseas Development Council, 1998); Douglas A. Irwin, *Free Trade Under Fire* (Princeton, NJ: Princeton University Press, 2003); Brink Lindsey, *Against the Dead Hand: The Uncertain Struggle for Global Capitalism* (Hoboken, NJ: Wiley Publishers, 2001); Daniel Yergin and Joseph Stanislaw, *The Commanding Heights: The Battle for the World Economy* (New York: Touchstone/Simon & Schuster, 2002); and Thomas L. Friedman, *The Lexus and the Olive Tree: Understanding Globalization* (New York: Anchor Books, 2000).

7 More critical economists and international political economy scholars who would like to reform neoliberal globalization include George Soros, *The Crisis of Global Capitalism* (New York: Public Affairs Books, 1998); Joseph E. Stiglitz, *Globalization and Its Discontents* (New York: W.W. Norton & Company, 2003); Jeffrey Sachs, *The End of Poverty: Economic Possibilities for Our Time* (New York: Penguin Books, 2005); Robert Gilpin, *The Challenge of Global Capitalism: The World Economy in the 21st Century* (Princeton, NJ: Princeton University Press, 2002); William Easterly, *The Elusive Quest for Growth: Economists' Adventures and Misadventures in the Tropics* (Cambridge, MA: MIT Press, 2002); Amartya Sen, *Development as Freedom* (New York: Anchor Books, 2000); and Pedro-Pablo Kuczynski *et al.*, eds., *After the Washington Consensus: Restarting Growth and Reform in Latin America* (Washington, DC: Institute for International Economics, 2003).

8 Keynesian, Polanyian, and other types of social democratic scholar-activists, many of which are affiliated with the International Forum on Globalization and are active in the social forums, include International Forum on Globalization (IFG), *Alternatives to Economic Globalization: A Better World Is Possible* (San Francisco, CA: Berrett-Koehler Publishers, 2002); Robin Broad, ed., *Global Backlash: Citizen Initiatives for a Just World Economy* (Lanham, MD: Rowman & Littlefield, 2002); David C. Korten, *When Corporations Rule the World* (San Francisco, CA: Berrett-Koehler Publishers, 2001); Colin Hines, *Localization: A Global Manifesto* (London: Earthscan, 2000); Maude Barlow and Tony Clarke, *Global Showdown: How the New Activists are Fighting Global Corporate Rule* (Toronto: Stoddart, 2001); Lori Wallach and Michelle Sforza, *Whose Trade Organization? Corporate Globalization and the Erosion of Democracy* (Washington, DC: Public Citizen, 1999); Susan George, *The Lugano Report* (London: Pluto, 1999); Vandana Shiva, *Protest or Plunder? Understanding Intellectual Property Rights* (London: Zed Books, 2001); Walden Bello, *Deglobalization: Ideas for a New World Economy* (London: Zed Books, 2003); Gerry Mander and Edward Goldsmith, eds., *The Case against the Global Economy* (San Francisco, CA: Sierra Club, 1996); George Monbiot, *In the Age of Consent: A Manifesto for a New World Order* (New York: HarperCollins, 2004); and Samir Amin, *The Liberal Virus: Permanent War and the Americanization of the World* (New York: Monthly Review Press, 2004).

9 See, for example, Alex Callinicos, *An Anti-Capitalist Manifesto* (Oxford: Blackwell, 2003); Michael Albert, *Parecon: Life after Capitalism* (London: Verso, 2004); Michael Hardt and Antonio Negri, *Empire* (Cambridge, MA: Harvard University Press, 2000); Michael Hardt and Antonio Negri, *Multitude: War and Democracy in the Age of Empire* (New York: Penguin Putnam, 2004); John Holloway, *Change the World without Taking Power: The Meaning of Revolution Today* (London: Pluto, 2002); Subcomandante Marcos, *Ya Basta! Ten Years of the Zapatista Uprising* (Oakland, CA: AK Press, 2004); and Subcomandante Marcos, *Our Word Is Our Weapon: Selected Writings* (New York: Seven Stories Press, 2002).

10 See, for example, Subcomandante Marcos, *Ya Basta!* and *Our Word Is Our Weapon*; Ralph Pettman, "Anti-Globalisation Discourses in Asia," in *Critical Theories, International Relations and "the Anti-Globalisation Movement": The Politics of Global Resistance*, eds. Catherine Eschle and Bice Maiguashca (London: Routledge, 2005), 121–38; various documents from the World March of Women, at www.marchemondiale.org/en/c_unesco.html; from Articulación Feminista Marcosur, at www.mujeresdelsur.org.uy/; and from Proutist Universal, at www.prout.org.

11 For works within this genre, see Richard P. Appelbaum and William I. Robinson, *Critical Globalization Studies* (London: Routledge, 2005); Eschle and Maiguashca, *Critical Theories*; Thomas Olesen, *International Zapatismo: The Construction of Solidarity in the Age of Globalization* (London: Zed Books, 2005); Neil Smith, *The End Game of Globalization* (London: Routledge, 2005); James H. Mittelman, *Whither Globalization? The Vortex of Knowledge and Ideology* (London: Routledge, 2004); James H. Mittelman, *Globalization Syndrome: Transformation and Resistance* (Princeton, NJ: Princeton University Press, 2000); Heikki Patomäki and Teivo Teivainen, *A Possible World: Democratic Transformation of Global Institutions* (London: Zed Books, 2004); Michael Mann, *Incoherent Empire* (London: Verso, 2003); V. Spike Peterson, *A Critical Rewriting of Global Political Economy: Integrating Reproductive, Productive and Virtual Economies* (London: Routledge, 2003); Stephen Gill, *Power and Resistance in the New World Order* (New York: Palgrave Macmillan, 2003); Robert W. Cox with Michael G. Schechter, *The Political Economy of a Plural World* (London: Routledge, 2002); Leslie Sklair, *Capitalism and its Alternatives* (Oxford: Oxford University Press, 2002); Anthony Giddens, *Runaway World: How Globalization Is Reshaping Our Lives* (London: Routledge, 2000); Barry Gills, ed., *Globalization and the Politics of Resistance* (New York: St. Martin's Press, 2000); Hardt and Negri, *Empire*; Mark Rupert, *Ideologies of Globalization: Contending Visions of a New World Order* (London: Routledge, 2000); Jan Aart Scholte, *Globalization: A Critical Introduction* (New York: St. Martin's Press, 2000); Richard Falk, *Predatory Globalization: A Critique* (Oxford: Blackwell, 1999); David Harvey, *Limits to Capital* (London: Verso, 1999); Saskia Sassen, *Globalization and Its Discontents* (New York: New Press, 1998); Susan Strange, *Mad Money: When Markets Outgrow Governments* (Ann Arbor, MI: University of Michigan Press, 1998); R. J. Johnson, Peter J. Taylor, and Michael J. Watts, *Geographies of Global Change: Remapping the World in the Late Twentieth Century* (Oxford: Blackwell, 1995); and Roland Robertson, *Globalization: Social Theory and Global Culture* (Newbury Park, CA: Sage, 1992).

12 I therefore follow critical globalization scholar Jim Mittelman in defining globalization as "a syndrome of political and material processes, including historical

transformations in time and space and the social relations attendant to them. It is also about ways of thinking about the world. Globalization thus constitutes a set of ideas centered on heightened market integration, which, in its dominant form, neoliberalism, is embodied in a policy framework of deregulation, liberalization, and privatization." In Mittelman, "Globalization: An Ascendant Paradigm," 2.

13 See Daniele Archibugi, David Held and Martin Kohler, *Re-imagining Political Community: Studies in Cosmopolitan Democracy* (Stanford, CA: Stanford University Press, 1998); Richard Falk, *Explorations at the End of Time: The Prospects for World Order* (Philadelphia, PA: Temple University Press, 1992); Martha Finnemore, *National Interests in International Society* (Ithaca, NY and London: Cornell University Press, 1996); Ann M. Florini, ed., *The Third Force: The Rise of Transnational Civil Society* (Washington, DC: Carnegie Endowment for International Peace, 2000); Chris Hann and Elizabeth Dunn, eds., *Civil Society, Challenging Western Models* (London: Routledge, 1996); John Keane, *Global Civil Society?* (Cambridge: Cambridge University Press, 2003); Margaret E. Keck and Kathryn Sikkink, *Activists beyond Borders: Advocacy Networks in International Politics* (Ithaca, NY: Cornell University Press, 1998); Ronnie Lipschutz, "Restructuring World Politics: The Emergence of Global Civil Society," *Millennium* 21, no. 3 (1992): 389–420; Craig N. Murphy, ed., *Egalitarian Politics in the Age of Globalization* (New York: Palgrave, 2002); Robert O'Brien *et al.*, eds., *Contesting Global Governance: Multilateral Economic Institutions and Global Social Movements* (Cambridge: Cambridge University Press, 2000); Thomas Risse, Stephen C. Ropp, and Kathryn Sikkink, eds., *The Power of Human Rights, International Norms and Domestic Change* (Cambridge: Cambridge University Press, 1999); Jackie Smith and Hank Johnston, eds., *Globalization and Resistance: Transnational Dimensions of Social Movements* (Lanham, MD: Rowman & Littlefield, 2002); Jackie Smith, Charles Chatfield, and Ron Pagnucco, eds., *Transnational Social Movements and Global Politics: Solidarity Beyond the State* (Syracuse, NY: Syracuse University Press, 1997); R. B. J. Walker, *One World, Many Worlds: Struggles for a Just World Peace* (Boulder, CO: Lynne Rienner, 1988); R. B. J. Walker, "Social Movements/World Politics," *Millennium* 23, no. 3 (1994): 669–700; and Paul Wapner, *Environmental Activism and World Civic Politics* (Albany, NY: SUNY Press, 1996).

14 Ann M. Florini and P. J. Simmons, "What the World Needs Now?," in *The Third Force*, ed. Ann M. Florini, 7.

15 Keane, *Global Civil Society*, 9.

16 Ibid., 11, 14.

17 Keck and Sikkink, *Activists beyond Borders*, 33–4, quoting Andrew Hurrell and Ngaire Woods, "Globalisation and Inequality," *Millennium* 24, no. 3 (1995): 468.

18 Social movement scholars tend to distinguish between transgressive or disruptive contention – or actions and goals that disobey laws or moral codes or breach certain limits of the bureaucratic political system – versus those that are routinized or contained within it, such as lobbying or participating in permitted marches. See, for example, Alberto Melucci, *Challenging Codes: Collective Action in the Information Age* (Cambridge: Cambridge University Press, 1996), 22–41; and William A. Gamson, *The Strategy of Social Protest* (Homewood, IL: Dorsey, 1975).

19 In the following methodological chapter (Chapter 2), I will detail the process of negotiating my dual role as a scholar-activist throughout the research project.

20 The Zapatistas are probably the most widely considered allies among anti-neoliberal activists, while armed factions within Iraq are the most controversial and distanced, just as groups like the Revolutionary Armed Forces of Colombia (FARC) fall somewhere in between.

21 Describing their pie flinging, "Subcomandante Tofutti" (sampling Margaret Mead) mused, "Never doubt that a small and dedicated group of people with pies can change the world. Indeed, it is the only thing that ever has." Notes from Nowhere, eds., *We are Everywhere: The Irresistible Rise of Global Anticapitalism* (London: Verso, 2003), 263. Innovative actions, plus commentary, such as this demonstrate the theatrical playfulness with which many activists approach direct action today, witnessed in the giant puppetry, flamboyant costumes, and political skits that have accompanied most street demonstrations, in addition to the wide variety of "culture jamming" techniques being deployed over the internet, on billboards, and in public spaces. See for example, Notes from Nowhere, *We are Everywhere*, and Kalle Lasn, *Culture Jam: How to Reverse America's Suicidal Consumer Binge – And Why We Must* (New York: Quill, 2000).

22 Aldijana Sisic, regional campaign coordinator, Europe and Central Asia, Amnesty International, workshop titled "The Role of Youth Activism in Creating Change," author's notes, European Social Forum, St. Denis, France, 13 November 2003.

23 W. Lance Bennett, "Social Movements beyond Borders: Organization, Communication, and Political Capacity in Two Eras of Transnational Activism," in *Transnational Protest and Global Activism: People, Passions, and Power*, eds. Donatella della Porta and Sidney G. Tarrow (Lanham, MD: Rowman & Littlefield, 2005), 203–26; Keck and Sikkink, *Activists beyond Borders*, 1998; and Smith, Chatfield, and Pagnucco, *Transnational Social Movements and Global Politics*.

24 Della Porta and Tarrow, *Transnational Protest and Global Activism*, 6.

25 Other scholars who have observed a transnationalizing trend in activism include: Bandy and Smith, *Coalitions across Borders*; Broad, *Global Backlash*; Donatella della Porta *et al.*, *Social Movements in a Globalizing World* (Houndmills: Macmillan, 1999); Philip G. Cerny, "Globalization and the Changing Logic of Collective Action," *International Organization* 49, no. 4 (1995): 595–625; della Porta and Tarrow, *Transnational Protest and Global Activism*; Michael Edwards and John Gaventa, eds., *Global Citizen Action* (Boulder, CO: Lynne Rienner, 2001); Eschle and Maiguashca, *Critical Theories*; Gills, *Globalization and the Politics of Resistance*; John A. Guidry *et al.*, *Globalizations and Social Movements: Culture, Power, and the Transnational Sphere* (Ann Arbor, MI: The University of Michigan Press, 2000); Pierre Hamel *et al.*, *Globalization and Social Movements* (Houndmills: Macmillan, 2001); Keck and Sikkink, *Activists beyond Borders*; Sanjeev Khagram, James V. Riker, and Kathryn Sikkink, eds., *Restructuring World Politics: Transnational Social Movements, Networks, and Norms* (Minneapolis: University of Minnesota Press, 2002); Smith and Johnston, *Globalization and Resistance*; Smith, Chatfield, and Pagnucco, *Transnational Social Movements and Global Politics*; Amory Starr, *Naming the Enemy: Anti-Corporate Movements Confront Globalization* (London and New York: Zed Books, 2000).

26 Jackie Smith, "Characteristics of the Modern Transnational Social Movement Sector," in *Transnational Social Movements and Global Politics*, 47, 52. These figures are

based on Smith's analysis of data from the Union of International Associations' *Yearbook of International Organizations*.

27 Ibid., 50–1.

28 In 1997 Russia officially joined the G7 industrialized nations' summits, thus changing the name to G8. However, since the Russian economy is considerably smaller than the others', it is not allowed to participate in most of the G7 economic and financial talks. So while the G8 summits have become a prime target of protests, the actual entity responsible for neoliberal policies continues to be the G7, whose finance ministers and central bankers meet at the G8 summit in addition to other times throughout the year as the G7. Therefore, my usage of each term throughout this work reflects this ambiguous overlap of G7 and G8.

29 From Mario Pianta, "Parallel Summits of Global Civil Society: An Update"; available from www.globalpolicy.org/ngos/role/conf.htm; internet; accessed 21 May 2004. This data is based on questionnaires distributed to hundreds of civil society organizations and on monitoring NGO publications, websites, newspapers, and journals. See also Pianta's related works: "Parallel Summits of Global Civil Society," in *Global Civil Society 2001*, eds. Helmut Anheier, Marlies Glasius, and Mary Kaldor (Oxford: Oxford University Press); *Globalizzazione del basso: Economia mondiale e movimenti sociali* (Rome: Manifestolibri, 2001); "I controvertici e gli eventi delle società civile globale," in *Capire i movimenti globali: Da Porto Alegre al Forum Sociale Europeo*, ed. Lunaria (Trieste: Asterios, 2002).

30 Ibid. But as we will learn throughout this work, sharing a "big tent" space such as the WSF and even becoming coalition partners does not signify the end of diversity and dissension. The reformist–radical gulf remains a real one in the various stances toward neoliberal globalization and capitalism.

31 Ibid.

32 Ali Hebshi, member of the Pittsburgh Social Forum, and Organizer, Clean Water Action, interview by author, tape recording, World Social Forum, Porto Alegre, Brazil, 28 January 2003.

33 John Cavanagh, director, Institute for Policy Studies, Washington, DC, interview by author, author's notes, Washington, DC, 31 July 2002.

34 World Social Forum, "Charter of Principles" (8 June 2002); available from www.forumsocialmundial.org.br/main.php?id_menu=4&cd_language=2; internet; accessed 25 December 2005; also reprinted in this work's appendix.

35 These groups are the Brazilian Association of Non-Governmental Organizations (ABONG), European and Brazilian branches of the Association for the Taxation of Financial Transactions for the Aid of Citizens (ATTAC), Brazilian Justice and Peace Commission (CBJP), Brazilian Business Association for Citizenship (CIVES), Central Trade Union Federation (CUT), Brazilian Institute for Social and Economic Studies (IBASE), Center for Global Justice (CJG), the MST, the Coalition against the MAI, the World Forum for Alternatives, and the Structural Adjustment Participatory Review International Network (SAPRIN).

36 Cavanagh, interview.

37 John Cavanagh, director, Institute for Policy Studies, Washington, DC, e-mail to author, August 2002.

38 Cavanagh, interview.
39 These groups are ABONG, ATTAC Brazil, CIVES, CUT, IBASE, MST, CBJP, and CJG.
40 These included ATTAC, the Coalition against the MAI, the World Forum for Alternatives, and SAPRIN.
41 These social movements are Brazil's MST, the Policy and Information Center for International Solidarity of South Korea, the National Federation of Farmers' Organizations from Burkina Faso, the Women's Movement from Quebec, and the Movement of the Unemployed from France.
42 WSF, "Charter of Principles."
43 Ibid.
44 Patomäki and Teivainen, *A Possible World*, 116.
45 Thomas Ponniah and William F. Fisher, "Introduction: The World Social Forum and the Reinvention of Democracy," in *Another World Is Possible: Popular Alternatives to Globalization at the World Social Forum*, eds. William F. Fisher and Thomas Ponniah (London: Zed Books, 2003), 1.
46 Bennett, "Social Movements beyond Borders," 225.
47 See links at ATTAC France's website, "Campagne pour la Victoire du NON"; available from www.france/.attac.org/r613; internet; accessed 1 September 2005.
48 For one of the first analyses of these restrictions, see Ruth Reitan, "Human Rights in U.S. Policy: A Casualty of the 'War on Terrorism'?" *International Journal of Human Rights* 7, no. 4 (2003): 51–62.
49 This loose network has met under a number of other names, including the Cairo Conferences and Declarations, the Jakarta Peace Consensus, the International Solidarity Forum and Tokyo Declaration, and the International Strategy Meeting of Anti-War and Anti-Globalization Movements and its Beirut Declaration.
50 For coalition troop withdrawals by country as of early 2005, see Richard Beeston, "Ranks Begin to Thin in Coalition of the Willing," *The Times*, UK, 15 March 2005.
51 Patrick E. Tyler, "A New Power in the Streets," *New York Times*, 17 February 2003, A1.
52 Thomas L. Friedman, "Senseless in Seattle," *New York Times*, 1 December 1999.
53 Thomas Olesen and James N. Rosenau, "The Reduction of Distance and the Construction of Proximity: Solidarity Movements and Globalization" (paper presented at the annual meeting of the International Studies Association, Honolulu, 1–5 March 2005), 1.
54 I wish to thank the scholars participating in the International Studies Association panel on "Violence and Democracy," Montreal, 17–21 March 2003, especially Barry Gills, who presented his work entitled "Global Hegemony, Structural Violence, and Legitimacy," for helping me grasp the importance of the concept of structural violence for my own work. See also recent works using the concept to analyze neoliberal globalization, including Branwen Gruffydd Jones, "Globalisations, Violences and Resistances in Mozambique: The Struggles Continue," in *Critical Theories, International Relations and 'the Anti-Globalisation Movement': The Politics of Global Resistance*, eds. Catherine Eschle and Bice Maiguashca (London: Routledge, 2005), 53–74; Sian Sullivan, "'We Are Heartbroken and Furious!': Violence and the (Anti-) Globalisation Movement(s)," in *Critical Theories, International Relations and 'the Anti-*

Globalisation Movement': The Politics of Global Resistance, eds. Catherine Eschle and Bice Maiguashca (London: Routledge, 2005), 174–94; Philippe Bourgois, "The Power of Violence in War and Peace: Post Cold War Lessons from El Salvador," *Ethnography* 2, no. 1 (2001): 5–34; and works by Paul Farmer, such as *Pathologies of Power: Health, Human Rights, and the New War on the Poor* (Berkeley, CA: University of California Press, 2003).

55 Johan Galtung, *Peace by Peaceful Means: Peace and Conflict, Development and Civilization* (Oslo: International Peace Research Institute and Sage Publications, 1996), 8, 197. Many critical scholars would argue that it is upon the very vestiges of colonialism that the structural violence of globalization found its base for expansion.

56 Ibid., 2.

57 Ibid., 200.

58 Quoted in Sue Branford and Jan Rocha, "Cutting the Wire: The Landless Movement of Brazil," in *We Are Everywhere: The Irresistible Rise of Global Anticapitalism*, ed. Notes from Nowhere (London: Verso, 2003), 122.

59 IFG, *Alternatives to Economic Globalization*, 8.

60 Nicolas Onuf, "Constructivism: A User's Manual," in *International Relations in a Constructed World*, eds. Vendulka Kubálková, Nicholas Onuf, and Paul Kowert (Armonk, NY: M. E. Sharpe, 1998), 58–78.

61 Peter Winch, *The Idea of Social Science* (London: Routledge and Kegan Paul, 1958); cited in Martin Hollis and Steve Smith, *Explaining and Understanding International Relations* (Oxford: Clarendon Press, 1991), 82–8.

62 Perti Alasuutari, *Researching Culture: Qualitative Method and Cultural Studies* (London: Sage, 1995), 35.

63 This definition of solidarity is taken from Eric L. Hirsh, "Sacrifice for the Cause: Group Processes, Recruitment, and Commitment in a Student Social Movement," *American Sociological Review* 55 (1990): 243.

64 For a visual depiction of these mechanisms constituting the scale shift process, please see Figure 2 in Chapter 2. The words in italics in this section signify the process's constituent mechanisms.

65 For an analytical table depicting the concepts discussed in this section on network composition and character, see Table 1 in Chapter 2. The words in italics in this section signify the table's analytical concepts.

66 The latter they term a solidarity model, constructed among a "community of shared fate." In Keck and Sikkink, *Activists beyond Borders*, 78.

67 Kathryn Sikkink, "Restructuring World Politics: The Limits and Asymmetries of Soft Power," in *Restructuring World Politics: Transnational Social Movements, Networks, and Norms*, eds. Sanjeev Khagram, James V. Riker, and Kathryn Sikkink (Minneapolis, MN: University of Minnesota Press, 2002), 313.

68 Olesen, *International Zapatismo*; Peter Waterman, "Of Saints, Sinners, and Compañeras: Internationalist Lives in the Americas Today" (The Hague, Netherlands: Institute of Social Studies, Working Paper Series, no. 286); available from www.antenna.nl/ ~waterman/saints.html; internet; accessed 1 February 2005; Ivana Eterovic and Jackie Smith, "From Altruism to a New Transnationalism? A Look at Transnational Social Movements," in *Political Altruism? Solidarity Movements in International Perspective*, eds. Marco Giugni and Florence Passy (Lanham, MD: Rowman & Littlefield, 2001).

69 Indeed, the observation that a common identity forms a potent solidarity is not new and dates back at least to the writings of Aristotle. Throughout the better part of the twentieth century, the identity of "worker" was privileged as the primary, and often sole legitimate, identity source for leftist transnational solidarity.

70 Bennett, "Social Movements beyond Borders."

71 Ibid., 213–17.

72 Massimo de Angelis, "Opposing Fetishism by Reclaiming our Powers," *International Social Sciences Journal* 182 (2004): 591; see also Jai Sen *et al.*, eds., *World Social Forum: Challenging Empires* (New Delhi: Viveka Foundation, 2004); Peter Waterman, "The Secret of Fire," in *World Social Forum: Challenging Empires*, eds. Jai Sen, *et al.* (New Delhi: Viveka Foundation, 2004), 148–60; Holloway, *Change the World without Taking Power*; Heikki Patomäki and Teivo Teivainen, "The World Social Forum: An Open Space or a Movement of Movements?," *Theory, Culture and Society* 21, no. 6 (2004): 145–54; Teivo Teivainen, "World Social Forum and Global Democratization: Learning from Porto Alegre," *Third World Quarterly* 23, no. 4 (2002): 621–32; Michael Hardt, "Today's Bandung?," in *A Movement of Movements: Is Another World Really Possible?*, ed. Tom Mertes (London: Verso, 2004), 230–6; Naomi Klein, "More Democracy – Not More Political Strongmen," *Guardian*, 3 February 2003; Francisco Whitaker, "Notes about the World Social Forum" (14 April 2003); available from www.forumsocialmundial.org.br/dinamic.asp?pagina=bal_whitaker_ing; internet; accessed 6 March 2005; Ponniah and Fisher, "Introduction."

2 Global Activism: methodology and scholarly review

1 See Steve Smith, "Singing Our World into Existence: International Relations Theory and September 11," *International Studies Quarterly* 48, no. 3 (2004): 499–515; and J. Ann Tickner's address to be published in *International Studies Quarterly*, forthcoming. I wish to thank Teivo Teivainen and Jackie Smith for inviting me to participate in a roundtable discussion entitled "Transnational Social Movements and Scholar Activism II: World Social Forum," at the 2005 ISA Convention in Honolulu, which first prompted me to reflect on my role as a scholar-activist, and for their ongoing encouragement in this endeavor.

2 Steve Smith makes a similar argument in "Singing Our World into Existence."

3 Willard Van Orman Quine, *From a Logical Point of View* (New York: Harper and Row, 1961).

4 Martin Hollis and Steve Smith, *Explaining and Understanding International Relations* (Oxford: Clarendon Press, 1991). Yet Hollis, in the same book, tends to disagree, as does Anthony Giddens, who, in his influential structuration theory, helped pave the way for constructivist approaches in international relations over the last decade. See Anthony Giddens, *Critical Issues in Social Theory* (London: Macmillan, 1979), ch. 2. The most notable recent attempt at this is Alexander Wendt's *Social Theory of International Politics* (Cambridge: Cambridge University Press, 1999).

5 See Stephen Kemmis and Robin McTaggart, "Participatory Action Research," in *Handbook of Qualitative Research*, eds. Norman K. Denzin and Yvonna S. Lincoln, 2nd edn. (London: Sage, 2000), 575–7; and Hollis and Smith, "Introduction: Two Traditions," in *Explaining and Understanding*, 1–15.

6 Ibid.
7 Each will be explained in greater detail later in the chapter and in the Appendixes at the end of the book.
8 Max Weber, *Economy and Society*, eds. Guenther Roth and Claus Wittich (Berkeley, CA: University of California Press, 1978); see also Guy Oakes, "The Verstehen Thesis and the Foundation of Max Weber's Methodology," *History and Theory* 16 (1977): 11–29.
9 Hollis and Smith, *Explaining and Understanding*, 80.
10 This definition of "comprehending" was derived from the Buddhist peace scholar and activist Thich Nhat Hanh's *Being Peace* (Berkeley, CA: Parallax Press, 1996), 35–9.
11 Kemmis and McTaggart, "Participatory Action Research," 568; see also Orlando Fals Borda and Muhammad Anisur Rahman, eds., *Action and Knowledge: Breaking the Monopoly with Participatory Action-Research* (New York: Apex, 1991); and Robin McTaggart, ed., *Participatory Action Research: International Contexts and Consequences* (Albany, NY: SUNY Press, 1997); Maria Mies, "Feminist Research: Science, Violence and Responsibility," in *Ecofeminism*, by Maria Mies and Vandana Shiva (London: Zed Books, 1993), 36–54; and Elizabeth Whitmore and Maureen Wilson, "Research and Popular Movements: Igniting Seeds of Fire," *Social Development Issues* 21, no. 1 (1999): 19–28.
12 Kemmis and McTaggart, "Participatory Action Research," 592.
13 Anthony Giddens, *Central Problems in Social Theory: Action, Structure, and Contradiction in Social Analysis* (London: Macmillan, 1979), 71.
14 Whitmore and Wilson, "Research and Popular Movements," 21.
15 Alasuutari, *Researching Culture*, 36.
16 Kemmis and McTaggart, "Participatory Action Research," 573.
17 Karen Olson and Linda Shopes, "Crossing Boundaries, Building Bridges: Doing Oral History among Working-Class Women and Men," in *Women's Words: The Feminist Practice of Oral History*, eds. Shurna B. Gluck and Daphne Patai (London: Routledge, 1991), 189–204; Rina Benmayor, "Testimony, Action Research, and Empowerment: Puerto Rican Women and Popular Education," In *Women's Words: The Feminist Practice of Oral History*, eds. Shurna B. Gluck and Daphne Patai (London: Routledge, 1991), 159–74.
18 Kemmis and McTaggart, "Participatory Action Research," 575, 578.
19 Ibid., 578.
20 Ibid., 574, 589–91.
21 Ibid., 581, 595.
22 See Alasuutari, *Researching Culture*, 2–3.
23 Kemmis and McTaggart, "Participatory Action Research," 579.
24 Ibid., 578. *Compañer@* is the politically correct version (in activist writing) of *compañera* and *compañero*, as the @ symbol contains both an "a" and an "o."
25 Ibid., 590.
26 Ibid., 596.
27 Ibid., 600.
28 Ibid., 595.
29 See for example the critique of international relations constructivists by Jeffrey T. Checkel, "Constructivist Turn in International Relations Theory," *World Politics* 50,

no. 2 (1998): 324–48; and Jeffrey T. Checkel, "Norms, Institutions and National Identity in Contemporary Europe," *International Studies Quarterly* 43 (1999): 83–114.

30 Indeed, as will be shown in the cases that follow, there is diversity and criticism across the spectrum of activism and within the sectors themselves: for example, in the splintering off of Jubilee South from the Jubilee 2000 network, the rebellion of the Via Campesina activists against development NGOs that had long sought to speak for peasants and funnel their claims into policy reform and research, and the ongoing challenge by the anarchistic Peoples' Global Action to make their own network – and spaces such as the WSF – more horizontal and actively oppositional to capitalism, the state, and all forms of hierarchy.

31 Annette-Aurélie Desmarais, "The Via Campesina: Peasants Resisting Globalization" (Ph.D. diss., University of Calgary, 2003), 12–15.

32 For works by other critical globalization scholars, see Chapter 1, note 11.

33 James H. Mittelman, "What Is a Critical Globalization Studies?" in *Critical Globalization Studies*, eds. Richard P. Appelbaum and William I. Robinson (London: Routledge, 2005), 24–5; and see also William I. Robinson, "What Is a Critical Globalization Studies? Intellectual Labor and Global Society," in *Critical Globalization Studies*, eds. Richard P. Appelbaum and William I. Robinson (London: Routledge, 2005), 11–18.

34 Catherine Eschle and Bice Maiguashca, eds., *Critical Theories, International Relations and 'the Anti-Globalisation Movement': The Politics of Global Resistance* (London and New York: Routledge, 2005), 5.

35 Catherine Eschle, "Constructing 'the Anti-Globalisation Movement,'" in *Critical Theories, International Relations and 'the Anti-Globalisation Movement': The Politics of Global Resistance*, eds. Catherine Eschle and Bice Maiguashca (London: Routledge, 2005), 33.

36 McAdam, Tarrow, and Tilly, *Dynamics of Contention*.

37 See, for example, Florence Passy, "Political Altruism and the Solidarity Movement: An Introduction," in *Political Altruism? Solidarity Movements in International Perspective*, eds. Marco Giugni and Florence Passy (Lanham, MD: Rowman & Littlefield, 2001); Jeffrey C. Alexander and Bernhard Giesen, "From Reduction to Linkage: The Long View of the Micro–Macro Debate," in *The Micro–Macro Link*, eds. Jeffrey C. Alexander *et al.* (Berkeley, CA: University of California Press, 1987), 1–42; Margaret S. Archer, *Realist Theory: The Morphogenetic Approach* (Cambridge: Cambridge University Press, 1995); Pierre Bourdieu, *Outline of a Theory of Practice* (Cambridge: Cambridge University Press, 1977); James S. Coleman, *Foundations of Social Theory* (Cambridge, MA: The Belknap Press of Harvard University Press, 1990); Anthony Giddens, *The Constitution of Society* (Cambridge: Polity Press, 1984); Mark Irving Lichbach, "Social Theory and Comparative Politics," in *Comparative Politics*, eds. Mark Irving Lichbach and Alan S. Zuckerman (Cambridge: Cambridge University Press, 1997), 239–76.

38 Its ambitious scope and agenda may explain some of the controversy it has caused, especially among scholars most firmly invested in specialized areas of study. A number of them, such as Mario Diani, Dieter Rucht, Ruud Koopmans, Pamela Oliver, and Verta Taylor, have put up a spirited defense of not abandoning existing concepts, theories, or camps for the DOC's "big tent." To get a sense of the scope and stakes of this debate, see the journal *Mobilization* 8, no. 1 (February 2003), which contains critiques and rebuttals from a book symposium on the DOC.

39 Namely, for reorienting the field toward the study of organizations, networks, power, and politics, shifting the view of movements to organized political phenomena rather than spontaneous expressions of personal and social disorganization, and developing rigorous methodologies that have allowed for the rapid accumulation of empirical findings.

40 This "turn" is still wending its way through the social sciences and has emerged in the last decade as constructivism in international relations. Sociologists tend to use the term constructionism, but both connote methodological attempts to overcome the agent–structure bifurcation by employing more dynamic or relational approaches.

41 Doug McAdam, John D. McCarthy, and Mayer N. Zald, "Social Movements," in *Handbook of Sociology*, ed. Neil J. Smelser (Newbury Park, CA: Sage, 1988), 695–738, quoted in Sidney Tarrow and Doug McAdam, "Scale Shift in Transnational Contention" (paper presented at conference entitled "Transnational Processes and Social Movements," Bellagio, Italy, 22–26 July 2003), 8.

42 Tarrow and McAdam, "Scale Shift in Transnational Contention."

43 McAdam, Tarrow, and Tilly, *Dynamics of Contention*, 331.

44 Tarrow and McAdam, "Scale Shift in Transnational Contention," 13.

45 Sidney Tarrow, "From Lumping to Splitting: Specifying Globalization and Resistance," in *Globalization and Resistance: Transnational Dimensions of Social Movements*, eds. Jackie Smith and Hank Johnston (Lanham, MD: Rowman & Littlefield, 2002), 235. The term "frame" originates with Erving Goffman, *Frame Analysis* (Cambridge: Harvard University Press, 1974), 21, and refers to a "schemata of interpretation" that allow individuals "to locate, perceive, identify, and label," rendering occurrences meaningful.

46 Tarrow, "From Lumping to Splitting," 238–45.

47 Ibid., 245; and Goffman, *Frame Analysis*, 308.

48 David Snow and Richard Machalek, "The Sociology of Conversion," in *Annual Review of Sociology*, eds. Ralph H. Turner and James F. Short (Palo Alto: Annual Reviews Inc., 1983), 265–6; and Tarrow, "From Lumping to Splitting," 246–7.

49 Michael Burawoy, "The Extended Case Method," *Sociological Theory* 16, no. 1 (1998): 4–33; Paul Lichterman, "Seeing Structure Happen: Theory-Driven Participant Observation," in *Methods of Social Movement Research*, eds. Bert Klandermans and Suzanne Staggenborg (Minneapolis, MN: University of Minnesota Press, 2002), 118–45; Barney Glaser and Anselm Strauss, *The Discovery of Grounded Theory* (Chicago: Aldine, 1967); and Anselm Strauss and Juliet Corbin, *Basics of Qualitative Research* (Newbury Park, CA: Sage, 1991).

50 See Kathleen M. Blee and Verta Taylor, "Semi-Structured Interviewing in Social Movement Research," in *Methods of Social Movement Research*, eds. Bert Klandermans and Suzanne Staggenborg (Minneapolis, MN: University of Minnesota Press, 2002), 92–117. See also Herbert J. Rubin and Irene S. Rubin, *Qualitative Interviewing: The Art of Hearing Data* (London: Sage, 1995); Aldon D. Morris, *The Origins of the Civil Rights Movement: Black Communities Organizing for Change* (New York: Free Press, 1984); Rick Fantasia, *Cultures of Solidarity: Consciousness, Action, and Contemporary American Workers* (Berkeley, CA: University of California Press, 1988); Doug McAdam, *Freedom Summer* (New York: Oxford University Press, 1988); Suzanne Staggenborg, *The Pro-Choice*

Movement (New York: Oxford University Press, 1991); Norman K. Denzin, *The Research Act: A Theoretical Introduction to Sociological Methods* (Englewood Cliffs, NJ: Prentice-Hall, 1989); Kathleen M. Blee, *Inside Organized Racism: Women in the Hate Movement* (Berkeley, CA: University of California Press, 2001); John Lofland and Lyn H. Lofland, *Analyzing Social Settings: A Guide to Qualitative Observation and Analysis*, 3rd edn. (Belmont, CA: Wadsworth, 1991); and Hank Johnston and Bert Klandermans, eds., *Social Movements and Culture* (Minneapolis, MN: University of Minnesota Press, 1995). Theory-driven semi-structured interviewing has also been undertaken by: Sidney G. Tarrow, *Between Center and Periphery: Grassroots Politicians in Italy and France* (New Haven, CT: Yale University Press, 1977); Thomas R. Rochon, *Mobilizing for Peace: The Antinuclear Movements in Western Europe* (Princeton, NJ: Princeton University Press, 1988); David S. Meyer, *A Winter of Discontent: The Nuclear Freeze and American Politics* (New York: Praeger, 1990); and Donatella della Porta, *Social Movements, Political Violence and the State: A Comparative Analysis of Italy and Germany* (Cambridge: Cambridge University Press, 1995).

51 Blee and Taylor, "Semi-Structured Interviewing," 93–7.

52 See Appendixes for fuller details. I also designed and distributed via e-mail three different questionnaires in English, Spanish, Portuguese, and French, reaching 240 WSF IC and Mobilizing Committee members, as well as participants in the Social Movements Assembly (SMA) affiliated with the forums. My intent was to more systematically elicit environmental, relational, and cognitive factors, or mechanisms, constituting a variety of processes, and to then *quadrangulate* these with evidence gathered through my other methods. But due to a response rate that was far too low to be statistically significant – 6 percent of questionnaires returned and only 5 percent of them usable – the received questionnaires were treated as qualitative evidence on par with that gathered through semi-structured interviews.

53 See Appendix 3, "Participant Observation and Interview Sites," for complete listing of activities in Washington, DC, and at European and World Social Forums.

54 See Appendix 2, "List of Interviews Conducted by Author." The criteria for selecting activists to be interviewed at the Florence ESF, to which I also adhered at the Brazilian WSF and Paris ESF, was to maximize diversity with respect to age, gender, and nationality. We also needed to share a common language. Interviews were therefore conducted primarily in English, but also in Spanish, Italian, and, with translators' assistance, in French. In order to gain consent and protect the identities of those I interviewed, I gave each respondent the choice of how they would like to be identified in my published works, with the overwhelming majority granting permission to use their names and organizational affiliations.

55 In the end this resulted in an amended scale shift model, depicted in Figure 2 later in the chapter.

56 Broad change processes and trigger events, according to McAdam, Tarrow, and Tilly, are environmental in the sense that they are changes that activists are responding to from "outside." The authors acknowledge that any environmental mechanism can itself be analyzed into constituent cognitive, relational, and other "structural" mechanisms if we chose to do so. Designating them as environmental simply reflects that our focus of inquiry lies elsewhere. McAdam, Tarrow, and Tilly

have identified change processes and triggers as key to sparking another process, that of mobilization. Including these as initiators of localized action is therefore both consistent with DOC's modeling of a related process, mobilization, and also crucial if we are to offer an explanation of *why* activism is going global. For it is by identifying activists' diverse claims as sharing a profound commonality – that of structural violence of neoliberal globalization in the form of change processes and triggers – that we are better able to explain not only how but also why the scale shift process is so pervasive in contemporary activism. See McAdam, Tarrow, and Tilly, *Dynamics of Contention*, 45.

57 The relational and non-relational distinction I adapted from Sidney Tarrow's most recent work on scale shift in *The New Transnational Activism* (Cambridge: Cambridge University Press, 2005). Here Tarrow identifies non-relational diffusion occurring when information passes from initiator to receiver without any direct ties between them, for example when the public learns from television news about a street demonstration, when curious net-surfers read an NGO website about their campaigns, or when stories of a riot spread by word of mouth. Relational diffusion and brokerage remain the same as in the original DOC conception.

58 My work in this area contributes to nascent scholarship on transnational mobilizing frames, such as that by Michael W. Hovey, "Interceding at the United Nations: The Human Right of Conscientious Objection," in *Transnational Social Movements and Global Politics: Solidarity Beyond the State*, eds. Jackie Smith, Charles Chatfield, and Ron Pagnucco (Syracuse, NY: Syracuse University Press, 1997), 214–24; David C. Atwood, "Mobilizing around the United Nations Special Sessions on Disarmament," in *Transnational Social Movements and Global Politics*, eds. Jackie Smith, Charles Chatfield, and Ron Pagnucco (Syracuse, NY: Syracuse University Press, 1997), 141–58; and David Cortright and Ron Pagnucco, "Limits to Transnationalism: The 1980s Freeze Campaign," in *Transnational Social Movements and Global Politics*, eds. Jackie Smith, Charles Chatfield, and Ron Pagnucco (Syracuse, NY: Syracuse University Press, 1997), 159–74. Social movement scholar John McCarthy has concluded that this level of framing is both exceedingly difficult and in need of comparative assessments, such as will be undertaken herein. See John D. McCarthy, "The Globalization of Social Movement Theory," in *Transnational Social Movements and Global Politics*, eds. Jackie Smith, Charles Chatfield, and Ron Pagnucco (Syracuse, NY: Syracuse University Press, 1997), 245.

59 For the first conception of "glocalization" in the social sciences, see Roland Robertson, "Glocalization: Time–Space and Homogeneity–Heterogeneity," in *Global Modernities*, eds. Mike Featherstone, Scott M. Lash, and Roland Robertson (London: Sage, 1996), 25–44.

60 Sidney Tarrow has also continued research on the scale shift process, and recently has proposed an amended model. See Sidney Tarrow, *The New Transnational Activism* (Cambridge: Cambridge University Press, 2005).

61 Fuyuki Kurasawa, "The Culture of Alternative Globalization and the Creation of Cosmopolitan Solidarity" (paper presented at the 45th Annual Convention of the International Studies Association, Montreal, Canada, 17–20 March 2004), 2; see also Fuyuki Kurasawa, "A Cosmopolitanism from Below: Alternative Globalization

and the Creation of a Solidarity Without Bounds," *European Journal of Sociology* 42, no. 2 (2004): 233–56; Pierre Bourdieu, "Pour un Nouvel Internationalisme," in *Contre-feux: Propos pour servir à la résistance contre l'invasion néo-libérale* (Paris: Raison d'agir, 1998), 66–75; Jacques Derrida, *On Cosmopolitanism and Forgiveness* (London: Routledge, 2001); Jürgen Habermas, *The Postnational Constellation: Political Essays* (Cambridge, MA: MIT Press, 2001); and Ulrich Beck, *World Risk Society* (London, Sage, 1999).

62 Dieter Rucht, "Distant Issue Movements in Germany: Empirical Description and Theoretical Reflections," in *Globalizations and Social Movements: Culture, Power, and the Transnational Public Sphere*, eds. John A. Guidry, Michael D. Kennedy, and Mayer N. Zald (Ann Arbor, MI: University of Michigan, 2000); and Olesen and Rosenau, "The Reduction of Distance."

63 See Mancur Olson, *The Logic of Collective Action* (New York: Schocken, 1968); and also Edward J. Walsh and Rex H. Warland, "Social Movement Involvement in the Wake of a Nuclear Accident: Activists and Free Riders in the TMI Area," *American Sociological Review* 48 (1983): 764–80.

64 See, for example, John D. McCarthy and Mayer N. Zald, "Resource Mobilization and Social Movements: A Partial Theory," *American Journal of Sociology* 82 (1977): 1212–41; and Charles Tilly, "Do Unto Others," in *Political Altruism*, eds. Giugni and Passy, 20.

65 Francis Fox Piven and Richard A. Cloward, *Poor People's Movements: Why They Succeed, How They Fail* (New York: Pantheon Books, 1979).

66 Waterman, "Of Saints"; Eterovic and Smith, "From Altruism to a New Transnationalism," 198; and see also Olesen, *International Zapatismo*, 108.

67 Such as Olesen, *International Zapatismo*; Waterman, "Of Saints"; Eterovic and Smith "From Altruism to a New Transnationalism,"; Donatella della Porta and Sidney Tarrow, "Transnational Processes and Social Activism: An Introduction," in *Transnational Protest and Global Activism* (Lanham, MD: Rowman & Littlefield: 2005), 1–20; and Donatella della Porta, "Multiple Belongings, Tolerant Identities, and the Construction of 'Another Politics': Between the European Social Forum and the Local Social Fora," in *Transnational Protest and Global Activism*, eds. Donatella della Porta and Sidney Tarrow (Lanham, MD: Rowman & Littlefield: 2005), 175–202.

68 Waterman, "Of Saints," 238.

69 Olesen, *International Zapatismo*, 109.

70 Della Porta and Tarrow, "Transnational Processes and Social Activism"; and della Porta, "Multiple Belongings."

71 Waterman, "Of Saints," 8.

72 Olesen, *International Zapatismo*, 111.

73 See, for example, Karl Marx, *The Civil Wars in France* (New York: International Publishers, 1935); Karl Marx, "The Class Struggles in France," in *Selected Works*, Karl Marx and Frederick Engels (Moscow: Foreign Languages, 1958), 139–242; and E.P. Thompson, *The Making of the English Working Class* (London: Gollancz, 1964).

74 Charles Tilly, Louise Tilly, and Richard Tilly, *The Rebellious Century: 1830–1930* (Cambridge, MA: Harvard University Press, 1975), 7.

75 These criticisms have been made by constructionist, new social movement scholars such as Alain Touraine and Alberto Melucci as well as by what can be called post-Marxists like Ernesto Laclau, Chantal Mouffe, Michael Hardt, and Antonio Negri.

76 Waterman, "Of Saints"; and see also Peter Waterman, *Globalization, Social Movements and the New Internationalisms* (London: Mansell, 1998).

77 In challenging the category of worker as the sole basis upon which identity solidarity is being forged, I am not asserting that the worker identity is not an extremely salient one in contemporary anti-neoliberal/anti-capitalist struggles. Indeed, there is a great and growing need for research into the various ways that unionized, flexible, and illegal workers alike are responding to the threats and opportunities of globalization as it touches down around the globe. Trade unions have been actively involved in recent mobilizations not only at the local and national levels but also at the transnational, and unions such as the CUT of Brazil, the Confederazione Generale Italiana del Lavoro (CGIL) and Comitati di Base (COBAS) of Italy, and the Center of Indian Trade Unions have been crucial in both organizing and participating in the world and regional social forums. Furthermore, "precarious" and illegal workers are attempting to overcome considerable obstacles to network across borders and within the space of the social forums. For recent works on the role of trade unions in the anti-neoliberal/anti-capitalist struggle, see Andreas Bieler and Adam David Morton, "'Another Europe Is Possible'? Labour and Social Movements at the European Social Forum," *Globalizations*, 1/2 (2004): 303–25; Andreas Bieler and Adam David Morton, "Canalising Resistance: The Historical Continuities and Contrasts of 'Anti-Capitalist' Movements and the Challenge of Neo-Liberal Globalisation," in *Labour, the State, Social Movements and the Challenge of Neo-liberal Globalisation*, eds. A. Gamble *et al.* (Manchester: Manchester University Press, forthcoming); Andreas Bieler, *The Struggle for a Social Europe: Trade Unions and EMU in Times of Global Restructuring* (Manchester: Manchester University Press, 2006); Peter Waterman, "Adventures of Emancipatory Labour Strategy as the New Global Movement Challenges," *Journal of World Systems Research* X, no. 1 (Winter 2004): 216–53; available from www.jwsr.ucr.edu/archive/vol10/number1/index.php; internet; accessed 18 October 2005; and Peter Waterman and Jill Timms, "Trade Union Internationalism and a Global Civil Society in the Making," in *Global Civil Society 2004–5*, eds. Helmut Anheier, Marlies Glasius, and Mary Kaldor (London: Sage, 2005), 175–202. For organizing on the part of illegal and precarious workers, see, for example, Virginie Guiraudon, "Weak Weapons of the Weak? Transnational Mobilization around Migration in the European Union," in *Contentious Europeans: Protest and Politics in an Emerging Polity*, eds. Doug Imig and Sidney Tarrow (Lanham, MD: Rowman & Littlefield, 2001), 163–86; Madjiguène Cissé, "The *Sans-Papiers*: A Woman Draws the First Lessons," in *We Are Everywhere: The Irresistible Rise of Global Anti-Capitalism*, ed. Notes from Nowhere (London: Verso, 2003), 38–45; and the No Border Network website; available from www.noborder.org; internet; accessed 28 December 2005.

78 On the role of social breakdown or disorganization in sparking collective action, which held sway especially in the 1960s, see William Kornhauser, *The Politics of Mass Society* (New York: Free Press, 1959); Neil Smelser, *Theory of Collective Behavior* (New York: Free Press, 1962); and James C. Davies, "Toward a Theory of Revolution," *American Sociological Review* 27 (1962): 5–29. On deprivation and grievances, see Ted Robert Gurr, *Rogues, Rebels, and Reformers: A Political History of Urban Crime and Conflict*

(Beverly Hills, CA: Sage, 1976); and Ted Robert Gurr, *Why Men Rebel* (Princeton, NJ: Princeton University Press, 1970). Scholarship that expanded on these traditions in various ways includes Piven and Cloward, *Poor People's Movements*; Bert Useem, "Solidarity Model, Breakdown Model, and the Boston Anti-Busing Movement," *American Sociological Review* 45 (1980): 357–69; Bert Useem, "Disorganization and the New Mexico Prison Riot of 1980," *American Sociological Review* 50 (1985): 667–88; and Edward J. Walsh, *Democracy in the Shadows: Citizen Mobilization in the Wake of the Accident at Three Mile Island* (Westport, CT: Greenwood, 1989). The main opposition to breakdown and deprivation theories came from resource mobilization scholarship, which critiqued the former by showing that grievances are sufficiently widespread across groups, disorganized groups are least likely to rebel due to their lack of resources, and, rather, that well-defined and well-resourced groups are more likely to organize politically. These works included John D. McCarthy and Mayer N. Zald, *The Trend of Social Movements in America: Professionalization and Resource Mobilization* (Morristown, NJ: General Learning Press, 1973); McCarthy and Zald, "Resource Mobilization and Social Movements"; and Tilly, Tilly and Tilly, *The Rebellious Century*. In the 1980s, scholars began searching for a middle ground between the social-psychological approaches such as breakdown and deprivation and the more structural-organizational resource mobilization theories. Both approaches were faulted for neglecting the process of interpreting grievances, for holding a static view on participation, and for failing to adequately explain participation-related processes. For works on such processes as frame alignment, micromobilization, and movement participation, see David A. Snow *et al.*, "Frame Alignment Processes, Micromobilization, and Movement Participation," *American Sociological Review* 51 (1986): 464–81; and David A. Snow and Robert D. Benford, "Master Frames and Cycles of Protest," in *Frontiers in Social Movement Theory*, eds. Aldon Morris and Carol M. Mueller (New Haven, CT: Yale University Press, 1992), 133–55.

79 Bennett, "Social Movements beyond Borders," 203, 212–15.

80 Ibid., 213.

81 See ibid., 203.

82 Martin Khor, "Commentary," in *South–North: Citizen Strategies to Transform a Divided World*, ed. John Cavanagh (San Francisco, CA: International Forum on Globalization, November 1995); reprinted in IFG, *Alternatives to Economic Globalization*, 13–14.

83 Nancy Fraser, "Social Justice in the Age of Identity Politics: Redistribution, Recognition and Participation," the Tanner Lectures on Human Values, Stanford University, 30 April–2 May 1996; pdf file available from www.tannerlectures.utah.edu/lectures/Fraser98.pdf; internet; accessed 7 May 2005; Nancy Fraser, *Adding Insult to Injury: Social Justice and the Politics of Recognition*, ed. Kevin Olson (London: Verso, 1999); and Nancy Fraser and Axel Honneth, *Redistribution or Recognition? A Political-Philosophical Exchange* (London: Verso, 2003).

84 Ibid., 3–5.

85 Ibid.

86 Fraser, *Adding Insult to Injury*, 42.

87 Bice Maiguashca makes a similar call to end this bifurcation, following Fraser, in "Globalisation and the 'Politics of Identity': IR Theory through the Looking Glass

of Women's Reproductive Rights Activism," in *Critical Theories*, eds. Eschle and Maiguashca, 117–36.

88 This is an ongoing source of tension, especially among some of the forum's founding member organizations. Recently Whitaker accused the assembly promoters – among them members of ATTAC France – of nearly hijacking the forum process, and a manifesto issued at the end of the 2004 WSF by a number of assembly participants further gave the impression that certain groups were attempting to speak on behalf of all, even though the manifesto's authors vehemently denied any such intention. With both the horizontals and the verticals weighing in, debate and critique continue around how "representative" the IC actually is of the global left today (the near-consensus answer is "not very"), as well as what, if anything, should be done to make it more reflective of the diversity of movements. There is a related discussion as to what ought to be the IC's proper role (no consensus seems forthcoming on the latter two points). These issues will be addressed in greater detail in subsequent chapters. For further reading, see Patomäki and Teivainen, "The World Social Forum"; Teivainen, "World Social Forum and Global Democratization"; Hardt, "Today's Bandung"; Klein, "More Democracy"; Whitaker, "Notes about the World Social Forum"; Sen, *World Social Forum*; de Angelis, "Opposing Fetishism"; Ponniah and Fisher, "Introduction"; Waterman, "The Secret of Fire"; and Holloway, *Change the World without Taking Power*.

3 Toward Jubilee 2000 and beyond

1 For an explanation of my usage of the terms G7 and G8 throughout this work, see Chapter 1, note 28.

2 See Fernando Henrique Cardoso and Enzo Faletto, *Dependency and Development in Latin America* (Berkeley, CA: University of California Press, 1979); Joel Migdal, *Strong States and Weak Societies: State–Society Relations and State Capabilities in the Third World* (Princeton, NJ: Princeton University Press, 1988); and John Walton, "Globalization and Popular Movements" (paper presented at "The Future of Revolutions in the Context of Globalization" conference, University of California, Santa Barbara, 25–27 January 2001).

3 For critical analyses of the debt crisis, see IFG, *Alternatives to Economic Globalization*; Robin Broad and John Cavanagh, "Development: The Market Is Not Enough," *Foreign Policy* 101 (Winter 1995–6); Elmar Altvater *et al.*, eds., *The Poverty of Nations: A Guide to the Debt Crisis from Argentina to Zaire* (London: Zed Books, 1991); Eric Toussaint and Arnaud Zacharie, "External Debt: Abolish the Debt in Order to Free Development," in *Another World Is Possible: Popular Alternatives to Globalization at the World Social Forum*, eds. William F. Fisher and Thomas Ponniah (London: Zed Books, 2003).

4 For differing analyses of SAPs, see World Bank, *Global Development Finance: Financing the Poorest Countries, 2002* (Washington, DC: World Bank, 2002); Stiglitz, *Globalization and Its Discontents*; IFG, *Alternatives to Economic Globalization*; and John Walton and Charles Ragin, "Global and National Sources of Political Protest: Third World Responses to the Debt Crisis," *American Sociological Review* 55 (December 1990): 876–90.

5 See John Walton and David Seddon, *Free Markets and Food Riots: The Politics of Global Adjustment* (Cambridge: Blackwell, 1994); John Walton, "Urban Protests and the

Global Political Economy: The IMF Riots," in *The Capitalist City: Global Restructuring and Community Politics*, eds. Michael Peter Smith and Joe R. Feagin (London: Basil Blackwell, 1987).

6 Gruffydd Jones, "Globalisations, Violences and Resistances," 53–73.

7 See Mridula Udayagiri and John Walton, "Global Transformation and Local Counter Movements: The Prospects for Democracy under Neoliberalism" (paper presented at the conference entitled "The Next Great Transformation? Karl Polanyi and the Critique of Globalization," University of California, Davis, 12–13 April 2002); pdf file available from www.sociology.ucdavis.edu/jtwalton/Walton/pdf/Polanyi_Conf.pdf; internet; accessed 14 September 2004; Jessica Woodroffe and Mark Ellis-Jones, *States of Unrest* (London: World Development Movement, 2000); Walton and Ragin, "Global and National Sources of Political Protest"; and Walton and Seddon, *Free Markets and Food Riots*.

8 Walton and Ragin, "Global and National Sources of Political Protest," 880.

9 René Coulomb, "Democratización de la gestión urbana," *Ciudades* (Mexico) 3 (January–March 1991): 39–44; and Udayagiri and Walton, "Global Transformation," 18–20.

10 Carole Collins, quoted in Fred Rosen, "Report on Global Finance: Doing Battle against the Debt," *NACLA Report on the Americas* 33, no. 1 (July–August 1999): 42–5.

11 Elizabeth A. Donnelly, "Proclaiming the Jubilee: The Debt and Structural Adjustment Network," UN Vision on Global Public Policy Networks, 24, 32–3; pdf available from www.globalpublicpolicy.net; internet; accessed 15 July 2004.

12 Alison Marshall, Head of Campaigns, CAFOD, London, interview by author, tape recording, WSF, Porto Alegre, Brazil, 28 January 2003.

13 Jan Bouke Wijbrandi, quoted in Novib, "What We Are Seeing Here Is the Globalisation of Civil Society," *Novib Network*, no. 2 (April 2003); available from www.novib.nl/en/content/?type=article&id=4012&bck=y; internet; accessed 22 April 2005.

14 Aldo Caliari, legal research scholar, Rethinking Bretton Woods Project, Center of Concern, Washington, DC, interview by author, tape recording, WSF, Porto Alegre, Brazil, 27 January 2003.

15 Donnelly, "Proclaiming the Jubilee," 8–23.

16 Ibid., 10–13.

17 Ibid., 33.

18 See Fifty Years Is Enough, "About Us" and "The Network"; available from http://www.50years.org/index.html; internet; accessed 17 July 2004; and ibid., 9–11.

19 Emphasis mine. Both reports are available from the World Bank's website: www.worldbank.org/research/sapri; internet; accessed 17 April 2005. The two other most significant Bank–civil society engagements, those of the World Commission on Dams and the Extractive Industries Review, have both soured in a similar way to the SAPRI. A statement signed by more than sixty groups, including Fifty Years Is Enough, Focus on the Global South, Jubilee South, Bretton Woods Project, Food and Information Action Network (FIAN), IBASE, Rede Brasil, Council of Canadians, Friends of the Earth International, Delhi Forum, ATTAC Japan, the Forum on African Alternatives, Global Exchange/Code Pink, and Public Citizen, among others, claimed: "In each of these initiatives, the Bank rejected the

exercise's ultimate findings when they turned critical of its operations and demonstrated a degree of bad faith so substantial as to cast suspicion on the Bank's motivations in any interaction with civil society." In "World Bank Courts NGOs as Wolfowitz Takes Helm" (22 April 2005); available from www.focusweb.org/finance/html/modules.php?op=modload&name=News&file=article&sid=276; internet; accessed 5 June 2005; and see also "World Bank Critics Denounce Civil Society Forum" (22 April 2005); available from www.focusweb.org/finance/html/Article275.html; internet; accessed 5 June 2005.

20 SAPRIN, "From Engagement to Protest: A Public Forum on Citizens' Challenges to the World Bank," public forum and discussion sponsored by SAPRIN, the Development GAP, Fifty Years Is Enough Network, and International Rivers Network, Rosslyn, Va., author's notes, 18–19 April 2002.

21 See Ann Pettifor, "Chapter 9/11? Resolving International Debt Crises – the Jubilee Framework for International Insolvency" (London: New Economics Foundation, A Report from Jubilee Research, February 2002): 21, n. 19; available from www.jubilee2000uk.org/; internet; accessed 18 April 2005; and Donnelly, "Proclaiming the Jubilee."

22 Madeleine Bunting, "Jubilee 2000: Churches Spread the Word on Debt," *Unesco Courier* 53, no. 1 (January 2000): 31–3.

23 Ibid.

24 The G7 Summit became the G8 that year, with the official admission of Russia to join the political, though not economic and financial, discussions.

25 Donnelly, "Proclaiming the Jubilee," 14.

26 Quoted in Rosen, "Report on Global Finance," 43.

27 Archbishop Njongonkulu Ndungane, quoted in Ann Pettifor, "The Jubilee 2000 Campaign" (presentation at SEDOS); available from www.sedos.org/english/pettifor.htm; internet; accessed 17 July 2004.

28 Pope John Paul II, quoted in Donnelly, "Proclaiming the Jubilee," 19–20.

29 Stephen Rand, quoted in Jubilee 2000 UK, "Jubilee Research: Analysis: How It Was Achieved: Humble Beginnings"; available from www.jubilee2000uk.org/analysis/repors/world_never_same_again/how.htm; internet; accessed 18 July 2004.

30 Ann Pettifor, "Meeting Series: Does Evidence Matter?" (transcription of a talk given at the Overseas Development Institute, 11 June 2003); available from www.odi.org.uk/RAPID/Meetings/Evidence/Presentation_15/Pettifor.html; internet; accessed 18 July 2004.

31 Bunting, "Jubilee 2000," 31–3.

32 Donnelly, "Proclaiming the Jubilee," 36.

33 Ibid., 47.

34 Carole Collins, "Break the Chain of Debt! International Jubilee 2000 Campaign Demands Deeper Debt Relief," *Review of African Political Economy* 26, no. 81 (September 1999): 419–22.

35 Pettifor, "Meeting Series."

36 This research suggests that frame transformation ought to be conceived more broadly than it has usually been by social movement scholars thus far. It is typically thought of as individuals undergoing or experiencing a "conversion," entailing a

radical transformation of consciousness, thus emphasizing individual, psychological characteristics. This research often focuses on techniques – notably *picking up*, *hooking*, *encapsulating*, and *effective* and *intensive interaction* – that recruiters utilize to convert their target. In this study, a global interpretive, transformative frame is seen more as an interactive, collective process in which widening circles of activists participate. In this sense it is a reasoned and principled expansion of awareness through group-level interactive processes of dialogue, debate, mutual learning, joint action, and reflection, rather than a cultish technique that is applied to a passive adherent. For traditional conceptions of transformative framing, see David A. Snow and Richard Machalek, "The Convert as a Social Type," *Sociological Theory* 1 (1983): 259–89; Richard Machalek and David S. Snow, "Conversion to New Religious Movements," in *Religion and The Social Order: The Handbook on Cults and Sects in America*, vol. 3B (Greenwich, CT: JAI Press, 1993), 53–79; and John Loflund, "Becoming a World-Saver Revisited," *Conversion Careers*, ed. James Richardson (London: Sage, 1978), 10–23.

37 Bunting, "Jubilee 2000," 31–3.
38 Donnelly, "Proclaiming the Jubilee," 18–30.
39 Collins, "Break the Chain of Debt!"
40 Rosen, "Report on Global Finance," 42–5.
41 Collins, "Break the Chain of Debt!"
42 Ann Pettifor, "The World Will Never Be the Same Again ... Because of Jubilee 2000"; available from www.jubilee2000uk.org; internet; accessed 18 July 2004.
43 Jubilee 2000 participant, quoted in Jubilee 2000 UK, "Jubilee Research."
44 Janet Thomas, *The Battle in Seattle: The Story behind and beyond the WTO Demonstrations* (Golden, CO.: Fulcrum Publishing, 2000), 107.
45 Peter Strimer, quoted in Thomas, *The Battle in Seattle*, 101.
46 Thomas, *The Battle in Seattle*, 96–102; Njoki Njehu, "Cancel the Debt," in *A Movement of Movements: Is Another World Really Possible?*, ed. Tom Mertes (London: Verso, 2004), 100.
47 Donnelly, "Proclaiming the Jubilee," 17–18.
48 Pettifor, "The World Will Never Be the Same Again."
49 For details of the various Bretton Woods initiatives for debt forgiveness and their comparisons with the Jubilee and other debt forgiveness and arbitration proposals, see Jubilee Research, "What Is the HIPC Initiative?"; available from www.jubilee2000uk.org/; internet; accessed 20 April 2005; Pettifor, "Chapter 9/11"; World Bank, "HIPC Debt Initiative"; available from www.worldbank.org/hipc/about/hipcbr/hipcbr.htm; internet; accessed 20 April 2005; and Heikki Patomäki and Teivo Teivainen, "Debt Arbitration Mechanism," in *A Possible World: Democratic Transformation of Global Institutions* (London: Zed Books, 2004): 150–62.
50 Pettifor, "Chapter 9/11"; and Patomäki and Teivainen, *A Possible World*, 159–60.
51 Jubilee Research, "Total Debt Relief Received by 42 HIPC Countries (in Nominal Terms)"; "Debt Relief by Country for the 42 HIPCS (in Nominal Terms)," 11 February 2004; and "What Is the HIPC Initiative"; all available from www.jubilee2000uk.org/; internet; accessed 18 April 2005.
52 Patomäki and Teivainen, *A Possible World*, 159.

53 Jubilee Research, "UK Chancellor Pledges L100 million for Multilateral Debt Cancellation: But Can We Really Cheer Twice?" (10 January 2004); available from www.jubilee2000uk.org/; internet; accessed 23 November 2004.

54 "World Bank Courts NGOs."

55 Pettifor, "Chapter 9/11," 21.

56 Donnelly, "Proclaiming the Jubilee," 19–20, 30.

57 Collins, "Break the Chain of Debt!" 419–22.

58 See Jubilee South website, www.jubileesouth.org/news/About_Us.shtml.

59 For these national coalitions, see various links on the Jubilee USA website; available from   www.jubileeusa.org/jubilee.cgi?path=/international_partners/international_ campaigns.

60 Pettifor, "Chapter 9/11," 21.

61 Ibid., 18.

62 Oxfam, "Press Release: Oxfam at the World Social Forum: World Leaders Must Act to Make a Breakthrough on Poverty in 2005" (25 January 2005); available from www.oxfam.org/eng/pr050125_wsf_brazil.htm; internet; accessed 18 April 2005.

63 Ibid. While the campaign has been successful in capturing media attention and attracting a number of high-profile people to lend their support, not everyone is convinced that it will yield results on any of its three issue areas. Ann Pettifor, for one, recently voiced concern that the three issues of trade, aid, and debt are too broad, and thus detract attention from the debt issue. Ann Pettifor, interview by author, tape recording, ESF, London, 16 October 2004.

64 See Make Poverty History webpage, at www.makepovertyhistory.org/; internet; accessed 20 April 2005; Barbara Stocking, director, Oxfam, interview by author, tape recording, ESF, London, 15 October 2004.

65 Oxfam, "Press Release: Celebrities at World Social Forum Publicly Support Global Call to Action against Poverty" (29 January 2005); available from www.oxfam.org/ eng/pr050129_wsf.htm; internet; accessed 18 April 2005.

66 Live8, "The Long Walk to Justice"; available from www.live8live.com/whattodo/ index.shtml; internet; accessed 2 November 2005.

67 Live8, "The Concerts"; available from www.live8live.com/theconcerts/index.shtml; internet; accessed 2 November 2005. Meanwhile, the British tabloids spilled much more ink over the pouting and jockeying that went on backstage among the big egos than over the debt, trade, and aid message behind the big event.

68 Firoze Manji (comment posted on London-based independent media site *Red Pepper*'s "Make the G8 History" weblog, 13 July 2005); available from www.redpepper. blogs.com/g8/2005/07/in_their_own_wo.html; internet; accessed 2 November 2005.

69 Ibid.

70 Ibid.

71 BBC News, "Cautious Welcome for G8 Debt Deal" (12 June 2005); available from www.news.bbc.co.uk/1/hi/business/4084574.stm; internet; accessed 24 June 2005.

72 Bob Geldof and Bono, quoted in IMCista, "Bono and Geldof Praise G8 Deal," *indymedia UK* (9 July 2005); available from www.indymedia.org.uk/en/2005/07/ 317651.html; internet; accessed 2 November 2005.

73 Oxfam, "Post-G8 Analysis: Steps in the Right Direction"; available from www.oxfam.org.uk/what_you_can_do/campaign/mph/g8/index.htm; internet; accessed 2 November 2005.

74 "One Reaction to G8 Summit Communique" (8 July 2005); available from http://releases.usnewswire.com/GetRelease.asp?id=50100; internet; accessed 2 November 2005.

75 "African Civil Society Groups Slam G8 Deal," comment posted on *Red Pepper* "Make the G8 History" weblog (19 July 2005); available from www.redpepper.blogs.com/g8/2005/07/african_civil_s.html; internet; accessed 2 November 2005.

76 Ibid.

77 See "In Their Own Words: How Campaigners Responded to the G8 Communique," at *Red Pepper* "Make the G8 History" weblog; available from www.redpepper.blogs.com/g8/2005/07/in_their_own_wo.html; internet; accessed 2 November 2005.

78 It is therefore not surprising that many Fifty Years Is Enough network members would side with the Southern partners when the latent tensions in J2000 came to a head, and would go on to become a key node in Jubilee South.

79 Keck and Sikkink, *Activists beyond Borders*, 78.

80 Jubilee South, "Jubilee South Pursues Campaign vs. Illegitimacy of Debt in World Social Forum III" (29 March 2003); available from www.jubileesouth.org/news/EpuAEApEyZYKMeAjLO.shtml; internet; accessed 5 January 2005.

81 Evert Bosman, "World Social Forum, Mumbai, India," *Novib Network*, no. 1 (February 2004); available from www.novib.nl/en/content/?type=article&id=5408&bck=y; internet; accessed 20 April 2005.

82 Wijbrandi, quoted in Novib, "What We Are Seeing Here."

83 Oxfam, "World Social Forum (WSF) 2004"; available from www.oxfam.org/eng/event_wsf04.htm; internet; accessed 20 April 2005.

84 Bart Monnens, "Novib at the World Social Forum," *Novib Network*, no. 1 (2005); available from www.novib.nl/content/?type=Article&id=6532&FromList=y; internet; accessed 20 April 2005.

85 Oxfam, "WSF 2004."

86 Bosman, "World Social Forum."

87 Jubilee South, "Jubilee South Pursues Campaign."

88 Jubilee South, "International Peoples' Tribunal on the Debt – Organization" (3 February 2001); available from www.jubileesouth.org/news/EpklpAZFEAPFfQzOvg.shtml; internet; accessed 5 January 2005; and Jubilee South, "People's Tribunal Declares External Debt Illegitimate, Calls for the Decommissioning of IMF–World Bank" (18 April 2002); available from www.jubileesouth.org/news/EpFVuVEFAZip HZbVcW.shtml; internet; accessed 5 January 2005.

89 Marita Hutjes, "There Is a Real Chance that We Can Win in Cancun and Stop the WTO Negotiations," *Novib Network*, no. 2 (April 2003); available from www.novib.nl/en/content/?type=article&id=4011&bck=y; internet; accessed 20 April 2005; and Monnens, "Novib at the World Social Forum."

90 This nascent coalition, calling itself "another Davos" or "anti-Davos," also included the Cairo-based World Forum of Alternatives, the French journal *Le Monde diplomatique* and the ATTAC network its editors had recently initiated, World March of

Women, the Brazilian MST representing the Via Campesina, the Hemispheric Social Alliance, and Euromarche. In François Houtart and François Poulet, eds. *The Other Davos* (London: Zed Books, 2001); Christophe Aguiton, Euromarche, WSF IC representative, conversation with author, author's notes, WSF IC meeting, Utrecht, Netherlands, 30 March 2005.

91 See Patomäki and Teivainen, *A Possible World*, 116–26.
92 See WSF, "Social Forums around the World"; available from www.forumsocial-mundial.org.br/dinamic.php?pagina=foruns_regiao_2005_i; internet; accessed 24 April 2005.
93 Jubilee South, "Reparations toward Another World" (30 August 2001); available from www.jubileesouth.org/news/EpklpEVAykoOBaDAFI.shtml; internet; accessed 5 January 2005.
94 Jubilee South, "Asia-Pacific Meeting Takes Hard Look at Impact of US War on Afghanistan" (20 October 2001); available from www.jubileesouth.org/news/EpEyZpkZFFMRXJYWqT.shtml; internet; accessed 5 January 2005.
95 Emphasis mine, WSF, "Charter of Principles."
96 Francisco Whitaker, comments at WSF IC and Committee meetings, Amsterdam, 31 March 2005.
97 Bosman, "World Social Forum"; WSF, "Background: The Events of 2001, 2002 and 2003"; available from www.forumsocialmundial.org.br/main.php?id_menu=2&cd_language=2; internet; accessed 20 April 2005; and Novib, "Novib Annual Report for 2002," *Novib Network*, no. 4 (July 2003); available from www.novib.nl/en/content/?type=article&id=4594&bck=y; internet; accessed 20 April 2005.

4   Our World Is Not For Sale

1 IFG, *Alternatives to Economic Globalization*, 44.
2 For details on this and other rulings, see Wallach and Sforza, *Whose Trade Organization?*
3 See Dani Rodrik, *Has Globalization Gone Too Far?* (Washington, DC: Institute for International Economics, 1997); and William Greider, *One World, Ready or Not: The Manic Logic of Global Capitalism* (New York: Touchstone, 1998).
4 Martin Khor, "The Hypocrisy of the North in the WTO," *Alternatives to Economic Globalization: A Better World Is Possible*, ed. IFG (San Francisco, CA: Berrett-Koehler Publishers, 2002), 50.
5 IFG, *Alternatives to Economic Globalization*, 118. On the WTO and regional trade agreements, see Wallach and Sforza, *Whose Trade Organization?*; and Ralph Nader *et al.*, *The Case against Free Trade: GATT, NAFTA, and the Globalization of Corporate Power* (San Francisco, CA: Earth Island Press, 1993).
6 Chakravarthi Raghavan, "Lamy Candidacy will Polarise WTO, May Endanger Trading System Itself" (8 December 2004); available from www.twnside.org.sg/title2/5705a.htm; internet; accessed 27 April 2005.
7 Kanaga Raja, "North Tactics to Split Developing-Country Alliances Exposed"; available from www.twnside.org.sg/title2/5623c.htm; internet; accessed 27 April 2005.
8 Walden Bello, "The Global South," in *A Movement of Movements: Is Another World Really Possible?*, ed. Tom Mertes (London: Verso, 2004), 55.

9 Ibid., 55–6.
10 See Focus's website; available from www.focusweb.org/main/html/index.php.
11 Bello, "The Global South," 55.
12 Ibid., 59.
13 See Tarrow, "From Lumping to Splitting," 243–5.
14 Bello, "The Global South," 57.
15 COC, "Our History," and "Vision Statement Background"; available from www.canadians.org; internet; accessed 17 August 2004.
16 Ibid.
17 COC, "Vision Statement Background."
18 FDP, "Spinoff & Associated Organizations: International Forum on Globalization"; available from www.deepecology.org/ifg.html; internet; accessed 18 August 2004.
19 Ibid.
20 Barlow and Clarke, *Global Showdown*, 24.
21 Craig Calhoun, "Community without Propinquity, Revisited: Communications Technology and the Transformation of the Urban Public Sphere," *Sociological Inquiry* 68 (1998): 382.
22 Ronald J. Deibert, "International Plug 'n' Play: Citizen Activism, the internet, and Global Public Policy," *International Studies Perspectives* 1 (2000): 261.
23 Ibid., 264–5.
24 Barlow and Clarke, *Global Showdown*, 24.
25 Ibid.
26 Ibid., 23.
27 Deibert, "International Plug 'n' Play," 264.
28 For a listing of many of the organizations present, see Thomas, *Battle in Seattle*, 66–7.
29 Other major coordinators of the week's actions included the American Federation of Labor–Congress of Industrial Organizations (AFL–CIO), which, along with major environmental groups like Friends of the Earth and Greenpeace, helped plan and take part in the official march of some 60,000 on "N30." As we saw in Chapter 3, the Jubilee 2000 network organized a prayer service and a human chain around the WTO meeting center on its opening night. Peoples' Global Action and Direct Action Network issued the internet call for a global day of action and spearheaded the direct protests in downtown Seattle. The Ruckus Society and Rainforest Action Network trained and took part in nonviolent civil disobedience. See Barlow and Clarke, *Global Showdown*, 9–14; and Thomas, *Battle in Seattle*.
30 Citizens' Trade Campaign, of which Public Citizen is a part, is a national coalition of consumer, environmental, labor, small farm, religious, and other NGOs that formed to coordinate US national and grassroots action against first the NAFTA, then the MAI, and all trade agreements to which the US would become a signatory since then. See the Citizens Trade Campaign website; available from www.citizenstrade.org.
31 Thomas, *Battle in Seattle*, 21. So autonomous and widespread were the Seattle-based preparations to counter the WTO that in the days leading up to the event the planning committee organized by Public Citizen's Soriano held a crowded meeting to which they invited local activists to "come and tell us what you are planning." Thomas, *Battle in Seattle*, 130.

32 Ibid., 124.

33 For a history of indymedia, see Christopher A. Shumway, "Participatory Media Networks: A New Model for Producing and Disseminating Progressive News and Information" (21 May 2002); available from www.reclaimthemedia.org/stories.php? story=02/05/21/6042306; internet; accessed 9 July 2004. For a local activist's account of the birth of Seattle's IMC and its role during protest week, see Miguel Bocanegra's interview with Jeff Perlstein, "Indymedia: Precursors and Birth," in *We Are Everywhere*, ed. Notes from Nowhere (London: Verso, 2003): 230–43.

34 Thomas, *Battle in Seattle*, 26, 192–3.

35 Ibid., 176.

36 Barlow and Clarke, *Global Showdown*, 15.

37 Timi Gerson, organizer/FTAA coordinator, Global Trade Watch, Public Citizen, representative to the WSF International Council, interview by author, tape recording, Washington, DC, 12 February 2003.

38 Naomi Klein, "Reclaiming the Commons," in *A Movement of Movements: Is Another World Really Possible?*, ed. Tom Mertes (London: Verso, 2004), 219.

39 Ian Hood, Globalize Resistance, Scotland, interview by author, tape recording, ESF, Paris, France, 16 November 2003.

40 Notes from Nowhere, *We Are Everywhere*, 22, 24.

41 Gerson, interview.

42 Desmarais, "Via Campesina: Peasants," 160–1.

43 OWINFS, "About Us"; available from www.ourworldisnotforsale.org/about.asp; internet; accessed 20 August 2004.

44 OWINFS, "New Updates"; available from www.ourworldisnotforsale.org/agri/ NewsUpdates/26.htm; internet; accessed 20 August 2004.

45 FDP, "Spinoff & Associated Organizations."

46 IFG, *Alternatives to Economic Globalization*. An edited, second edition was released in 2005.

47 IFG, "Recent Events"; available from www.ifg.org/events/recent.htm; internet; accessed 18 August 2004; and 4 May 2005.

48 Desmarais, "Via Campesina: Peasants," 139, 161–5.

49 OWINFS, "Cancun Planning Meeting"; available from www.ourworldisnotforsale.org/ articles.asp?cat=action&id=62; internet; accessed 5 January 2005.

50 OWINFS, "September 13: Worldwide Day of Action against Corporate Globalization and War"; available from www.ourworldisnotforsale.org/cancun/WTO/cancun/ 03.htm; internet; accessed 20 August 2004.

51 Benny Kuruvilla, "Farmers and Other Civil Society Groups Give a Wake Up Call to the G-20 – But Are They Listening?" (9 April 2005); available from www.ourworld-isnotforsale.org/showarticle.asp?search=169; internet; accessed 27 April 2005; and TWN, "TWN Info Service on WTO and Trade Issues" (21 March 2005); available from www.ourworldisnotforsale.org/showarticle.asp?search=44; internet; accessed 27 April 2005.

52 Raja, "North Tactics."

53 Daniel Pruzin, "Canada to Host WTO Senior Officials 'Mini-Ministerial' in Geneva April 18–19," *International Trade Daily*; available from www.ourworldisnotforsale.org/ showarticle.asp?search=611; internet; accessed 27 April 2005; and Peoples' Food

Sovereignty Network, "Groups Offer Alternative to WTO's Trade Liberalisation Policies: Plan Needed to Protect People's Food Sovereignty," Sign-on Statement; available from www.focusweb.org/trade/html/Article241.html; internet; accessed 5 June 2005.

54 Brid Brennan, Asia Program coordinator, Transnational Institute and WSF IC member, interview by author, tape recording, WSF IC meeting, Utrecht, Netherlands, 1 April 2005.
55 Brennan, interview.
56 Friends of the Earth Europe member, interview by author, tape recording, ESF, London, England, 15 October 2004.
57 Brennan, interview.
58 Ibid.
59 Kuruvilla, "Farmers and Other Civil Society Groups,"; and TWN, "TWN Info Service on WTO and Trade Issues."
60 Ibid.
61 Interfaith Working Group on Trade and Investment, "Religious Organizations Oppose CAFTA," Press Release (20 April 2005); pdf file available from www.citizenstrade.org/; internet; accessed 27 April 2005.
62 Brennan, interview.
63 Ibid.
64 Gemma Galdon, "After Seattle and Cancun ... Next Stop: Hong Kong, *Znet* (8 March 2005); available from www.ourworldisnotforsale.org/showarticle.asp?search= 293; internet; accessed 26 April 2005.
65 Nicola Bullard, Focus on the Global South and WSF IC representative, conversation with author, author's notes, WSF IC meeting, Utrecht, Netherlands, 1 April 2005.
66 Brennan, interview.
67 Ibid.
68 Ibid.
69 Ibid.
70 Ibid.
71 Ibid.
72 Ibid.
73 Ibid.
74 Ibid.
75 Gerson, interview.
76 Korean People's Action against the FTA and WTO, "We Propose an 'Asian Peoples and Social Movements Assembly against War and Neoliberal Globalization' to Take Place During World Social Forum 2005" (6 January 2005); available from www.our worldisnotforsale.org/showarticle.asp?search=119; internet; accessed 16 November 2005.
77 Helena Tagesson, ATTAC Sweden, interview by author, tape recording, WSF, Porto Alegre, Brazil, 28 January 2003.
78 Social Movements International Secretariat, "Porto Alegre Call for Mobilization" (2001); available from www.movsoc.org/htm/call_2001_english.htm; internet; accessed 21 November 2005.

79 Social Movements Assembly, "Call from Social Movements for Mobilizations against the War, Neoliberalism and Exclusion: Another World Is Possible" (31 January 2005); available from www.movsoc.org/htm/call_2005_english.htm; internet; accessed 19 November 2005.

80 Tagesson, interview.

81 Emphasis mine. Francisco Whitaker, "Lessons from Porto Alegre" (24 August 2002); available from www.forumsocialmundial.org.br/DINAMIC/eng_balanco_ChicoW.asp; internet; accessed 24 March 2005.

82 Francisco Whitaker, "Memorial WSF 2003: Notes about the World Social Forum" (14 April 2003); available from www.forumsocialmundial.org.br/dinamic.asp?pagina=bal_whitaker_ing; internet; accessed 24 March 2005.

83 The G19 include Tariq Ali of Pakistan, Samir Amin of Egypt, Walden Bello from the Philippines, Frei Betto and Emir Sader of Brazil, Atilio Boron and Adolfo Pérez Esquivel from Argentina, Bernard Cassen of France, Eduardo Galeano of Uruguay, Francois Houtart and Armand Mattelart from Belgium, Riccardo Petrella and Roberto Savio of Italy, Ignacio Ramonet from Spain, Samuel Ruiz Garcia of Mexico, José Saramago and Bonaventura de Sousa Santos from Portugal, Animata Traoré of Mali, and Immanuel Wallerstein of the United States.

84 "Porto Alegre Manifesto," quoted in Debra Anthony and José Antonio Silva, "The Consensus of Porto Alegre?" (30 January 2005); available from www.ipsnews.net/interna.asp?idnews=27250; internet; accessed 18 November 2005.

85 Summarized at Wikipedia, "Porto Alegre Manifesto"; available from www.en.wikipedia.org/wiki/Porto_Alegre_Manifesto; internet; accessed 17 November 2005.

86 Ignacio Ramonet, quoted in Anthony and Silva, "The Consensus of Porto Alegre."

87 Patrick Bond, "Discussing the Porto Alegre Manifesto," *Znet* (22 February 2005); available from www.zmag.org/sustainers/content/2005-02/22bond.cfm; internet; accessed 20 November 2005.

88 TerraViva Team, "A Divisive Consensus" (31 January 2005); available from www.ipsterraviva.net/tv/wsf2005/viewstory.asp?idnews=179; internet; accessed 22 November 2005.

89 Anthony and Silva, "The Consensus of Porto Alegre."

90 Ibid.

5   Via Campesina

1 John Kinsman, "John Kinsman's Via Campesina Presentation to the 4th Congress of the National Agricultural Confederation (CAN) in Coimbra, Portugal" (9 March 2003); available from www.familyfarmdefenders.org/whatwere%20doing/johnkinsman.html; internet; accessed 30 July 2004.

2 Vandana Shiva, "Wars against Nature and the People of the South," in *Views from the South: The Effects of Globalization and the WTO on the Third World*, ed. Sarah Anderson (Oakland, CA: Food First Books and IFG, 2000).

3 John Ross, *The War against Oblivion: The Zapatista Chronicles 1994–2000* (Monroe, Maine: Common Courage Press, 2000); see also Stiglitz, *Globalization and Its Discontents*; and João Pedro Stedile, "Brazil's Landless Battalions: The Sem Terra

Movement," in *A Movement of Movements: Is Another World Really Possible?*, ed. Tom Mertes (London: Verso, 2004), 16–48.

4 Desmarais, "Via Campesina: Peasants," 89.

5 UNEP, quoted in Darrell Addison Posey, ed., *Cultural and Spiritual Values of Biodiversity* (London: Intermediate Technology Publications, 1999).

6 Stedile, "Brazil's Landless Battalions," 46.

7 See Maude Barlow, *Blue Gold: The Global Water Crisis and the Commodification of the World's Water Supply* (San Francisco, CA: IFG, 2001).

8 Victoria Tauli-Corpuz, "Cultural Diversity: The Right of Indigenous Peoples to Remain Different and Diverse," in *Alternatives to Economic Globalization: A Better World Is Possible*, ed. IFG (San Francisco, CA: Berrett-Koehler Publishers, 2002), 65–8.

9 IFG, *Alternatives to Economic Globalization*, 64. See also Vandana Shiva, *Biopiracy: The Plunder of Nature and Knowledge* (Boston, MA: South End Press, 1997); Andrew Kimbrell, *The Human Body Shop: The Engineering and Marketing of Life* (San Francisco, CA: Harper San Francisco, 1993); Vandana Shiva, "From Commons to Corporate Patents on Life," in *Alternatives to Economic Globalization: A Better World Is Possible*, ed. IFG (San Francisco, CA: Berrett-Koehler Publishers, 2002).

10 Annette-Aurélie Desmarais, "The Via Campesina: Consolidating an International Peasant and Farm Movement," *Journal of Peasant Studies* 29, no. 2 (January 2002): 91–124.

11 Notes from Nowhere, *We are Everywhere*, 122; and Stedile, "Brazil's Landless Battalions," 20.

12 Miguel Carter, "The Origins of Brazil's Landless Rural Workers' Movement (MST): The Natalino Episode in Rio Grande do Sul (1981–84). A Case of Ideal Interest Mobilization," Working Paper CBS-43-2003 (Oxford: University of Oxford Centre for Brazilian Studies, Working Paper Series, 2003): 4; pdf file available from www.brazil.ox.ac.uk/carter43.pdf.12; internet; accessed 30 July 2004.

13 Stedile, "Brazil's Landless Battalions," 20.

14 Ibid.

15 Ibid., 18.

16 Ibid., 21.

17 Desmarais, "Via Campesina: Consolidating," 93–7.

18 Sue Branford and Jan Rocha, "Cutting the Wire: The Landless Movement of Brazil," in *We Are Everywhere: The Irresistible Rise of Global Anticapitalism*, ed. Notes from Nowhere (London: Verso, 2003), 129.

19 Notes from Nowhere, *We are Everywhere*, 122.

20 Stedile, "Brazil's Landless Battalions," 39.

21 Ibid., 42–3.

22 Notes from Nowhere, *We are Everywhere*, 154–5; and Udayagiri and Walton, "Global Transformation," 8.

23 PGA, "Report from Peoples' Global Action Meeting in Bombay" (29 January 2004); available from www.indybay.org/news/2004/01/1669069.php; internet; accessed 1 September 2005; and Notes from Nowhere, *We are Everywhere*, 158.

24 Udayagiri and Walton, "Global Transformation," 8; and Notes from Nowhere, *We are Everywhere*, 154.

25 Udayagiri and Walton, "Global Transformation," 10.
26 Notes from Nowhere, *We are Everywhere*, 154.
27 Udayagiri and Walton, "Global Transformation," 11.
28 Ibid., 12.
29 Ibid., 13; and Notes from Nowhere, *We are Everywhere*, 152. Destroying GMO crops through burning or pulling up plants has quickly spread throughout India and much further a field (literally): In addition to VC members emulating the tactic across the world, environmentalists such as Greenpeace have incorporated the "crop pull" into their repertoire in places like the UK.
30 Professor Nanjundaswamy, President of KRRS, "Cremating Monsanto: Genetically Modified Fields on Fire," in *We are Everywhere: The Irresistible Rise of Global Anticapitalism*, ed. Notes from Nowhere (London: Verso, 2003), 152–4.
31 Norm Diamond, "Roquefort Rebellion," in *We are Everywhere: The Irresistible Rise of Global Anticapitalism*, ed. Notes from Nowhere (London: Verso, 2003), 278–85.
32 Desmarais, "Via Campesina: Consolidating," 97.
33 Judit Bodnar, "Roquefort vs. Big Mac: Globalization and Its Others," *European Journal of Sociology* XLIV, no. 1 (2003): 69.
34 José Bové, "A Farmers' International?," in *Movement of Movements*, ed. Mertes, 140–1.
35 Diamond, "Roquefort Rebellion."
36 Bové, "Farmers' International," 142.
37 *Wall Street Journal*, "A Child of Seattle," editorial, *Wall Street Journal*, 6 July 2000: A26.
38 Ibid.
39 Desmarais, "Via Campesina: Peasants," 185. It is important to note that Bové was also a founding member of ATTAC France, which provided him with not only considerable domestic sympathy but also transnational support. For example, ATTAC Japan delivered some 3,000 signatures to French President Chirac appealing for Bové's pardon and release. In Vicki Birchfield and Annette Freyberg-Inan, "Organic Intellectuals and Counter-Hegemonic Politics in the Age of Globalisation: The Case of ATTAC," in *Critical Theories, International Relations and 'the Anti-Globalisation Movement': The Politics of Global Resistance*, eds. Catherine Eschle and Bice Maiguashca (London: Routledge, 2005), 169.
40 Desmarais, "Via Campesina: Peasants," 89.
41 Bové, "Farmers' International," 142; Bodnar, "Roquefort vs. Big Mac"; and see European Farmers Coordination website, www.cpefarmers.org.
42 Desmarais, "Via Campesina: Peasants," 90.
43 Ibid., 93; and Desmarais, "Via Campesina: Consolidating," 93–7.
44 "NFU-UNAG Women's Committee," quoted in Desmarais, "Via Campesina: Peasants," 92.
45 Desmarais, "Via Campesina: Consolidating," 97.
46 "Managua Declaration," quoted in Desmarais, "Via Campesina: Peasants," 88.
47 Desmarais, "Via Campesina: Consolidating," 95–6.
48 Ibid., 116, n. 8.
49 See Desmarais, "Via Campesina: Peasants," 117–22, for a discussion of this history.
50 For research on NGO–grassroots social movement conflicts, see, for example, Sonia E. Alvarez, "Latin American Feminisms 'Go Global': Trends of the 1990s and

Challenges for the New Millennium," in *Culture of Politics of Cultures: Re-visioning Latin American Social Movements*, eds. Sonia E. Alvarez *et al.* (Boulder, CO: Westview Press, 1998); Marc Edelman, *Peasants against Globalization: Rural Social Movements in Costa Rica* (Stanford, CA: Stanford University Press, 1999); Anthony Bebbington, "Movements, Modernizations and Markets," in *Liberation Ecologies: Environment, Development and Social Movements*, eds. Richard Peet and Michael Watts (London and New York: Routledge, 1996); Annette Desmarais, "Organizing for Change: Peasant Women in Bolivia and Honduras" (research report prepared for the Canadian Bureau for Education, 1994); and James Petras and Henry Veltmeyer, *Globalization Unmasked: Imperialism in the 21st Century* (Halifax and New York: Fernwood Publishing and Zed Books, 2001).

51 For an in-depth analysis of the divergences and conflict between the VC and the IFAP, see Desmarais, "Via Campesina: Peasants."

52 Paul Nicholson, quoted in Desmarais, "Via Campesina: Consolidating," 96.

53 Via Campesina, "Bangalore Declaration of the Via Campesina" (declaration at the Third International Conference of the Via Campesina, 3–6 October, 2000), 1–2.

54 Family Farm Defenders website; available from www.familyfarmdefenders.org/ whatwere%20doing/johnkinsman.html; internet; accessed 30 July 2004.

55 Family Farm Defenders, "Welcome to Via Campesina! – The World's Largest Peasant Farmer Movement!"; available from www.familyfarmdefenders.org/whoweworkwith/ viacampesina.html; internet; accessed 30 July 2004.

56 Desmarais, "Via Campesina: Consolidating," 116, n. 2.

57 Stedile, "Brazil's Landless Battalions," 43.

58 Ibid.

59 Desmarais, "Via Campesina: Consolidating," 105.

60 Ibid., 112.

61 Ibid., 104.

62 Ibid., 93, 98.

63 Jeffrey St. Clair, "Jeffrey St. Clair's Seattle Diary: It's a Gas, Gas, Gas," in *5 Days that Shook the World: Seattle and Beyond*, eds. Alexander Cockburn, Jeffrey St. Clair, and Allan Sekula (London: Verso, 2000), 20.

64 See World Forum on Agrarian Reform website; available from www.fmra.org; internet; accessed 1 September 2005.

65 Desmarais, "Via Campesina: Peasants," 103–7.

66 See Via Campesina website; available from www.viacampesina.org/welcome_english. php3; internet; accessed 1 September 2005.

67 Kinsman, "John Kinsman's Via Campesina Presentation."

68 Desmarais, "Via Campesina: Peasants," 203–22.

69 Via Campesina, "Declaration of the Second International Assembly of Rural Women – June 13"; available from www.viacampesina.org/art_fr.php3?id_article= 448; internet; accessed 2 August 2004.

70 Desmarais, "Via Campesina: Consolidating," 99.

71 Bové, "Farmers' International," 145–6.

72 Via Campesina, "Struggle for Agrarian Reform and Social Changes in the Rural Areas. Via Campesina III Int. Conference"; available from www.viacampesina.org/ art_english.php3?id_article=43; internet; accessed 1 August 2004.

73 Emphasis mine. Via Campesina, "Struggle for Agrarian Reform."
74 Via Campesina, "Draft Via Campesina Position Paper: International Relations and Strategic Alliances," quoted in Desmarais, "Via Campesina: Peasants," 155.
75 Desmarais, "Via Campesina: Peasants," 155–7; and 174, n. 26.
76 Ibid., 158.
77 Paul Nicholson, quoted in Desmarais, "Via Campesina: Peasants," 160.
78 Desmarais, "Via Campesina: Peasants," 159–60; and Bové, "Farmers' International," 145.
79 Desmarais, "Via Campesina: Consolidating," 108–9.
80 On "glocalization," see, for example, Roland Robertson, "Glocalization: Time–Space and Homogeneity–Heterogeneity," in *Global Modernities*, eds. Mike Featherstone, Scott M. Lash, and Roland Robertson (London: Sage, 1996), 25–44.
81 Desmarais, "Via Campesina: Consolidating," 13, 102.
82 Nettie Wieber, Via Campesina regional coordinator for North America, quoted in ibid., 108.
83 Desmarais, "Via Campesina: Consolidating," 107–8.
84 Via Campesina, "Struggle for Agrarian Reform."
85 Via Campesina, "Via Campesina Will Be Present in Mumbai, India"; available from www.viacampesina.org/art_english.php3?id_article=273; internet; accessed 6 January 2005.
86 Desmarais, "Via Campesina: Peasants," 1, 161.
87 Ibid., 180–1.
88 Via Campesina, "Program 18–19 January Debate with Venues"; available from www.viacampesina.org/art_sp.php3?id_article=297; internet; accessed 6 January 2005; and Via Campesina, "'Space' in Mumbai, India" (18–19 January 2004); available from www.peoplesfoodsovereignty.org/activity/2004/01-WSF.htm; internet; accessed 4 June 2005.
89 Desmarais, "Via Campesina: Peasants," 180–1.
90 See, for example, Marco Sibaja, "Brazilian Farmers Storm Monsanto, Uproot Plants" (26 January 2005); available from www.njpcgreens.org/brasil.html; internet; accessed 25 November 2005; and Associated Press, "Brazil Relents on Expulsion of French Anti-Globalization Activist" (31 January 2001); available from www.thecampaign.org/newsupdates/jan00x.htm; internet; accessed 25 November 2005.
91 Brennan, interview.
92 Friends of the Earth International member, interview by author, tape recording, WSF IC meeting, Utrecht, Netherlands, 2 April 2005.
93 This collaboration led to the VC women's committee inviting WMW activists to attend their international conference in Brazil in June 2005. Diane Matte, coordinator, WMW and WSF IC member, interview by author, tape recording, WSF IC meeting, Utrecht, Netherlands, 30 March 2005.
94 Mumbai Resistance appears to have consisted mainly of Maoist and other far left factions within India, led by the Peoples' War Group of the Communist Party India (ML). Claiming to be the sole, legitimate "organized resistance against imperialist globalization and imperialist wars," they derided the WSF for its privileging of "reflective thinking and debate" rather than revolutionary action, and for lacking or

refusing a vanguard, which they purported to be. See Aditya Nigam, "The Old Left in a New World: The Mumbai 'Resistance'?" *indymedia India* (18 January 2004); available from www.india.indymedia.org/en/2004/01/208739.shtml; internet; accessed 25 November 2005.

95 Via Campesina, "'Space' in Mumbai, India."

96 Ibid.

97 Monsanto's statement, quoted in Sibaja, "Brazilian Farmers."

98 In Linden Farrer, "World Forum Movement: Abandon or Contaminate"; available from www.nadir.org/nadir/initiativ/agp/free/wsf/worldforum.htm#a25; internet; accessed 25 November 2005.

6   Zapatista-inspired Peoples' Global Action

1 English translation: Zapatista National Liberation Army.

2 See Justin Paulson, "Peasant Struggles and International Solidarity: The Case of Chiapas"; available from www.yorku.ca/socreg/paulson01.html; internet; accessed 28 November 2004.

3 Chiapas Link, "The Zapatista Movement: Roots of Rebellion"; available from www.chiapaslink.ukgateway.net/ch1.html#roots; internet; accessed on 27 November 2004.

4 EZLN, "First Declaration from the Lacandon Jungle: EZLN's Declaration of War"; available from www.geocities.com/SamppaS/chiapas.html; internet; accessed on 27 November 2004.

5 Notes from Nowhere, *We Are Everywhere*, 24, paraphrasing John Berger.

6 Subcomandante Marcos, quoted in Notes from Nowhere, *We Are Everywhere*, 24.

7 Notes from Nowhere, *We Are Everywhere*, 22; and Chiapas Link, "Zapatista Movement."

8 This indigenous network continued to play an important role in subsequent negotiations toward accords with the Mexican government (which the government ultimately reneged on), and fostered a revival in indigenous and peasant struggles throughout the Americas. See Harry Cleaver, "Zapatistas in Cyberspace: A Guide to Analysis & Resources"; available from www.eco.utexas.edu/faculty/Cleaver/zapsincyber.html; internet; accessed 28 November 2004.

9 See Harry Cleaver, "The Chiapas Uprising and the Future of Class Struggle in the New World Order"; available from www.eco.utexas.edu/facstaff/Cleaver/chiapa-suprising.html; internet; accessed 28 November 2004; Harry Cleaver, "The Zapatistas and the Electronic Fabric of Struggle"; available from www.eco.utexas.edu/faculty/Cleaver/zaps.html; internet; accessed 28 November 2004; and Olesen, *International Zapatismo*. For a comprehensive guide to web-based groups and information on the EZLN, see Cleaver, "Zapatistas in Cyberspace: A Guide."

10 Olesen, *International Zapatismo*, 144.

11 EZLN, "First Declaration of La Realidad," 1996, trans. and quoted in Olesen, *International Zapatismo*, 137.

12 Chiapas Link, "Resistance to Globalisation"; available from www.chiapaslink.ukgateway.net/ch13.htm; internet; accessed 27 November 2004.

13 Paulson, "Peasant Struggles."

14 Ana Esther Ceceña, "Neoliberalismo e Insubordinación," *Chiapas* 4 (1997): 34; trans. and quoted in Paulson, "Peasant Struggles."
15 Chiapas Link, "Resistance to Globalisation."
16 Cleaver, "Zapatistas in Cyberspace: A Guide."
17 Sidney Tarrow and Doug McAdam, "Scale Shift in Transnational Contention," in *Transnational Protest and Global Activism*, eds. Donatella della Porta and Sidney Tarrow (Lanham, MD: Rowman & Littlefield, 2005), 142; Judith Adler Hellman, "Real and Virtual Chiapas: Realism and the Left," in *Socialist Register*, eds. Leo Panitch and Colin Leys (London: Merlin Press, 1999), 166–74.
18 Notes from Nowhere, *We Are Everywhere*, 22–3.
19 Paulson, "Peasant Struggles."
20 Nick Higgins, "Lessons from the Indigenous: Zapatista Poetics and a Cultural Humanism for the Twenty-First Century," in *Critical Theories, International Relations and 'the Anti-Globalisation Movement': The Politics of Resistance*, eds. Catherine Eschle and Bice Maiguashca (London: Routledge, 2005), 97; and Yvon Le Bot, *Subcomandante Marcos: El Sueño Zapatista* (Barcelona: Plaza y Janes Editores, 1997), 195–6; and see also Ross, *War against Oblivion*, 44–5.
21 Notes from Nowhere, *We Are Everywhere*, 115–19.
22 Paulson, "Peasant Struggles."
23 Ibid.
24 Chiapas Link, "Resistance to Globalisation."
25 Paulson, "Peasant Struggles."
26 Subcomandante Marcos, quoted in Le Bot, *Submcomandante Marcos*, 149–50.
27 Ibid., 145–6.
28 EZLN, "Dignity Cannot be Studied; You Live It or It Dies," in *Our Word is Our Weapon: Selected Writings, Subcomandante Marcos*, ed. Juana Ponce de Leon (London: Serpent's Tail, 2001), 265, quoted in Olesen, *International Zapatismo*, 120; see also Kathleen Bruhn, "Antonio Gramsci and the *palabra verdadera*: The Political Discourse of Mexico's Guerilla Forces," *Journal of Interamerican Studies and World Affairs* 41, no. 2 (1999): 49.
29 Cleaver, "The Zapatistas and the Electronic Fabric of Struggle"; and for a detailed investigation of the transnational Zapatista solidarity network, see Olesen, *International Zapatismo*.
30 This also helps explain the early involvement of VC members with the PGA. Via Campesina, "Report of the Coordinator of the Activities Commission and 1994 Proposals" (report prepared by Paul Nicholson, Brussels, CPE), quoted in Desmarais, "Via Campesina: Peasants," 128.
31 On "hactivism" and "culture jamming," see, for example, Tim Jordan, *Activism! Direct Action, Hactivism and the Future of Society* (London: Reaktion Books, 2002); and Kalle Lasn, *Culture Jam: How to Reverse America's Suicidal Consumer Binge – and Why We Must* (New York: Quill, 2000).
32 Notes from Nowhere, *We Are Everywhere*, 28.
33 Ibid., 64–5.
34 See Ross, *War against Oblivion*, 171–3. A second American continental encounter was held in Belém in the Brazilian Amazon in early December 1999, which attracted some 3,000 participants from two dozen American and European countries. See

"Second American Encounter against Neoliberalism and for Humanity"; available from www.eco.utexas.edu/faculty/Cleaver/2ndencounteren.html; internet; accessed 28 November 2004; and "Declaración final del II encuentro americano por la humanidad y contra el neoliberalismo"; available from www.laneta.apc.org/consultaEZLN/belem/declara.htm; internet; accessed 28 November 2004.

35 Quoted in Peter Brown, "Zapatistas Launch International of Hope" (3 August 1996); available from www.geocities.com/CapitolHill/3849/enpeterb.html; internet; accessed 3 August 2004.

36 Ross, *War against Oblivion*, 191.

37 Ibid., 190–1.

38 María Elena Martínez, executive director of CorpWatch, San Francisco, interview by author, tape recording, World Social Forum, Porto Alegre, Brazil, 25 January 2003.

39 EZLN, "Second Declaration of La Realidad (Reality) for Humanity against Neoliberalism" (3 August 1996); available from www.afn.org/~iguana/archives/1997_02/19970209.html; internet; accessed 11 January 2006.

40 Cleaver, "Zapatistas in Cyberspace: A Guide."

41 Cleaver, "Zapatistas in Cyberspace: II. Internet Lists, Conferences & Newsgroups"; available from www.eco.utexas.edu/faculty/Cleaver/zapsincyberinternetlists.html; internet; accessed 28 November 2004.

42 See Il Encuentro por la Humanidad y Contra el Neoliberalismo website; available from www.nodo50.org/encuentro/; internet; accessed 2 December 2004; and Ross, *War against Oblivion*, 225–6.

43 Emphasis mine, quoted in Chiapas Link, "Resistance to Globalisation."

44 Bennett, "Social Movements beyond Borders," 203–26.

45 See, for example, Dissent! Network, "Introduction to the Dissent! Network"; available from www.dissent.org.uk/content/view/62/52/; internet; accessed 28 June 2005.

46 "Documento di consenso sulla rete di resistenze redatto dai delegati dei sei blocchi di lavoro ed approvato dall'assemblea plenaria del II incontro intercontinentale per l'umanitá e contro il neoliberismo nel corso dell'atto conclusivo" (2 August 1997); available from www.tmcrew.org/chiapas/docfin.htm; internet; accessed 28 November 2004.

47 Ross, *War against Oblivion*, 226.

48 Since their founding meeting, PGA have convened macro-regional conferences in South and North America, Asia, and Europe, including most recently in Belgrade and Bangladesh, as well as international conferences in Bangalore and Cochabamba. They are currently trying to organize North African and Middle Eastern networks, centered on the Palestinian issue.

49 See PGA, "Letter from the Geneva Welcoming Committee," *PGA Bulletin* 1 (March 1997); available from www.nadir.org/nadir/initiativ/agp/en/pgainfos/bulletin1.html#1; internet; accessed 28 November 2004; and David Graeber, "The New Anarchists," in *A Movement of Movements: Is Another World Really Possible?*, ed. Tom Mertes (London: Verso, 2004), 205.

50 PGA, "Peoples' Global Action Manifesto"; available from www.nadir.org/nadir/initiativ/agp/en/pgainfos/manifest.htm; internet; accessed 3 December 2004.

51 Their tactics, as well as the challenges they pose to alliance formation with other networks resisting neoliberalism, will be explored in greater detail in subsequent sections.

52 In Europe, their main listserve is pga_europe_process<\\>@>squat.net. There are also North American and international lists, for general news and information, and around four campaigns, including against state militarism and terrorism, for self-determination of peoples and land sovereignty, fighting privatization, and for alternative models to capitalism. There is also a list for Latin America, for Brazil, and for the Pacific. They also publish their Infopoint newsletters on their website in English, German, and French. In a reinvigorated effort to facilitate transnational learning and emulation, as well as attribution of similarity, PGA have recently set up an electronic journal on their webpage, to be administered by the support group, where they invite members to send articles concerning their situations so that different movements can then compare, learn from each other, emulate and improvise on what is being done. See links at www.riseup.net/agp.na/comms.html; and www.nadir.org/nadir/initiativ/agp/free/listas/index.htm; and PGA, "PGA Europe Infopoint Contact List"; available from www.nadir.org/nadir/initiativ/agp/pgaeurope/infopoints.htm; internet; accessed 28 November 2004.

53 For a complete list of their calls for global days of action, along with links, see PGA, "Days of Global Action against Capitalism"; available from www.nadir.org/nadir/initiativ/agp/free/global/index.htm; internet; accessed 4 December 2004. For their G8 2005 call, see also PGA, "Resist the G8//Global Action Callout//Wednesday July 6th 2005"; available from www.nadir.org/nadir/initiativ/agp/resistg8/index.htm; internet; accessed 28 June 2005.

54 For a comprehensive list of coordinated actions on that day in roughly sixty cities around the world, see PGA, "Global Days of Action against 'Free' Trade and the WTO – May 1998," *PGA Bulletin* 2 (June 1998); available from www.nadir.org/nadir/initiativ/agp/en/pgainfos/bulletin2/bulletin2b.html; internet; accessed 28 November 2004.

55 Notes from Nowhere, *We Are Everywhere*, 154–9; and Udayagiri and Walton, "Global Transformation."

56 Other PGA caravans include the Colombian Black Communities tour and the Peoples' Caravan from Cochabamba to Colombia.

57 Katharine Ainger, "Life Is Not Business: The Intercontinental Caravan," in *We Are Everywhere: The Irresistible Rise of Global Anticapitalism*, ed. Notes from Nowhere (London: Verso, 2003), 160–1. Other Indian movements taking part in the caravan included Bharat Kishan Union, the Joint Action Forum of Indian People against the WTO and Anti-People-Policy (JAFIP), the Narmada Bachao Andolan (Save the Narmada Movement), and the National Forum of Fishworkers. In Squat!net, "Brief Description of Indian Movements Participating in the ICC"; available from www.squat.net/caravan/ICC-en/movements.htm; internet; accessed 6 January 2005.

58 Ainger, "Life Is Not Business," 162.

59 Vijay Jawandhia, quoted in ibid.

60 On the varieties of guerrilla gardening, see Notes from Nowhere, *We Are Everywhere*, 134–9, 150–1, 469.

61 On street reclaiming, see ibid., 50–61.

62 Subcomandante Marcos, quoted in ibid., 233.
63 Jeff Perlstein, quoted in Miguel Bocanegra, "Indymedia: Precursors and Birth," in *We Are Everywhere: The Irresistible Rise of Global Anticapitalism*, ed. Notes from Nowhere (London: Verso, 2003), 233.
64 Ibid., 234–5.
65 ibid., 234.
66 See indymedia, "Declaration in Support of the Indymedia Network and against the Seizure of Its Servers"; available from www.solidarity.indymedia.org.uk; internet; accessed 4 December 2004.
67 Spokescouncils are but one of the many innovative tools that activists have developed to reach group consensus. Others include affinity groups, break-outs, brainstorming sessions, fishbowls, strawpolls, blocks and stand-asides. For an overview of the anarchistic, consensus-reaching toolbox, see Graeber, "New Anarchists," 213–14.
68 Notes from Nowhere, *We Are Everywhere*, 309.
69 PGA, "3. Plans of Action," *PGA Bulletin* 1 (March 1997); available from www.nadir.org/nadir/initiativ/agp/en/pgainfos/bulletin1.html#1; internet; accessed 28 November 2004; see also PGA, "A Call for Global Action in Europe"; available from www.nadir.org/nadir/initiativ/agp/en/pgainfos/pga-call.htm; internet; accessed 28 November 2004.
70 See John Arquilla and David F. Ronfeldt, *Networks and Netwar: The Future of Terror, Crime and Militancy* (Washington, DC: Rand Corporation, 2002).
71 On the logic of the swarm and networks, see Notes from Nowhere, *We Are Everywhere*, 63–73.
72 WOMBLES, "Background: Lessons Learned: Personal Reflections and Opinions on S26" (November 2000); available from www.wombles.org.uk/background/lessons.php; internet; accessed 26 June 2005. One of the first academic treatments of the fluffy vs. spiky contingents, without naming it as such, is by Kate O'Neill, "Transnational Protest: States, Circuses, and Conflict at the Frontline of Global Politics," *International Studies Review* 6, no. 2 (June 2004): 233–51.
73 Rhythms of Resistance, "Why We Do It"; available from www.rhythmsof resistance.co.uk/?lid=52; internet; accessed 30 November 2005.
74 On the importance of carnival to anarchist actions, see Notes from Nowhere, *We Are Everywhere*, 173–83.
75 Brian Holmes, "Touching the Violence of the State," in *We Are Everywhere: The Irresistible Rise of Global Anticapitalism*, ed. Notes from Nowhere (London: Verso, 2003), 346.
76 Kate Evans, "It's Got to Be Silver and Pink: On the Road with Tactical Frivolity," in *We Are Everywhere: The Irresistible Rise of Global Anticapitalism*, ed. Notes from Nowhere (London: Verso, 2003), 291.
77 ROR's website also provides practical information on how to start a band and make homemade instruments; available from www.rhythmsofresistance.co.uk/; internet; accessed 30 November 2005.
78 Infernal Noise Brigade agit-prop is on their website; available from www.infernal-noise.org; quoted in Jennifer Whitney, "Infernal Noise: The Soundtrack to

Insurrection," in *We Are Everywhere: The Irresistible Rise of Global Anticapitalism*, ed. Notes from Nowhere (London: Verso, 2003), 224.

79 Whitney, "Infernal Noise," 218–19.

80 Showing their ideological affinity with Antonio Negri, their demands mirror those that Hardt and Negri put forward in their final chapter of *Empire*, "The Multitude Against Empire."

81 See, for example, Notes from Nowhere, *We Are Everywhere*, 38, 428–9; and the No Borders website, at www.noborder.org.

82 Tute Bianche, "A Busload of Lies Exposed, Appended with a Vivid Depiction of the Italian Scene and a Lot of Links and References: Who Are the White Overalls? And Why Are They Slandered by People Who Call Themselves 'Anarchists'?"; available from www.nadir.org/nadir/initiativ/agp/free/genova/busload.htm; internet; accessed 5 August 2004.

83 See the WOMBLES website; available from www.wombles.org.uk/.

84 Infoshop, "Black Blocs for Dummies: Frequently Asked Questions" (31 January 2004); available from www.infoshop.org/blackbloc.html; internet; accessed 30 November 2005; see also Wikipedia, "Black Bloc"; available from www.en.wikipedia.org/wiki/Black_bloc; internet; accessed 25 June 2005

85 St. Clair, "Jeffrey St. Clair's Seattle Diary," 29.

86 Infoshop, "Black Blocs for Dummies"; see also WOMBLES, "Background: Lessons Learned: Personal Reflections and Opinions on S26" (November 2000); available from www.wombles.org.uk/background/lessons.php; internet; accessed 26 June 2005; and Wikipedia, "Black Bloc." It must be stressed, however, that black bloc tactics are not supported by all, or even many, of the PGA, who often prefer "white" or "pink" tactics. Yet because some PGAers, such as members of the UK's WOMBLES, at times use or at least support black bloc tactics, it seems appropriate to include them here.

87 St. Clair, "Jeffrey St. Clair's Seattle Diary," 47.

88 Carl Pope and Medea Benjamin, quoted in ibid., 47–8.

89 Barbara Rimml, ATTAC Switzerland, interview by author, tape recording, Potsdam, Germany, 9 January 2004.

90 Sian Sullivan, "'We Are Heartbroken and Furious!': Violence and the (Anti) Globalisation Movement(s)," in *Critical Theories, International Relations and 'the Anti-Globalisation Movement': The Politics of Global Resistance*, eds. Catherine Eschle and Bice Maiguashca (London: Routledge, 2005), 174–94; this chapter also appears in a longer form under the title "'We Are Heartbroken and Furious!' (#2): Violence and the (Anti-)Globalisation Movement(s)" (University of Warwick: Centre for the Study of Globalisation and Regionalisation, Working Paper No. 133/04, May 2004); pdf available from www.warwick.ac.uk/fac/soc/csgr/research/workingpapers/2004/wp13304.pdf; internet; accessed 27 November 2005.

91 Jeff Juris, "The London ESF and the Politics of Autonomous Space," *Znet* (2 November 2004); available from www.zmag.org/content/showarticle.cfm?SectionID=41&ItemID=6552; internet; accessed 7 January 2006.

92 PGA, "Report."

93 This view, however, is not an entirely fair one, for it denies the long, unique gestation process out of which the WSF grew. When asked about the connections between the Zapatista *encuentros* and the social forum, Chico Whitaker responded that the inspiration for the forum as a space came from the ideas of Paulo Freire and, to a lesser extent, from the '68 generation. The Brazilian founders had very little contact with Mexican groups, either in Chiapas or elsewhere. But recently they have been actively seeking relations with them. Through their informal contacts, they encouraged Mexicans to host the 2006 WSF, but activists were not yet prepared to do so. Francisco "Chico" Whitaker, conversation with author, author's notes, WSF IC meeting, Utrecht, Netherlands, 1 April 2005.

94 Jeff Juris, "London ESF"; and Hub Project, "Summary from Final Plenary of the Hub, Firenze" (10 November 2002); available from www.nadir.org/nadir/initiativ/agp/space/finalplenary.htm; internet; accessed 25 November 2005.

95 Juris, "London ESF."

96 WOMBLES, "Reflections & Analysis: The WOMBLES, the ESF & beyond" (December 2004); available from www.wombles.org.uk/auto/reflections.php?PHPSESSID=0b793d5649decd5dd5dcd6b1e97cadbf; internet; accessed 24 June 2005.

97 WOMBLES, "Beyond ESF: 5 Days & Nights of Anti-Authoritarian Ideas and Action: A Short Analysis of the Socio-Political Role of the WSF–ESF"; available from www.wombles.org.uk/auto/esfcritique.php; internet; accessed 24 June 2005.

98 WOMBLES, "News: Beyond ESF – Programme, Posted 14:53 08 October 2004: Beyond ESF: Programme & Timetable, Wednesday 13th–Sunday 17th October"; available from www.wombles.org.uk/news/article_2004_10_8_5355.php; internet; accessed 24 June 2005.

99 WOMBLES, "Beyond ESF: 5 Days & Nights."

100 Ibid.

101 Ezequiel Adamovsky, Cid Campeador Neighborhood Assembly, Buenos Aires, "The World Social Forum's New Project: 'The Network of the World's Social Movements'"; available from www.nadir.org/nadir/initiativ/agp/free/wsf/newproject.htm; internet; accessed 15 November 2005.

102 Ezequiel Adamovsky, "Another Forum Is Possible: Whose Bridges Are We Building? Do We Need a New International?" (February 2003); available from www.nadir.org/nadir/initiativ/agp/free/wsf/anotherforum.html internet; accessed 15 October 2005.

103 Adamovsky, "Another Forum Is Possible."

104 Adamovsky, "The World Social Forum's New Project."

105 Open Democracy, "A luta continua"; available from www.opendemocracy.typepad.com/wsf/2005/01/neither_bang_no.html; internet; accessed 22 November 2005.

106 Farrer, "World Forum Movement."

107 Emiliano, coletivo contra-a-corrente, "We Will Not Go to the World 'Social' Forum! And We Are Not Alone!" (6 December 2000); available from www.nadir.org/nadir/initiativ/agp/free/wsf/nowsf.htm; internet; accessed 25 November 2005.

108 Emiliano, "We Will Not Go."

109 Adamovsky, "The World Social Forum's New Project."

110 Ibid.

111 Jason Adams, "WSF 2002: Hopes for a True International," *Znet* (13 February 2002); available from www.zmag.org/content/VisionStrategy/AdamsWSF.cfm; internet; accessed 15 December 2005; and Farrer, "World Forum Movement."

112 CIRCA Clown no. 1, interview by author, tape recording, European Social Forum, London, 16 October 2004.

113 Juris, "The London ESF."

114 WOMBLES, "Reflections & Analysis."

115 Adamovsky, "Another Forum is Possible."

116 Francisco "Chico" Whitaker, comments made at WSF IC meetings, author's notes, Amsterdam and Utrecht, Netherlands, 28 March–1 April 2005.

117 Ibid.

118 With a possible exception in the case of Roberto Savio, who should be made to wait until he is eighty to speak again as punishment for signing the G19 Manifesto!

7 Concluding reflections on present and future scholarship and activism

1 De Angelis, "Opposing Fetishism," 591.

2 Charles Tilly, "From Interactions to Outcomes in Social Movements," in *How Social Movements Matter*, eds. Marco Giugni, Doug McAdam, and Charles Tilly (Minneapolis, MN: University of Minnesota, 1999), 253–70.

Appendix

1 Available from www.forumsocialmundial.org.br/main.php?id_menu=4&cd_language=2; Internet; accessed 14 September 2005.

Bibliography

Adamovsky, Ezequiel. "Another Forum Is Possible: Whose Bridges Are We Building? Do We Need a New International?" (February 2003). Available from www.nadir.org/nadir/initiativ/agp/free/wsf/anotherforum.html. Internet. Accessed 15 October 2005.

—— "The World Social Forum's New Project: 'The Network of the World's Social Movements'." Available from www.nadir.org/nadir/initiativ/agp/free/wsf/newproject.htm. Internet. Accessed 15 November 2005.

Adams, Jason. "WSF 2002: Hopes for a True International." *Znet* (13 February 2002). Available from www.zmag.org/content/VisionStrategy/AdamsWSF.cfm. Internet. Accessed 15 December 2005.

"African Civil Society Groups Slam G8 Deal." Comments posted on *Red Pepper*, "Make the G8 History," weblog (19 July 2005). Available from www.redpepper.blogs.com/g8/2005/07/african_civil_s.html. Internet. Accessed 2 November 2005.

Ainger, Katharine. "Life Is Not Business: The Intercontinental Caravan." In *We Are Everywhere: The Irresistible Rise of Global Anticapitalism*, edited by Notes from Nowhere. London: Verso, 2003.

Alasuutari, Perti. *Researching Culture: Qualitative Method and Cultural Studies*. London: Sage, 1995.

Albert, Michael. *Parecon: Life after Capitalism*. London: Verso, 2004.

Alexander, Jeffrey C., and Bernhard Giesen. "From Reduction to Linkage: The Long View of the Micro–Macro Debate." In *The Micro–Macro Link*, edited by Jeffrey C. Alexander, Bernhard Ciesen, Richard Munch, and Neil J. Smelser. Berkeley: University of California Press, 1987.

Altvater, Elmar, Kurt Hübner, Jochen Lorentzen, and Raúl Rojas, eds. *The Poverty of Nations: A Guide to the Debt Crisis from Argentina to Zaire*. London: Zed Books, 1991.

Alvarez, Sonia E. "Latin American Feminisms 'Go Global': Trends of the 1990s and Challenges for the New Millennium." In *Culture of Politics of Cultures: Re-visioning Latin American Social Movements*, edited by Sonia E. Alvarez, Evelina Dagnino, and Arturo Escobar. Boulder, CO: Westview Press, 1998.

Amin, Samir. *The Liberal Virus: Permanent War and the Americanization of the World*. New York: Monthly Review Press, 2004.

Anthony, Debra, and José Antonio Silva. "The Consensus of Porto Alegre?" (30 January 2005). Available from www.ipsnews.net/interna.asp?idnews=27250. Internet. Accessed 18 November 2005.

Appelbaum, Richard P., and William I. Robinson. *Critical Globalization Studies*. London: Routledge, 2005.

Archer, Margaret S. *Realist Theory: The Morphogenetic Approach*. Cambridge: Cambridge University Press, 1995.

Archibugi, Daniele, David Held and Martin Kohler. *Re-imagining Political Community: Studies in Cosmopolitan Democracy*. Stanford, CA: Stanford University Press, 1998.

Arquilla, John, and David F. Ronfeldt. *Networks and Netwar: The Future of Terror, Crime and Militancy*. Washington, DC: Rand Corporation, 2002.

Associated Press. "Brazil Relents on Expulsion of French Anti-Globalization Activist" (31 January 2001). Available from www.thecampaign.org/newsupdates/jan00x.htm. Internet. Accessed 25 November 2005.

ATTAC France. "Campagne pour la Victoire du NON." Available from www.france/.attac.org/r613. Internet. Accessed 1 September 2005.

Atwood, David C. "Mobilizing around the United Nations Special Sessions on Disarmament." *Transnational Social Movements and Global Politics*, edited by Jackie Smith, Charles Chatfield, and Ron Pagnucco. Syracuse, NY: Syracuse University Press, 1997.

Bandy, Joe, and Jackie Smith, eds. *Coalitions across Borders: Transnational Protest and the Neoliberal Order*. Lanham, MD: Rowman & Littlefield, 2004.

Barlow, Maude. *Blue Gold: The Global Water Crisis and the Commodification of the World's Water Supply*. San Francisco, CA: International Forum on Globalization, 2001.

Barlow, Maude, and Tony Clarke. *Global Showdown: How the New Activists are Fighting Global Corporate Rule*. Toronto: Stoddart, 2001.

BBC News. "Cautious Welcome for G8 Debt Deal" (12 June 2005). Available from www.news.bbc.co.uk/1/hi/business/4084574.stm. Internet. Accessed 24 June 2005.

Bebbington, Anthony. "Movements, Modernizations and Markets." In *Liberation Ecologies: Environment, Development and Social Movements*, edited by Richard Peet and Michael Watts. London: Routledge, 1996.

Beck, Ulrich. *World Risk Society*. London, Sage, 1999.

Beeston, Richard. "Ranks Begin to Thin in Coalition of the Willing." *The Times*, UK, 15 March 2005.

Bello, Walden. *Deglobalization: Ideas for a New World Economy*. London: Zed Books, 2003.

—— "The Global South." In *A Movement of Movements: Is Another World Really Possible?*, edited by Tom Mertes. London: Verso, 2004.

Benmayor, Rina. "Testimony, Action Research, and Empowerment: Puerto Rican Women and Popular Education." In *Women's Words: The Feminist Practice of Oral History*, edited by Shurna B. Gluck and Daphne Patai. London: Routledge, 1991.

Bennett, W. Lance. "Social Movements beyond Borders: Organization, Communication, and Political Capacity in Two Eras of Transnational Activism." In *Transnational Protest and Global Activism: People, Passions, and Power*, edited by Donatella della Porta and Sidney G. Tarrow. Lanham, MD: Rowman & Littlefield, 2005.

Bhagwati, Jagdish. *In Defense of Globalization*. Oxford: Oxford University Press, 2004.

Bieler, Andreas. *The Struggle for a Social Europe: Trade Unions and EMU in Times of Global Restructuring*. Manchester: Manchester University Press, 2006.

Bieler, Andreas, and Adam David Morton. "'Another Europe Is Possible'? Labour and Social Movements at the European Social Forum." *Globalizations* 1/2 (2004): 303–25.

—— "Canalising Resistance: The Historical Continuities and Contrasts of 'Anti-Capitalist' Movements and the Challenge of Neo-Liberal Globalisation." In *Labour, the State, Social Movements and the Challenge of Neo-liberal Globalisation*, edited by Andrew Gamble, Steve Ludlam, Andrew Taylor and Stephen Wood. Manchester: Manchester University Press, forthcoming.

Birchfield, Vicki, and Annette Freyberg-Inan. "Organic Intellectuals and Counter-Hegemonic Politics in the Age of Globalisation: The Case of ATTAC." In *Critical Theories, International Relations and 'the Anti-Globalisation Movement': The Politics of Global Resistance*, edited by Catherine Eschle and Bice Maiguashca. London: Routledge, 2005.

Blee, Kathleen M. *Inside Organized Racism: Women in the Hate Movement*. Berkeley, CA: University of California Press, 2001.

Blee, Kathleen M., and Verta Taylor. "Semi-Structured Interviewing in Social Movement Research." In *Methods of Social Movement Research*, edited by Bert Klandermans and Suzanne Staggenborg. Minneapolis, MN: University of Minnesota Press, 2002.

Bocanegra, Miguel. "Indymedia: Precursors and Birth." In *We Are Everywhere*, edited by Notes from Nowhere. London: Verso, 2003

Bodnar, Judit. "Roquefort vs. Big Mac: Globalization and Its Others." *European Journal of Sociology* XLIV, no. 1 (2003): 68–79.

Bond, Patrick. "Discussing the Porto Alegre Manifesto." *Znet* (22 February 2005). Available from www.zmag.org/sustainers/content/2005-02/22bond.cfm. Internet. Accessed 20 November 2005.

Bosman, Evert. "World Social Forum, Mumbai, India." *Novib Network*, no. 1 (February 2004). Available from www.novib.nl/en/content/?type=article&id=5408&bck=y. Internet. Accessed 20 April 2005.

Bourdieu, Pierre. *Outline of a Theory of Practice.* Cambridge: Cambridge University Press, 1977.

—— "Pour un Nouvel Internationalisme." In *Contre-feux: Propos pour servir à la résistance contre l'invasion néo-libérale.* Paris: Raison d'agir, 1998.

Bourgois, Philippe. "The Power of Violence in War and Peace: Post Cold War Lessons from El Salvador." *Ethnography* 2, no. 1 (2001): 5–34.

Bové, José. "A Farmers' International?" In *A Movement of Movements: Is Another World Really Possible?*, edited by Tom Mertes. London: Verso, 2004.

Branford, Sue, and Jan Rocha. "Cutting the Wire: The Landless Movement of Brazil." In *We Are Everywhere: The Irresistible Rise of Global Anticapitalism*, edited by Notes from Nowhere. London: Verso, 2003.

Broad, Robin, ed. *Global Backlash: Citizen Initiatives for a Just World Economy.* Lanham, MD: Rowman & Littlefield, 2002.

Broad, Robin, and John Cavanagh. "Development: The Market Is Not Enough." *Foreign Policy* 101 (Winter 1995–6).

Brown, Peter. "Zapatistas Launch International of Hope" (3 August 1996). Available from www.geocities.com/CapitolHill/3849/enpeterb.html. Internet. Accessed 3 August 2004.

Bruhn, Kathleen. "Antonio Gramsci and the *palabra verdadera:* The Political Discourse of Mexico's Guerilla Forces." *Journal of Interamerican Studies and World Affairs* 41, no. 2 (1999): 29–57.

Bunting, Madeleine. "Jubilee 2000: Churches Spread the Word on Debt." *Unesco Courier* 53, no. 1 (January 2000): 31–3.

Burawoy, Michael. "The Extended Case Method." *Sociological Theory* 16, no. 1 (1998): 4–33.

Calhoun, Craig. "Community without Propinquity, Revisited: Communications Technology and the Transformation of the Urban Public Sphere." *Sociological Inquiry* 68 (1998): 373–97.

Callinicos, Alex. *An Anti-Capitalist Manifesto.* Oxford: Blackwell, 2003.

Cardoso, Fernando Henrique, and Enzo Faletto. *Dependency and Development in Latin America.* Berkeley, CA: University of California Press, 1979.

Carter, Miguel. "The Origins of Brazil's Landless Rural Workers' Movement (MST): The Natalino Episode in Rio Grande do Sul (1981–84). A Case of Ideal Interest Mobilization." Working Paper CBS-43-2003. Oxford: University of Oxford Centre for Brazilian Studies, Working Paper Series, 2003. Pdf file available from www.brazil.ox.ac.uk/carter43.pdf.12. Internet. Accessed 30 July 2004.

Cerny, Philip G. "Globalization and the Changing Logic of Collective Action." *International Organization* 49, no. 4 (1995): 595–625.

Checkel, Jeffrey T. "Constructivist Turn in International Relations Theory." *World Politics* 50, no. 2 (1998): 324–48.

—— "Norms, Institutions and National Identity in Contemporary Europe." *International Studies Quarterly* 43 (1999): 83–114.

Chiapas Link. "Resistance to Globalisation." Available from www.chiapaslink.ukgateway.net/ch13.htm. Internet. Accessed 27 November 2004.

—— "The Zapatista Movement: Roots of Rebellion." Available from www.chiapaslink.ukgateway.net/ch1.html#roots. Internet. Accessed 27 November 2004.

Cissé, Madjiguène. "The *Sans-Papiers*: A Woman Draws the First Lessons." In *We Are Everywhere: The Irresistible Rise of Global Anticapitalism*, edited by Notes from Nowhere. London: Verso, 2003.

Cleaver, Harry. "The Chiapas Uprising and the Future of Class Struggle in the New World Order." Available from www.eco.utexas.edu/facstaff/Cleaver/chiapasuprising.html. Internet. Accessed 28 November 2004.

—— "The Zapatistas and the Electronic Fabric of Struggle." Available from www.eco.utexas.edu/faculty/Cleaver/zaps.html. Internet. Accessed 28 November 2004.

—— "Zapatistas in Cyberspace: A Guide to Analysis & Resources." Available from www.eco.utexas.edu/faculty/Cleaver/zapsincyber.html. Internet. Accessed 28 November 2004.

—— "Zapatistas in Cyberspace: II. Internet Lists, Conferences & Newsgroups." Available from www.eco.utexas.edu/faculty/Cleaver/zapsincyberinternetlists.html. Internet. Accessed 28 November 2004.

Coleman, James S. *Foundations of Social Theory*. Cambridge, MA: The Belknap Press of Harvard University Press, 1990.

Collins, Carole. "Break the Chain of Debt! International Jubilee 2000 Campaign Demands Deeper Debt Relief." *Review of African Political Economy* 26, no. 81 (September 1999): 419–22.

Cortright, David, and Ron Pagnucco. "Limits to Transnationalism: The 1980s Freeze Campaign." In *Transnational Social Movements and Global Politics*, edited by Jackie Smith, Charles Chatfield, and Ron Pagnucco. Syracuse, NY: Syracuse University Press, 1997.

Coulomb, René. "Democratización de la gestión urbana." *Ciudades* (Mexico) 3 (January–March 1991): 39–44.

Council of Canadians. "Our History." Available from www.canadians.org. Internet. Accessed 17 August 2004.

—— "Vision Statement Background." Available from www.canadians.org. Internet. Accessed 17 August 2004.

Cox, Robert. "A Perspective on Globalization." In *Globalization: Critical Reflections*, edited by James Mittelman. Boulder, CO: Lynne Rienner, 1996.

Cox, Robert W., with Michael G. Schechter. *The Political Economy of a Plural World*. London: Routledge, 2002.

Davies, James C. "Toward a Theory of Revolution." *American Sociological Review* 27 (1962): 5–29.

de Angelis, Massimo. "Opposing Fetishism by Reclaiming Our Powers." *International Social Sciences Journal* 182 (2004): 591–604.

"Declaración final del II encuentro americano por la humanidad y contra el neoliberalismo." Available from www.laneta.apc.org/consultaEZLN/belem/declara.htm. Internet. Accessed 28 November 2004.

Deibert, Ronald J. "International Plug 'n' Play" Citizen Activism, the Internet, and Global Public Policy." *International Studies Perspectives* 1 (2000): 255–72.

della Porta, Donatella. "Multiple Belongings, Tolerant Identities, and the Construction of 'Another Politics': Between the European Social Forum and the Local Social Fora." In *Transnational Protest and Global Activism*, edited by Donatella della Porta and Sidney G. Tarrow. Lanham, MD: Rowman & Littlefield, 2005.

—— *Social Movements, Political Violence and the State: A Comparative Analysis of Italy and Germany*. Cambridge: Cambridge University Press, 1995.

della Porta, Donatella, Hanspeter Kriesi, and Dieter Rucht. *Social Movements in a Globalizing World*. Houndmills: Macmillan, 1999.

della Porta, Donatella, and Sidney Tarrow. "Transnational Processes and Social Activism: An Introduction." In *Transnational Protest and Global Activism*. Lanham, MD: Rowman & Littlefield: 2005.

—— eds. *Transnational Protest and Global Activism: People, Passions, and Power.* Lanham, MD: Rowman & Littlefield, 2005.

Denzin, Norman K. *The Research Act: A Theoretical Introduction to Sociological Methods.* Englewood Cliffs, NJ: Prentice-Hall, 1989.

Derrida, Jacques. *On Cosmopolitanism and Forgiveness.* London: Routledge, 2001.

Desmarais, Annette. "Organizing for Change: Peasant Women in Bolivia and Honduras." Research report prepared for the Canadian Bureau for Education, 1994.

—— "The Via Campesina: Consolidating an International Peasant and Farm Movement." *Journal of Peasant Studies* 29, no. 2 (January 2002): 91–124.

—— "The Via Campesina: Peasants Resisting Globalization." Ph.D. diss., University of Calgary, 2003.

Diamond, Norm. "Roquefort Rebellion." In *We Are Everywhere: The Irresistible Rise of Global Anticapitalism*, edited by Notes from Nowhere. London: Verso, 2003.

Dissent! Network. "Introduction to the Dissent! Network." Available from www.dissent.org.uk/content/view/62/52/. Internet. Accessed 28 June 2005.

Docena, Herbert. "How the US Got Its Neo-Liberal Way in Iraq." *Asia Times Online*, 1 September 2005.

"Documento di consenso sulla rete di resistenze redatto dai delegati dei sei blocchi di lavoro ed approvato dall'assemblea plenaria del II incontro intercontinentale per l'umanitá e contro il neoliberismo nel corso dell'atto conclusivo" (2 August 1997). Available from www.tmcrew.org/chiapas/docfin.htm. Internet. Accessed 28 November 2004.

Donnelly, Elizabeth A. "Proclaiming the Jubilee: The Debt and Structural Adjustment Network." UN Vision on Global Public Policy Networks, no. 24. Pdf file available from www.globalpublicpolicy.net. Internet. Accessed 15 July 2004.

Easterly, William. *The Elusive Quest for Growth: Economists' Adventures and Misadventures in the Tropics*, Cambridge, MA: MIT Press, 2002.

Economist. "Let's All Go to the Yard Sale." *Economist*, 25 September 2003.

Edelman, Marc. *Peasants Against Globalization: Rural Social Movements in Costa Rica.* Stanford, CA: Stanford University Press, 1999,

Edwards, Michael, and John Gaventa, eds. *Global Citizen Action.* Boulder, CO: Lynne Rienner, 2001.

Ejército Zapatista de Liberación Nacional. "Dignity Cannot be Studied; You Live It or It Dies." In *Our Word Is Our Weapon: Selected Writings, Subcomandante Marcos*, edited by Juana Ponce de Leon. London: Serpent's Tail, 2001.

—— "First Declaration from the Lacandon Jungle: EZLN's Declaration of War." Available from www.geocities.com/SamppaS/chiapas.html. Internet. Accessed 27 November 2004.

—— "Second Declaration of La Realidad (Reality) for Humanity against Neoliberalism" (3 August 1996). Available from www.afn.org/~iguana/archives/1997_02/19970209.html. Internet. Accessed 11 January 2006.

Emiliano [no last name given]. "We Will Not Go to the World 'Social' Forum! And We Are Not Alone!" (6 December 2000). Available from www.nadir.org/nadir/initiativ/agp/free/wsf/nowsf.htm. Internet. Accessed 25 November 2005.

Eschle, Catherine. "Constructing 'the Anti-Globalisation Movement'." In *Critical Theories, International Relations and 'the Anti-Globalisation Movement': The Politics of Global Resistance*, edited by Catherine Eschle and Bice Maiguashca. London: Routledge, 2005.

Eschle, Catherine, and Bice Maiguashca, eds. *Critical Theories, International Relations and 'the Anti-Globalisation Movement': The Politics of Global Resistance.* London: Routledge, 2005.

Eterovic, Ivana, and Jackie Smith. "From Altruism to a New Transnationalism? A Look at Transnational Social Movements." In *Political Altruism? Solidarity Movements in International Perspective*, edited by Marco Giugni and Florence Passy. Lanham, MD: Rowman & Littlefield, 2001.

Evans, Kate. "It's Got to Be Silver and Pink: On the Road with Tactical Frivolity." In *We Are Everywhere: The Irresistible Rise of Global Anticapitalism*, edited by Notes from Nowhere. London: Verso, 2003.

Falk, Richard. *Explorations at the End of Time: The Prospects for World Order.* Philadelphia, PA: Temple University Press, 1992.

——— *Predatory Globalization: A Critique.* Oxford: Blackwell, 1999.

Fals Borda, Orlando, and Muhammad Anisur Rahman, eds. *Action and Knowledge: Breaking the Monopoly with Participatory Action-Research.* New York: Apex, 1991.

Family Farm Defenders. "Welcome to Via Campesina! – The World's Largest Peasant Farmer Movement!" Available from www.familyfarmdefenders.org/whoweworkwith/viacampesina.html. Internet. Accessed 30 July 2004.

Fantasia, Rick. *Cultures of Solidarity: Consciousness, Action, and Contemporary American Workers.* Berkeley, CA: University of California Press, 1988.

Farmer, Paul. *Pathologies of Power: Health, Human Rights, and the New War on the Poor.* Berkeley, CA: University of California Press, 2003.

Farrer, Linden. "World Forum Movement: Abandon or Contaminate." Available from www.nadir.org/nadir/initiativ/agp/free/wsf/worldforum.htm#a25. Internet. Accessed 25 November 2005.

Fifty Years Is Enough. "About Us." Available from www.50years.org/index.html. Internet. Accessed 17 July 2004.

——— "The Network." Available from www.50years.org/index.html. Internet. Accessed 17 July 2004.

Finnemore, Martha. *National Interests in International Society.* Ithaca, NY and London: Cornell University Press, 1996.

Fisher, William F., and Thomas Ponniah, eds. *Another World Is Possible: Popular Alternatives to Globalization at the World Social Forum.* London: Zed Books, 2003.

Florini, Ann M., ed. *The Third Force: The Rise of Transnational Civil Society.* Washington, DC: Carnegie Endowment for International Peace, 2000.

Florini, Ann M., and P. J. Simmons. "What the World Needs Now?" In *The Third Force: The Rise of Transnational Civil Society,* edited by Ann M Florini. Washington, DC: Carnegie Endowment for International Peace, 2000.

Foundation for Deep Ecology. "Spinoff & Associated Organizations: International Forum on Globalization." Available from www.deepecology.org/ifg.html. Internet. Accessed 18 August 2004.

Fraser, Nancy. "Social Justice in the Age of Identity Politics: Redistribution, Recognition and Participation." The Tanner Lectures on Human Values, Stanford University, 30 April–2 May 1996. Pdf file available from www.tannerlectures.utah.edu/lectures/Fraser98.pdf. Internet. Accessed 7 May 2005.

——— *Adding Insult to Injury: Social Justice and the Politics of Recognition,* edited by Kevin Olson. London: Verso, 1999.

Fraser, Nancy, and Axel Honneth. *Redistribution or Recognition? A Political-Philosophical Exchange.* London: Verso, 2003.

Friedman, Thomas L. "Senseless in Seattle." *New York Times,* 1 December 1999.

——— *The Lexus and the Olive Tree: Understanding Globalization.* New York: Anchor Books, 2000.

Galdon, Gemma. "After Seattle and Cancun ... Next Stop: Hong Kong." *Znet* (8 March 2005). Available from www.ourworldisnotforsale.org/showarticle.asp?search=293. Internet. Accessed 26 April 2005.

Galtung, Johan. *Peace by Peaceful Means: Peace and Conflict, Development and Civilization.* Oslo: International Peace Research Institute and Sage Publications, 1996.

Gamson, William A. *The Strategy of Social Protest.* Homewood, IL: Dorsey, 1975.

George, Susan. *The Lugano Report.* London: Pluto, 1999.

Giddens, Anthony. *Central Problems in Social Theory: Action, Structure, and Contradiction in Social Analysis.* London: Macmillan, 1979.

——— *Critical Issues in Social Theory.* London: Macmillan, 1979.

——— *The Constitution of Society.* Cambridge: Polity Press, 1984.

——— *Runaway World: How Globalization Is Reshaping Our Lives.* London: Routledge, 2000.

Gill, Stephen. "Globalization, Market Civilization, and Disciplinary Neoliberalism." *Millennium: Journal of International Studies* 24, no. 3 (1995): 399–423.

—— *Power and Resistance in the New World Order.* New York: Palgrave Macmillan, 2003.

Gills, Barry, ed. *Globalization and the Politics of Resistance.* New York: St. Martin's Press, 2000.

Gilpin, Robert. *The Challenge of Global Capitalism: The World Economy in the 21st Century.* Princeton, NJ: Princeton University Press, 2002.

Giugni, Marco, and Florence Passy, eds. *Political Altruism? Solidarity Movements in International Perspective.* Lanham, MD: Rowman & Littlefield, 2001.

Glaser, Barney, and Anselm Strauss. *The Discovery of Grounded Theory.* Chicago, IL: Aldine, 1967.

Goffman, Erving. *Frame Analysis.* Cambridge, MA: Harvard University Press, 1974.

Graeber, David. "The New Anarchists." In *A Movement of Movements: Is Another World Really Possible?*, edited by Tom Mertes. London: Verso, 2004.

Greider, William. *One World, Ready or Not: The Manic Logic of Global Capitalism.* New York: Touchstone, 1998.

Gruffydd Jones, Branwen. "Globalisations, Violences and Resistances in Mozambique: The Struggles Continue." In *Critical Theories, International Relations and 'the Anti-Globalisation Movement': The Politics of Global Resistance,* edited by Catherine Eschle and Bice Maiguashca. New York: Routledge, 2005.

Guidry, John A., Michael D. Kennedy, and Mayer Zald. *Globalizations and Social Movements: Culture, Power, and the Transnational Sphere.* Ann Arbor, MI: The University of Michigan Press, 2000.

Guillén, Mauro F. "Is Globalization Civilizing, Destructive or Feeble? A Critique of Five Key Debates in the Social-Science Literature." *Annual Review of Sociology* 27 (2001): 235–60.

Guiraudon, Virginie. "Weak Weapons of the Weak? Transnational Mobilization around Migration in the European Union." In *Contentious Europeans: Protest and Politics in an Emerging Polity,* edited by Doug Imig and Sidney Tarrow. Lanham, MD: Rowman & Littlefield, 2001.

Gurr, Ted Robert. *Why Men Rebel.* Princeton, NJ: Princeton University Press, 1970.

—— *Rogues, Rebels, and Reformers: A Political History of Urban Crime and Conflict.* Beverly Hills, CA: Sage, 1976.

Habermas, Jürgen. *The Postnational Constellation: Political Essays.* Cambridge, MA: MIT Press, 2001.

Hamel, Pierre, Henri Lustiger-Thaler, Jan Nederveen Pieterse, and Sasha Roseneil. *Globalization and Social Movements.* Houndmills: Macmillan, 2001.

Hanh, Thich Nhat. *Being Peace.* Berkeley, CA: Parallax Press, 1996.

Hann, Chris, and Elizabeth Dunn, eds. *Civil Society, Challenging Western Models.* London: Routledge, 1996.

Hardt, Michael. "Today's Bandung?" In *A Movement of Movements: Is Another World Really Possible?*, edited by Tom Mertes. London: Verso, 2004.

Hardt, Michael, and Antonio Negri. *Empire.* Cambridge, MA: Harvard University Press, 2000.

—— *Multitude: War and Democracy in the Age of Empire.* New York: Penguin Putnam, 2004.

Harvey, David. *Limits to Capital.* London: Verso, 1999.

Held, David, and Anthony McGrew, eds. *The Global Transformations Reader: An Introduction to the Globalization Debate.* Cambridge: Polity Press, 2000.

Held, David, Anthony G. McGrew, David Goldblatt, and Jonathan Perraton. *Global Transformations: Politics, Economics and Culture.* Stanford, CA: Stanford University Press, 1999.

Hellman, Judith Adler. "Real and Virtual Chiapas: Realism and the Left." In *Socialist Register,* edited by Leo Panitch and Colin Leys. London: Merlin Press, 1999: 166–74.

Higgins, Nick. "Lessons from the Indigenous: Zapatista Poetics and a Cultural Humanism for the Twenty-First Century." In *Critical Theories, International Relations and 'the Anti-*

Globalisation Movement': The Politics of Resistance, edited by Catherine Eschle and Bice Maiguashca. London: Routledge, 2005.

Hines, Colin. *Localization: A Global Manifesto.* London: Earthscan, 2000.

Hirsh, Eric L. "Sacrifice for the Cause: Group Processes, Recruitment, and Commitment in a Student Social Movement." *American Sociological Review* 55 (1990): 243–55.

Hollis, Martin, and Steve Smith. *Explaining and Understanding International Relations.* Oxford: Clarendon Press, 1991.

Holloway, John. *Change the World without Taking Power: The Meaning of Revolution Today.* London: Pluto, 2002.

Holmes, Brian. "Touching the Violence of the State." In *We Are Everywhere: The Irresistible Rise of Global Anticapitalism*, edited by Notes from Nowhere. London: Verso, 2003.

Houtart, François, and François Poulet, eds. *The Other Davos.* London: Zed Books, 2001.

Hovey, Michael W. "Interceding at the United Nations: The Human Right of Conscientious Objection." In *Transnational Social Movements and Global Politics: Solidarity Beyond the State*, edited by Jackie Smith, Charles Chatfield, and Ron Pagnucco. Syracuse, NY: Syracuse University Press, 1997.

Hub Project. "Summary from Final Plenary of the Hub, Firenze" (10 November 2002). Available from www.nadir.org/nadir/initiativ/agp/space/finalplenary.htm. Internet. Accessed 25 November 2005.

Hurrell, Andrew, and Ngaire Woods. "Globalisation and Inequality." *Millennium* 24, no. 3 (1995): 447–70.

Hutjes, Marita. "There Is a Real Chance that We Can Win in Cancun and Stop the WTO Negotiations." *Novib Network*, no. 2 (April 2003). Available from www.novib.nl/en/content/?type=article&id=4011&bck=y. Internet. Accessed 20 April 2005.

IMCista. "Bono and Geldof Praise G8 Deal." *indymedia UK* (9 July 2005). Available from www.indymedia.org.uk/en/2005/07/317651.html. Internet. Accessed 2 November 2005.

"In Their Own Words: How Campaigners Responded to the G8 Communique." Comments posted on *Red Pepper*, "Make the G8 History," weblog. Available from http://redpepper.blogs.com/g8/2005/07/in_their_own_wo.html. Internet. Accessed 2 November 2005.

indymedia. "Declaration in Support of the Indymedia Network and against the Seizure of Its Servers." Available from http://solidarity.indymedia.org.uk. Internet. Accessed 4 December 2004.

Infoshop. "Black Blocs for Dummies: Frequently Asked Questions." 31 January 2004. Available from www.infoshop.org/blackbloc.html. Internet. Accessed 30 November 2005.

Interfaith Working Group on Trade and Investment. "Religious Organizations Oppose CAFTA." Press Release, 20 April 2005. Pdf file available from www.citizenstrade.org/ Internet. Accessed 27 April 2005.

International Forum on Globalization. *Alternatives to Economic Globalization: A Better World Is Possible.* San Francisco, CA: Berrett-Koehler, 2002.

—— "Recent Events." Available from www.ifg.org/events/recent.htm. Internet. Accessed 18 August 2004; and 4 May 2005.

Irwin, Douglas A. *Free Trade Under Fire.* Princeton, NJ: Princeton University Press, 2003.

Johnson, R. J., Peter J. Taylor, and Michael J. Watts. *Geographies of Global Change: Remapping the World in the Late Twentieth Century.* Oxford: Blackwell, 1995.

Johnston, Hank, and Bert Klandermans, eds. *Social Movements and Culture.* Minneapolis, MN: University of Minnesota Press, 1995.

Jordan, Tim. *Activism! Direct Action, Hactivism and the Future of Society.* London: Reaktion Books, 2002.

Jubilee 2000 UK. "Jubilee Research: Analysis: How It Was Achieved: Humble Beginnings." Available from www.jubilee2000uk.org/analysis/repors/world_never_same_again/how.htm. Internet. Accessed 18 July 2004.

Jubilee Research. "UK Chancellor Pledges L100 million for Multilateral Debt Cancellation: But Can We Really Cheer Twice?" (10 January 2004). Available from www.jubilee2000uk.org/. Internet. Accessed 23 November 2004.

—— "Debt Relief by Country for the 42 HIPCS (in Nominal Terms)" (11 February 2004). Available from www.jubilee2000uk.org/. Internet. Accessed 18 April 2005.

—— "Total Debt Relief Received by 42 HIPC Countries (in Nominal Terms)." Available from www.jubilee2000uk.org/. Internet. Accessed 18 April 2005.

—— "What is the HIPC Initiative?" Available from www.jubilee2000uk.org/. Internet. Accessed 20 April 2005.

Jubilee South. "Asia-Pacific Meeting Takes Hard Look at Impact of US War on Afghanistan" (20 October 2001). Available from www.jubileesouth.org/news/EpEyZpkZFFMRXJYWqT.shtml. Internet. Accessed 5 January 2005.

—— "International Peoples' Tribunal on the Debt – Organization" (3 February 2001). Available from www.jubileesouth.org/news/EpklpAZFEAPFfQzOvg.shtml. Internet. Accessed 5 January 2005.

—— "Reparations toward Another World" (30 August 2001). Available from www.jubileesouth.org/news/EpklpEVAykoOBaDAFI.shtml. Internet. Accessed 5 January 2005.

—— "People's Tribunal Declares External Debt Illegitimate, Calls for the Decommissioning of IMF–World Bank" (18 April 2002). Available from www.jubileesouth.org/news/EpFVuVEFAZipHZbVcW.shtml. Internet. Accessed 5 January 2005.

—— "Jubilee South Pursues Campaign vs. Illegitimacy of Debt in World Social Forum III" (29 March 2003). Available from www.jubileesouth.org/news/EpuAEApEyZYMeAjLO.shtml. Internet. Accessed 5 January 2005.

Juris, Jeff. "The London ESF and the Politics of Autonomous Space." *Znet* (2 November 2004). Available from www.zmag.org/content/showarticle.cfm?SectionID=41&ItemID=6552. Internet. Accessed 7 January 2006.

Keane, John. *Global Civil Society?* Cambridge: Cambridge University Press, 2003.

Keck, Margaret E., and Kathryn Sikkink. *Activists Beyond Borders: Advocacy Networks in International Politics*. Ithaca, NY: Cornell University Press, 1998.

Kemmis, Stephen, and Robin McTaggart. "Participatory Action Research." In *Handbook of Qualitative Research*, edited by Norman K. Denzin and Yvonna S. Lincoln. 2nd edn. London: Sage, 2000.

Khagram, Sanjeev, James V. Riker, and Kathryn Sikkink, eds. *Restructuring World Politics: Transnational Social Movements, Networks, and Norms*. Minneapolis, MN: University of Minnesota Press, 2002.

Khor, Martin. "Commentary." In *South–North: Citizen Strategies to Transform a Divided World*, edited by John Cavanagh. San Francisco, CA: International Forum on Globalization, November 1995.

—— "The Hypocrisy of the North in the WTO." In *Alternatives to Economic Globalization: A Better World Is Possible*, edited by International Forum on Globalization. San Francisco, CA: Berrett-Koehler Publishers, 2002.

Kimbrell, Andrew. *The Human Body Shop: The Engineering and Marketing of Life*. San Francisco, CA: Harper San Francisco, 1993.

Kinsman, John. "John Kinsman's Via Campesina Presentation to the 4th Congress of the National Agricultural Confederation (CAN) in Coimbra, Portugal" (9 March 2003). Available from www.familyfarmdefenders.org/whatwere%20doing/johnkinsman.html. Internet. Accessed 30 July 2004.

Klandermans, Bert, and Jackie Smith. "Survey Research: A Case for Comparative Designs." In *Methods of Social Movement Research*, edited by Bert Klandermans and Suzanne Staggenborg. Minneapolis, MN: University of Minnesota Press, 2002.

Klein, Naomi. "More Democracy – Not More Political Strongmen." *Guardian*, 3 February 2003.

—— "Reclaiming the Commons." In *A Movement of Movements: Is Another World Really Possible?*, edited by Tom Mertes. London: Verso, 2004.

Korean People's Action against the FTA and WTO. "We Propose an 'Asian Peoples and Social Movements Assembly against War and Neoliberal Globalization' to Take Place During World Social Forum 2005" (6 January 2005). Available from www.ourworldis-notforsale.org/showarticle.asp?search=119. Internet. Accessed 16 November 2005.

Kornhauser, William. *The Politics of Mass Society.* New York: Free Press, 1959.

Korten, David C., *When Corporations Rule the World.* San Francisco, CA: Berrett-Koehler Publishers, 2001.

Kuczynski, Pedro-Pablo and John Williamson, eds. *After the Washington Consensus: Restarting Growth and Reform in Latin America.* Washington, DC: Institute for International Economics, 2003.

Kurasawa, Fuyuki. "A Cosmopolitanism from Below: Alternative Globalization and the Creation of a Solidarity Without Bounds." *European Journal of Sociology* 42, no. 2 (2004): 233–56.

—— "The Culture of Alternative Globalization and the Creation of Cosmopolitan Solidarity." Paper presented at the 45th Annual Convention of the International Studies Association, Montreal, Canada, 17–20 March 2004.

Kuruvilla, Benny. "Farmers and Other Civil Society Groups Give a Wake Up Call to the G-20 – But Are They Listening?" (9 April 2005). Available from www.ourworldisnot-forsale.org/showarticle.asp?search=169. Internet. Accessed 27 April 2005.

Lasn, Kalle. *Culture Jam: How to Reverse America's Suicidal Consumer Binge – And Why We Must.* New York: Quill, 2000.

Le Bot, Yvon. *Submcomandante Marcos: El Sueño Zapatista.* Barcelona: Plaza y Janes Editores, 1997.

Lechner, Frank J., and John Boli. *The Globalization Reader.* Oxford: Blackwell, 2000.

Lichbach, Mark Irving. "Social Theory and Comparative Politics." In *Comparative Politics*, edited by Mark Irving Lichbach and Alan S. Zuckerman. Cambridge: Cambridge University Press, 1997.

Lichterman, Paul. "Seeing Structure Happen: Theory-Driven Participant Observation." In *Methods of Social Movement Research*, edited by Bert Klandermans and Suzanne Staggenborg. Minneapolis, MN: University of Minnesota Press, 2002.

Lindsey, Brink. *Against the Dead Hand: The Uncertain Struggle for Global Capitalism.* Hoboken, NJ: Wiley Publishers, 2001.

Lipschutz, Ronnie. "Restructuring World Politics: The Emergence of Global Civil Society." *Millennium* 21, no. 3 (1992): 389–420.

Live8. "The Concerts." Available from www.live8live.com/theconcerts/index.shtml. Internet. Accessed 2 November 2005.

—— "The Long Walk to Justice." Available from www.live8live.com/whattodo/index.shtml. Internet. Accessed 2 November 2005.

Loflund, John. "Becoming a World-Saver Revisited." In *Conversion Careers*, edited by James Richardson. London: Sage, 1978.

Lofland, John, and Lyn H. Lofland. *Analyzing Social Settings: A Guide to Qualitative Observation and Analysis.* 3rd edn. Belmont, CA: Wadsworth, 1991.

McAdam, Doug. *Freedom Summer.* New York: Oxford University Press, 1988.

McAdam, Doug, John D. McCarthy, and Mayer N. Zald. "Social Movements." In *Handbook of Sociology*, edited by Neil J. Smelser. Newbury Park, CA: Sage, 1988.

McAdam, Doug, Sidney Tarrow, and Charles Tilly. *Dynamics of Contention.* Cambridge: Cambridge University Press, 2001.

McCarthy, John D. "The Globalization of Social Movement Theory." In *Transnational Social Movements and Global Politics*, edited by Jackie Smith, Charles Chatfield, and Ron Pagnucco. Syracuse, NY: Syracuse University Press, 1997.

McCarthy, John D., and Mayer N. Zald. "Resource Mobilization and Social Movements: A Partial Theory." *American Journal of Sociology* 82 (1977): 1212–41.

—— *The Trend of Social Movements in America: Professionalization and Resource Mobilization.* Morristown, NJ: General Learning Press, 1973.

Machalek, Richard, and David S. Snow. "Conversion to New Religious Movements." In *Religion and the Social Order: The Handbook on Cults and Sects in America*, vol. 3B. Greenwich, CT: JAI Press, 1993.

McTaggart, Robin, ed. *Participatory Action Research: International Contexts and Consequences*. Albany, NY: SUNY Press, 1997.

Maiguashca, Bice. "Globalisation and the 'Politics of Identity': IR Theory through the Looking Glass of Women's Reproductive Rights Activism." In *Critical Theories, International Relations and 'the Anti-Globalisation Movement': The Politics of Global Resistance*, edited by Catherine Eschle and Bice Maiguashca. London: Routledge, 2005.

Mander, Gerry, and Edward Goldsmith, eds. *The Case against the Global Economy*. San Francisco, CA: Sierra Club, 1996.

Manji, Firoze. Comment posted on *Red Pepper*, "Make the G8 History," weblog (13 July 2005). Available from www.redpepper.blogs.com/g8/2005/07/in_their_own_wo.html. Internet. Accessed 2 November 2005.

Mann, Michael. *Incoherent Empire*. London and New York: Verso, 2003.

Marx, Karl. *The Civil Wars in France*. New York: International Publishers, 1935.

—— "The Class Struggles in France." In *Selected Works*, by Karl Marx and Frederick Engels. Moscow: Foreign Languages, 1958.

Melucci, Alberto. *Challenging Codes: Collective Action in the Information Age*. Cambridge: Cambridge University Press, 1996.

Meyer, David S. *A Winter of Discontent: The Nuclear Freeze and American Politics*. New York: Praeger, 1990.

Mies, Maria. "Feminist Research: Science, Violence and Responsibility." In *Ecofeminism*, by Maria Mies and Vandana Shiva. London: Zed Books, 1993.

Migdal, Joel. *Strong States and Weak Societies: State–Society Relations and State Capabilities in the Third World*. Princeton, NJ: Princeton University Press, 1988.

Mittelman, James H. *Globalization Syndrome: Transformation and Resistance*. Princeton, NJ: Princeton University Press, 2000.

—— "Globalization: An Ascendant Paradigm?" *International Studies Perspectives* 3, no. 2 (2002): 1–14.

—— *Whither Globalization? The Vortex of Knowledge and Ideology*. London: Routledge, 2004.

—— "What Is a Critical Globalization Studies?" In *Critical Globalization Studies*, edited by Richard P. Appelbaum and William I. Robinson. London: Routledge, 2005.

Monbiot, George. *In the Age of Consent: A Manifesto for a New World Order*. New York: HarperCollins, 2004.

Monnens, Bart. "Novib at the World Social Forum." *Novib Network*, no. 1 (2005). Available from www.novib.nl/content/?type=Article&id=6532&FromList=y. Internet. Accessed 20 April 2005.

Morris, Aldon D. *The Origins of the Civil Rights Movement: Black Communities Organizing for Change*. New York: Free Press, 1984.

Murphy, Craig N., ed. *Egalitarian Politics in the Age of Globalization*. New York: Palgrave, 2002.

Nader, Ralph, *et al*. *The Case against Free Trade: GATT, NAFTA, and the Globalization of Corporate Power*. San Francisco, CA: Earth Island Press, 1993.

Nanjundaswamy, Professor, President of Karnataka State Farmers' Association. "Cremating Monsanto: Genetically Modified Fields on Fire." In *We Are Everywhere: The Irresistible Rise of Global Anticapitalism*, edited by Notes from Nowhere. London: Verso, 2003.

Nigam, Aditya. "The Old Left in a New World: The Mumbai 'Resistance'?" *indymedia India* (18 January 2004). Available from www.india.indymedia.org/en/2004/01/208739.shtml. Internet. Accessed 25 November 2005.

Njehu, Njoki. "Cancel the Debt." In *A Movement of Movements: Is Another World Really Possible?*, edited by Tom Mertes. London: Verso, 2004.

Norberg, Johan. *In Defense of Globalization*. Washington, DC: Cato Institute, 2003.

Notes from Nowhere, eds. *We Are Everywhere: The Irresistible Rise of Global Anticapitalism*. London: Verso, 2003.

Novib. "Novib Annual Report for 2002." *Novib Network*, no. 4 (July 2003). Available from www.novib.nl/en/content/?type=article&id=4594&bck=y. Internet. Accessed 20 April 2005.

—— "What We Are Seeing Here Is the Globalisation of Civil Society." *Novib Network*, no. 2 (April 2003). Available from www.novib.nl/en/content/?type=article&id=4012& bck=y. Internet. Accessed 22 April 2005.

O'Brien, Robert, Anne Marie Goetz, Jan Aart Scholte, and Marc Williams. *Contesting Global Governance: Multilateral Economic Institutions and Global Social Movements.* Cambridge: Cambridge University Press, 2000.

O'Neill, Kate. "Transnational Protest: States, Circuses, and Conflict at the Frontline of Global Politics." *International Studies Review* 6, no. 2 (June 2004): 233–51.

Oakes, Guy. "The Verstehen Thesis and the Foundation of Max Weber's Methodology." *History and Theory* 16 (1977): 11–29.

Olesen, Thomas. *International Zapatismo: The Construction of Solidarity in the Age of Globalization.* London: Zed Books, 2005.

Olesen, Thomas, and James N. Rosenau. "The Reduction of Distance and the Construction of Proximity: Solidarity Movements and Globalization." Paper presented at the annual meeting of the International Studies Association, Honolulu, 1–5 March 2005.

Olson, Karen, and Linda Shopes. "Crossing Boundaries, Building Bridges: Doing Oral History among Working-Class Women and Men." In *Women's Words: The Feminist Practice of Oral History*, edited by Shurna B. Gluck and Daphne Patai. London: Routledge, 1991.

Olson, Mancur. *The Logic of Collective Action.* New York: Schocken, 1968.

"One Reaction to G8 Summit Communique" (8 July 2005). Available from www.releases. usnewswire.com/GetRelease.asp?id=50100. Internet. Accessed 2 November 2005.

Onuf, Nicolas. "Constructivism: A User's Manual." In *International Relations in a Constructed World*, edited by Vendulka Kubálková, Nicholas Onuf, and Paul Kowert. Armonk, NY: M. E. Sharpe, 1998.

Open Democracy. "A luta continua." Available from www.opendemocracy.typepad.com/ wsf/2005/01/neither_bang_no.html. Internet. Accessed 22 November 2005.

Our World Is Not for Sale. "About Us." Available from www.ourworldisnotforsale.org/ about.asp. Internet. Accessed 20 August 2004.

—— "New Updates." Available from www.ourworldisnotforsale.org/agri/NewsUpdates/ 26.htm. Internet. Accessed 20 August 2004.

—— "September 13: Worldwide Day of Action against Corporate Globalization and War." Available from www.ourworldisnotforsale.org/cancun/WTO/cancun/03.htm. Internet. Accessed 20 August 2004.

—— "Cancun Planning Meeting." Available from www.ourworldisnotforsale.org/articles. asp?cat=action&id=62. Internet. Accessed 5 January 2005.

Oxfam. "Post-G8 Analysis: Steps in the Right Direction." Available from www.oxfam. org.uk/what_you_can_do/campaign/mph/g8/index.htm. Internet. Accessed 2 November 2005.

—— "Press Release: Celebrities at World Social Forum Publicly Support Global Call to Action against Poverty" (29 January 2005). Available from www.oxfam.org/eng/ pr050129_wsf.htm. Internet. Accessed 18 April 2005.

—— "Press Release: Oxfam at the World Social Forum: World Leaders Must Act to Make a Breakthrough on Poverty in 2005" (25 January 2005). Available from www.oxfam.org/eng/pr050125_wsf_brazil.htm. Internet. Accessed 18 April 2005.

—— "World Social Forum (WSF) 2004." Available from www.oxfam.org/eng/ event_wsf04.htm. Internet. Accessed 20 April 2005.

Passy, Florence. "Political Altruism and the Solidarity Movement: An Introduction." In *Political Altruism? Solidarity Movements in International Perspective*, edited by Marco Giugni and Florence Passy. Lanham, MD: Rowman & Littlefield, 2001.

Patomäki, Heikki, and Teivo Teivainen. *A Possible World: Democratic Transformation of Global Institutions.* London: Zed Books, 2004.

—— "The World Social Forum: An Open Space or a Movement of Movements?" *Theory, Culture and Society* 21, no. 6 (2004): 145–54.

Paulson, Justin. "Peasant Struggles and International Solidarity: The Case of Chiapas." Available from www.yorku.ca/socreg/paulson01.html. Internet. Accessed 28 November 2004.

Peoples' Food Sovereignty Network. "Groups Offer Alternative to WTO's Trade Liberalisation Policies: Plan Needed to Protect People's Food Sovereignty." Sign-on Statement. Available from www.focusweb.org/trade/html/Article241.html. Internet. Accessed 5 June 2005.

Peoples' Global Action. "3. Plans of Action." *PGA Bulletin* 1 (March 1997). Available from www.nadir.org/nadir/initiativ/agp/en/pgainfos/bulletin1.html#1. Internet. Accessed 28 November 2004.

—— "Global Days of Action against 'Free' Trade and the WTO – May 1998." *Bulletin* 2 (June 1998). Available from www.nadir.org/nadir/initiativ/agp/en/pgainfos/bulletin2/bulletin2b.html. Internet. Accessed 28 November 2004.

—— "Letter from the Geneva Welcoming Committee." *PGA Bulletin* 1 (March 1997). Available from www.nadir.org/nadir/initiativ/agp/en/pgainfos/bulletin1.html#1. Internet. Accessed 28 November 2004.

—— "A Call for Global Action in Europe." Available from www.nadir.org/nadir/initiativ/agp/en/pgainfos/pga-call.htm. Internet. Accessed 28 November 2004.

—— "Days of Global Action against Capitalism." Available from www.nadir.org/nadir/initiativ/agp/free/global/index.htm. Internet. Accessed 4 December 2004.

—— "Peoples' Global Action Manifesto." Available from www.nadir.org/nadir/initiativ/agp/en/pgainfos/manifest.htm. Internet. Accessed 3 December 2004.

—— "PGA Europe Infopoint Contact List." Available from www.nadir.org/nadir/initiativ/agp/pgaeurope/infopoints.htm. Internet. Accessed 28 November 2004.

—— "Report from Peoples' Global Action Meeting in Bombay" (29 January 2004). Available from www.indybay.org/news/2004/01/1669069.php. Internet. Accessed 1 September 2005.

—— "Resist the G8//Global Action Callout//Wednesday July 6th 2005." Available from www.nadir.org/nadir/initiativ/agp/resistg8/index.htm. Internet. Accessed 28 June 2005.

Peterson, V. Spike. *A Critical Rewriting of Global Political Economy: Integrating Reproductive, Productive and Virtual Economies.* London: Routledge, 2003.

Petras, James, and Henry Veltmeyer. *Globalization Unmasked: Imperialism in the 21st Century.* Halifax and New York: Fernwood Publishing and Zed Books, 2001.

Pettifor, Ann. "Chapter 9/11? Resolving International Debt Crises – the Jubilee Framework for International Insolvency." London: New Economics Foundation. A report from Jubilee Research, February 2002. Available at www.jubilee2000uk.org/. Internet. Accessed 18 April 2005.

—— "Meeting Series: Does Evidence Matter?" Transcription of a talk given at the Overseas Development Institute, 11 June 2003. Available from www.odi.org.uk/RAPID/Meetings/Evidence/Presentation_15/Pettifor.html. Internet. Accessed 18 July 2004.

—— "The Jubilee 2000 Campaign." Presentation at SEDOS. Available from www.sedos.org/english/pettifor.htm. Internet. Accessed 17 July 2004.

—— "The World Will Never Be the Same Again ... Because of Jubilee 2000." Available from www.jubilee2000uk.org. Internet. Accessed 18 July 2004.

Pettman, Ralph. "Anti-Globalisation Discourses in Asia." In *Critical Theories, International Relations and 'the Anti-Globalisation Movement': The Politics of Global Resistance,* edited by Catherine Eschle and Bice Maiguashca. London: Routledge, 2005.

Pianta, Mario. *Globalizzazione del basso: Economia mondiale e movimenti sociali.* Rome: Manifestolibri, 2001.

—— "Parallel Summits of Global Civil Society." In *Global Civil Society 2001*, edited by Helmut Anheier, Marlies Glasius, and Mary Kaldor. Oxford: Oxford University Press, 2001.

—— "I controvertici e gli eventi delle societa civile globale." In *Capire i movimenti globali: Da Porto Alegre al Forum Sociale Europeo*, edited by Lunaria. Trieste: Asterios, 2002.

—— "Parallel Summits of Global Civil Society: An Update." Available from www.globalpolicy.org/ngos/role/conf.htm. Internet. Accessed 21 May 2004.

Piven, Francis Fox, and Richard A. Cloward. *Poor People's Movements: Why They Succeed, How They Fail*. New York: Pantheon Books, 1979.

Ponniah, Thomas, and William F. Fisher. "Introduction: The World Social Forum and the Reinvention of Democracy." In *Another World Is Possible: Popular Alternatives to Globalization at the World Social Forum*, edited by William F. Fisher and Thomas Ponniah. London: Zed Books, 2003.

Posey, Darrell Addison, ed. *Cultural and Spiritual Values of Biodiversity*. London: Intermediate Technology Publications, 1999.

Pruzin, Daniel. "Canada to Host WTO Senior Officials 'Mini-Ministerial' in Geneva April 18–19." *International Trade Daily*, 18 March 2005. Available from www.ourworldisnotforsale.org/showarticle.asp?search=611. Internet. Accessed 27 April 2005.

Raghavan, Chakravarthi. "Lamy Candidacy Will Polarise WTO, May Endanger Trading System Itself" (8 December 2004). Available from www.twnside.org.sg/title2/5705a.htm. Internet. Accessed 27 April 2005.

Raja, Kanaga. "North Tactics to Split Developing-Country Alliances Exposed." Available from www.twnside.org.sg/title2/5623c.htm. Internet. Accessed 27 April 2005.

Reitan, Ruth. "Human Rights in U.S. Policy: A Casualty of the 'War on Terrorism'?" *International Journal of Human Rights* 7, no. 4 (2003): 51–62.

Rhythms of Resistance. "Why We Do It." Available from www.rhythmsofresistance.co.uk/?lid=52. Internet. Accessed 30 November 2005.

Risse, Thomas, Stephen C. Ropp, and Kathryn Sikkink, eds. *The Power of Human Rights, International Norms and Domestic Change*. Cambridge: Cambridge University Press, 1999.

Robertson, Roland. *Globalization: Social Theory and Global Culture*. Newbury Park, CA: Sage, 1992.

—— "Glocalization: Time–Space and Homogeneity–Heterogeneity." In *Global Modernities*, edited by Mike Featherstone, Scott M. Lash, and Roland Robertson. London: Sage, 1996.

Robinson, William I. "What Is a Critical Globalization Studies? Intellectual Labor and Global Society." In *Critical Globalization Studies*, edited by Richard P. Appelbaum and William I. Robinson. London: Routledge, 2005.

Rochon, Thomas R. *Mobilizing for Peace: The Antinuclear Movements in Western Europe*. Princeton, NJ: Princeton University Press, 1988.

Rodrik, Dani. *Has Globalization Gone Too Far?* Washington, DC: Institute for International Economics, 1997.

—— *The New Global Economy and Developing Countries: Making Openness Work*. Washington, DC: Overseas Development Council, 1998.

Rosen, Fred. "Report on Global Finance: Doing Battle Against the Debt." *NACLA Report on the Americas* 33, no. 1 (July–August 1999): 42–5.

Ross, John. *The War against Oblivion: The Zapatista Chronicles 1994–2000*. Monroe, Maine: Common Courage Press, 2000.

Roy, Arundhati. "Come September." In *War Talk*. Cambridge, MA: South End Press, 2003.

Rubin, Herbert J., and Irene S. Rubin. *Qualitative Interviewing: The Art of Hearing Data*. London: Sage, 1995.

Rucht, Dieter. "Distant Issue Movements in Germany: Empirical Description and Theoretical Reflections." In *Globalizations and Social Movements: Culture, Power, and the Transnational Public Sphere*, edited by John A. Guidry, Michael D. Kennedy, and Mayer N. Zald. Ann Arbor, MI: University of Michigan, 2000.

Rupert, Mark. *Ideologies of Globalization: Contending Visions of a New World Order.* London: Routledge, 2000.

Sachs, Jeffrey. *The End of Poverty: Economic Possibilities for Our Time.* New York: Penguin Books, 2005.

St. Clair, Jeffrey. "Jeffrey St. Clair's Seattle Diary: It's a Gas, Gas Gas." In *5 Days that Shook the World: Seattle and Beyond,* edited by Alexander Cockburn, Jeffrey St. Clair, and Allan Sekula. London: Verso, 2000.

Sassen, Saskia. *Globalization and Its Discontents.* New York: New Press, 1998.

Scholte, Jan Aart. *Globalization: A Critical Introduction.* New York: St. Martin's Press, 2000.

"Second American Encounter Against Neoliberalism and for Humanity." Available from www.eco.utexas.edu/faculty/Cleaver/2ndencounteren.html. Internet. Accessed 28 November 2004.

Sen, Amartya. *Development as Freedom.* New York: Anchor Books, 2000.

Sen, Jai, Anita Anand, Arturo Escobar, and Peter Waterman, eds. *World Social Forum: Challenging Empires.* New Delhi: Viveka Foundation, 2004.

Shiva, Vandana. *Biopiracy: The Plunder of Nature and Knowledge.* Boston: South End Press, 1997.

—— "Wars against Nature and the People of the South." In *Views from the South: The Effects of Globalization and the WTO on the Third World,* edited by Sarah Anderson. Oakland, CA: Food First Books and International Forum on Globalization, 2000.

—— *Protest or Plunder? Understanding Intellectual Property Rights.* London: Zed Books, 2001.

—— "From Commons to Corporate Patents on Life." In *Alternatives to Economic Globalization: A Better World Is Possible,* edited by International Forum on Globalization. San Francisco, CA: Berrett-Koehler Publishers, 2002.

Shumway, Christopher A. "Participatory Media Networks: A New Model for Producing and Disseminating Progressive News and Information" (21 May 2002). Available from www.reclaimthemedia.org/stories.php?story=02/05/21/6042306. Internet. Accessed 9 July 2004.

Sibaja, Marco. "Brazilian Farmers Storm Monsanto, Uproot Plants" (26 January 2005). Available from www.njpcgreens.org/brasil.html. Internet. Accessed 25 November 2005.

Sikkink, Kathryn. "Restructuring World Politics: The Limits and Asymmetries of Soft Power." In *Restructuring World Politics: Transnational Social Movements, Networks, and Norms,* edited by Sanjeev Khagram, James V. Riker, and Kathryn Sikkink. Minneapolis, MN: University of Minnesota Press, 2002.

Sisic, Aldijana, regional campaign coordinator for Europe and Central Asia, Amnesty International. "Author's notes." Workshop entitled "The Role of Youth Activism in Creating Change," European Social Forum, St. Denis, France, 13 November 2003.

Sklair, Leslie. *Sociology of the Global System.* Baltimore, MD: Johns Hopkins University Press, 1995.

—— *Capitalism and Its Alternatives.* Oxford: Oxford University Press, 2002.

Smelser, Neil. *Theory of Collective Behavior.* New York: Free Press, 1962.

Smith, Jackie. "Characteristics of the Modern Transnational Social Movement Sector." In *Transnational Social Movements and Global Politics,* edited by Jackie Smith, Charles Chatfield, and Ron Pagnucco. Syracuse, NY: Syracuse University Press, 1997.

Smith, Jackie, and Hank Johnston, eds. *Globalization and Resistance: Transnational Dimensions of Social Movements.* Lanham, MD: Rowman & Littlefield, 2002.

Smith, Jackie, Charles Chatfield, and Ron Pagnucco, eds. *Transnational Social Movements and Global Politics: Solidarity Beyond the State.* Syracuse, NY: Syracuse University Press, 1997.

Smith, Neil. *The End Game of Globalization.* London: Routledge, 2005.

Smith, Steve. "Singing Our World into Existence: International Relations Theory and September 11." *International Studies Quarterly* 48, no. 3 (2004): 499–515.

Snow, David A., and Robert D. Benford. "Master Frames and Cycles of Protest." In *Frontiers in Social Movement Theory,* edited by Aldon Morris and Carol M. Mueller. New Haven, CT: Yale University Press, 1992.

Snow, David A., and Richard Machalek. "The Convert as a Social Type." *Sociological Theory* 1 (1983): 259–89.

—— "The Sociology of Conversion." In *Annual Review of Sociology*, edited by Ralph H. Turner and James F. Short. Palo Alto, CA: Annual Reviews Inc., 1983.

Snow, David A., E. Burke Rochford, Steven K. Worden, and Robert D. Benford. "Frame Alignment Processes, Micromobilization, and Movement Participation." *American Sociological Review* 51 (1986): 464–81.

Social Movements Assembly. "Call from Social Movements for Mobilizations against the War, Neoliberalism and Exclusion: Another World is Possible" (31 January 2005). Available from www.movsoc.org/htm/call_2005_english.htm. Internet. Accessed 19 November 2005.

Social Movements International Secretariat. "Porto Alegre Call for Mobilization" (2001). Available from www.movsoc.org/htm/call_2001_english.htm. Internet. Accessed 21 November 2005.

Soros, George. *The Crisis of Global Capitalism.* New York: Public Affairs Books, 1998.

Squat!net. "Brief Description of Indian Movements Participating in the ICC." Available from www.squat.net/caravan/ICC-en/movements.htm. Internet. Accessed 6 January 2005.

Staggenborg, Suzanne. *The Pro-Choice Movement.* New York: Oxford University Press, 1991.

Starr, Amory. *Naming the Enemy: Anti-Corporate Movements Confront Globalization.* London and New York: Zed Books, 2000.

Stedile, João Pedro. "Brazil's Landless Battalions: The Sem Terra Movement." In *A Movement of Movements: Is Another World Really Possible?*, edited by Tom Mertes. London: Verso, 2004.

Stiglitz, Joseph E. *Globalization and Its Discontents.* New York: W. W. Norton, 2002.

Strange, Susan. *Mad Money: When Markets Outgrow Governments.* Ann Arbor, MI: University of Michigan Press, 1998.

Strauss, Anselm, and Juliet Corbin. *Basics of Qualitative Research.* Newbury Park, CA: Sage, 1991.

Structural Adjustment Participatory Review Initiative Network. "From Engagement to Protest: A Public Forum on Citizens' Challenges to the World Bank." Public forum and discussion. Author's notes. Rosslyn, Va., 18–19 April 2002.

—— "The Policy Roots of Economic Crisis and Poverty: A Multi-Country Participatory Assessment of Structural Adjustment." Washington, DC: SAPRIN, April 2002. Pdf available from www.saprin.org/SAPRI_Findings.pdf. Internet. Accessed 11 January 2006.

Subcomandante Marcos. *Our Word Is Our Weapon: Selected Writings.* New York: Seven Stories Press, 2002.

—— *Ya Basta! Ten Years of the Zapatista Uprising.* Oakland, CA: AK Press, 2004.

Sullivan, Sian. "'We Are Heartbroken and Furious!' (#2): Violence and the (Anti-)Globalisation Movement(s)." University of Warwick: Centre for the Study of Globalisation and Regionalisation, Working Paper No. 133/04, May 2004. Pdf available from www.warwick.ac.uk/fac/soc/csgr/research/workingpapers/2004/wp13304.pdf. Internet. Accessed 27 November 2005.

—— "'We Are Heartbroken and Furious!': Violence and the (Anti-)Globalisation Movement(s)." In *Critical Theories, International Relations and 'the Anti-Globalisation Movement': The Politics of Global Resistance*, edited by Catherine Eschle and Bice Maiguashca. London: Routledge, 2005.

Tarrow, Sidney G. *Between Center and Periphery: Grassroots Politicians in Italy and France.* New Haven, CT: Yale University Press, 1977.

—— "From Lumping to Splitting: Specifying Globalization and Resistance." In *Globalization and Resistance: Transnational Dimensions of Social Movements*, edited by Jackie Smith and Hank Johnston. Lanham, MD: Rowman & Littlefield, 2002.

—— "Confessions of a Recovering Structuralist." *Mobilization* 8, no. 1 (2003): 134–41.

——— *The New Transnational Activism*. Cambridge: Cambridge University Press, 2005.

Tarrow, Sidney, and Doug McAdam. "Scale Shift in Transnational Contention." Paper presented at a conference entitled "Transnational Processes and Social Movements," Bellagio, Italy, 22–26 July 2003.

——— "Scale Shift in Transnational Contention." In *Transnational Protest and Global Activism*, edited by Donatella della Porta and Sidney Tarrow. Lanham, MD: Rowman & Littlefield, 2005.

Tauli-Corpuz, Victoria. "Cultural Diversity: The Right of Indigenous Peoples to Remain Different and Diverse." In *Alternatives to Economic Globalization: A Better World Is Possible*, edited by International Forum on Globalization. San Francisco, CA: Berrett-Koehler Publishers, 2002.

Teivainen, Teivo. "World Social Forum and Global Democratization: Learning from Porto Alegre." *Third World Quarterly* 23, no. 4 (2002): 621–32.

TerraViva Team. "A Divisive Consensus" (31 January 2005). Available from www.ipsterraviva.net/tv/wsf2005/viewstory.asp?idnews=179. Internet. Accessed 22 November 2005.

Third World Network. "TWN Info Service on WTO and Trade Issues" (21 March 2005). Available from www.ourworldisnotforsale.org/showarticle.asp?search=44. Internet. Accessed 27 April 2005.

Thomas, Janet. *The Battle in Seattle: The Story behind and beyond the WTO Demonstrations*. Golden, Colo.: Fulcrum Publishing, 2000.

Thompson, E. P. *The Making of the English Working Class*. London: Gollancz, 1964.

Tilly, Charles. "From Interactions to Outcomes in Social Movements." In *How Social Movements Matter*, edited by Marco Giugni, Doug McAdam, and Charles Tilly. Minneapolis, MN: University of Minnesota, 1999.

——— "Do Unto Others." In *Political Altruism? Solidarity Movements in International Perspective*, edited by Marco Giugni and Florence Passy. Lanham, MD: Rowman & Littlefield, 2001.

——— "Foreword." In *Coalitions across Borders: Transnational Protest and the Neoliberal Order*, edited by Joe Bandy and Jackie Smith. Lanham, MD: Rowman & Littlefield, 2004.

Tilly, Charles, Louise Tilly, and Richard Tilly. *The Rebellious Century: 1830–1930*. Cambridge, MA: Harvard University Press, 1975.

Toussaint, Eric, and Arnaud Zacharie. "External Debt: Abolish the Debt in Order to Free Development." In *Another World Is Possible: Popular Alternatives to Globalization at the World Social Forum*, edited by William F. Fisher and Thomas Ponniah. London: Zed Books, 2003.

Tute Bianche. "A Busload of Lies Exposed, Appended with a Vivid Depiction of the Italian Scene and a Lot of Links and References: Who Are the White Overalls? And Why Are They Slandered by People Who Call Themselves 'Anarchists'?" Available from www.nadir.org/nadir/initiativ/agp/free/genova/busload.htm. Internet. Accessed 5 August 2004.

Tyler, Patrick E. "A New Power in the Streets." *New York Times*, 17 February 2003.

Udayagiri, Mridula, and John Walton. "Global Transformation and Local Counter Movements: The Prospects for Democracy under Neoliberalism." Paper presented at the conference entitled "The Next Great Transformation? Karl Polanyi and the Critique of Globalization," University of California, Davis, 12–13 April 2002. Pdf file available from www.sociology.ucdavis.edu/jtwalton/Walton/pdf/Polanyi_Conf.pdf. Internet. Accessed 14 September 2004.

Useem, Bert. "Solidarity Model, Breakdown Model, and the Boston Anti-Busing Movement." *American Sociological Review* 45 (1980): 357–69.

——— "Disorganization and the New Mexico Prison Riot of 1980." *American Sociological Review* 50 (1985): 667–88.

Van Orman Quine, Willard. *From a Logical Point of View*. New York: Harper and Row, 1961.

Via Campesina. "Bangalore Declaration of the Via Campesina." Declaration at the Third International Conference of the Via Campesina, 3–6 October 2000.

——— "'Space' in Mumbai, India" (18–19 January 2004). Available from www.peoples-foodsovereignty.org/activity/2004/01-WSF.htm. Internet. Accessed 4 June 2005.

——— "Struggle for Agrarian Reform and Social Changes in the Rural Areas. Via Campesina III Int. Conference." Available from www.viacampesina.org/art_english.php3?id_article=43. Internet. Accessed 1 August 2004.

——— "Declaration of the Second International Assembly of Rural Women – June 13." Available from www.viacampesina.org/art_fr.php3?id_article=448. Internet. Accessed 2 August 2004.

——— "Program 18–19 January Debate with Venues." Available from www.viacampesina.org/art_sp.php3?id_article=297. Internet. Accessed 6 January 2005.

——— "Via Campesina Will Be Present in Mumbai, India." Available from www.viacampesina.org/art_english.php3?id_article=273. Internet. Accessed 6 January 2005.

Walker, R. B. J. *One World, Many Worlds: Struggles for a Just World Peace.* Boulder, CO: Lynne Rienner, 1988.

——— "Social Movements/World Politics." *Millennium* 23, no. 3 (1994): 669–700.

Wall Street Journal. "A Child of Seattle." Editorial. *Wall Street Journal,* 6 July 2000: A26.

Wallach, Lori, and Michelle Sforza. *Whose Trade Organization? Corporate Globalization and the Erosion of Democracy.* Washington, DC: Public Citizen, 1999.

Walsh, Edward J. *Democracy in the Shadows: Citizen Mobilization in the Wake of the Accident at Three Mile Island.* Westport, CT: Greenwood, 1989.

Walsh, Edward J., and Rex H. Warland. "Social Movement Involvement in the Wake of a Nuclear Accident: Activists and Free Riders in the TMI Area." *American Sociological Review* 48 (1983): 764–80.

Walton, John. "Urban Protests and the Global Political Economy: The IMF Riots." In *The Capitalist City: Global Restructuring and Community Politics,* edited by Michael Peter Smith and Joe R. Feagin. London: Basil Blackwell, 1987.

——— "Globalization and Popular Movements." Paper presented at "The Future of Revolutions in the Context of Globalization" conference, University of California, Santa Barbara, 25–27 January 2001.

Walton, John, and Charles Ragin. "Global and National Sources of Political Protest: Third World Responses to the Debt Crisis." *American Sociological Review* 55 (December 1990): 876–90.

Walton, John, and David Seddon. *Free Markets and Food Riots: The Politics of Global Adjustment.* Cambridge: Blackwell, 1994.

Wapner, Paul. *Environmental Activism and World Civic Politics.* Albany, NY: SUNY Press, 1996.

Waterman, Peter. *Globalization, Social Movements and the New Internationalisms.* London: Mansell, 1998.

——— "The Secret of Fire." In *World Social Forum: Challenging Empires,* edited by Jai Sen, Anita Anand, Arturo Escobar, and Peter Waterman. New Delhi: Viveka Foundation, 2004.

——— "Adventures of Emancipatory Labour Strategy as the New Global Movement Challenges." *Journal of World Systems Research* X, no. 1 (Winter 2004): 216–53.

——— "Of Saints, Sinners, and Compañeras: Internationalist Lives in the Americas Today." The Hague, Netherlands: Institute of Social Studies, Working Paper Series, no. 286. Available from www.antenna.nl/~waterman/saints.html. Internet. Accessed 1 February 2005.

Waterman, Peter, and Jill Timms. "Trade Union Internationalism and a Global Civil Society in the Making." In *Global Civil Society 2004–5,* edited by Helmut Anheier, Marlies Glasius and Mary Kaldor. London: Sage, 2005.

Weber, Max. *Economy and Society.* Edited by Guenther Roth and Claus Wittich. Berkeley, CA: University of California Press, 1978.

Wendt, Alexander. *Social Theory of International Politics.* Cambridge: Cambridge University Press, 1999.

Whitaker, Francisco. "Lessons from Porto Alegre" (24 August 2002). Available from www.forumsocialmundial.org.br/DINAMIC/eng_balanco_ChicoW.asp. Internet. Accessed 24 March 2005.

—— "Memorial WSF 2003: Notes about the World Social Forum" (14 April 2003). Available from www.forumsocialmundial.org.br/dinamic.asp?pagina=bal_whitaker_ing. Internet. Accessed 24 March 2005.

—— "Notes about the World Social Forum" (14 April 2003). Available from www.forum socialmundial.org.br/dinamic.asp?pagina=bal_whitaker_ing. Internet. Accessed 6 March 2005.

—— Comments made at the World Social Forum International Council meetings. Author's notes. Amsterdam and Utrecht, Netherlands, 28 March–1 April 2005.

Whitmore, Elizabeth, and Maureen Wilson. "Research and Popular Movements: Igniting Seeds of Fire." *Social Development Issues* 21, no. 1(1999): 19–28.

Whitney, Jennifer. "Infernal Noise: The Soundtrack to Insurrection." In *We Are Everywhere: The Irresistible Rise of Global Anticapitalism*, edited by Notes from Nowhere. London: Verso, 2003.

Wikipedia. "Black Bloc." Available from www.en.wikipedia.org/wiki/Black_bloc. Internet. Accessed 25 June 2005.

—— "Porto Alegre Manifesto." Available from www.en.wikipedia.org/wiki/Porto_Alegre_Manifesto. Internet. Accessed 17 November 2005.

Williamson, John. *The Progress of Policy Reform in Latin America*. Washington, DC: Institute for International Economics, 1990.

Winch, Peter. *The Idea of Social Science*. London: Routledge and Kegan Paul, 1958.

Wolf, Martin. *Why Globalization Works*. New Haven, CT: Yale University Press, 2004.

WOMBLES. "Background: Lessons Learned: Personal Reflections and Opinions on S26" (November 2000). Available from www.wombles.org.uk/background/lessons.php. Internet. Accessed 26 June 2005.

—— "Reflections & Analysis: The WOMBLES, the ESF & beyond" (December 2004). Available from www.wombles.org.uk/auto/reflections.php?PHPSESSID=0b793d5649decd5dd5dcd6b1e97cadbf. Internet. Accessed 24 June 2005.

—— "Beyond ESF: 5 Days & Nights of Anti-Authoritarian Ideas and Action: A Short Analysis of the Socio-Political Role of the WSF–ESF." Available from www.wombles.org.uk/auto/esfcritique.php. Internet. Accessed 24 June 2005.

—— "News: Beyond ESF – Programme, Posted 14:53 08 October 2004: Beyond ESF: Programme & Timetable, Wednesday 13th–Sunday 17th October." Available from www.wombles.org.uk/news/article_2004_10_8_5355.php. Internet. Accessed 24 June 2005.

Woodroffe, Jessica, and Mark Ellis-Jones. *States of Unrest*. London: World Development Movement, 2000.

World Bank. "Adjustment from Within: Lessons from the Structural Adjustment Participatory Review Initiative." Paper presented at the Second Global SAPRI Forum, 30–31 July 2001. Pdf available from www.worldbank.org/research/sapri/WB_SAPRI_Report.pdf. Internet. Accessed 11 January 2006.

—— *Global Development Finance: Financing the Poorest Countries, 2002*. Washington, DC: World Bank, 2002.

—— "HIPC Debt Initiative." Available from www.worldbank.org/hipc/about/hipcbr/hipcbr.htm. Internet. Accessed 20 April 2005.

"World Bank Courts NGOs as Wolfowitz Takes Helm" (22 April 2005). Available from www.focusweb.org/finance/html/modules.php?op=modload&name=News&file=article&sid=276. Internet. Accessed 5 June 2005.

"World Bank Critics Denounce Civil Society Forum" (22 April 2005). Available from www.focusweb.org/finance/html/Article275.html. Internet. Accessed 5 June 2005.

World Social Forum. "Charter of Principles" (8 June 2002). Available from www.forumsocial
mundial.org.br/main.php?id_menu=4&cd_language=2. Internet. Accessed 25
December 2005.
—— "Background: The Events of 2001, 2002 and 2003." Available from www.forumsocial
mundial.org.br/main.php?id_menu=2&cd_language=2. Internet. Accessed 20 April
2005.
—— "Social Forums around the World." Available from www.forumsocialmundial.org.br/
dinamic.php?pagina=foruns_regiao_2005_i. Internet. Accessed 24 April 2005.
Yergin, Daniel, and Joseph Stanislaw. *The Commanding Heights: The Battle for the World
Economy*. New York: Touchstone (Simon & Schuster), 2002.

Interviews by author

Aguiton, Christophe, Euromarche, World Social Forum International Council representa-
tive. Conversation with author. Author's notes. World Social Forum International
Council meeting, Utrecht, Netherlands, 30 March 2005.
ATTAC delegate. Interview by author. Tape recording. World Social Forum, Porto Alegre,
Brazil, 28 January 2003.
Brennan, Brid, Asia program coordinator, Transnational Institute and World Social
Forum International Council member. Interview by author. Tape recording. World
Social Forum International Council meeting, Utrecht, Netherlands, 1 April 2005.
Bullard, Nicola, Focus on the Global South and World Social Forum International
Council representative. Conversation with author. Author's notes. World Social Forum
International Council meeting, Utrecht, Netherlands, 1 April 2005.
Caliari, Aldo, legal research scholar, Rethinking Bretton Woods Project, Center of
Concern. Interview by author. Tape recording. World Social Forum, Porto Alegre,
Brazil, 27 January 2003.
Cavanagh, John, director, Institute for Policy Studies. Interview by author. Author's notes.
Washington, DC, 31 July 2002.
CIRCA Clown no. 1. Interview by author. Tape recording. European Social Forum,
London, 16 October 2004.
Comité Mercosur de Organizaciones de Trabajo Social. Interview by author. Tape
recording, World Social Forum, Porto Alegre, Brazil, 24 January 2003.
Friends of the Earth Europe member. Interview by author. Tape recording. European
Social Forum, London, England, 15 October 2004.
Friends of the Earth International member. Interview by author. Tape recording. World
Social Forum International Council meeting, Utrecht, Netherlands, 2 April 2005.
Gerson, Timi, organizer/FTAA coordinator, Global Trade Watch, Public Citizen, repre-
sentative to the World Social Forum International Council. Interview by author. Tape
recording. Washington, DC, 12 February 2003.
Hebshi, Ali, Pittsburgh Social Forum and organizer, Clean Water Action. Interview by
author. Tape recording. World Social Forum, Porto Alegre, Brazil, 28 January 2003.
Hood, Ian. Globalize Resistance, Scotland. Interview by author. Tape recording. European Social Forum, Paris, France, 16 November 2003.
Madre de la Plaza de Mayo de la Linea Fundadora, Cucuey Province, Argentina. Interview by author. Tape recording. World Social Forum, Porto Alegre, Brazil, 25 January
2003.
Marshall, Alison, head of campaigns, Catholic Agency for Overseas Development. Interview
by author. Tape recording. World Social Forum, Porto Alegre, Brazil, 28 January 2003.
Martínez, María Elena, executive director of CorpWatch. Interview by author. Tape
recording. World Social Forum, Porto Alegre, Brazil, 25 January 2003.
Matte, Diane, coordinator, World March of Women and World Social Forum International Council member. Interview by author. Tape recording. World Social Forum
International Council meeting, Utrecht, Netherlands, 30 March 2005.

Pettifor, Ann. Interview by author. Tape recording. European Social Forum, London, 16 October 2004.

Rajan, W. R. Varada, national secretary of the Centre of Indian Trade Unions. Interview by author. Tape recording. World Social Forum, Porto Alegre, Brazil, 25 January 2003.

Rimml, Barbara, ATTAC Switzerland. Interview by author. Tape recording. Potsdam, Germany, 9 January 2004.

Stocking, Barbara, director, Oxfam. Interview by author. Tape recording. European Social Forum, London, 15 October 2004.

Tagesson, Helena, ATTAC Sweden. Interview by author. Tape recording. World Social Forum, Porto Alegre, Brazil, 28 January 2003.

Whitaker, Francisco. Conversation with author. Author's notes. World Social Forum International Council meeting, Utrecht, Netherlands, 1 April 2005.

Index

Acción Zapatista 210
accompaniment 33
Action Aid 94
ActionAid Alliance 126
Action Canada Network 116
activism 250–8
activists *see* global activists
activist swarms 211–17
actor constitution 232, 248
affective response 51–2, 237
Africa Growth and Opportunity Act 109
African Network and Forum on Debt and
    Development (AFRODAD) 73
agriculture 164–5
Ali, Muhammad 79
alterglobalization 48
altruism 52–3
altruistic solidarity 20, 52–3, 237
American Association of Jurists 102
Amnesty International 192
anarchism 3
Anglican Christian Aid 75
Annan, Kofi 85
anti-globalization movement 2; *see also
    individual organizations*
anti-neoliberalism 8–10
Anti-Privatization Forum 75
Arab NGO Network for Development 128
armed militants 6
armed uprising 9
Asian Campaign on Debt and Structural
    Adjustment 74
Asia-Pacific Economic Cooperation 109
Asia-Pacific Research Network 108
Asociación Nacional de Agricultores
    Pequenas 170
Asociación de Organizaciones Campesinas
    Centroamericanas para la Cooperación
    y el Desarrollo 154
ASOCODE 166–7, 170, 180

Association for the Taxation of Financial
    Transactions for the Aid of Citizens
    (ATTAC) 12, 14, 48, 208, 215
attribution 193, 231; of interconnectedness
    19; of similarity 19, 41, 43, 48, 231,
    236; of worthiness 19, 192, 231
austerity policies 69

Bachus, Spencer 79
Barker, Debi 117
Barlow, Maude 115–17, 119, 123
Battle in Seattle 13, 83–4, 120–5, 176,
    214–15
Beck, Ulrich 53
belief amplification 43
Belize Association of Producers
    Organization 170
Bello, Walden 113–14, 117, 145, 246
Benjamin, Medea 215
Bennett, W. Lance 6, 57–8, 97, 240
biopiracy 150
bivalence 63, 238
black bloc 214–17
Blee, Kathleen 44
Bolivia 14, 69
Bond, Patrick 145, 186
Bono 91, 93
Bourdieu, Pièrre 53
Bové, José 159, 161, 163–4, 171, 174
Brazil 17, 69, 150; Movimento dos Sem
    Terra 17, 151–6, 183; Natalino
    Crossing 153–4; Pastoral Land
    Commission 153; Social Network for
    Justice and Human Rights 75
Brazilian Workers' Party 185
Bread for the World 71, 77
Brennan, Brid 130, 183
Bretton Woods 2, 67, 85–6, 99, 114
bricolage 35
broad change processes 231, 233

brokerage 19, 41–2, 48, 112–15, 165–6, 231
Brown, Gordon 78–9, 91
Burns, Reverend Thomas 71
Burrawoy, Michael 44

Call of Renewal 83
Call of the Social Movements/Social Movements Assembly 65
Campinas Declaration 71
Canadian Inter-Church Committee on Human Rights in Latin America 192
Canadian National Farmers' Union 167
Cancun ministerial 128–9, 176
capacity-building 114
capitalism 3–4, 8–9, 23–4, 56, 59–60, 99, 156, 188–9, 197–8, 206–7, 209, 213, 216–17, 219, 221–3, 225, 230, 235, 239, 241, 245, 247–8, 256–8
Carter, Isabel 75, 153
Cassen, Bernard 12
Catholic Agency for Overseas Development (CAFOD) 72, 75, 77, 94, 109
Catholic Bishops of Chiapas 192
Cavanagh, John 11, 117
Center of Concern 72, 77
Central American Free Trade Agreement (CAFTA) 90, 109, 131
chain of equivalence 240, 250
Chatfield, Charles 7
Chavez, Hugo 106
Chiapas 9, 28, 121, 164, 189–90, 193–6
Chile 69
Chilean Asociación Nacional de Mujeres Rurales e Indígenas 170
Christian Aid 77, 94
Christian aid organizations 71–3
church networks 76–9
Citizens' Agenda 116
civil disobedience 6
claims 57
Clandestine Insurgent Rebel Clown Army (CIRCA) 226–7
Clarke, Tony 119
Cleaver, Harry 192
Cloward, Richard 53
Comic Relief 92
Committee for the Abolition of Third World Debt 102
Common Agricultural Policy 165
competition 141–7
comprehending 32, 34, 41, 44–5; participatory action research 32–4

Confédération Nationale des Syndicats de Travailleurs Paysans 160, 166
Confédération Paysanne 126, 151, 159–64
Congreso Nacional Indígena 192
conscience constituents 239
Continental Campaign against the FTAA 142
Continental Encounters of Indigenous Peoples 192
convergence centers 211
Coordinadora Latinoamericana de Organizaciones del Campo (CLOC) 154, 166
coordinated action 42–3; *see also* transnational collective action
Coordination Paysanne Européene 165–6, 170, 180
Council of Canadians 108, 111–12, 115–16
crossovers 38
Cuba: Asociación Nacional de Agricultores Pequeñas 170
cultural harms 61
cultural politics of difference 61–2
cultural recognition 22, 57, 238
cultural violence 17

de Angelis, Massimo 23
Debt Action Coalition 74
Debt Crisis Network 71, 73, 75
debt forgiveness 85, 92–3
Debt Study Group 74
Debt Treaty movement 74
decentering 38
della Porta, Donatella 7, 54, 111
democracy 28
Dent, Martin 75
Derrida, Jacques 53
Desmarais, Annette 38, 178
Development GAP 71
diffusion 19, 41–2, 48, 112–15, 165–6, 192–3
dignity 199
direct action: black bloc 214–17; fluffy 212; pink bloc 212–13; spiky 212; white bloc 213–14
Direct Action Network 212
direct activism: social justice model 57; social justice networks 21
direct violence 17
discrimination 188
Doha meeting 128
Dolan, Mike 121
domain-specific policy reform 60
Drop the Debt 66, 86

Durito 194
dynamics of contention 40–1, 231–2

Earth First! 199
economic distribution 61
economic harms 61
economic redistribution 22, 57
Ecuador 69
Ejército Zapatista de Liberación Nacional
    164, 188, 200; *aguascalientes* 201; *Durito*
    194; formation of 200–2; framing and
    diffusing 192–3; *intergaláctica* 201–2,
    218; transnational solidarity evoked by
    191–2
empathy 20, 52, 237
empire 46
emulation 42–3, 49
encounter space 140–1, 182–4, 243
encuentros 200–2
Enlace Civil 192
episodes 40–1
erklären 32
Eschle, Catherine 39
Eterovic, Ivana 20, 53–4
Europe 73–5
European Network on Debt and
    Development 73
European Social Forums 45, 221
European Union 7; Common Agricultural
    Policy 165
evolution 59

Fahamu 92
faith-based organizations 76–9, 96
Family Farm Defenders 172
Fédération Nationale des Syndicats
    Paysans 160
Federation of Peasant Organizations of
    Indonesia 170
feminist perspective 3–4
Fifty Years Is Enough 74–5, 84, 94, 96,
    103, 128
Financial Crimes 81
'first-generation' advocacy networks 20,
    57–8
Fisher, William 13
Five Interested Parties 129–30
Florini, Ann 4
fluffy direct action 212
Focus on the Global South 13, 75, 103,
    108, 111–13, 136, 142, 176
Food and Agricultural Organization 149
Food First 108, 113

Food and Information Action Network
    177, 180
food riots 69
food sovereignty 171, 174
Ford Foundation 107
Fortune 500 5
Forum for African Alternatives 75
Forum on Debt and Development
    (FONDAD) 73
Foundation for Deep Ecology 117
frame alignment 19, 42, 231
frame amplification 43, 79, 193, 234
frame bridging 42, 81, 234
frame extension 43, 234
frame transformation 43, 234
framing 112–15, 170–1, 192–3
France: Confédération Nationale des
    Syndicats de Travailleurs Paysans 160;
    Confédération Paysanne 126, 151,
    159–64; Fédération Nationale des
    Syndicats Paysans 160
Fraser, Nancy 60–3, 242
Freedom from Debt Coalition 74
free horizontal articulation 247
Freeing the Media Conference 210
Free Speech TV 210
free trade 110
Free Trade Area of the Americas (FTAA)
    3, 8, 109
Freire, Paulo 33, 154
Frente Zapatista de Liberación Nacional 192
Friedman, Thomas L. 15
Friends of the Earth International 48,
    108, 126, 176, 183, 241

G7/G8 countries 7, 98
G8 Summits 66, 77–8, 82, 209
G19 246–7
G33 131
G90 131
Galeano, Eduardo 201
Galtung, Johan 17, 232, 234
Gandhi, Mahatma 157
Gaymard, Hervé 91
Geldof, Bob 73, 79, 91
General Agreement on Tariffs and Trade
    (GATT) 2, 109, 149–50, 164–5
General Assembly of the Anti-War
    Movement (GAAWM) 15, 208
general strikes 69
genetically modified crops 158
genetically modified foods 126
genetically modified organisms 120

Giddens, Anthony 33
Glaser, Barney 44
global activism 1–65
global activists 4–7
Global Assembly on Food Security 171
Global Call to Action Against Poverty 53,
    89–94, 98, 101
Global Campaign for Agrarian Reform
    177, 184
global capitalism *see* capitalism
global civil society 106, 246
global days of action 208
global debt 67–9
Global Exchange 215
global interpretive transformative frames 235
globalization 4; of hope 28; neoliberal *see*
    neoliberal globalization; of
    neoliberalism 1–24
Global Justice Movement 10, 16
Global Policy Forum 86
glocalization 49, 236
'glocal' networks 177–8
going global 19; realization of need to go
    231
Grajew, Oded 12
Greenpeace 113, 118
gross domestic product 150
Grzybowski, Candido 14
Guadalajara 133–4

Habermas, Jürgen 53
hacktivism 199
Haiti 69
Hemispheric Social Alliance 135, 142
highly indebted poor countries 73–4, 85
historicism 38
holism 30–1
Hong Kong ministerial 132–3
horizontalism 64, 246
Human Rights Watch 192
Hungry for Change campaign 73
hybrid networks 21, 238
hyper-organizations 137

identity 55; sharing of 52
identity solidarity 20, 54–5, 237, 239
inclusive diversity 241
India: KRRS *see* Karnataka State Farmers'
    Association; People's Agenda 131
Indian Patent Act (190) 157
individualism 30–1
indymedia 122, 199, 210–11
Infernal Noise Brigade 213

Institute for Agriculture and Trade Policy
    117
Institute for Policy Studies 71, 117
Interchurch Coordinating Committee on
    Development Projects 73
interconnectedness 49, 231, 233, 236
Intercontinental Network of Alternative
    Communication 202
Interfaith Working Group on Trade and
    Investment 131
intergaláctica 201–2, 218
International Day of Peasant and Farmers'
    Struggle 171
International Federation of Agricultural
    Producers 168
International Finance Facility 90
International Forum on Globalization
    (IFG) 18, 116–17; *Alternatives to Economic
    Globalization* 140; anti-MAI campaign
    118–20; role of 127
International Gender and Trade Network
    126
International Monetary Fund (IMF) 1–2,
    7, 18, 49, 67, 70, 72, 230; IMF riots
    9, 69
International People's Tribunal on the
    Debt 102, 243
International Society for Ecology and
    Culture 117
international solidarity 197
International Via Campesina Space 184–5
Internet 80–1, 172, 192
Italy: Rifondazione Comunista 223; Tute
    Bianche 199, 213–14; Ya Basta! 199,
    205, 213

Jesuit's Center of Concern 71
Jobs with Justice 83
Johnston, Donald 119
Jubilee 2000 14, 27, 48, 66–107; Battle in
    Seattle 83–4; beginnings of 75–6;
    breakup of 86–9; foundations of 71–3;
    media attention 79–80; objects and
    aims 76–81; transnational collective
    action 19, 81–2; *see also* structural
    adjustment programs
Jubilee 2000 Northwest 84
Jubilee Debt Campaign 94
Jubilee Foundation 75
Jubilee Framework 66, 89–94, 252–3
Jubilee networks 1
Jubilee South 22, 28, 94, 98, 100–2, 237,
    240, 243–4, 251, 253–4

Jubilee South Africa 104, 244
Jubilee South-Latin America 104
Jubilee USA 102

Kairos-Canada 102
Karnataka State Farmers' Association
    (KRRS) 14, 151, 156–9, 170;
    Operation Cremation Monsanto 158;
    peoples' caravans 208–9
Keane, John 5
Keck, Margaret 5, 7, 20, 54, 97
Kemmis, Stephen 33, 36
Keynesianism 2–3
Khor, Martin 59, 105, 110, 117, 137, 241,
    254
Klein, Naomi 123
Korean People's Action against the
    Korea-Japan Free Trade Agreement
    and the World Trade Organization
    (KOPA) 108, 140
Korten, David C. 117
Krueger, Anne 85
Kurasawa, Fukuyi 52–3

land disputes 188
landlessness 149–50
Larzac movement 159–61
Le Monde diplomatique 145
liberated zones 196
Lichterman, Paul 44
literature review 39–40
Live 8 concerts 53, 92
LiveAid 73
Livingstone, Ken 226
localized collective action 41–2
localized resistance 19
Loong, Au 132

Maastricht Treaty 109, 195, 205
McAdam, Doug 40, 45, 231, 233
McCarthy, John 40, 234
McDonalds 161–3
McTaggart, Robin 33, 36
Maiguashca, Bice 39
Make Poverty History 91, 98, 104
Malhotra, Kamal 113
Mandela, Nelson 91, 110
Mander, Gerry 117
Maple Leaf Summit 115
Maradiaga, Archbishop Oscar Rodriguez 79
Marcos, Subcomandante Insurgente 189,
    191, 194–6, 210
Marxism 3, 55

mass mobilization 207–17; activist swarms
    211–17; convergence centers 211;
    global days of action 208; indymedia
    122, 199, 210–11; peoples' caravans
    208–9; street reclaiming 209
Matte, Diane 183–4
Mayo, Ed 76
mechanisms 40–1
Melucci, Alberto 40
Methodist Church Women United 71
Mexico: localized resistance in 189; Unión
    Nacional de Organizaciones
    Regionales Campesinas Autónomas
    166; Zapatista uprising 188, 190–1
Millennium Development Goals 90
Minghella, Anthony 79
Mittelmann, James 38
mobilization 232–3
Mobilization for Global Justice 45
Monsanto 14, 150, 156, 158–9, 171, 182,
    185, 245, 256
Morocco 69
movement entrepreneurs 231, 234
Movimento dos Sem Terra 17, 151–6,
    183
MST 170
Mulroney, Brian 115
Multilateral Agreement on Investment
    (MAI) 8; IFG's compaign against
    118–20
Multilateral Debt Coalition 74, 77
multinationals 8
multi-sector structural transformation 57, 60
multitude 46
mutual solidarity 54

Natalino Crossing 153–4
national campaigns, strengthening and
    coordinating 131–2
National Family Farm Coalition 166
National Farmers' Union 170
N'Dour, Youssou 79
Ndungane, Archbishop Njongonkulu 77–8
neoliberal globalization 1–24, 56, 69–70,
    191; debate over 3–4; as public enemy
    194, 198; trade agreements and SAPs
    151–2
neoliberalism *see* neoliberal globalization
neoliberal triumvirate 230
networking 8
Network Institute for Global
    Democratization 85
network model 57–8, 238

network of networks 8–10, 13–15, 60, 101, 125, 140–1, 147, 188, 230
Network Opposed to the WTO 121
networks: composition and character 237–42; transnational *see* transnational networks
new internationalisms 56, 238–9
NGO advocacy 21, 57
NGOs *see* nongovernmental organizations
Nicaragua: Unión Nacional de Agricultores y Ganaderos 166–7
Nicholson, Paul 169
Njehu, Njoki 84
No Borders network 214, 221
nongovernmental organizations 1, 5, 20, 71, 175, 238; *see also individual organizations*
No One Is Illegal initiative 214
Norberg-Hodge, Helena 117
North American Free Trade Agreement (NAFTA) 3, 8, 109, 115–16, 136; Zapatista uprising in Mexico 190–1
North Atlantic Treaty Organization (NATO) 7
Novib 72–3, 101–2

Olesen, Thomas 16, 20, 53–5, 231
Olson, Mancur 53
O'Neill, Paul 85
Onuf, Nicolas 18
operational paradigm 57, 59–60, 238
Operation Cremation Monsanto 158
Orange, Reverend James 83
Organization for Economic Cooperation and Development (OECD) 7
Organization of the Petroleum Exporting Countries (OPEC) 67
Our World Is Not For Sale (OWINFS) 1,13, 27, 48, 108–47, 138–9, 176, 180, 240–1, 254–5; *Alternatives to Economic Globalization* 243; claims against WTO 125; and free trade promoters 127–9; launch of 124–5; lobbying WTO headquarters 132; localized actors 111–12; South-North information exchange 133–5; strategy of 129–35; website 125–6
Oxfam 72, 75, 77, 92, 101, 103–4, 107, 113, 243; Hungry for Change campaign 73
Oxfam International Fund 107
Oxfam-Solidarité 175

Pagnucco, Ron 7
Paulo Freire Stichting 167

Paper Tiger 210
Paris Club 7
participatory action research 32–4, 249; in critical globalization scholarship 38–9; critique of 36–8; reflexive dialectical perspective 34–6
PASMOC 51
Pastoral Land Commission 153
Patomäki, Heikki 13, 85
Paulson, Justin 192
PeaceNet 192
People Centered Development Forum 117
People for Fair Trade 121
People's Alliance Against the WTO 132, 135
peoples' caravans 208–9
Peoples' Global Action (PGA) 1,14, 27, 176, 188–229, 240; establishment of 203–7; involvement with WSF 219–20; mass mobilization by 207–17; as transnational network 217–19
perceived connection 52, 237
Perlstein, Jeff 210
personal suffering 52, 237
perspectival dualism 63
Peru 69; Confederación Campesina del Peru 166
Petros, Hannah 83–4
Pettifor, Ann 75, 80, 84, 86
pink bloc 212–13
Piven, Francis Fox 53
Plan Puebla Panama 109
polarization 232
politics of recognition 61
Ponniah, Thomas 13
Pope, Carl 215
Pope John Paul II 79; *Tertio Millennio Adveniente* 78
Porto Alegre Manifesto 141, 145, 224–5, 245–6; *see also* World Social Forum
posse 46
Prasartsert, Suthy 113
privatization of commons 149–50
Pro-Canada Network 115
processes 40–1
proletariat 55
protest entrepreneurs 111, 151
proximity to problem 51–2, 237
Public Citizen 108, 121, 126; Global Trade Watch 13, 108; MAI-Not list 118
Public Grassroots Media Conference 210
Public Services International 108, 126

Ramonet, Ignacio 145

Rasmussen, Poul Nyrup 91
realization of need to 'go global' 231
reciprocal solidarity 20, 239
reciprocity 20–1, 49, 52, 54
Reclaim the Streets 199, 205, 212
recovering neoliberals 3
reflexive dialectical perspective 34–6
reflexivity 38
reformism 241
regional trade agreements 109–11
Religious Working Group on World Bank
    and IMF 74–5, 77, 82
Research Foundation for Science,
    Technology and Ecology 117, 126
resistance farming 159
RICA 202–3
Rifondazione Comunista 223
Ritchie, Mark 117
Rosenau, James 16, 53, 231
Ross, John 201
Rucht, Dieter 53

Sachs, Jeffrey 81
St Clair, Jeffrey 215
scale shift process 41–3, 50
Schengen Treaty 205
scholar-activism 248–50
scholar-activists 26; audience 31–2;
    individualism vs holism 30–1;
    normative commitments of 26–9
Schroeder, Gerhard 79
Seattle to Brussels network 134
Seattle, WTO ministerial meeting *see* Battle
    in Seattle
second-generation, direct activism social
    justice networks 57–8, 206, 238
shared fate 35
shifting scale 231–7
Shiva, Vandana 117, 149
Sikkink, Kathryn 5, 7, 20, 54, 97
Simmons, P.J. 4
Sisters of the Holy Cross 75
Smith, Jackie 7, 20, 53–4
Smith, Steve 25
Social Movements Assembly 15, 44, 143,
    223, 235; calls for mobilization 141–2
Social Movements International Network 142
Social Movements World Network 223
Social Network for Justice and Human
    Rights 75
social politics of equality 61–2
Solidarité et Luttes Paysannes
    Internationales 167

solidarity 19–20, 48, 51–2, 193, 231, 236;
    altruistic 20, 52–3, 237; identity 20,
    54–5, 237, 239; international 197;
    movement-based, people-driven 135;
    mutual 54; reciprocal 20, 52, 239;
    substitution 53–4; transnational 52–7;
    see also transnational collective action;
    transnational networks
Solidarity Network 115
Soriano, Sally 121
Southern Christian Leadership
    Conference 83
Southern Cone 47
South-North information exchange 133–5
Sovereign Debt Restructuring Mechanism
    85
spikey direct action 212
state actors 5
state allies 5
Stedile, João 153
STOP-MAI list 118
strategic transformations 38
Strauss, Anselm 44
street protests 6
Strimer, Reverend Peter 83
Structural Adjustment Policy Review
    Initiative (SAPRI) 75
structural adjustment programs (SAPs) 1,
    7–8, 67–70, 73–5, 151–2
structural transformation 22
structural violence 16, 18, 27, 46, 233, 242
substitution solidarity 53–4
Sudan 69
Sullivan, Sian 217
Sweeney, John 84
sympathy 52, 237

Tarrow, Sidney 7, 16, 40, 45, 111, 231, 233
Taylor, Verta 44
Tearfund 76
Teivainen, Teivo 13, 85
Thatcher, Margaret 2
theory of communicative action 34
Third World debt 67
Third World Network 13, 59, 110
Tickner, J. Ann 25
Tilly, Charles 40, 45, 231, 233
Touraine, Alain 201
trade agreements 151–2
Trade-Related Aspects of Intellectual
    Property Rights (TRIPs) agreement 90
transformation 241; in parts 59
transformative frame 81

transition 241
transitional paradigm 22, 60
transnational activist networks 20–3
transnational civil society 4–7
transnational collective action 19, 81–2,
    231, 236; against WTO 126; nature of
    171–2; pyrrhic victory 84–6
transnational corporations 8–9, 99, 113, 205
Transnational Institute 130, 175, 255
transnational left activism 7–8
transnational networks: composition and
    character 50–1, 94–100; involvement
    with WSF 100–7; nature of claims 60–3;
    operational paradigm 57, 59–60;
    PASMOC 51; World Social Forum 63–5
triggers 231, 233
Turkey 69
Tute Bianche 199, 213–14

UK: Debt Crisis Network 71, 73, 75; Earth
    First! 199; Reclaim the Streets 199,
    205, 212; Tactical Frivolity 212
United Nations 7; Environment Program
    149; Food and Agricultural
    Organization 149
UNORCA 170
US: Conference of Catholic Bishops 77;
    National Family Farm Coalition 166
US-Canada Free Trade Agreement 115
Ustawi 102

value amplification 43
verticalism 65, 246
Via Campesina 1, 6, 14, 17, 21, 27, 38, 48,
    108, 128, 131, 135, 142, 148–87, 237,
    240, 244, 255–6; communication 172–4;
    composition and character 178–81;
    demands of 170–1; founding of 167–8;
    as 'glocal' network 177–8; independence
    and autonomy 168; involvement with
    WSF 181–2; role of women in 173;
    strategic ties 175–7; ties with other
    peasant groups 170

Wallach, Lori 117
Wallis, Jim 83
Washington Consensus 2
water, buying up of 150
Waterman, Peter 20, 53–6
Waters, Maxine 84
Weber, Max 32
Whitaker, Francisco "Chico" 12, 106,
    143–4, 146, 227–8

White Overalls Movement Building
    Libertarian Effective Struggles
    (WOMBLES) 212, 214, 221, 223, 227
Wijbrandi, Jan Bouke 101
Winch, Peter 18
Windward Islands Farmers' Association 170
Wolfensohn, James 75
Wolfowitz, Paul 91
women: feminist perspective 3–4; role of
    173
World Bank 1–2, 7–8, 18, 49, 67, 70, 72,
    230
World Council of Churches 77, 102
World Development Movement 76
World Economic Forum 7, 12
World Food Summit 171, 176
World Forum on Agrarian Reform 171–2,
    185–6, 244
World Forum of Fisherpeople 108, 128
World March of Women 14, 48, 102, 183,
    241
World Social Forum 1, 5, 7, 10–13, 27–8,
    63–5, 139–40; Call of the Social
    Movements 47; Charter of Principles
    10, 106, 259–61; contention and
    confrontation 222–9; as encounter
    space 140–1, 182–4, 243; fostering of
    competition by 141–7, 184–7;
    International Council 11, 44;
    involvement of PGA with 219–20;
    involvement with transnational
    networks 100–7; involvement of Via
    Campesina with 181–2; Porto Alegre
    46, 102–3; and transnationalizing
    activity 23–4, 242–8
World Trade Organization 1, 6–8, 18, 49,
    72, 109–11, 170–1, 230; Cancun
    ministerial 128–9, 176; claims of
    OWINFS against 125; Doha meeting
    128; Hong Kong ministerial 132–3;
    Seattle ministerial *see* Battle in Seattle;
    transnational collective action against
    126
World Wildlife Fund 118

Ya Basta! 199, 205, 213
Yo Mango 222

Zald, Mayer 40
Zapata, Emiliano 190
zapatismo 195–9, 257; *encuentros* 200–2
Zapatista solidarity network 199–300
Zaragoza, Federico Mayor 91

Lightning Source UK Ltd.
Milton Keynes UK
UKOW021045240212

187845UK00002B/43/A